P9-CDV-388

THE INTERPRETATION OF AGREEMENTS AND WORLD PUBLIC ORDER

OF RELATED INTEREST

Harold D. Lasswell and Abraham Kaplan
POWER AND SOCIETY. 1950

Myres S. McDougal and Associates
STUDIES IN WORLD PUBLIC ORDER. 1960

Myres S. McDougal and Florentino P. Feliciano
LAW AND MINIMUM WORLD PUBLIC ORDER:
The Legal Regulation of International Coercion. 1961

Myres S. McDougal and William T. Burke
THE PUBLIC ORDER OF THE OCEANS:
A Contemporary International Law of the Sea. 1962

Myres S. McDougal, Harold D. Lasswell, and Ivan A. Vlasic
LAW AND PUBLIC ORDER IN SPACE. 1963

Douglas M. Johnston
THE INTERNATIONAL LAW OF FISHERIES:
A Framework for Policy-Oriented Inquiries. 1965.

B. F. Murty
THE IDEOLOGICAL INSTRUMENT OF COERCION AND WORLD PUBLIC ORDER. 1967

THE INTERPRETATION OF AGREEMENTS AND WORLD PUBLIC ORDER

Principles of Content and Procedure

by Myres S. McDougal, Harold D. Lasswell, and James C. Miller

NEW HAVEN AND LONDON, YALE UNIVERSITY PRESS, 1967

Set in Baskerville type,

and printed in the United States of America by

the Vail-Ballou Press, Inc., Binghamton, N.Y.

Distributed in Canada by McGill University Press.

Library of Congress catalog card number: 67-13442

ACKNOWLEDGMENTS

Our debts for criticism and other assistance in the preparation of this book are numerous. Mary Ellen Caldwell collaborated indispensably in testing an evolving manuscript against the understanding of several generations of students. William T. Burke was a sharp critic of both the initial formulations and the final manuscript. Layman Allen contributed directly to the statement of the principles of logic, and otherwise. Dennis O'Connor translated Russian sources and offered creative suggestions. Fritz Scharpf aided with German translations. Cynthia Crawford Lichtenstein made an early study of some of the more important principles.

Other friends and associates who offered suggestions affecting text or footnotes include Oscar Schachter, Michael Reisman, Egon Schwelb, Leon Lipson, Florentino Feliciano, Oliver Lissitzyn, Arthur J. Brodbeck, Richard M. Goodman, Peter Liacouras, Pauli Murray, Maurice Merrill, David Daube, Benjamin Forman, Karl Krastin, Ernest Jones, Alan Karabus, Cynthia Miller, and Harold Cunningham.

Among the many former students, too numerous for complete mention, who contributed helpful comment or information are Theodore Jakaboski, Richard Helgesen, Martin Lowy, Peter Zimroth, Henning Wegener, and Fred Scharf.

John Henderson, with the effective help of James Golden and Robert Brooks of the Library staff, assisted in the checking of the final manuscript, and Elise Kelso and Isabel Malone survived a difficult secretarial burden.

The Stimson Fund of Yale University has been our principal source of financial support, and was characteristically generous.

The skilled and empathetic editing of Marian Ash continues to be an inspiration for authorship.

Myres S. McDougal
Harold D. Lasswell
James C. Miller

April 1, 1967

CONTENTS

INTRODUCTION xi

1. DELIMITATION OF THE PROBLEM: THE PROCESSES OF AGREEMENT, CLAIM, AND DECISION AS CONTEXT 3
   - The Process of Agreement 13
   - The Process of Claim 21
   - The Constitutive Process of Authoritative Decision 27

2. CLARIFICATION OF THE GOALS AND STRATEGIES OF INTERPRETATION 35
   - Necessity for Interpretation Inherent in Communication 35
   - The Postulated Goals of Interpretation 39
   - Strategies of Interpretation 45
     - *Principles of Content* 50
     - *Principles of Procedure* 65

3. TRENDS IN CONCEPTIONS OF GOALS AND STRATEGIES OF INTERPRETATION 78
   - Recognition of the Necessity of Interpretation 78
   - The Goals of Interpretation 82
   - Functions Ascribed to Principles of Interpretation 111

4. TRENDS IN THE MANAGEMENT OF PRINCIPLES OF CONTENT 119
   - The Contextuality Principle 119
     - *Preliminary Events* 122
     - *Subsequent Conduct* 132
   - Principles Relating to the Process of Agreement 144
     - *Participants* 144
       - The Principle of Involvement 144
       - The Relevance of Characteristics 148

Objectives 154
The Relevance of Value Range 154
The Principle of Projecting Genuine Expectations 156
The Principle of the Anticipated Solution 186
Situations 188
The Principle of Assessing the Particular Interactions of the Parties in Reference to the General Pattern of the Setting 188
Base Values 193
The Principle of Assessing the Value Positions of the Parties 193
Strategies 194
The Principle of Including All Strategic Acts 194
The Principle of the Preferred Mode of Expression 197
The Principle of Logical Relationships 199
The Principle of Adapting the Level of Generality or Particularity to the Other Features of the Context 200
Outcomes 206
The Principle of the Distinctive Phase of Agreements 206
Post-Outcomes 215
Principles Relating to the Context of Factors Affecting the Process of Agreement 216
The Principle of the Largest Shared Audience 216
The Principle of the Probability of Agreement 252
Principles Relating to the Decision Process 258
Officials 258
The Principle of Impartiality 258
Objectives 260
The Principle of Primary Interpretation 260
The Principle of Supplementing Expectations by Public Order Goals 260
The Principle of Constitutive Priority 261
The Principle of Stable Future Expectations 262
Base Values 263
The Principle of Making Decisions Effective 263
Strategies 265
The Principle of Explicit Rationality 265
Outcomes 267
The Principle of Comprehensive Mobilization of Authority Functions 267

5. TRENDS IN THE MANAGEMENT OF PRINCIPLES OF PROCEDURE 270
The Contextuality Principle 273
The Operation of Adjusting Effort to Importance 302
The Operation of Identifying the Focal Agreement 307
The Historical Operation 309
The Lexical Operation 319
The Logical Operation 330
The Operation of Assessing Gesture and Deed 343
The Operation of Assessing Scientific Credibility 350
The Operation of Estimating Agreement Probability 351
The Operation of Estimating the Effects of Decision 353
The Operation of Examining the Self for Bias 356

6. PAST INADEQUACIES AND FUTURE PROMISE 360
Past Inadequacies 361
Factors Conditioning Past Inadequacies 369
Possible Future Developments 378
Recapitulation of Recommended Alternatives 382
The Future Promise of Interpretation 391

TABLE OF CASES 397

NAME INDEX 401

SUBJECT INDEX 406

INTRODUCTION

Whatever the system of public order, whether that of the world community in its entirety or of a regional, national, or subnational component of the whole, the task of interpretation would appear to be fundamentally the same for all types of prescriptions—international agreements, constitutions, statutes, precedents, and customary prescriptions—and even for private agreements. When we explore the history of any prescription or agreement whatsoever, it becomes evident that every such outcome in social process is most conveniently described as the culminating event in a sequence of communication; and in every particular controversy authorized decision-makers who are charged with the task of interpretation must proceed within the frame of reference provided by the basic prescriptions of all the public order systems to which they are responsible. Every type of prescription or agreement, as a communication in which parties seek through signs and deeds to mediate their subjectivities, would appear to present to an interpreter comparable difficulties or infirmities in abstractness, contradiction, ambiguities, and degrees of completeness. Similarly, since these difficulties infect even the most basic constitutional prescriptions of any community, authorized decision-makers charged with responsibility for applying all the different types of prescriptions and agreements in particular controversies would appear to have comparable opportunities for relating the decisions they make to the basic goal values of preferred public order.

Inquiry about the interpretation of international agreements, as about that of other prescriptions and agreements, which would be realistic and consequential must, accordingly, begin with a clear working conception of what is involved in a process of communication, at least a preliminary indication of what is meant by interpretation, and some specification of the role of interpretation, so defined, in the more comprehensive decision process of *application* in which the policy of giving deference to agreements is related to, and integrated with, all other community policies. In the pages immediately following we offer certain initial clarifications of all three indispensable concepts—communication, interpretation, and application—and will hope that, as our book develops, the general framework we recommend will take on more clarity and substantiality.

The Process of Communication

Fortunately the study of communication has been one of the most rapidly expanding fields in the modern social, behavioral, and engineering sciences. We are able to benefit from the analytic clarity that has been a result of vigorous debate in linguistics, logic, and mathematics, and of extensive empirical research on the role of communicative activities in social process. Since the decision process is an inseparable part of this larger context, and perpetually interacts with it, whatever advances of knowledge illuminate the life of society cannot fail to light the path of the law. We propose to exploit contemporary developments as fully as they prove profitable for the difficult and delicate task of interpretation.

Communication is a comprehensive process in which *communicators* and *audiences* are both involved. Or, to phrase the relationship more precisely, participants usually play two supplementary roles, one that of the initiator of messages, the other that of the recipient. In great mass-communication enterprises the full-time specialists on radio-T.V., film, and press may disseminate far more than they receive from a given target audience. But two diplomatic negotiators move quickly back and forth between the initiating and the receiving roles, giving and receiving messages throughout the sequence of the negotiation.

It is not difficult to identify the characteristic that distinguishes a social interaction that is chiefly to be regarded as an act of communication from what is primarily to be viewed as something else. To communicate is to make use of *signs*. Signs are materials or energies that are specialized to the task of mediating between the subjective events of two or more persons. The signs on which we principally rely are linguistic, the sounds comprising the words of language systems. But these are supplemented by gestures, and by such equivalents as written characters and pictures. A sign is most readily classified according to the group whose members are expected to understand it. Hence we identify the words of the English language by reference to those who are assumed to speak English; and we discover the terms of art distinctive of English law by examining the vocabulary of trained English lawyers.

The subjective events that are called up by the signs of a system of communication are *symbols.* In the most generalized sense, symbols are often referred to as "interpretations" of signs. In our analysis we shall keep the concept of interpretation much narrower than this, restricting it to the usage that is well established in the discourse of jurisprudence and international law. But it is a pertinent step toward objectivity to perceive the role that a similar though more generalized definition has played in the fundamental theory of communication.

We find it important to locate any specific sequence of signs and symbols in the aggregate situation of which it is part. Hence many *forums* may be identified, such as the forum that includes the elite of the nation-states, the international intergovernmental organizations, and all other major participants in the world community. Forums arise whenever communicative acts become at least partially stabilized. Reflection will show that it is sometimes useful to identify such micro-forums as occur between two people—as for example, between Winston Churchill and Franklin D. Roosevelt during World War II. No one can doubt the significance of such relationship for the flow of international agreement or for the occurrence of problems of interpretation.

It is also essential to take into account the *objectives* sought by participants in a forum. Often these objectives are highly explicit subjective events, comprising value demands whose realization it is proposed to optimize through acts of communication. Examination also shows that the perspectives of demand are closely tied to expectations about the way in which the preferred events can be made to take place. These are the strategic expectations that guide the intermediate steps of the communicators in seeking to influence one another and to modify the resource environment. Expectations and demands are themselves arranged in an order of some kind by each communicator for himself. Taken in conjunction with the self-symbol of the individual or group, these perspectives comprise the self-systems of all participants in the social and political process. Besides the highly explicit objectives referred to, attention must often be given to marginally conscious and unconscious demands, expectations, and identities that affect the statements that are made (or omitted) in international or local affairs.

All who participate in a given forum have various *base values* at their disposal at a particular time. The asset values may include access to the network of communication facilities available in the situation (telstar, underwater cables, and the like). Political authority and control may be indispensable prerequisites to access; and the chances are perhaps enhanced if religious, family, social class, scientific, educational, and welfare advantages are at hand. Instead of assets, communicators may have liabilities which can be inventoried in terms of our reference list of basic categories: wealth, power, rectitude, affection, respect, enlightenment, skill, well-being. It may be noted that the base values include personnel that is specialized to the technological requirements of the media. Although these individuals typically lack the discretionary impact on a collective process that is exerted by the initiators and ultimate recipients of communication, an exhaustive list of participants would certainly include the media handlers.

The several *strategies* of communication encompass all the modes of managing base values to affect outcomes. A double sequence is implied which may be called, respectively, assembling and processing. The values under the control of a communicator may not at first be in a usable form for the transmittal of messages. It may therefore be necessary to take financial assets and employ them to procure the office space and facilities needed to draft possible agreement, and to prepare presentations favorable to its acceptance. Skilled personnel is required; and enlightened understanding of the policy situation is also essential if full advantage is taken of the predispositions present in the arena. The prospects of success may be enhanced by the tireless cultivation of powerful, distinguished, and upright friends.

In processing the content of communication two characteristic features require strategic attention. Statements can be analyzed *syntactically* and *semantically*. In the former case the problem is to disclose the interrelations among statements when they are viewed as a closed universe, a family of meaning. From this standpoint statements can be classified according to the degree of abstractness involved, or to implied contradiction or compatibility. Semantic analysis, on the other hand, is concerned with the references found in statements regardless of the location of the referent inside or outside of the total message. We may see, for instance, that the chief topics in an agreement are industrial development and trade, both of which are plainly semantic.

Even in social interactions where the manipulation of signs is a conspicuous feature, acts of collaboration, which by definition go beyond communication, are not entirely absent. A combined strategic campaign may involve diplomatic entertainment, gifts to key officials, and many other measures that go beyond signs in the strict sense, thus integrating the signs in patterns of practice that give great variety to the total significance of the communication component.

The *outcomes* of a communication process often diverge widely from one another in completeness of shared subjectivity and in other respects that may come to be regarded as important to the immediate participants or to others who are ultimately affected. From the standpoint of a scientific observer who is enabled to use all known methods of research to establish the best possible basis of inference concerning a communication outcome, it may appear that the parties do indeed match the symbols elicited by the visible signs. From this relatively perfect state of accord every conceivable degree of divergence may be discerned. Perhaps the participants are under the false impression that they enjoy shared subjectivities; or in some cases the false impression is that specific differences obtain. Differences may reach some theoretical limit of irrelevance to one another; or, analyzed in another dimension, they may be in explicit and intense contradiction.

From the standpoint of the task of interpretation the most sweeping point to be made is the contextuality of any process of communication. Every feature may affect the outcome by facilitating the appearance of shared subjectivities, or by interfering in greater or less degree with such a result. Contextuality implies that any interpreter of an outcome must be ready and able to explore the possible influence in concrete circumstances of the identity of communicators and audiences, of inclusive forums, of significant objectives, of base values and strategies. For many purposes, although not necessarily interpretation, post-outcome effects may be the factors most worthy of investigation.

Perhaps this review of the communication process is enough to suggest that it is a mistake to trust blindly to the assumption that the presence or absence of shared subjectivity at the end of a sequence of communication is to be read off in simple fashion from the manifest content of particular words embossed or imprinted. Interpretation is a far more realistic and subtle challenge.

The Process of Interpretation

The essential feature of genuine interpretation has been implied in the preceding sketch of communication. If the culminating statements in a stream of assertion and counterassertion are to be properly understood, they must be put in the setting of all the preceding events that are likely to have affected the final result in any significant way.

In different contexts the various components of a communication process take on distinctive relationships. Hence it is impossible to succeed in any attempt to impute a valid unvarying weight to particular features of the process. In one negotiation, for instance, a critical issue may arise in connection with the encoding and decoding of final texts. In the making of other agreements a key issue may relate to the fullness with which salient facts were disclosed by the parties to one another. And so on through every interaction that arises; subsequent questions may refer to any one of them.

Hence there can be no arbitrary weightings or fixed hierarchies of signification that, when chosen by the interpreter in advance, remove ambiguity from the contents of communication. This follows implacably from the contextual principle that each detail in the whole of an act of communication is affected by, and in turn affects, all other details; and further, that the direction and intensity of the effect is to be ascertained by investigating the specific situation, not by pretending to dispose of the problem by arbitrary rules.

The primary aim of a process of interpretation by an authorized and controlling community decision-maker can be formulated in the following proposition: discover the shared expectations that the parties to the relevant communication succeeded in creating in each other. It would be an act of distortion on behalf of one party against another to ascertain and to give effect to his version of a supposed agreement if investigation shows that the expectations of this party were not matched by the expectations of the other. And it would be an obvious travesty on interpretation for a community decision-maker to disregard the shared subjectivities of the parties and to substitute arbitrary assumptions of his own.

It is the grossest, least defensible exercise of arbitrary formalism to arrogate to one particular set of signs—the text of a document—the role of serving as the exclusive index of the parties' shared expectations. We join with those who condemn textualism of this kind as a violation of the human dignity to choose freely. It does violence to the policy of directing community decision-makers to make themselves an instrument of the dignity of man by acting in harmony with a strong presumption to respect the preferences of as many members of the community as possible on as many occasions as possible. Instead of seeking to constrict the alternatives open to particular parties in relation to one another, the appropriate aim is to search out, and assist in expressing, the permissible options exercised by world community members. Any level of performance that falls short of this standard is an act of coercion against the parties whose shared expectations are frustrated.

The concern of an interpreter who represents a public order of human dignity—and such an order is approximated on many matters in world affairs—is to give encouragement to individuality, inventiveness, and diversity. These are interconnected manifestations of the abounding resources of man and his inexhaustible potential for creativity. Unless individuals are permitted to express themselves distinctively, they cannot achieve new forms. Inventiveness is a means of proceeding further along the path of individuality by bringing new patterns into the picture. The growth of distinctive combinations is fostered by the cultivation of innovation and originality of style in arranging old and new.

In connection with every interpretative problem one is well advised to adopt a critical and realistic rather than a perfectionist expectation in regard to results. After all, the subjectivities of one human mind are not open to direct observation by another. Hence we spend our lives becoming adept in varying measure in drawing inferences about the moods and images of others, automatically formulating and testing hypotheses that are based on posture, body movement, gesture, speech, and overt participation in a great range of social situations. Hypotheses can rarely be put to the test of utterly unambiguous confirmation, unless the topic is quite trivial. But the order of confirmation of even profound assumptions about the inner lives of other persons, though of differing magnitude, may be consensually high.

One assumes, therefore, that characterizations of subjectivity will be approximations, and that any degree of approximation is to be preferred to undisciplined and arbitrary preclusion of relevant indices of expectation. If the light cannot be dazzling there is no reason for sulking in the dark.

No one should jump to the conclusion that the difference between goals set in terms of conscientious and competent approximation to genuine shared subjectivities and textuality is slight. Textuality stops short with words; or, rather, with an ascription of meaning to words taken as final. The approach which seeks genuine shared expectations does not neglect the words of a purportedly final text, if any exists. It does, however, regard any initial version of their relation to shared expectations as provisional, and requires that the interpreter engage in a course of sustained testing and revision of preliminary inferences about the pertinent subjectivities. And of course this calls for scrutiny of the whole context of communication.

The execution of such a program demands that the interpreter suspend any act of final choice until all the evidence is in, and the commitment can be made with an eye to all that has entered efficaciously into the final outcomes and affected its purport.

Such a program demands further that the interpreter open himself fully to experiences that may sweep away many initial prejudgments. Thoroughly understood, interpretation is a two-pronged and interconnected process. One approach arranges the manifest content of the statements that appear in relevant texts—including more than a putatively final text—according to harmony or contradictions, and abstractness. The further approach examines each pertinent expression in the order in which it was made and also in relation to any information that helps to establish the perspectives of the communicator and his audience. The interpreter is thereby exposing himself to an agenda of experiences that aid in modifying the initial picture of the subjectivities of the parties.

The twofold principles of interpretation can be formulated in terms of *content,* or the analysis of statement message, and of *procedure,* or the exposure of the interpreter to an orderly reconstruction of the situation that affects his ultimate appraisal of its character and significance for the shared subjectivities of the participants. The latter dimension of the interpreter's approach allows him to permit changes to occur and to be recognized in the continuing, never-ending sequence of events that compose the self. No inconsiderable act of readiness is required if the interpreter is to allow himself to empathize—with minimum distortion—with the perspectives of others.

The Process of Application

The process of interpretation that most concerns us here, as observers of the role of international agreements in world public order is, it may require emphasis, part of the more inclusive function that occurs, or can be expected to occur, at the application phase of community decision. The primary sense that we have assigned to the word "interpretation" is that of designating the shared subjectivities of communicators. Such a problem is pertinent to the application phase of community decision only when a controversy arises that demands the determination of public order policies as they refer to the particularities of a concrete case in which a prior agreement is alleged and denied.

The scope of our present analysis of interpretation, therefore, does not explicitly extend to the other phases of decision even though in these phases also questions may arise about shared perspectives. The prescriptive phase, for example, includes the elucidation of assumptions about the allocations of constitutive authority among the various participants in the power process itself. The promotional phase is almost entirely devoted to the hammering out of a consensus about what community policies ought to be seriously considered for adoption. Without describing the whole process of decision further, the present point is served by emphasizing our concern with the distinctive features of application. A concrete issue is joined concerning the specific content of an agreement assumed to have been made. Hence the initial part of the problem of application is *primary interpretation* in the sense of ascertaining the shared expectations of the parties, which is the task we have been stressing.

Application also calls for the *supplementation* of many demonstrable agreements in ways that cure omissions or vagueness which obviously come within the objectives sought by the parties, and give rise to unnecessary value deprivations if denied. No one acquainted with the complex facts of life ever imagines that a sequence of words can be arranged to designate in concrete and minute intimacy the entire features of a situation, though they can be at least approximately indicated by reasonably careful language. Life is too short to trap all the abundance of history; hence we must be content with sketches, not thumb prints.

When the task of supplementation has been accomplished and the shared expectations of the parties are as clear as they can be made, the decision-maker in his role of applier turns to another major component of his problem. We refer to *policing and integration* to include all considerations that appropriately enter into the problem of relating each specific controversy about an agreement to the total context of public policy. Sometimes the need is to diminish rather than to supplement the explicit references of an agreement. Circumstances may have arisen that under the fulfillment of the letter of an arrangement exceedingly onerous for one of the parties. Changes may have occurred that could not reasonably have been foreseen. The aims of public policy would be foiled if a party were constrained to do exactly what on allegedly liberal interpretation he appeared to have agreed to do. We note, too, that when expectations are brought into clear focus it may be apparent that they contradict accepted goal values and instrumental specifications of public order. Community decision-makers would be remiss if they failed to *withhold* the sanction of public power from such expectations. Similarly, the optimum exercise of the application function may on occasion require a measure of *exemption* of an overcommitted party, if important enterprises are not to be destroyed and future commitments inhibited. Finally, there may be purely *mechanical or clerical errors* which need to be corrected in order to permit the original expectation to be executed. The policy of avoiding unnecessary burdens on the implementation of choice is obviously served in this way.

The appropriate performances of these tasks in supplementing and policing primary interpretation will of course vary with many different types of specific claims or controversies between parties about the processes of agreement and decision. Hence the entire sequence of events leading up to controversy and comprising the process of claim are not without potential relevance. In future study it may be appropriate to amplify the scope of the present book by reviewing the different ways in which the many varieties of claim and the numerous variations in the claims process, raising very different community policy issues, influence the performance of the several tasks involved in the application of an international agreement.

The performance of these several tasks in application must also be affected by many different features of the more comprehensive process of authoritative decision of which it is a part. A systematic analysis of these features would identify the established decision-makers, locate them in the structures of authority maintained by the community, specify the objectives for which they are maintained, indicate the bases of power made available to them, and so on. Some of the more significant variables will be noted as we proceed.

The Present Treatment

Despite the complexities that show themselves when the problem of interpretation is dealt with even within the limits of authoritative application, we approach the problems involved in a sanguine frame of mind. It is at least feasible to identify and to take note of the many factors that affect shared expectations, rather than to turn aside in despair from the relationships involved. Despite the defeatist notes that have not infrequently been sounded by many past scholars and decision-makers, we join with those who take a more confident standpoint. We believe that the past is a storehouse of experience that may enable contemporary observers to devise improved principles to assist the decision-maker in his tasks.

The more detailed organization of our book is elaborated and explained in Chapter 1, in which we seek to relate the interpretation of agreements to the larger context of world public order. It may bear emphasis that in the subsequent chapters in which we sample and survey past decision, practice, and opinion our purpose is more to increase insight, by demonstrating the potentialities of appropriate goal and principles, than to attempt a comprehensive and definitive summary of past failures and successes.

THE INTERPRETATION OF AGREEMENTS AND WORLD PUBLIC ORDER

1. DELIMITATION OF THE PROBLEM: THE PROCESSES OF AGREEMENT, CLAIM, AND DECISION AS CONTEXT

Even in a community which aspires only to minimum public order, in the sense of the prevention and repression of unauthorized violence, agreements are of central importance: agreements, explicit and implicit, are indispensable for establishing a stability in peoples' expectations which lessens predispositions for arbitrary resort to violence.[1] In a community which projects, beyond minimum order, the goals of an optimum public order, in the sense of the greatest production and widest sharing of all human values, agreements assume an even greater significance. In such a community agreements serve both to secure that values are shaped and shared more by persuasion than coercion and to organize initiatives for the effective employment of resources in the maximum production and distribution of valued social outcomes.[2]

1. This thesis is comprehensively documented in McDougal and Feliciano, *Law and Minimum World Public Order* (1961). The potential role of agreements is outlined in Ch. 4. More abundant illustration is offered in Clark and Sohn, *World Peace Through World Law* (2d rev. ed. 1960).

The need for stability in expectations is of course pervasive for all interactions transcending state lines, not merely in relation to the control of coercion and violence. An appropriate stress upon this need for stability is made by De Visscher in *Problèmes d'Interprétation Judiciaire en Droit International Public* (1963).

2. For amplification, see McDougal and Lasswell, "The Identification and Appraisal of Diverse Systems of Public Order," 53 *Am. J. Int'l L.* 1 (1959). The importance of agreements for world public order is strongly—perhaps too strongly—emphasized in Rosenne, "Some Diplomatic Problems of the Codification of the Law of Treaties," 41 *Wash. L. Rev.* 261, 273 (1966). He writes:

> one must remember that in terms of sheer quantity, treaty law today exceeds in bulk and in practical importance customary international law. The

The important role of agreements in the most comprehensive contemporary community of mankind relates, thus, to both minimum order and optimum order. It is by agreement most broadly conceived—that is, when agreement is conceived to include the whole flow of peoples' collaborative behavior—that the effective participants in earth-space power processes establish an overall "constitutive process"—identifying authoritative decision-makers, projecting fundamental community objectives, affording structures of authority, providing bases of power in authority and other values, legitimizing or condemning different strategies in persuasion and coercion, and allocating competence among effective participants over different authority functions and value interactions—for the maintenance of a modest minimum order.[3] It is by agreement, further, when agreement is no less broadly conceived, that the established decision-makers perform the important authority function of prescribing, of "legislating," general community policies about the detailed activities which comprise world social process in pursuit of all values.[4] It is by agreement also, when the basic constitutive process of the general community is appropriately maintained, that the many different participants in the world social process—territorially organized communities, international governmental organizations, political parties, pressure groups, private associations, and individuals—express their creative initiatives and organize their base values to get on with the world's work in producing and distributing new values.[5]

> greater part of the day-to-day international legal relations of States are now governed by treaty and not by customary law. This is so both for bilateral relations and for multilateral relations.

Some documentation of importance is offered in Toscano, *The History of Treaties and International Policies* (1966).

3. What is meant by "constitutive process" is indicated in more detail in McDougal, Lasswell, and Vlasic, *Law and Public Order in Space* Ch. 1 (1963). See also McDougal and Feliciano, op. cit. supra note 1, Ch. 4.

4. Kaplan and Katzenbach, *The Political Foundations of International Law* 236 (1961).

5. Ample evidence may be found in any collection of treaties or in any standard treatise upon private international law. For historical background, see Niemeyer, *Law Without Force* (1941).

Two points may require emphasis:

First, the agreements with which we are concerned in this study are not simply those between nation-states or governments but also include those between any participants in world community process, even those between individuals and

Given this important role of agreements in contemporary earth-space public order, the urgent need for appropriate general community procedures and principles to facilitate the making and application of agreements can scarcely require elaboration. The urgency of this need can, further, be expected to accelerate in proportion as the interdependences of peoples accelerate in the emerging new space-atomic era, with both its threats of potentially comprehensive destruction and its promises of a productivity in all values hitherto beyond fantasy.

The world constitutive process of authoritative decision does today, fortunately, afford certain established procedures and a well-tested body of principles designed to facilitate and police the making, performance, and termination of many different types of agreements between many different participants in world social process. These procedures and principles comprise what are conventionally known as the public international law of treaties, the law (as yet sometimes unnamed) of concessions and other state contracts with private parties, the private international law relating to choice of law about agreements, and the internal law of contracts of the different states.[6]

Among the procedures and principles of critical importance about the *application* of international agreements are, of course, those designed to guide and assist in the interpretation of such agreements.[7]

---

private associations, which have effects transcending nation-state lines and importantly affect world public order. A comparably broad conception of international agreements appears in Jessup, *A Modern Law of Nations* Ch. 6 (1946).

Secondly, the line between expectations created by cooperative activity—sometimes called "customary" behavior—and explicit agreement is often difficult to draw. Much of what we will have to say about the interpretation of "international" agreements is no less applicable to "customary" international prescriptions. These interrelations are being developed in a separate study. See Raman, "The International Court of Justice and the Development of International Customary Law," 1965 *A.S.I.L. Proceedings* 169.

6. Perhaps the most useful statement of procedures and compilation of principles is still Harvard Research in International Law, *Law of Treaties: Draft Convention With Comment* (1935). Other types of agreements are discussed in Wolff, *Private International Law* (2d ed. 1950); Nussbaum, *Principles of Private International Law* (1943); Jenks, *The Common Law of Mankind* (1958); Carlston, "International Role of Concession Agreements," 52 *Nw. U. L. Rev.* 618 (1957).

7. The more important traditional principles are collected in Harvard Research, op. cit. supra note 6.

More recent studies include International Law Commission, "Report on the

Deference to human dignity, when taken seriously, requires the application, within the limits of overriding community policies, of the genuine choice of the parties (whether group or individual), and not of an imposed choice. The goal which envisions world social processes ordered more by persuasion than coercion must remain illusion in the degree that the genuine shared expectations of the parties to agreements are not in fact applied to the events with respect to which they seek to project their policies.

Contemporary professional opinion, scholarly and other, is, however, today much confused about both the feasible goals of interpretation and the possibilities of achieving useful principles of interpretation to guide and assist decision-makers. Among the multitudinous commentators upon the feasibility of an application of international agreements designed to secure the genuine shared expectations of the parties to such agreements, and upon the potentialities of principles of interpretation in assisting such application, there may be discerned two diametrically opposed views, enshrouding various intermediate degrees of confusion. The one view is that the application of an international agreement to facts in controversy is easy, almost to the point of being automatic, and that little, if any, interpretation

---

Laws of Treaties," U.N. Gen. Ass. Off. Rec., 19th Sess., Supp. No. 9 (A/5809), p. 25 (1964); Degan, *L'Interprétation des Accords en Droit International* (1963); De Visscher, op. cit. supra note 1; Bernhardt, *Die Auslegung völkerrechtliches Verträge* (1963); Bentivoglio, *La Funzione Interpretatina Nell' Ordinamento Internazionale* (1958); Grossen, *Les Présomptions en Droit International Public* (1954); Neri, *Sull' Interpretazione Dei Trattati Nel Diritto internazional* (1958); Ehrlich, *Interpretorcju Traktatow* (1957). The earlier Ehrlich, "Interprétation des Traités," 24 *Recueil des Cours* 5 (1928) is still useful. The interrelations of interpretation and application are developed by Silving, "A Plea for a Law of Interpretation," 98 *U. Pa. L. Rev.* 499 (1950).

The Russians do not, surprisingly, appear to have developed comprehensive and systematic theories about interpretation. Some illustrative discussions are Pereterskiy, *Tolkovaniye Mezhdunarodnikh Dogovorov* (The Interpretation of International Treaties) (1959); Shurshalov, *Osnovniye Voprosy Mezhdunarod-Nogo Dogovora* (Basic Questions of the International Treaty) (1959); "Interpretation of Treaties," in Kozhevnikov (ed.), *International Law* 277–78 (English transl., 1961); and "Interpretation of the International Treaty," in Kozhevnikov (ed.), *Mezhdunarodnoye Pravo* (International Law) 347–50 (1964).

For views not unlike those presented in this book, see Haraszti, *A nemzetközi szerzodések értelmézésenek alpavetö kérdései* (Budapest, 1965) (English summary in back.).

and few principles of interpretation are required.[8] The other view is that, when the genuine shared expectations of the parties are postulated as the goal, the process is so difficult as to approach the impossible and that principles of interpretation, however carefully they may be formulated and refined, can do little to lessen the difficulty.[9]

The view that interpretation is so easy as to be almost automatic developed early in the literature of international law, and is expressed in various forms. Perhaps the oldest and most frequently invoked formulation of this view, described by the Harvard Research as "fundamental" among principles of interpretation, is the famous maxim of Vattel: "It is not permissible to interpret what has no need of interpretation."[10] Still other formulations, also frequently invoked, are the varying expressions of a principle of interpretation, alleged to have priority over all other principles, which emphasizes the "clear," "natural," "plain," or "ordinary" meanings of the words in an international agreement, in explicit disregard of other significant features of the context of communication.[11] A striking illustration of this type of formulation is offered by the International Court of Justice in its opinion in the *Second Admissions* case:[12]

> When the Court can give effect to a provision of a treaty by giving to the words used in it their natural and ordinary mean-

8. For examples of this view, see Lawrence, *The Principles of International Law* 302 (75th ed. 1928); 1 Westlake, *International Law* 282–83 (1904).

9. Stone, "Fictional Elements in Treaty Interpretation—A Study in the International Judicial Process," 1 *Sydney L. Rev.* 344, 344–47, 359–63 (1955). This position has also been taken, in effect, by Fairman, "The Interpretation of Treaties," 20 *Transact. Grot. Soc'y* 123 (1934); 1 Schwartzenberger, *International Law* 488–97 (3d ed. 1957); Yü, *The Interpretation of Treaties* 27–29, 37–38, 52–58, 203–04, et seq. (1927).

For recent review of varying attitudes toward interpretation, with citations, see Gordon, "The World Court and the Interpretation of Constitutive Treaties," 59 *Am. J. Int'l L.* 794 (1965); Lissitzyn, "The Law of International Agreements in the Restatement," 41 *N.Y.U. L. Rev.* 96, 107 (1966); Tammelo, *Treaty Interpretation and Practical Reason* (The Australian Society of Legal Philosophy, Preliminary Working Paper, No. 3, 1965).

10. Vattel, *The Law of Nations* 199 (Fenwick trans. ed. of 1758, 1916); Harvard Research, op. cit. supra note 6, at 940.

11. Many versions of this principle will be discussed below. For citations, see Stone, supra note 9, at 345.

12. *Competence of the General Assembly for the Admission of a State to the United Nations,* [1950] I.C.J. Rep. at 4.

> ing, it may not interpret the words by seeking to give them some other meaning. In the present case the Court finds no difficulty in ascertaining the natural and ordinary meaning of the words in question and no difficulty in giving effect to them.[13]

Somewhat more subtle, though no less illustrative, is a statement by Sir Gerald Fitzmaurice, in giving reasons for rejecting a direct quest for the intention of the parties:

> It [the direct quest] ignores the fact that the treaty was, after all, drafted precisely in order to give expression to the intentions of the parties, and must be presumed to do so. Accordingly, this intention is, *prima facie,* to be found in the text itself, and therefore the primary question is not what the parties intended by the text, but what the text itself means: whatever it clearly means on an ordinary and natural construction of its terms, such will be deemed to be what the parties intended.[14]

The view that the task of interpretation, when directed toward the goal of approximating the genuine shared expectations of the parties, is so difficult as to defy achievement, and that principles of interpretation can be of little utility, is also expressed in various forms. Sometimes, upon an apparent assumption that the intent of the parties is nearly always fictitious, the feasibility of the stipulated goal is doubted.[15] More often, however, doubts are related merely to the

13. Id. at 8.

14. Fitzmaurice, "The Law and Procedure of the International Court of Justice 1951–54: Treaty Interpretation and Other Treaty Points," 33 *Brit. Yb. Int'l L.* 203, 205 (1957).

An often quoted passage from Lord Asquith in *In the Matter of An Arbitration Between Petroleum Development (Trucial Coast) Ltd. and the Sheikh of Abu Dhabi,* reported in 1 *Int'l & Comp. L. Q.* 247 (1952), offers a principle of economy in justification:

> the English rule which attributes paramount importance to the actual language of the written instrument in which the negotiations result seems to me no mere idiosyncrasy of our system, but a principle of ecumenical validity. Chaos may obviously result if that rule is widely departed from; and if, instead of asking what the words used mean, the inquiry extends at large to what each of the parties meant them to mean, and how and why each phrase came to be inserted. Id. at 251.

An appropriate apotheosis in application of the plain and rational meaning principle and the Vattel maxim was surely achieved by Mr. Justice Owle in the

principles of interpretation, with the utility of either certain important or all principles being questioned. Thus Sir Hersch Lauterpacht, as Oppenheim's editor, remarked that he retained his predecessor's list of interpretative rules "more out of piety than conviction," noting that such rules often provide only "the form in which the judge cloaks a result arrived at by other means." [16] Similarly, Professor Verzijl concludes: "In principle they [the principles of interpretation] are all correct, but on concrete application they often abrogate each other and frequently appear worthless." [17] An often quoted statement, asserting the same view, is that of Professor Fairman:

> Formal maxims do not decide concrete cases: no one of the so-called rules of interpretation is so inexorable that it actually dominates the process of giving a meaning to an instrument. Indeed it is easy to see that in the application of the familiar canons one is often in competition with another. It is believed that the matter is put in its proper light if it is realised that in the actual order of judicial decision the conclusion is reached

---

recent case of *Brigitte Bardot M.P.?* See A. P. Herbert, *Bardot M.P.? and Other Misleading Cases* (1964). The learned Justice said:

> Sir Anthony then offered to call evidence from Brussels which would show that in the minds of the Treaty-makers the "liberal professions" meant "the arts and sciences, teaching, law, medicine", and so on. But as I had to remind him, and now remind the world, though this was once a foreign Treaty, *it is now a British statute:* and I conceive it my duty to interpret it as we interpret every Act of Parliament, by the plain contemporary meaning of the words. It is not our custom to peep around corners, to poke our noses into Parliamentary debates or the proceedings of committees, in order to discover what the lawmaker meant: and it will be an ill day when we do. "No English judge," Lord Mildew said in *Scott* v. *the Thames Conservancy* (1937), "looks under the bed." (pp. 166–67).

Later he added: "If I may quote Lord Mildew again: 'If Parliament does not mean what it says it must say so.' " (*Bluff* v. *Father Gray.*) (pp. 167–68).

15. Beckett, "Comments on the Report of Sir Hersh Lauterpacht," 43 *Annuaire de l'Institut de Droit International* [I] 435, 438–39 (1950). For further discussion of this view, see pages 88–104 below.

16. Lauterpacht, "Restrictive Interpretation and the Principle of Effectiveness in the Interpretation of Treaties," 26 *Brit. Yb. Int'l L.* 48, at 49, 53 (1949).

17. Speech before the Royal Netherlands Academy of Science (*Mededeelingen der Afdeeling Letterkunde, nievwe Reeks D1, No. 2*) 144. Verzijl went on to call

> before the maxim is invoked. A rule of construction is a way of stating the result rather than a way of arriving at the result. By a subtle process which may take many competing considerations into account, the mind comes to rest at a conclusion which seems proper in the case; it is then recognized that that mode of reasoning falls under one of the accepted rules of construction. This rule is then invoked to explain the conclusion.[18]

It is our belief that both of these views, in all their multiple versions, are unrealistic and unnecessarily destructive of community and individual values.[19] Despite the fact that the subjectivities (demands, identifications, and expectations) of one human being are not open to direct observation by another, the postulation for community decision-makers, confronted with the task of interpreting an international agreement, of the goal of the closest possible approximation to the genuine shared expectations of the particular parties to the agreement appears an entirely feasible goal. The mere fact that individuals and peoples can and do join in complex, noncoercive, cooperative activity is sufficient evidence of their capacity to formulate and communicate some shared subjectivities, even by simple collaboration. The historic record of such activity exhibits, it may bear emphasis, not merely cooperation, but cooperation of a most intense and successful kind in pursuit of all the values cherished by man. Similarly, the fact that, when disputes occur about the interpretation of agreements, intervention by community-established decision-makers can be, and often is, made to facilitate, rather than disrupt, co-

---

interpretation as reference to principles a "clever word game" to help the judge rationalize his decision actually made on the basis of "other factors": "The judge . . . is already prejudiced before he draws up his sentence, in the sense that at that moment—led by an intuitive, uncontrollable, and to himself probably obscure preference—he has already chosen the starting-point decisive to the judgment." Id. at 145.

18. Fairman, supra note 9, at 134.

19. For agreement on this point see Schechter, *Interpretation of Ambiguous Documents by International Administrative Tribunals* 110–13 (1964). Schechter at p. 112 writes: "In particular, the idea of a neat and antiseptic separation of decision-making and rules of interpretation is dubious. The worm that gnaws at the highly polished and undoubtedly intellectual apple of the opponents of rules of interpretation is, simply, that no recurrent thought process can be wholly and permanently detached from the explanation given in each concrete application of the process."

operative activities is sufficient evidence that third parties are sometimes able effectively to infer the shared subjectivities, or lack thereof, of parties to agreements. It cannot, on the other hand, be emphasized too much that the effective interpretation of an international agreement is not, and cannot be made, a simple and mechanical routine. The communications which constitute an international agreement, like all other communications, are functions of a larger context, and the realistic identification of the content of these communications must require a systematic, comprehensive examination of all the relevant features of that context, with conscious and deliberate appraisal of their significance.

Clarification both of the very real difficulties and of the constructive potentialities of interpretation must of course begin with a closer examination of precisely what is involved in an act of interpretation. Decision-makers who are asked to interpret an international agreement have their attention directed to a series of events designated by claimants as embracing an agreement of certain alleged content.[20] The events so designated may include many diverse participants, having many varying characteristics. The participants may project and demand many different future policies, relating to many different values and value phases, and act in many different situations and at varying times. They may employ many different base values to affect each others' expectations, and may create expectations in each other both by signs of varying comprehensiveness and precision in reference (exhibiting or not exhibiting contradictions, gaps, and ambiguities) and by collaborative acts admitting of multiple inferences about accompanying subjectivities. They may achieve outcomes in apparent agreement of many different degrees of genuine shared expectation about future commitment, and may pursue many different courses of subsequent conduct. The context of conditions in which this focal agreement-making process goes forward may, further, include many, or all, of the variables of the multiple social processes of the comprehensive earth-space arena. Similarly, the specific claims which the parties to agreements, or others, make for their interpretation may arise either directly or indirectly (in controversies affecting many different community policies) : directly, in ex-

20. It has been suggested that the task confronting a decision-maker who must characterize certain coercive acts as "aggression" or "self-defense" is entirely comparable. McDougal and Feliciano, op. cit. supra note 1, at 59–67.

plicit demands for determinations of whether shared expectations of commitments were in fact created and of what the content of any such shared expectations was; indirectly, in demands relating to other types of controversies, such as with respect to the formalities of commitment, competency, protection of third parties, transfer of benefit, performance, termination by the parties or by the community, and subjection to community claims. The decision-makers which world constitutive process establishes as authorized to interpret international agreements may, finally, be located in various structures of authority, international and national, and may have varying conceptions of the overriding community objectives for which they are maintained and of the conditions under which they must make decision. From even this brief orientation, two things should presumptively, at least, be obvious: first, that the degree to which the participants in an agreement-making process can in fact achieve shared subjectivities about commitment may be affected by any and all of the variables in the process of agreement and its context, and, secondly, that the degree to which an authoritative decision-maker, who is later called upon to ascertain the degree and content of this commitment, will in fact possess the capabilities and predispositions to do so, may be affected by his perception of these same variables, as well as by all the important variables in the processes of claim and authoritative decision.

It is the purpose of this study, in rejection both of the complacency and narrowness of the "plain and natural meaning" or "textuality" school and of the nihilism of the arbitrary-decision school, to establish that principles of interpretation, relating to both content (events to be observed) and procedure (order and techniques of observation), are either presently available, or can readily by adapted, greatly to facilitate the task of interpretation for authoritative decision-makers who are bona fide committed to the overriding community goal of achieving the closest possible approximation of the genuine shared expectations of the particular parties to an agreement.

In pursuit of this purpose, and for the indication and recommendation of specific appropriate principles to guide and assist in interpretation, we propose to proceed by the following steps:

> First, we seek a more careful delimitation of the problem, through an outline of some of the more significant features of the process of agreement, claim, and decision.

Next, we recommend a particular clarification of the fundamental community policies at stake in the interpretation of international agreements, considering both the appropriate goals of interpretation and particular principles for implementing such goals.

Next, we offer a brief survey of the past practices of decision-makers in the management of principles of interpretation, noting trends in degrees of approximation to our recommended policies and, where possible, the factors which appear to have affected decision.

Finally, we summarize both our appraisals of past practices and our recommendations of more economic alternatives for securing preferred general community policies.[21]

We turn first to the more careful delimitation of the problem of interpretation, and for this purpose offer brief and somewhat impressionistic, though schematic outlines of the processes of agreement, claim, and decision.

THE PROCESS OF AGREEMENT

The international agreements with which we are concerned embrace all agreements, whoever the parties and whatever the type, which are intended to order, or do in fact have an impact upon the ordering of, value shaping and sharing which transcends nation-state lines. The "process of agreement," by which we generalize our reference to all such agreements, is an integral part of a more comprehensive world social process in which groups and individuals employ strategies both of persuasion and of coercion to attain their goals.[22] By persuasive strategies we refer to strategies which afford their targets many alternatives, at low cost and with high probabilities of gain. By coercive strategies we refer to those which afford their targets few alternatives, at high cost and with low probabilities in gain. By agreement we refer to outcomes of commitment, both explicit and implicit in social

21. The intellectual tasks, or skills in thought, we regard as relevant to policy-oriented inquiry about any problem are indicated in somewhat more detail in McDougal and Lasswell, supra note 2.

22. The broad outlines of the more comprehensive world social process are indicated in McDougal and Lasswell, supra note 2. See also McDougal, Lasswell, and Vlasic, op. cit. supra note 3, Ch. 1.

process, which are achieved by strategies consisting more of persuasion than coercion.[23]

In the most comprehensive world social process, embracing all value processes and both types of strategy, many different participants, for numerous objectives, in varying situations of international impact, employ many different base values, by diverse strategies in communication, to achieve many different outcomes in degree and content of shared commitment.[24] An appropriate understanding of the range of factors in this process that may affect both the shared expectations of commitment which the parties are able to achieve and the realism with which a subsequent interpreter may hope to approximate their shared expectations requires a more systematic review of the various phases of the process and its context. We itemize some of the more representative factors.

The Distinctive Process of Agreement

Participants

PRELIMINARY IDENTIFICATION

The participants in processes of persuasion, as in processes of coercion, are group and individual. The most important group participants, in terms of the value impacts of the agreements they make, remain of course the nation-state and lesser territorially organized communities. Of increasing importance, however, are international governmental organizations, private associations devoted to wealth and other values, political parties, and pressure groups.

The individual human being is a participant both simply *qua* individual, as when he subordinates and manages all his group roles for private interest without regard for any particular group interest, and

23. Some notion of what we mean by a *process* of making and performing agreements may be obtained from Iklé, *How Nations Negotiate* (1964). This book, though not as systematically organized as we might wish, contains much relevant factual material.

For further discussion and citations, see Gould, "Laboratory, Law, and Anecdote: Negotiations and the Integration of Data," 18 *World Politics* 92 (1965) (reviewing the Iklé work). A helpful broader context is offered in Davison, *International Political Communication* (1965).

24. A parallel description of coercive interactions is made in McDougal and Feliciano, op. cit. supra note 1, Ch. 2.

as the ultimate actor in all group interactions. Even when states make agreements, the subjectivities which are important to shared commitment, and which a subsequent interpreter must seek, are the subjectivities of individual human beings, the authoritative and controlling negotiators and their constituencies.

MORE DETAILED CHARACTERISTICS

Certain specific characteristics of both group participants and individuals may affect demand for, and expression and understanding of, commitment.

GROUPS

States

Significant characteristics may include size or aggregate strength, degree of governmentalization of internal power processes, types of base values controlled, degree of industrialization, alliances and affiliations with other states, and type of world public order demanded.

International Governmental Organizations

Significant characteristics may include geographic compass (universal, regional), comprehensiveness of purpose in relation to values (general, specialized), scope of authority and weight of other base values, and modalities of internal structures.

Private Associations

Significant characteristics may include specialization to scope value (wealth, rectitude, enlightenment, or other), organizational structure, base values, range of geographic operations, and authority relations to differing nation-states.

INDIVIDUALS

The role of particular individuals may be affected either by certain specific characteristics, such as their nationality, community affiliation, and formal authority, their skill and intelligence, and their sex, age, marital status, and so on, or by more general conditioning factors, such as culture, class, interest, personality, and past exposure to crises.

Objectives

The most general objective of parties in making an international agreement is to project a common policy with respect to a future distribution of values.

The more detailed objectives of the parties may relate to any value category (power, wealth, enlightenment, respect, well-being, skill, affection, rectitude) or to any phase of a particular value process (participation, situations, base values, strategies, outcomes, and (effects).

The great range of values sought in international agreements may be illustrated by quick reference to some of the more important types of agreements made by states: treaties of alliance (power); treaties of friendship, commerce, and navigation (wealth); communications conventions (enlightenment); agreements for the protection of minorities (respect); sanitary conventions (health); agreements for the exchange of technical personnel (skill); agreements promoting freedom of religion (rectitude); and agreements for the protection of marital and family rights (affection).

The range in phases of particular value processes sought to be affected in international agreements may be illustrated, similarly, by reference to agreements which states commonly make about power: multilateral agreements about the recognition of states or their admission to international organizations (participants); charters establishing international organizations (arenas); cessions of territory (bases of power); conventions renouncing war or regulating the conduct of hostilities (strategies); agreements relating to jurisdiction or extradition (outcomes); agreements concerning state succession effects).

The intensities with which the different parties to an agreement affirm their demands, and the relative importance which they may attach to different demands in cases of conflict or contradiction, may of course vary with different values and different phases of a particular value process, as well as with other features of the context.

The important difficulties for interpretation stem from this variability in the demands of participants and from the absence, among both group and individual participants, of any uniform hierarchy of objectives, transcending the more specific features of the context. Even the shared objectives of parties may also of course vary greatly in their compatibility or incompatibility with overriding general community policies.

Situations

GENERAL FEATURES

The situations (particular contexts of confrontation) in which international agreements are negotiated and performed differ greatly in features relevant to the communication of demands and expectations about commitment. The more important features may be conveniently categorized as those relating to spatial position, time, degree of institutionalization, and intensities in exposures to crisis.

PARTICULAR RELEVANCE

SPATIAL POSITION

Factors relating to spatial location may affect the number of participants to whom communications may be made, possible modes of communication and their effectiveness, the use of base values, and the objectives which may realistically be entertained.

TIME FACTORS

The duration of the interactions (negotiations and subsequent conduct) may affect expectations about commitment, and the lapse of time between alleged agreement outcomes and controversies about interpretation may affect the realism of interpretation.

INSTITUTIONALIZATION

The degree to which interactions are stable or unstable, patterned or unpatterned, organized or unorganized, may affect the degree to which expectations are standardized or eccentric.

CRISIS LEVEL

Degrees in expectations of violence or other destruction from rapid change may affect demands for and expectations about commitment.

Base Values

Potentially, all values may be employed as base values in processes of negotiation, and the relative positions of the parties in control over particular base values may affect both the degree and content of their commitment.

The importance of differences in power position is a matter of common observation. Scarcely less relevant are differences in wealth (capabilities for the production of goods and services), enlightenment (scientific development, intelligence services), skill (the capabilities of statesmen, negotiators), affection (solidarity in community, loyalty of allies), rectitude (sense of right, affiliation to moral world public order), and so on.

Strategies

By strategies we refer to the sequence of negotiations and other activities by which the parties mediate their subjectivities (demands, identifications, expectations) to achieve outcomes in shared commitment. The communications the parties make to each other may be either direct (expressed through the use of words or other signs) or indirect (expressed in deeds or acts of collaboration).[25]

Whether expressed in signs or deeds, the communications may exhibit certain characteristic infirmities, thus magnifying the tasks of interpretation.

SIGNS

The infirmities of signs as instruments of communication include at least the following difficulties of reference:

- Varying levels of abstraction
- Varying aspects of complementarity, (contradiction) in expression
- Varying degrees of ambiguity
- Varying degrees of completeness (gaps)

When different languages are employed by different parties, there are of course the added problems of translation.

25. Pei, *The Story of Language* Ch. 1 (1949) offers some interesting observations on non-linguistic modes of communication.

DEEDS

The infirmities of acts of collaboration as instruments of communication entirely parallel those of signs. As bases for the inference of subjectivities, they admit of vagaries in all of the following items:

Degrees of inclusivity

Degrees of complementarity

Degrees of unequivocality

Degrees of completeness

When the parties are of different cultures the difficulties in inference are obviously increased.

Outcomes

GENERAL FEATURES

The outcome phase in a process of agreement is a culminating event or sequence of events. It is the moment or moments, after past differences have been reconciled and before future differences arise, when the parties integrate and express their shared expectations of common commitment to a future policy. It is to be distinguished both from pre-outcome phases (preliminary negotiations) and from post-outcome phases (subsequent conduct and performance). The policy projected may relate to any of the great range of objectives, goal values, or particular phases of value processes indicated above, and may be expressed, through any of the possible strategies, in many differing degrees of particularity, ranging from the most generic to the most precise. Sometimes at this phase the parties exchange a document, presumptively embodying their focal agreement.

PARTICULAR RELEVANCE

The peculiar importance of the outcome phase stems from the parties' perception of it as the culminating point, at which they crystallize and consolidate their consensus and render prior differences irrelevant. This perception they frequently symbolize by a ceremony or ritual (handshake, signature, seal, sharing of provisions, exchange of document, transfer of a clod of dirt or peppercorn) which indicates clearly the point in time of irreversibility, of final commitment.

The omnipresent ambiguities, gaps, and contradictions exhibited in the manifestations of this final commitment continue of course to provide opportunity for the initiation and development of subsequent controversies about the content of commitment.

Effects

GENERAL FEATURES

The longer-term value consequences of outcomes in commitment relate both to the parties to an agreement and to the various communities in which they interact.

For the parties, such consequences are reflected in the course of subsequent conduct by which they interpret and apply the agreement to their interrelations. The course of performance or nonperformance between them may indeed require analysis and description as comprehensive and detailed as that here offered for the making of the agreement.

For the various communities of which the parties are members, the consequences of an agreement may relate to any value and exhibit many differing degrees of intensity and importance.

PARTICULAR RELEVANCE

The distinctive significance of the conduct of the parties subsequent to the outcome phase is in its reflection of the parties' continuing consensus, or want thereof, about the content of their commitment.

The significance of the effects upon the communities in which the parties are members depends upon the degree of conformity or nonconformity of such effects with the overriding policies of the more comprehensive public orders of these communities. One consequence of agreement may of course be change in overriding community policies.

The Context of Conditions

GENERAL FEATURES

The features of the larger context, embracing the process of agreement, which may significantly affect the sequence and content of communication will of course vary from agreement to agreement. Most comprehensively considered, for all international agreements, this context includes the whole world social process, with all its participants, their perspectives, the sustaining patterns of institutional practice in communication and collaboration, and the features of the resource environment. Different participants in the agreement-making process may belong to many different subcommunities.

An economic mode of categorization for specific inquiry, as has been suggested, is by value process and phase of value process.[26]

RELEVANCE

The more comprehensive process both shapes the predispositions of particular agreement-makers and constitutes the environment which expands or limits their effective capabilities in strategies of persuasion. It affects not only demands for commitment (including freedom or compulsion in choice) and capabilities for fulfillment, but also the modalities by which the parties mediate their subjectivities and the degree of their common perception and understanding.

With respect to these latter effects—upon the modalities of communication and shared understanding—the different territorial communities and different functional interest groupings to which the various parties belong are of especial significance. Consider, for example, how differently the same words are employed in nontotalitarian and totalitarian countries.

THE PROCESS OF CLAIM

In the course of making and performing international agreements, controversies may arise between the original parties, or their successors in interest, with respect to many different aspects of alleged commitment. Quite commonly the parties to these controversies,

26. For illustration in detail, see McDougal, Lasswell, and Vlasic, op. cit. supra note 3, Ch. 1.

when they cannot achieve settlement among themselves, appeal to the established community processes of authoritative decision for resolution of their differences and for many different types of remedy for asserted injury. Almost any of these controversies may, and most of them do, present demands for the interpretation of the agreement, in the sense of an effort to ascertain the genuine shared expectations of the parties, and sometimes this demand for interpretation is raised directly, as the principal issue in controversy, relatively free of other encumbering claims about the application of the agreement to events subsequent to the outcome in commitment.

For convenience in inquiry, we may generalize a process of claim, comparable to that of agreement, and consider briefly the claimants, their objectives, specific types of controversies, strategies in presentment, outcomes, and the conditions which peculiarly affect claim.

Claimants

The claimants to authoritative decision in controversies involving demands for the interpretation of international agreements commonly include, from the standpoints both of the scientific observer and of their self-description, the original parties to the agreement, designated beneficiaries, successors in interest, strangers to the agreement, and representatives of the organized general community.

The significant characteristics of all these claimants, group and individual, are entirely comparable to those previously indicated for the original parties to the agreement and may be observed in the same categories as were recommended for such parties. When the claimants are the manifest original parties, any changes in their internal constitutive processes of authority may require special notice.

Objectives

The most general objective of claimants in invoking the processes of community decision in controversies about agreement is of course to secure an application of general community policies—including that of giving the highest possible deference, compatible with overriding community goals, to the genuine shared expectations of the parties about commitment—in the resolution of such controversies. The range in detailed demand extends from that for identification of the parties to the commitment, through that for fulfillment of alleged shared expectations, to that for the partial or complete termination of such expectations. What appears as manifest demands for interpretation may of course upon occasion be disguised strategies for the achievement of other ends, such as the mere harassment of an adversary.

The more detailed objectives of claimants may be most economically described in terms of certain particular types of controversies. A categorization of controversies in terms of differences between claimants and their objectives, and in relation to the different phases of the process of agreement, may permit scholars and decision-makers to clarify community policies and to study trends in decision and factors affecting decision in ways which are comparable through time and in relation to different communities.

Specific Types of Controversy

The recurrent types of controversy—any one of which may include demands for interpretation—relate, as has been suggested, to every phase of the process of agreement, including performance or nonperformance. Hence the most convenient mode of categorization is in terms of such phases. The itemization which follows is intended to be illustrative only.

Claims Concerning Participants

- Claims that a certain body politic, international governmental organization, private association, or individual is (or is not) directly involved in the making of an agreement
- Claims that an alleged party is (or is not) competent by community standards
  - General community standards
  - National community standards
- Claims that an alleged party is (or is not) involved in a commitment through the action of a designated representative

Claims Concerning Objectives

- Claims that the alleged objectives of an agreement are (or are not) within the policy limits established by the general community for the scope of agreements

Claims Concerning Situations

Claims that because of certain standardized features of a situation (e.g. monopoly control) the expectations of the parties must be regarded as standardized

Claims Concerning Base Values

Claims that a party is (or is not) free of obligation because of gross disparity in bargaining power during the course of negotiations

Claims Concerning Strategies

Claims that a party did (or did not) employ duress

Claims that a party did (or did not) misrepresent certain features of the context

Claims that the parties were (or were not) mistaken about certain features of the context

Mutual mistake
Unilateral mistake

Claims Concerning Outcomes

Claims that shared expectations of commitment were (or were not) in fact created

Claims that the parties did (or did not) observe community-prescribed formalities for certain types of commitments

Claims that the content of a commitment is (or is not) of a certain described specification

Relating to anticipated contingencies
Relating to unanticipated contingencies

Claims Concerning Effects

Claims that a commitment has (or has not) been fully performed by the parties

Claims that a tendered performance is (or is not) in conformity with the provisions of the agreement

Claims that the benefit of an agreement has (or has not) been assigned

Claims that the parties to an agreement should (or should not) be protected in enjoyment against nonparties

Claims that the parties have (or have not) appropriately modified or terminated a commitment

Claims Concerning Conditions

Claims that the performance of an agreement has (or has not) become impossible or been frustrated

Claims that because of certain changes in the context of conditions the general community may authorize the termination of commitment

Claims Concerning the Process of Decision

Claims for the granting or withholding of certain remedies or enforcement measures for the securing of various goals in community policy

The type of controversy which most directly raises problems of interpretation is of course the third subcategory in relation to outcomes, which calls explicitly for determination of the specific content of an alleged commitment. It is sometimes suggested that the distinction we make in relation to this type of controversy, between anticipated and unanticipated contingencies, is an artificial one. The degree to which the parties did in fact anticipate and provide for certain contingencies may be the most controversial issue, and the indices afforded of the parties' shared expectations may be most meager. It must of course be agreed that this dichotomy, like most other dichotomies, points in its detailed reference to a continuum in degrees, with anticipation and failure of anticipation shading imperceptibly into each other. As will be developed below, we do not, however, believe that this fact causes any unique difficulty for decision. Whatever the precise bounds in any particular instance between anticipation and failure of anticipation, the community decision-maker is required, whether for supplementing faulty anticipation or policing explicit anticipation, to apply overriding community policies in resolving the particular controversy before him.

The special relevance of the type of controversy to the task of interpretation resides of course in the fact that the general community, quite appropriately, prescribes very different policies, both for supplementing the defective and policing the effective communications of the parties, for application to different types of controversies.

Strategies

The strategies employed by claimants in invoking community processes of decision are mainly diplomatic, that is, verbal appeals to small audiences of officials, and include the presentation of assertions about (a) the claimants' versions of the events precipitating controversy (the significant features of the process of agreement), (b) authoritatively required remedies (including definitive interpretation, damages, specific performance, injunction, recision, restitution, and so on), and (c) justifications of demands in terms of alleged community policies, technical and value-oriented, including the whole arsenal of principles of interpretation.

Outcomes

The important outcome of the invocation of community processes is, if not negotiated settlement, the submission of the dispute to an authorized decision-maker for the application of relevant general community policies, including the authoritatively determined, and lawful, shared expectations of the parties to the agreement.

The Context of Conditions

The factors in world social process which may affect the continuing consensus of the parties to an agreement, and their predispositions to invoke community processes of authoritative decision for the resolution of any differences, are of course much the same as those affecting original commitment, and may be analyzed in the same way. Of especial relevance is the degree of confidence which potential claimants have in the impartiality and effectiveness of available processes of decision.

THE CONSTITUTIVE PROCESS OF AUTHORITATIVE DECISION

The process of authoritative decision to which claimants may turn for resolution of controversies about international agreements is that same "constitutive process" of the world arena to which we alluded above—in itself in some measure established by agreement as well as by customary prescription—and sometimes inadequately known as "international law." [27] The features of this process particularly important for the resolution of controversies about the interpretation of international agreements may be synoptically recalled by brief reference to the identities and characteristics of the authorized decision-makers, the objectives for which the community establishes them, the arenas of decision, base values at the disposal of authority, the strategies employed in decision, the outcomes achieved, the effects of such outcomes upon the participants and their communities, and the conditions which shape the entire process of decision.[28]

Decision-Makers

The decision-makers who are established to apply, and hence interpret, international agreements include both international and national officials.

27. The inadequacy in past conception to which we refer stems from the failure of many writers to recognize the comprehensive and all-pervasive features of constitutive process of decision in the world arena. See McDougal and Reisman, "The Changing Structure of International Law: Unchanging Theory for Inquiry," 65 *Col. L. Rev.* 810 (1965).

The world arena, as any particular national arena, requires decisions which "constitute" its most comprehensive process of authoritative decision. Most broadly conceived, "international law" includes of course both constitutive process and the flow of particular public order decisions emanating from that process.

An excellent introduction to the literature on decision processes, with references, is Mayo and Jones, "Legal-Policy Decision Process: Alternative Thinking and the Predictive Function," 33 *Geo. Wash. L. Rev.* 318 (1964).

28. Our concern in this study is more for the principles which guide, or could guide, interpretation and application than for the details of the structures of authority in which interpretation and application go forward. It is believed that the same or comparable principles of interpretation may be usefully employed in many different structures of authority.

For brief consideration of the problem see Harvard Research, op. cit. supra

Despite the relative absence of centralized executive and judicial agencies, and of compulsory jurisdiction in such agencies as exist, a substantial competence for the application and interpretation of international agreements is in fact established by a wide variety of constitutional charters in many different agencies. Such agencies include the International Court of Justice, the various branches of the United Nations, the specialized agencies of the United Nations, and many other international governmental organizations. In addition, for the resolution of particular controversies which are impervious to negotiated settlement, special arbitral tribunals of international composition are established with great frequency.

The most important appliers and interpreters of international agreements, however, are still perhaps nation-state officials. In the absence of appropriate centralized structures of authority with compulsory jurisdiction, world constitutive process continues to confer upon each state a competence unilaterally to interpret the agreements to which it is a party, and in many instances effective interpretation can only proceed by synthesis of a series of unilateral decisions. What restraint there is upon arbitrary decision, and it is not insignificant, is afforded by the same sanction which supports all international law: common interest, policed by need for reciprocity and fear of retaliation. The state officials who participate in the application and interpretation of international agreements may be located in many different structures of authority—structures conventionally named as executive, administrative, judicial, and even legislative.

In the exercise of authority functions which bear quite directly upon application and interpretation, such as intelligence-serving, recommending, and invoking, many participants in world social process other than officials, such as private associations, political parties, pressure groups, and individual human beings, may of course play important roles.

The significant characteristics of decision-makers may vary in the same ways as indicated for the parties to international agreements. For the individual official these ways include, it may be recalled, both certain specific characteristics—effective authority, personal capabilities, age, sex, marital status, and so on—and certain more general con-

---

note 6, at 973; Briggs, *The Law of Nations: Cases, Documents, and Notes* 896, 897 (2d ed. 1952).

ditioning factors, including culture, class, interest, personality, and past exposure to crises.

Objectives

The most general objective, in relation to the application of international agreements, for which the larger community, through its effective power processes, establishes and maintains authoritative decision-makers is of course to secure the application of such agreements to specific events in the modalities most compatible with the community's basic, "constitutional" prescriptions.

In the degree that the contemporary world community genuinely projects the goals of minimum and optimum order, as we have specified them above, it also projects, as one of its basic constitutional policies, the goal of giving the utmost possible deference, compatible with other constitutional policies, to the genuine shared expectations of the parties to international agreements.

The more detailed execution of the community's most general objective in relation to the application of international agreements may thus be seen to involve two interrelated, but analytically separable, subgoals: (a) primary and supplementing interpretation, and (b) policing and integration.

PRIMARY AND SUPPLEMENTING INTERPRETATION

By interpretation we refer to responsible effort to ascertain the degree and content of the genuine shared expectations of the parties to an international agreement. Since the subjectivities of the parties are never open to direct observation, bona fide effort at interpretation can only be directed toward signs and acts of collaboration from which subjectivities may be inferred. In principle, of course, the more comprehensive, and the more systematic, the observation and weighing of relevant indices which are possible, and undertaken, the more genuine the interpretation. It must be recognized, however, that the availability and accessibility of relevant indices of subjectivities will vary greatly from case to case, and in some instances may be meager or confusing in the inferences they suggest. In these latter instances, even the most conscientious interpreter can have no recourse other than to eke out inferred subjectivities by reference to basic, general community policies.

POLICING AND INTEGRATION

By policing we refer, in contrast, to the explicit appraisal of the parties' shared expectations, in whatever degree of clarity or genuineness they may be ascertained, for their compatibility with basic, constitutional, community policies, and the rejection of any expectations which are found incompatible with such policies. The contemporary world constitutive process exhibits but few policies regarded as sufficiently basic to override the explicit agreement of particular states, but these few are important to both minimum and optimum order, and it is a widely accepted goal that agreements in contravention of these policies should not be honored in application. Parties other than states are of course subjected to many more constitutional restrictions upon the agreements they may make in hope of general community assistance with respect to application.

It need be no cause for anxiety, when it is recalled that the overriding goal in decision is comprehensive application of *all* basic community policies, that the precise interrelations and requirements of the subgoals of interpretation and policing may in particular instances be somewhat uncertain. In a particular instance of comprehensive application it may of course be difficult to distinguish between the appraisal and rejection of the genuine shared expectations of the parties and the supplementation of such expectations, when bases of inference are meager or missing, by reference to general community policies—just as we found above that it is often difficult to distinguish between contingencies which the parties did or did not anticipate, and hence between the making of genuine inferences about shared subjectivities and the supplementation of such inferences by recourse to community policies. When, however, accepted goals direct a decision-maker both to all available, important indices of shared subjectivities and to all relevant community policies, basic community policies may be rationally and fully served without the delimitation of sharp, and perforce illusory, boundaries between interrelated subgoals. The requirements of a world public order of human dignity are not that all expressions of shared subjectivities, even the most explicit, must be made effective, but only that a genuine effort be made to achieve the closest possible approximation to such subjectivities and that those which are in accord with basic, constitutional policies be made effective.[29]

Arenas

The arenas in which controversies about the application and interpretation of international agreements are resolved include all the familiar arenas of the world constitutive process of authoritative decision, both external and internal to particular states, both continuous and especially constituted, and both organized and unorganized.

Base Values

The base values at the disposal of the established interpreters of international agreements include all those at the disposal of both international governmental organizations and states, for all their varying purposes. For international governmental organizations such bases include grants of authority from states and control over military forces, resources, skills, enlightenment, well-being, loyalties, and conceptions of rectitude. For states assessment may be made in terms of control over people, resources, and institutional arrangements.

The significance of base values relates to the expectations created, or not created, about potentialities for securing conformity to decision.

Strategies

The detailed strategies available to interpreters of international agreements embrace all those generally employed by the different officials performing the application function in world constitutive processes of authority. The most important emphasis is commonly put upon the diplomatic instrument, with attempted persuasion in small group audiences by means of the familiar principles of interpretation.

The more important of these principles, as will be developed in detail below, both make reference to varying features of the parties'

29. A more explicit statement of the appropriate interrelationship of these various goals is attempted in the next chapter.

communications and the context of their communications and purport to assign rough weightings to such features in terms of their relevance to the task of interpretation. One set of principles, including Vattel's maxim that "it is not permissible to interpret what has no need of interpretation" and the associated formulation that the terms of an agreement are to be interpreted in their "plain" and "natural" meanings, is designed to focus attention upon any text alleged to incorporate the parties' expectations and to limit an interpreter's operations largely to the consideration of such a text. Still other principles, such as those relating to *travaux préparatoires* and "subsequent conduct," emphasize the relevance of broader contextual features, both pre-outcome and post-outcome, to the parties' genuine shared expectations and authorize recourse to such features. Two broad, complementary principles, the principles of effectiveness and of restrictive interpretation, spotlight the especial relevance of the parties' objectives, as major and minor and as expressed in varying levels of generality. Still other principles, which will be indicated in detail below, invoke the significance of varying syntactic and semantic references by the parties and of varying policy considerations.[30]

Outcomes

The outcomes in the process of authoritative decision relevant to problems of interpretation are the particular choices in application

30. An excellent history of the slow and tortuous development of these principles, with references and discussion, is offered by Degan, op. cit. supra note 7, at 27 et seq.

It may not be irrelevant to our theme that the interpretation of all prescriptions and agreements is attended by comparable difficulties and opportunities to note that entirely comparable principles have been developed for constitutions, statutes, precedents, and private agreements.

An indication of the range of principles employed in interpreting the constitution of the United States can apparently be found only in scattered articles. See, for examples, Merrill, "Constitutional Interpretation: The Obligation to Respect the Text," in Pound, Griswold, and Sutherland (eds.), *Perspectives of Law; Essays for Austin Wakeman Scott* (1964); Llewellyn, "The Constitution as Institution," 34 *Col. L. Rev.* 1 (1934); Beth, "Technical and Doctrinal Aids to Constitutional Interpretation," 18 *U. Pitt. L. Rev.* 108 (1950).; ten Broek, "Admissibility and Use by the United States Supreme Court of Extrinsic Aids in Constitutional Construction," 26 *Calif. L. Rev.* 287, 437, 664 (1937); Hamilton, "The Constitution—Apropos of Crosskey," 21 *U. Chi. L. Rev.* 79 (1953); Miller,

of general community policies, including both the demanded deference for the genuine shared expectations of the parties and any relevant overriding policies, to the events in controversy between the parties. Such outcomes may be described, within the limits of practi-

---

"Notes on the Concept of the 'Living' Constitution," 31 *Geo. Wash. L. Rev.* 881 (1963).

It is surprising how little explicit attention is given to principles of interpretation in the many recent books which seek to define the appropriate role of the Supreme Court in our scheme of government. The discussion is largely tangential even in such distinguished books as Wechsler, *Principles, Politics and Fundamental Law* (1960); Black, *The People and the Court* (1960); Bickel, *The Least Dangerous Branch* (1962); Rostow, *The Sovereign Prerogative: The Supreme Court and the Quest for Law* (1962); and Freund, *On Understanding the Supreme Court* (1950).

Our inheritance of principles for the interpretation of statutes closely parallels that for the interpretation of treaties. For convenient summary and references, see Johnstone, "An Evaluation of the Rules of Statutory Interpretation," 3 *U. of Kans. L. Rev.* 1 (1954); Lenhoff, "On Interpretation Theories: A Comparative Study in Legislation," 27 *Tex. L. Rev.* 312 (1949); Cohen and Cohen, *Readings in Jurisprudence and Legal Philosophy* 497–527 (1951); "A Symposium on Statutory Construction," 3 *Vand. L. Rev.* 365 (1950). Some of the more controversial issues are debated in Radin, "Statutory Interpretation," 43 *Harv. L. Rev.* 863 (1930); Landis, "A Note on 'Statutory Interpretation,'" 43 *Harv. L. Rev.* 886 (1930); Wellington and Alpert, "Statutory Interpretation and the Political Process: A Comment on *Sinclair* v. *Atkinson*," 72 *Yale L. J.* 1547 (1963); Bishin, "The Law Finders: An Essay in Statutory Interpretation," 38 *So. Cal. L. Rev.* 1 (1965); Stevens, "Statutory Interpretation, Restrictive Practices and the 'New' House of Lords," 27 *Mod. L. Rev.* 337 (1964); Silving, "In the Nature of a Compact—A Note on Statutory Interpretation," 20 *Revista del Collegio de Abogados de Puerto Rico* 159 (1960).

Principles for interpreting precedents (the communications in past decisions), though cast in somewhat different terms, are easily translated into equivalents of the more important principles with respect to treaties. The traditional principles are presented, with ample references in Llewellyn, *The Common Law Tradition: Deciding Appeals* (1960); Cross, *Precedent in English Law* (1961); Levi, *An Introduction to Legal Reasoning* (1948); Patterson, *Jurisprudence* Chs. 11, 19 (1953); Goodhart, "Determining the Ratio Decidendi of a Case," 40 *Yale L. J.* 16 (1930); Clark and Trubek, "The Creative Role of the Judge," 71 *Yale L. J.* 255 (1961). Some of the potentialities of reformulation are indicated in Lasswell, "Review" [of Llewellyn, supra], 61 *Col. L. Rev.* 931 (1961).

The familiar principles and techniques customarily employed in the interpretation of private agreements are summarized in Patterson, "The Interpretation and Construction of Contracts," 64 *Col. L. Rev.* 833 (1964). See also 3 Corbin, *On Contracts* Ch. 24 (1960).

cal enquiry, in terms of the degree to which they approach conformity to the objectives specified above.

Effects

The longer-term consequences of the outcomes in particular applications, taken in aggregate, obviously affect not merely the distribution of values among the immediate claimants and the lesser communities in which they interact, but also the kind of comprehensive public order, human dignity or other, which the general community can achieve. Of especial significance are trends in the narrowing or widening of the range of events to which the processes of consent, as contrasted with coercion, are made applicable. Expectations may also be created about the probable course of future decision in the interpretation and application of agreements.

The Context of Conditions

The conditions which may in measure affect the world constitutive process of authoritative decision in the application and interpretation of international agreements are obviously the same as those affecting the process generally, and again include the whole of world social process.

Factors which may have an especially direct impact upon the application and interpretation of agreements include:

> changes in the relative strength of the various contending world public orders, which honor persuasion and coercion as instruments of social change in differing degree;
>
> changes in the interdependences, and in the recognition of interdependences, among peoples, affecting the potentialities of sanctions;
>
> changes in the composition of territorial communities and functional groups, affecting both the modalities of communication and the perception of common meanings; and
>
> changes in the technology of communication and the recording of communication;
>
> changes in cooperative strategies in the shaping and sharing of particular values, affecting expectations about the future modalities of such cooperation.

2. CLARIFICATION OF THE GOALS AND STRATEGIES OF INTERPRETATION

In our efforts to clarify the more fundamental community policies at stake in the interpretation of international agreements, we consider first the necessity for interpretation as inherent in any process of communication, next the goals in interpretation which appear most compatible with the postulated overriding policies of a public order of human dignity, and finally, in much greater detail, the principles of interpretation which would appear best designed to secure the clarified goals.

NECESSITY FOR INTERPRETATION INHERENT IN COMMUNICATION

The discussion in the previous chapter of the processes of agreement, claim, and decision should have made it overwhelmingly obvious why, despite the continued contrary claims by certain commentators, some interpretation is always necessary in the application of international agreements to particular circumstances of controversy. In any particular instance of application, a decision-maker must draw inferences from one complex process of communication, the making and performance of an agreement, and relate these inferences to still other inferences from even more complex processes of communication, the basic constitutive process of the community and all relevant public order communications.

An authoritative decision-maker is not drawn into a problem of application unless the parties to an agreement, or others claiming through the parties, are in dispute about the relation between past expectations and present or prospective events. In many cases, perhaps the typical case, a decision-maker is asked to apply the communications in a document that all parties accept as embodying their original understanding. For the aggregate flow of cases, it would, however, be a mistake to attribute paramount or exclusive importance to written texts, because texts are often ambiguous and since controversies frequently arise over *deeds* or gestures that are also alleged to have established or exhibited original expectations of the parties. Latent in every controversy is the question of what sequence of communications the decision-maker is to regard as "the focal agreement." We employ this expression—the focal agreement—for the purpose of having a ready means of distinguishing "what is being interpreted" from the "context employed in the interpretation" or the "interpretation" made by the decision-maker.

The candid decision-maker cannot, as the preceding discussion has emphasized, in advance exclude any events from the potential context to be employed in the interpretation, since judgments of relevancy must continually be made throughout the deciding process. The decision-maker may, however, find it economic *provisionally* to specify a body of words and deeds that he is willing to take as the focal agreement which he is engaged in interpreting. We say "provisionally" in view of the possibility that the decision-maker may revise his conception of the focal agreement as he becomes more fully acquainted with the context.

Part of our task is to make a relatively complete and formal statement of the modes of inference open to the decision-maker who is seeking to ascertain the expectations of the parties to the agreement. As a preliminary to this task it is important to underline the crucial fact that the decision-maker is always acting *subsequent* to the events—even the practically contemporaneous events in agreement and controversy—that he is responsible for describing and interpreting. Moreover, these earlier events always involve *communication* if in fact an agreement was made, i.e. if shared expectations of commitment were in fact created. The complete task of applying an agreement in a particular instance must also require the relation of the communication in the agreement to the larger flow of communications in the comprehensive constitutive process by which basic community policies are established.

Let us, in development of the theme anticipated in our introduction, speak more precisely about the characteristics of communication. A sequence of communication events occurs when *someone says something to someone in a channel with some effect.*[1] The process may be one-way, as when the initiator receives no answer and hence does not become a member of the audience of someone in his own audience. Two-way communication occurs when participants make audiences of one another. We do not speak of an "agreement," of course, unless the original parties have had two-way communication.

In the terminology of communication analysis the subjectivities of communicator and audience are "mediated" by gestures, signals, and languages.[2] These mediating events are not subjective events; however, they are specialized to the inducing of such events. We speak of them as "signs," such as the physical movements made in a "gesture of rejection," or the fire signal employed to indicate that the "enemy sues for peace," or the spoken sounds uttered in saying "I agree." The gesture, signal, and speech pattern constitute sign systems when they call up relatively standardized symbol events, which are the subjectivities constituting the interpretation of signs. Some gestures are not part of a system in the sense that they do not conform to the expectations current in a social situation about the expressive movements that people make. Such idiosyncratic movements may eventually be interpreted—by a psychiatrist, for instance—and prove to be part of a system of gesture that an individual has developed on his own.[3] Sig-

1. The formula "who says what in what channel to what audience with what effect" has been employed in many expositions of communication. The components are condensed or expanded to fit the convenience of the investigator in dealing with particular problems. See, for example, Lasswell, Casey, and Smith, *Propaganda and Promotional Activities: An Annotated Bibliography* (1935); Smith, Lasswell, and Casey, *Propaganda, Communication, and Public Opinion: A Comprehensive Reference Guide* (1946); Katz, Cartwright, Eldersveld, and Lee (eds.), *Public Opinion and Propaganda* (1954). For a general discussion of communication as the basis of personal interaction see Hartley and Hartley, *Fundamentals of Social Psychology,* Part I (1952).

Relevant studies include Deutsch, *Nationalism and Social Communication* (1953) and *The Nerves of Government* (1963); Doob, *Communication in Africa* (1961); Hurley, "The Role of Communications Technology in Democracy," George Washington University Program of Policy Studies in Science and Technology, Paper No. 9 (1965).

2. See Morris, *Signs, Language and Behavior* (1946); Sapir, "Communication" (1931), 4 *Encyclopaedia of the Social Sciences* 78; "Symbolism" (1934), 14 id. 492, *Language* (1921); Miller, *Language and Communication* (1951); Brown, *Words and Things* (1958).

3. Sullivan stressed the role of symbol, as in *The Interpersonal Theory of Psychiatry* (1953). See Ruesch and Bateson, *Communication: The Social Matrix of Psychiatry* (1950).

nals and languages are by definition systems of signs; that is, they are comprised of units which are manipulated according to conventional rules and interpreted with at least a minimum stability in a given social setting.

The same symbol or symbol sequence can be called up by a variety of signs. The interpretation "He says, 'I agree,' " for instance, can be made by one who listens to spoken words or observes a code of hand signals, or sees a gesture that lacks the stereotyped patterning of a code but is nonetheless conventionally recognizable. Similarly, the same sign may, in different contexts, call up very different symbol events.

It is thus evident that no act of communication is ever solely "subjective" or entirely "nonsubjective." [4] It is necessarily both. Communication is a sequence that we define as beginning with subjective events—the intention to participate in a given activity in a certain way—and proceeding through expression—which consists in such nonsubjective events as using one's voice or shaking one's head—to the subjective events eventually occurring in an audience, which are preceded by physical orientation toward a channel and the transmission of sensory events to the brain. At any cross section in a communication sequence an observer-participant must recognize that subjective and nonsubjective events occur simultaneously.[5] Even as he introspects, a trained person is aware that the "awareness of awareness" occurs in a context of brain cells, or that it is affected by the sensations initiated by the black letters of a document.

Two kinds of indices are required, therefore, for describing any act of communication: indices that refer directly to subjective events; and indices that refer to nonsubjective events. Since the subjectivities of other people cannot be directly observed the index is always hypo-

4. The distinction between "subjective" and "objective" interpretation sometimes put forward—as for example in Degan, *L'Interprétation des Accords en Droit International Public* 151 et seq. (1963) makes no reference to the realities of a process of communication. Ascertainment of the expectations created by a communication is always a matter of inference. The difference between the two views, so metaphorically labeled, can only be in the range of the features of a context which are regarded as permissible bases of inference. The labels are of no policy relevance to choice.

5. See Pribram, "A Review of Theory in Physiological Psychology," 11 *Annual Review of Psychology* 1 (1960), which puts the work on brain chemistry, neurology, and brain simulation in perspective, giving regard among others to the work of Ashby, Bruner, Gerard, Hebb, Klüver, MacKay, von Neumann, McCulloch, and Pitts.

thetical when applied to them, although it may be highly probable. In referring to one's own subjectivities, the index is *not* hypothetical. However, one makes a record that from the point of view of other observers must be employed by them as a hypothetical index of the subjectivities of the one who prepared the record.

It need scarcely be said that the description of intersubjective events is a precarious matter. Some of the many features in the context that may affect the sharing of subjectivities by the parties to an agreement have been indicated in the previous chapter. When it is added that the details of every sequence of communication are always changing in relation to the whole context of which they are a part, and that the foresight of the parties to an agreement is seldom adequate to anticipate and provide in minute detail for the evolving future, the precariousness of any subsequent interpretation is obvious.[6] Yet the fact that social life does go on suggests, as we have developed above, that the difficulties are in necessary degree surmountable.

THE POSTULATED GOALS OF INTERPRETATION

Our recommended goals of interpretation are based on the fundamental expectation that future events cannot fail to be affected in some degree by any decision outcome. The decision-maker who engages in acts of interpretation is in search of the past and present; but the past and present are pursued as a way of accomplishing a future result. Obviously, decision of the particular case calls for action

6. The point is eloquently and fully documented in Schachter, "The Relation of Law, Politics and Action in the United Nations," *Recueil des Cours* [I] 1963, p. 169. He writes (p. 196):

> Certainly the words of the Charter must be the starting point, but as we have seen, in relatively few cases can the words provide a substantial part of the answer. In most cases the dictionary and the texts themselves can do little to resolve the issues which are presented as a result of generality, indeterminancy, conflicts and inconsistencies of the Charter norms. It is apparent from the various types of norms that the range of relevant considerations will vary considerably from problem to problem, but it is also clear that in a great many cases the organs have to evaluate complex situations in terms of a diversity of factors, including some which clearly involve judgements of 'reasonableness', importance, intent, expectations and 'necessity'.

A comparable demonstration both of the necessity for interpretation and of the necessity for departure from a "textualist" approach is offered by Hexner,

affecting the future relations of the parties, and particular consequences are expected to follow the decision. Results are not, however, restricted to the fate of the immediate parties, even when precautions are taken to circumscribe the significance of the decision as precedent. The chain of effect may prove to be visible for a very short time or it may be discerned for long periods and in many jurisdictions. In any event, effects are not to be eliminated by wishing or pretending that they will not occur.

The goals of interpretation that we propose take into consideration the obligation of any decision-maker to act rationally in harmony with the fundamental objectives of the community whose authoritative spokesman he is. Decision outcomes have consequences that can and ought to be affected by deliberate efforts to further the realization of the basic pattern of value distribution and the fundamental institutions that are compatible with the preferred system of public order.

The particular goals we here suggest recognize the opportunities that decision-makers often enjoy to give effect to the goals of a public order of human dignity. At the level of verbal commitment many authoritative decision-makers of the contemporary world community have associated themselves with the overriding objectives of such a public order system. In concrete controversies such decision-makers may find themselves able to bring the facts of life more into accord with their proclaimed purposes.

The primary or initial goal of interpretation we recommend is thus both in accord with a great historic tradition and highly distinctive of a system of public order in which human dignity is conscientiously sought. This primary, distinctive goal stipulates that decision-makers undertake a disciplined, responsible effort to ascertain the genuine shared expectations of the particular parties to an agreement. The link with fundamental policy is clear: to defend the dig-

---

"Teleological Interpretation of Basic Instruments of Public International Organizations," in Engel (ed.), *Law, State and International Legal Order: Essays in Honor of Hans Kelsen* (1964).

For other recent indications of difficulties in a "textualist" approach to important types of agreements, see Schwelb, "The Nuclear Test Ban Treaty and International Law," 58 *Am. J. Int'l. L.* 642 (1964); O'Connell, "State Succession and Problems of Treaty Interpretation," 58 id. 41 (1964); DeVries, "Choice of Language," 3 *Va. J. Int'l. L.* 26 (1963).

nity of man is to respect *his* choices and not, save for overriding common interest, to impose the choices of others upon him.[7]

As a second or ancillary goal, in support of search for the genuine shared expectations of the parties, we recommend that in instances when such search must falter or fail because of gaps, contradictions, or ambiguities in the parties' communication, a decision-maker should supplement or augment the relatively more explicit expressions of the parties by making reference to the basic constitutive policies of the larger community which embraces both parties and decision-maker. It would appear that no conceivable alternative goal is in accord with the aspiration to defend and expand a social system compatible with the overriding objectives of human dignity.

A final major goal must of course, for the protection of overriding common interests, stipulate that when grave contradictions are found between the explicit expectations of the parties to an agreement and the requirements of fundamental community policy, decision-makers should refuse to give effect to the expectations of the parties. This "policing," or integrative goal would appear inherent in the general community expectation that an authoritative decision-maker who lives up to his full obligation must examine the significance of every specific controversy for the entire range of policy purposes sought by the total system to which he is responsible. Beyond its negative or

7. Some of the modern rejections of this goal appear to derive from Mr. Justice Holmes. In a much quoted essay "The Theory of Legal Interpretation," 12 *Harv. L. Rev.* 417, 418 (1899), reprinted in *Collected Legal Papers* (1920) 203, 204, Holmes insists that the task of an interpreter of a document is not "to discover the particular intent of the individual, to get into his mind and bend what he said to what he wanted" but rather to ask "what those words would mean in the mouth of a normal speaker of English." In justification he asserts that since the "normal speaker of English" is "external to the particular writer," "a reference to him as the criterion is simply another instance of the externality of the law."

The answer to this is of course that an interpreter does not have to achieve "externality" to the parties to an agreement. He has such externality thrust upon him by the fact that he cannot directly observe the subjectivities of the parties. The relevant questions are what goal is to be established for interpretation and what bases of inference are to be examined in pursuit of that goal. The position taken by Holmes would impose upon the parties purposes other than their own and drastically limit the features of the context open for examination as bases for inferring expectation. It might be noted, further, that the criterion of the "prudent man" (another version of the "plain and natural meaning" rule) does not escape the necessity of inferring subjectivities: for the subjectivities of the parties, it merely substitutes the subjectivities imputed to the whole community.

"policing" function, requiring the rejection of the parties' explicit expectations which contradict constitutive policies, this residuary integrative goal has certain important affirmative functions.

Among the important affirmative functions of the integrative goal is that of strengthening peoples' expectations that their decision processes will be impartial and competent. This goal is common to all decision-making; but it is peculiarly significant when the interpretation of agreements is at stake. For agreements are acts of communication which are widely admitted to present delicate problems that make heavy claims upon the good faith and skill of those who settle disputes concerning their application.

We may further specify our recommended integrative goals by emphasizing the consequences of interpretation for the aggregate agreement process. Since clarity of expectation may be encouraged in future agreement-making if decision-makers give deference to carefully worked out arrangements, we include among the objectives of interpretation the encouragement of deliberate efforts among the parties to future agreements to obtain definiteness of expectation.

Decision-makers who act as interpreters have unusual opportunities to promote mutuality of understanding in the agreement process by seeking to nullify the impact of obscurity-producing factors. Experienced observers know that participants in many international agreements are likely to differ greatly in knowledge and skill. The decision-makers of powerful industrialized states are in a position to exert disproportionate influence upon the outcome of controversies that involve diverging constructions of an agreement. Hence the norms of the industrial powers tend to affect the result; and unless the parties have had equal knowledge of these norms, and equal skill in applying them, the original agreement may eventually work to the disadvantage of the weaker and less industrialized power. This applies whether the stronger participant is commonly described as "socialist" or "capitalist."

Fortunately the decision-makers of the international community are sometimes able—especially when the process of applying agreements occurs in a judicial arena which is as a matter of public policy somewhat sheltered from the effect of short-range pressures—to act with relatively long-range policy goals in view. If such decision-makers systematically examine the position of the agreement-making parties for the purpose of discovering the degree to which they were in possession of equal knowledge and skill and, further, act explicitly to modify the consequences of handicap, the world of agreement-makers will be put on notice. It is not oversanguine to suggest that the participants who are in control of knowledge and talent (of the kind suitable to modern industrial culture) will be influenced to refrain from fully exploiting a one-sided situation. Already there are examples of voluntary assistance given by counselors who represent strong corporate negotiators to less experienced negotiators who are acting on behalf of weaker parties.

The suggestion is often put forward—especially by persons who resent the subtleties involved in every act of communication—that interpreters ought to give a standard meaning to the same terms or rituals and in this way reduce the uncertainties of agreement-making. To a modest extent this is a feasible objective. It is practicable—as the history of judicial decision amply shows—presumptively to defer to the expectations that ordinarily accompany terms of art in the legal vocabulary of the agreement-makers' communities. This is most obviously true when the parties have had competent professional assistance in negotiation.

Nevertheless, the potentialities of the "standard meaning" objective are severely limited, especially when we take into consideration the ambiguous character of such terms. They often assume factual contingencies whose occurrence or nonoccurrence is in controversy. If community decision-makers are so enamoured of the "standard meaning" aim that they jump to the conclusion that the presence of a standard term attests the presence of certain "facts," the interpreter fails to perform his proper task. Subject to the fundamental principle that *all* objectives of interpretation are to be applied, a limited role can, however, be recommended to the encouraging of standard modes of expressing recurrent relationships.

Even though further mention may give the point disproportionate emphasis, we might call attention to the standardizing and simplifying tendencies that are exhibited in languages. Where the participants in a process of communication employ the same linguistic signs, the most frequently used signs tend to become more and more economical in terms of psychophysical characteristics. The most frequently used words are shorter than the words less often employed. This has been generalized by Zipf as an empirical law of least effort. We can safely predict that as world experience becomes more uniform, and as communication is more intense, the number of short terms of legal art will increase; and the formal significance of each term—its relation to other terms—will be generally understood. However, interpreters cannot hope to wait for this process to work itself out; nor can they expect to be exempted from the task of verifying in the concrete case all hypotheses regarding the expectations of the parties that are suggested by whatever terms of art were employed.

Our recommended goals of interpretation may thus be summarized in the following specifications:

THE GOALS OF INTERPRETATION

General statement: The goal is application of international agreements in terms of all community policies, including the policy of according the highest possible deference, compatible with other constitutional policies, to the genuine shared expectations of the particular parties.

More specific statement

- Primary interpretation
  - Give deference to the genuine shared expectations of the particular parties to an agreement.
- Supplementing interpretation
  - When expectations are ambiguous or vague, complete the argument in accordance with the goals of public order.
- Policing and integrating interpretation
  - Negative
    - Do not give effect to the expectations of the parties when they conflict with the goals of the system of public order.
  - Affirmative
    - Encourage the conformity of future agreement-making with the goals of public order.
      - By explaining criteria of judgment, strengthen expectations that the decision process can be relied upon to be impartial and competent.
      - Encourage deliberate efforts to obtain definiteness of expectation among the parties to future agreement by re-

warding, where possible, careful agreement-making in the past.

Promote mutuality of expectation in the agreement process by seeking to nullify the impact of obscurity-producing factors (such as those growing out of discrepancies in the knowledge and skills available to the parties) by calling attention to community policies that might contribute to the result sought.

Reduce the uncertainties of agreement-making by giving deference to terms of art employed by competent negotiators (subject to investigations to ascertain the occurrence of implied contingencies in the concrete case).

STRATEGIES OF INTERPRETATION

From clarification of the goals of interpretation, we turn to the invention of more appropriate strategies for securing such goals. For decision-makers concerned to make interpretations which promote the overriding goals of an international order of human dignity—whether in minimum or maximum degree—we commend the systematic employment of a comprehensive set of principles of interpretation. The principles we recommend have their origin of course in the experience of interpreters authoritatively charged with the application of international agreements. Since, however, the contemporary study of communication and decision processes provides a clearer map than has hitherto been available of the relevant task and potential resources, these principles are presented in more detail and somewhat more systematically than has been customary in the past.

If principles are successfully put into words they enter the stream of communication that affects the preparation and conduct of the decision process, and contribute to the level of performance of any individual interpreter, or to any corrective arrangements for interpretation. We are chiefly concerned in the present analysis with the problem-solving task that faces the individual decision-maker.[8]

8. In his distinguished articles on "The International Court: Rules of Treaty Interpretation," in 43 *Minn. L. Rev.* 369, 44 id. 5 (1959), Professor James F. Hogg has sought to demonstrate that principles of interpretation serve the purpose of limiting the arbitrary discretion of decision-makers.

It may require emphasis that our design is broader. We seek to demonstrate

The decision-maker moves from a starting point in time—the opening gambits of a controversy—to the final announcement of his response. His response is a commitment to one or more of the diverse claims brought before him by contending parties, modified by his obligation to integrate the agreement in the frame of reference supplied by the various goals of public order.

On reflection it is evident that two basic questions are explicitly—or tacitly—solved by every decision-maker. There is the question of content: What shall I think about? And there is the question of procedure: How shall I think about it? [9] Principles of interpretation are helpful if they provide guidance to the interpreter in the performance of his delicate task of disposing of particular controversies over agreements.

Principles of content are addressed to the choice of subject matter that is relevant to the alternatives of policy open to a decision-maker. From the beginning of his connection with a controversy the interpreter acts selectively, since he is aware of the obligation to come up at the end with a declaration that some claims are more in harmony with relevant public policy than rival claims. Hence he is continually engaged in an evaluative sequence that culminates in a terminal crystallization of judgment. The principles of content provide reminders of the criteria to be used in preferring one alternative to another. They are phrased with explicit reference to the objectives of the decision-maker that we have formulated above as objectives of primary, supplementary, and integrative interpretation. The principles in regard to content will particularize the evaluative task by directing attention to potentially significant features of the processes of agreement, claim, and decision and to the obligation to prefer one response to another when rival interpretations are put before the decision-maker.

The principles of procedure, though intimately intertwined with content, deal with the agenda used by the problem-solver in bringing relevant subject matter to the center of his attention. Included are

---

that principles of interpretation can be devised and employed to promote all of a community's basic goals, including that of ascertaining and implementing the genuine shared expectations of parties to agreements.

9. The distinction made between principles of content and procedure is developed by Lasswell, "Clarifying Value Judgment: Principles of Content and Procedure," 2 *Inquiry* 87 (1958).

the technical devices by which controversial pre-arena events (events prior to the submission of the dispute to the decision-maker) can be described. Concerning questions of agenda, for instance, it is helpful to emphasize the importance of establishing a provisional statement of the original agreement—and of arriving at this formulation early in the proceedings. The choice of technical procedures is pertinent when rival methods are relied on by the parties to assert the presence of shared expectations. Throughout the decision process the official is giving preference, not only to alternative content, but to alternative procedures.

It will be apparent that we lay great stress on considering the entire context of events in which an alleged agreement took place, and which may affect the future of public order. The contextual point is so significant for both content and procedure, in fact, that we give it first mention.

STRATEGIES OF INTERPRETATION

General statement: The probability of maximizing the realization of the goals sought by interpretation is increased if individual decision-makers employ a comprehensive set of principles of interpretation that include principles of both content and procedure. Principles of content guide the choice of subject matter relevant to evaluating the alternatives of policy open to the decision-maker. Principles of procedure are agendas and techniques for bringing pertinent content to the focus of the decision-maker's attention.

Principles of Content

General statement: In performing the tasks of primary, supplementary, and integrative interpretation of agreements, give preference to policy alternatives that have been considered in the context of factors that affect the processes of agreement and claim, and all community policies at stake.

More specific statements

In the task of primary interpretation, give preference to the interpretation that has been evaluated by the decision-maker for degree of approximation to the expectations shared by the parties during the course of their interaction, as indicated by the context as a whole (as against interpretations not so evaluated).

Observe the interactions among the parties at phases of the process of agreement (participants, objectives, situations, base values, strategies, outcomes, effects).

Note influence upon the interactions (among the parties) of the context of factors that affect the process of agreement at every phase.

In the task of integrating agreements, give preference, by considering relevant features of the processes of claim and decision, to interpretations that harmonize most fully with public order prescriptions and that will probably do most to influence future agreements toward harmony with public order goals.

Principles of Procedure

General statement: In making primary, supplementary, and final interpretation of agreements, give preference to procedures that are most likely, as indicated below, to disclose relevant content in the most clarifying order.

More Specific Statement

In making primary interpretations

At each stage of the consideration of the agreement process, proceed by paired comparison of procedural alternatives, giving preference, when it can be economically done, to the procedure that is the more intensive and the more competently executed.

Before final commitment, review the provisional selection of procedures in the whole available context, and give preference to the results obtained by the procedures that are most intensive and competently executed.

At each stage of the consideration of the agreement process, in employing principles of content, proceed by paired comparison of alternative interpretations, giving provisional preference to the interpretation that appears to provide the most accurate estimate of the expectations of the parties.

Before final commitment, review provisional choices in the light of the whole, giving final preference to the interpretation that appears to provide the most accurate estimate of the expectations of the parties.

In integrating agreements (with community policies)

At each stage in evaluating past or prospective events according to a policy objective, give preference to the procedure that is most intensive and competently executed for establishing the policy and the pertinent objective.

Before final commitment, review the provisional selection of procedures in the light of the whole available context, giving preference to the results of procedures that are most intensive and competently executed.

At each stage of the consideration of past or prospective events according to a policy objective, give provisional preference to the alternatives most in harmony with policy, and most likely to further its future realization.

Before final commitment, review the provisional preferences in the light of the total context, giving preference to the alternatives that appear most in harmony with all policy objectives and pertinent information.

In the illustrations that follow we focus largely on the task of primary interpretation, leaving principles of integration for development elsewhere. Our aim here is, further, to be suggestive only,[10] and not exhaustive, of the possible formulation of helpful principles. It may perhaps bear emphasis also that the principles are to be applied in relation to each other and that none of them is to be construed as purporting to dictate particular outcomes in interpretation, irrespective of reference to the total context. We begin with proposed principles of content and then turn to principles of procedure.

10. Degan, op. cit. supra note 4, at 74, offers a "système entier" which might be compared with what we outline. In the absence of clearly postulated goals for interpretation, he has no criteria or techniques for relating different principles to each other, and the particular itemizations he offers are far from homogeneous in their references to the processes of agreement, claim, and decision.

Principles of Content

The Contextual Principle

Interpret the focal agreement according to the expectations shared by the parties during the course of their interaction, including both the making and performance of the agreement, as indicated by the context considered as a whole.[11]

This is the most comprehensive guide to the decision-maker. It is of far-reaching importance, since it reminds him to beware of permitting any details exclusively to dominate his judgment before they have been viewed in the total context. It implies the consideration of all relevant signs and deeds occurring at any time prior to, at the time of, or subsequent to outcome. Beyond this, it requires consideration also of the entire process of agreement and its context of conditioning factors, as well as of the processes of claim and decision and of possible future impacts upon various expectations of the current decision process.

Principles Relating to Phases of the Process of Agreement

PARTICIPANTS

Identify the parties to the agreement, observing their degree of involvement and their varying characteristics.

THE PRINCIPLE OF INVOLVEMENT

It sometimes happens that several parties are alleged to have participated in the formation and in the subsequent benefits and burdens of an agreement. In identifying the parties, those with little involvement in the process of agreement-making are to be given a weight in the examination of expectations commensurate with the role they have played.[12]

11. Awareness of context is the principal characteristic of scientific fields previously occupied with "itemistic" ways of thinking. Among modern innovators—in addition to Freud and psychoanalysts—are Koffka, Köhler, Wertheimer, Lewin, Piaget, Tolman.

12. The degree of involvement of an individual in an interaction is one of the most important factors (or factor combinations) to be taken into account in as-

THE RELEVANCE OF CHARACTERISTICS

Group

Account should be taken of the differing characteristics of the various group participants, such as nation-states, international organizations, and private associations. Allowance should be made, thus, for the difference in perspectives when one of the parties is a state, representing a whole body politic, and the other is a private association, primarily dedicated to the scope value of wealth (that is, wealth as the primary value sought).[13]

Individual

Appropriate account should be taken of characteristic differences in the perspectives of individual participants related to different cultures, classes, interest groupings, personality forms, and exposures to crises.[14] Where the parties have comparable characteristics, subjectivities are more likely to be shared. In cases of alleged conflicting subjectivities, prefer meanings suggested by characteristics common to the parties.

OBJECTIVES

THE RELEVANCE OF VALUE RANGE

Consideration should be given to the whole range of values alleged by the parties, or observed by the interpreter, to be at stake in the

---

sessing the specific strategies that he uses. The degree of identification of participants with one another is pertinent; see among the many current discussions Stein, Vidich, and White (eds.), *Identity and Anxiety: Survival of the Person in Mass Society* (1960), especially papers by Erikson and Fromm-Reichmann. In the context of decision studies, see Edwards, "The Theory of Decision Making," 51 *Psychological Bulletin* 380 (1954). For general theories of motivation, see Brown, *The Motivation of Behavior* (1961), and Hall, *Psychology of Motivation* (1961).

13. See Marvick (ed.), *Political Decision-makers* (1961), especially contributions of Marvick, Lasswell, and Pye. The bibliography is a helpful guide to the perspectives of political elite (and some non-elite) groups.

14. On such points see the volume by Marvick, id., and studies by Shils, Dogan, Guttsman, Eulau, and associates.

making and performance of the agreement. The genuineness of asserted value objectives may be tested by relating them to other features of the context, such as the initial value positions of the parties and the magnitude of potential gains and losses. No hierarchical ordering of objectives should be substituted for the ordering by participants.[15]

It is necessary also to appraise the compatibility of the different objectives of the parties with the constitutive policies of the general community and the goal values of a public order of human dignity. Asserted objectives contrary to constitutive policies should of course be rejected. In cases of conflict between asserted objectives, or doubt about objectives, presume in favor of objectives most in accord with human dignity goals.

THE PRINCIPLE OF PROJECTING EXPECTATIONS

Interpret in accordance with the major objectives of the parties, considering varying intensities in demand and attributions of importance. (Traditionally this has been called the principle of effectiveness and has received particular emphasis among the guides available to community decision-makers.) In establishing the major objectives, do not impose upon the parties objectives beyond the expectations that they genuinely shared. (Traditionally this is one formulation of the principle of restrictive interpretation).

The major and minor objectives of parties may be distinguished in varying ways. Explicit statements by the parties may indicate what they regard as major or minor, nuclear or peripheral. When explicit statement is missing or ambiguous, note may be taken, with respect to verbal communications, of such factors as generality and elaborateness in mode of statement, prominence in position or location among statements, and amount of repetition; and in regard to communications conveyed by collaborative acts, of such factors as intensity of effort, amount of repetition, and the sum of all values expended. The most explicitly stated, most elaborated, most repeated, and most prominently displayed objectives should be given at least a presumptive priority over those that are less explicitly stated, less elaborated, less repeated, and less prominently displayed.

15. On the diversity of human values in concrete circumstances, see Albert and Kluckhohn, *A Selected Bibliography on Values, Ethics, and Esthetics in The Behavioral Sciences and Philosophy, 1920–1958* (1959).

Another distinction is between objectives which relate to demanded outcomes in value processes ("scope values" or "ends") and those which relate to the strategies to be employed in pursuit of such values ("employing base values," "means"). When conflicts are alleged between objectives relating to demanded outcomes and those relating to preferred strategies, a tentative presumption might, upon the principle of the equivalency of alternative strategies, be made to avail in favor of the former.

THE PRINCIPLE OF THE ANTICIPATED SOLUTION

Many contingencies are often explicitly mentioned by the parties during negotiation which are not expressly incorporated in what the parties regard as the final agreement. Interpreters should take into account solutions that were anticipated, and not rejected, during the agreement process. If these solutions were not included by the parties in order to keep the agreement simple and short, a presumption favors giving effect to them. If, on the contrary, such solutions were rejected on other grounds, the presumption is against them.

It is common experience that various contingencies may be mentioned in the course of negotiation which the parties fail to elaborate at the "outcome" phase of the original agreement, not because the specification is uncongenial to the parties, but because they attach importance to a short and simple statement. In such instances, decision-makers are well advised to take into account anticipated solutions that were not spelled out. When the failure to elaborate an alternative was the result of disagreement among the parties about its acceptability, the presumption should be emphatically against giving effect to such rejected solutions.

SITUATIONS

THE PRINCIPLE OF ASSESSING THE PARTICULAR INTERACTIONS AMONG THE PARTIES IN REFERENCE TO THE GENERAL PATTERNS IN THE SETTING

The expectations of the parties may be unclear if attention is limited to isolated interactions in the agreement process. These unclarities may disappear, or tend to disappear, if the characteristics of the situation which might affect shared subjectivities are taken into account.

Spatial Position

Observe the geographical features of the interaction and the degree of direct confrontation, or separation, of the parties during the course of the mediation of their subjectivities. Note the technological instruments employed by the parties and the possible bearing of these instruments upon communication.[16] Preferences should be given to inferences drawn from situations in which the parties have achieved the fullest psychophysical confrontation.[17]

Time Features

Observe the duration of negotiations and subsequent collaborative behavior, considering the frequency of contact of participants. Note especially the lapse of time between the outcome phase of agreement and the rise of controversy. Prefer the inferences as to subjectivities derived from enduring and repeated interactions to those from briefer and more episodic interplay.

Institutionalization

Observe the degree to which the interactions and expectations of the parties about the particular type of agreement are routinized (perhaps even prescribed) by the community.[18] Identify the specific

16. "Information theory" is concerned with the physical features of the channel through which the pattern of signs introduced as "input" must pass until it becomes "output." The theory emphasizes "noise" phenomena that interfere with the transmittal of "bits" of information. In the U.S. the most important mathematical analysis of the problem was made by telephone engineers. See Shannon and Weaver, *The Mathematical Theory of Communication* (1949); Cherry, *On Human Communication* (1957); Ayer et al., *Studies in Communication* (1955).

17. The dangers of overloading a channel or system of communication has been repeatedly stressed by Deutsch in several studies, beginning with *Nationalism and Social Communication* (1953).

18. A guide to the role of agreement-making in folk societies is Hoebel, *The Law of Primitive Man: A Study in Comparative Legal Dynamics* (1954); Pospisil, *Kapauku Papuans and Their Law* (1958); Llewellyn and Hoebel, *The Cheyenne Way* (1941); Malinowski, *Crime and Custom in Savage Society* (1926); Barton, *Ifugao Law* (1919); Gutmann, *Chagga Law* (1926).

features of routinization or prescription for the particular type of agreement (as, e.g., in the case of insurance contracts and other contracts of adhesion). Prefer the community-established expectations for routinized agreements in the absence of evidence that the particular parties shared different expectations.

Crisis Level

Consider the varying intensities of crisis during the interactions of the parties and the potential impacts of crisis upon the shared subjectivities of the parties. It is obvious that the importance to be accorded crisis factors will vary with many other features of the context and especially with different types of agreements (e.g., contrast agreements for alliance with those relating to wealth).[19]

BASE VALUES

THE PRINCIPLE OF ASSESSING THE VALUE POSITIONS OF THE PARTIES

Uncertainties regarding the expectations of parties may be lessened by taking into consideration the different categories of values controlled by the parties and the degree of their equality or inequality in value position.[20] It is necessary to observe the values at the disposal of each party and to consider the bearing of each value upon potential communication. Thus enlightenment and skill may affect understanding and capability for communication; power may affect the "fullness" of communication; respect position may affect styles; and so on. Upon the assumption that the stronger party is likely to have access to more talent and to exercise more effective control over

19. Detailed documentation of the contrast between crisis and intercrisis agreement-making is obtainable from the literature of diplomacy (war and peace), business fluctuation (prosperity and depression), family relations (marriage and divorce), and so on through all value-institution components of the social process.

20. Modern social research is describing the distribution of values in communities of different size and location. For example: Janowitz (ed.), *Community Political Systems* (1961); Verba, *Small Groups and Political Behavior: A Study of Leadership* (1961); Sprout and Sprout, *Foundations of National Power* (1945, rev. 1951).

channels of communication, when the parties are highly unequal, a modest presumption may be indulged in favor of the interpretations urged by the weaker party.

STRATEGIES

THE PRINCIPLE OF INCLUDING ALL STRATEGIC ACTS

Acts of communication are to be described in terms of signs and deeds; and, since the entire sequence of acts and deeds may be relevant to shared subjectivities, an interpreter should include in his consideration all the signs and deeds throughout the negotiations that culminated in commitments, as well as during the course of performance. When contradictions, ambiguities, gaps, and varying levels of abstraction appear in communications by words, or their equivalents in communications by deeds, recourse must be had to other features of the context for clarification of the parties' shared subjectivities.

THE PRINCIPLE OF PREFERRED MODE OF EXPRESSION

When contradictory results are given by sources of equal credibility that refer to different modes of expression (language, gesture, deed), give priority to the sources that depend on the most important mode of expression employed by the parties in arriving at the focal agreement.

We take cognizance of the fact that decision-makers are often confronted by a text that is accepted by the parties as constituting their focal agreement, though they differ in the meaning to be attributed to it. It is also recognized that part at least of the focal agreement may be inferred from gestures alleged to have been employed by the parties; or inferences may be based on activities or a course of conduct. It is not within the scope of the principle of preferred mode of expression to serve as a guide in sifting the evidence for or against the alleged occurrence of a word, gesture, or deed. Rather the rule is intended to assume that the words, gestures, or deeds have been satisfactorily described, but that when attention is given to inferences that largely depend upon each category separately, contradictions appear. Thus one party may confront textual statements with contradictory evidence from gesture or deed. This principle suggests that when such contradictions are found, priority is to be given to sources relating to language when the focal agreement is a text, to sources pertaining to gesture when the agreement relied principally upon gesture, and to sources relating to course of conduct when the focal agreement is generalized primarily from course of conduct.

THE PRINCIPLE OF LOGICAL RELATIONSHIP

If the controversy relates to alleged logical contradictions, ambiguities, or gaps, choose the logical inferences that appear to have been shared by the parties during the course of interaction. As an aid in elucidating the logical structure of the focal agreement (and of any other pertinent statements), use may be made of formal methods of analysis.

Care should be taken, however, not to substitute esoteric possibilities for the relationships actually intended by the parties. The methods developed by modern logicians are so refined that they are capable of disclosing the existence of relationships in the logical structure of focal agreements that might have been overlooked or ignored by common consent when the parties made the original understanding. The decision-maker should therefore consider the interpretations that were prevalent among persons of approximately the same characteristics as the parties at the time when what we now regard as a logical gap or ambiguity occurred.[21]

THE PRINCIPLE OF ADAPTING THE LEVEL OF GENERALITY OR PARTICULARITY TO THE OTHER FEATURES OF THE CONTEXT

Signs may be employed at any level of generality. When general or particular statements regarding expectations are available, the task of the decision-maker is to determine by reference to other factors in context which level of generality most nearly represents the parties' shared expectations. Importance should be given to any emphasis

21. See Allen, "Symbolic Logic: A Razor Edged Tool for Drafting and Interpreting Legal Documents," 66 *Yale L. J.* 833 (1957) and *M.U.L.L.*, the newsletter initiated by the Electronic Data Retrieval Committee of the American Bar Association and the Yale Law School. See also Jensen, *The Nature of Legal Argument* (1957); Levi, *An Introduction to Legal Reasoning* (1948).

upon goal and to repetition, prominence, and elaboration. By examining the whole concatenation of factors arbitrariness may be avoided.

OUTCOMES

THE PRINCIPLE OF THE DISTINCTIVE PHASE OF AGREEMENTS

When sources of equal credibility give contradictory results concerning the expectations that prevailed at the pre-outcome and outcome phases of the agreement process, assign priority to the expectations shared at the outcome phase. The outcome phase—that denoting the parties' final commitment upon the projection of a future policy—may be identified by the parties' explicit statement or from various features of the context, such as ceremonies, attachment of signatures or seals, delivery of an object, and so on.

The point of stressing the significance of the outcome phase is, in part, the prominent position that it presumably occupies in the perspectives of the parties to an agreement. In many instances the final outcome is reached after protracted negotiations in which incomplete or even equivocal indications may be used as part of the strategy by which a favorable result was sought. Presumably the parties are optimally alert to their total value position when final phrasings are being accepted and adopted.

The considerations in favor of stressing the outcome phase weaken to the degree that such a phase was indistinct in the perspectives of the parties. Many "customary" practices bring about expectations by a gradual process containing few if any discernible episodes to alert the parties to the precise character of their favorable or unfavorable position.

EFFECTS (POST-OUTCOMES)

THE PRINCIPLE OF SUBSEQUENT CONDUCT

Take into account the whole sequence of acts of communication and collaboration that have occurred since the outcome phase. Action by the parties in reliance upon asserted or implicit interpretations during the course of performing an agreement is appropriately regarded as reliable evidence of shared subjectivities and may be given priority over contradictory evidence even from the outcome phase.

THE PRINCIPLE OF ASSESSING IMPACTS ON THE VALUE POSITIONS OF THE PARTIES

Consider the impact on the relative value positions of the parties of accepting or rejecting alternative interpretations. Although inferences are to be made with caution, a presumption is appropriately indulged in favor of interpretations that equalize burdens among the parties and against interpretations that impose disproportionate deprivations upon one party. It is not to be assumed that parties seeking in general to improve their net value position will make "preposterous" agreements.

Principles Relating to the Context of Factors That Affect the Process of Agreement

The purpose of the following statement is to make explicit the principles that apply to every feature of the setting in which the parties interact with one another at the pre-outcome, outcome, and post-outcome phases of the agreement process.

THE PRINCIPLE OF THE LARGEST SHARED AUDIENCES

Unless persuasive evidence is established to the contrary, assume that the terms of an agreement are intended to be understood as they are generally understood by the largest audience contemporary to the agreement to which both parties belong. The probabilities are that the more people who share a meaning, the more likely the particular parties are to have had that meaning. The burden should be upon the one who alleges special meanings to prove that such meanings in fact represent the genuine shared expectations of the parties.

Agreements occur within the larger framework that is provided by the system of public order which includes the parties. The system is available for the "umpiring" of disagreements. Although decision-makers are made accessible to settle disputes it is evident that limits must be set to the degree to which community resources are committed for the purpose of disposing of any particular controversy.

The principle of the largest shared audience makes explicit one of the criteria to be employed in choosing among rival interpretations. By emphasizing the priority of the largest shared audience the decision-maker is enabled to limit, when limitation becomes necessary, the context on which his interpretations depend. The rule also increases the probability that the decision-maker's judgment can be rationally appraised by those affected directly and indirectly by the result.

The parties to the agreement may share some languages, dialects, and special usages in common. Where the focal agreement is open to rival constructions the present principle calls for judgments made according to the usages that were current among the largest groups to which the parties belonged.

THE PRINCIPLE OF THE PROBABILITY OF AGREEMENT

Agreements are rarely of great novelty. It is typical to find that any particular arrangement is part of a stream of arrangements entered into in a given social context under comparable factual circumstances by parties whose characteristics have much in common with one another. Hence whenever ambiguities arise concerning the expectations of parties to a particular agreement it is enlightening to consider the practices that were current at the time the arrangement was made, especially as these practices throw light upon the obligations and risks that equivalent parties usually took in order to obtain benefits of the kind anticipated. As a basis for estimating the genuine expectations of the parties, attention should be given to the information at the disposal of the agreement-makers, and of agreement-makers with similar characteristics. Was such information typically a basis for assuming burdens and benefits of the kind alleged? Furthermore, is there evidence of other agreements entered into by the parties under comparable conditions?

Principles Relating to the Decision Process[22]

OFFICIALS

THE PRINCIPLE OF IMPARTIALITY

Since decisions cannot but influence values we underline the requirement of rational decision-making that an overriding goal, the goal of human dignity, be adopted as a guide in the resolution of controversies. Hence every party is entitled to equality of consideration. If this principle of impartiality is to be applied, decision-makers must make themselves conscious of, and counterbalance as far as possible, any interfering predispositions resulting from such factors as culture, class, interest, personality, and prior exposure to crisis.

OBJECTIVES

THE PRINCIPLE OF PRIMARY INTERPRETATION .

Decision-makers should give deference to the genuine shared expectations of the particular parties to an agreement, insofar as these

22. It will be observed that we do not include principles of content relating to the different types of controversies itemized in our description of the process of claim. This is a concession to expediency only for the purpose of keeping this inquiry and presentation within manageable limits.

Certainly it can be supposed that the particular type of controversy is highly relevant to outcomes in interpretation. When the indices of the parties' shared expectations are meager or give rise to conflicting inferences, decision-makers are required, as we have seen, to supplement expectations by reference to community policies. Similarly, in all instances, whatever the clarity in expression of shared expectations, decision-makers are required to appraise alleged expectations for their conformity to the more basic community policies. The different types of particular controversies which we have suggested, if our categorizations achieve their purpose, raise very different issues in comprehensive community policy; hence it could not be surprising that decision-makers in their tasks of interpretation might perform their tasks of supplementation and appraisal differently in regard to different particular types of controversies.

The kinds of principles of content about particular types of controversies we might suggest, were we to extend our inquiry, may be briefly illustrated.

(a) Participation: Participants who create reasonable expectations that they are becoming parties to an agreement should be made to honor these expectations. In more particular, when states become apparent parties to an agreement,

are compatible with the basic constitutional policies of the general community.

THE PRINCIPLE OF SUPPLEMENTING EXPECTATIONS IN HARMONY WITH PUBLIC ORDER GOALS

When a decision-maker discovers gaps, ambiguities, and contradictions among the indices of the parties' expectations, he should remedy these inadequacies by presuming expectations to give effect to objectives that further common community values. Hence the decision-maker will assess the probable impact of alternative interpretations on these common values. Community goals are expressed in the basic constitutive objectives. When such objectives are unclearly expressed, decision-makers should have recourse to the basic policies of a public order of human dignity.

THE PRINCIPLE OF CONSTITUTIVE PRIORITY

Decision-makers should in all their applications of agreements appraise the genuine shared expectations of the parties for their con-

---

they should not be permitted to assert internal constitutional defects as a defense against obligation.

(b) Objectives: Community sanction should be denied agreements which are incompatible with the provisions of the United Nations Charter for the maintenance of minimum order or which derogate from the common interests of all peoples in the enjoyment of sharable resources, such as the oceans or outer space.

(c) Situations: When agreement-making and performance occur in highly institutionalized situations, such as with respect to the exploitation of monopolized resources, a presumption should favor widely shared, standardized expectations.

(d) Base values: When agreements are alleged to be invalid because of initial disparity in the bargaining position of the parties, the importance of protecting stability in parties' expectations must be balanced against that of protecting them from improvident bargains.

(e) Strategies: Duress, misrepresentation, or mistake which destroys the genuineness of consent should be regarded as precluding enforceability.

(f) Outcomes: Formal requirements for establishing commitment should be interpreted to serve the complementary policies both of insuring that spurious agreements are not imposed upon parties and of making certain that parties do not arbitrarily deny genuine commitments. And so on.

The type of controversy described under "outcomes" as relating to determination of the content of a commitment is of course that upon which we more comprehensively focus in this inquiry and for which we suggest an abundance of principles.

formity to the established constitutive goals of the general community and should deny sanction to all expectations found to contravene such goals.[23]

THE PRINCIPLE OF PROMOTING STABLE FUTURE EXPECTATIONS

One goal of the decision-maker who is committed to the public order of human dignity is, as we have indicated more comprehensively above, that the expectations of those who enter into lawful agreements are to be given effect. In a current controversy the attention of decision-makers may be drawn to questions which if officially clarified would aid, in all the ways indicated above, in stabilizing the expectation of future agreement-makers. In the absence of other significant consequences contrary to public policy, the decision-maker should seize the opportunity to affect future agreement processes.

BASE VALUES

THE PRINCIPLE OF ENFORCEABLE DECISION

A fundamental goal of decision-makers is to strengthen the acceptance of the decision process itself. In part this depends on the expectation that authoritative outcomes will be put into effect. In concrete circumstances the enforceability of an official response depends on the availability of base values adequate to the degree of resistance

23. The final appraisal of a proposed interpretation of an international agreement, like that of a proposed application of a customary rule, must of course be made in terms of a comprehensive set of preferred community values. Thus Schachter, supra note 6, at 197, after insisting that all interpretation involves an act of choice, adds: "But my main submission is that the act of choice must be validated and justified in terms of 'shared values' which have been expressed in the Charter or manifested through other consensual procedures."

The more general point was well made by the late Felix Cohen, "Transcendental Nonsense and the Functional Approach," 35 *Col. L. Rev.* 809, 848 (1935). "The prospect of determining the consequences of a given rule of law appears to be an infinite task, and it is indeed an infinite task, unless we approach it with some discriminating criterion of what consequences are *important*. Now a criterion of *importance* presupposes a criterion of values, which is precisely what modern thinkers of the 'sociological' and 'realistic' schools of jurisprudence have never had." It needs only to be added that a relevant comprehensive set of values is close to hand in any community in its flow of public order communications.

likely to be encountered. Calculations will include the possibility that if assets for enforcement are at once visible potential challengers will be deterred, and that impermissible activities will be brought to a halt and permissible relationships restored. Decision-makers will likewise consider the significance of the base values at their disposal for such other sanctioning objectives as rehabilitation, prevention, reconstruction, and correction.

STRATEGIES

THE PRINCIPLE OF EXPLICIT RATIONALITY

For the guidance of future agreement-makers and interpreters, as well as for their own guidance and self-knowledge, decision-makers should make as explicit as possible the principles of interpretation and application which influence their decision.

OUTCOMES

THE PRINCIPLE OF COMPREHENSIVELY MOBILIZED AUTHORITY FUNCTIONS

Decision-makers engaged in applications, which include interpretations, should employ all other policy functions, such as the intelligence and recommending functions, in ways best designed to promote successful interpretation.[24]

24. Complete exposition of the principles which should guide decision-makers in the supplementation of incomplete indexes of expectation and in policing and integrating even the most highly explicit expectations would of course require survey, among other public order communications, of all the more important principles of international law. This is what is demanded in the common insistence that interpretations be made "in the light of the general principles of international law."

It is conceivable, however, that a useful brief checklist of principles could be formulated in relation to both minimum order and optimum order.

In relation to minimum order, the most important principle would, as indicated in the previous note, require interpretations designed to promote community security and rejection of even explicit commitments requiring violation of basic community policies (such as the prohibition of aggression and the regulations concerning the conduct of hostilities) about minimum order. Another principle (suggested to us by Dean Karl Krastin of the University of Toledo)

Principles of Procedure

We turn now to the recommendation of principles to guide the decision-maker in arranging the sequence of events that he admits into his focus of attention while he is engaged in the interpretative process. The general questions are in what order and by what detailed techniques is it most advantageous for him to bring the relevant content to his purview.

The Contextual Principle

In parallel with the comparable content principle, the first admonition to the decision-maker is that he use procedures calculated to bring all relevant content to the focus of his attention in the order best adapted to exhibiting relevance. An appropriate concern for contextuality must require, further, that the decision-maker, though continuously engaged in evaluation, suspend final commitment until he has examined the whole of the relevant context.

The Operation of Adjusting Effort to Importance

Adjust the time and facilities devoted to the act of interpretation according to the importance of the values at stake in the controversy and to community policies.

The community decision-maker has limited resources of time, energy, and facilities available to meet the community's demands upon

---

might seek to exclude meaning not consensual in fact, when disparity in the power position of the parties and other features of the context establish that the process of commitment partook more of coercion than persuasion.

In relation to optimum order, principles might be formulated both to promote the continued consensus between, and collaboration of, parties to agreements and the widest possible participation in all value processes. Thus principles might stipulate in favor of open, rather than closed, access to situations of value shaping and sharing; equality of opportunity for acquisition of base values; competitive rather than monopolistic strategies; inclusive rather than exclusive enjoyment; and so on. A more extensive statement of relevant principles of this order of abstraction may be found in Part Two of McDougal, Lasswell, and Vlasic, *Law and Public Order in Space* (1963).

him. It is a matter of common observation that the consideration of any controversy can be stretched out interminably or, on the contrary, condensed to a degree that arouses a sense of grievance. Throughout the interpretative process the provocation is always present to incline toward one extreme or the other. A rational perspective calls for estimates to be made of the gains and losses to be expected by proceeding further or turning from the current inquiry. Hence the operation of adjusting effort to importance is not a "once-and-for-all" estimate. Rather, it occurs intermittently as the decision process goes forward. The purpose of the formulation of the present principle is to bring more clearly to the focus of attention the operations that are inescapable from any act of judgment. If the "cut-off" points along the sequence of decision are to rest upon deliberate choices, the decision-maker has the responsibility of giving careful consideration to the magnitude of the values at stake from the standpoint of community policy. It is not part of the policy of a public order of the type we commend to neglect the individual case and to concentrate solely on the "larger issues." A public order that defends human dignity gives heavy emphasis to the obligation of the community to treat individual claims with deference. We are calling attention here to the obvious necessity of recognizing limits on deliberation, and proposing that the decision-maker face these choices candidly as he goes along. The various specific operations by which new information is made available vary greatly in money cost; hence one of the ever-present features of judgment is whether relatively high costs will add much to the context that will legitimately affect one's final judgment.[25]

The Operation of Identifying the Focal Agreement

We referred above to the importance of establishing a working formulation of the agreement to be interpreted. The focal agreement, as provisionally determined, may be modified in the course of the decision process as the decision-maker becomes better acquainted with the entire context. In preliminary identification of the focal agree-

25. The strategy of decision is discussed in Bross, *Design for Decision* (1953); Williams, *The Compleat Strategyst, Being a Primer on the Theory of Games Strategy* (1954); Rapaport, *Games and Decision* (1961).

ment, the decision-maker may note any express statements by the parties, any formalization of communication at the outcome phase, and all indices of any preferred mode of commitment by the parties.

The Historical Operation

Consider the focal agreement in the light of the context by moving attention back to the period of negotiating the agreement and forward to date.

It is "natural" in our civilization to think historically in the sense that we seek to understand any present situation in human affairs by examining the steps through time by which it became what it is. This is manifestly of great significance to the interpreter of an agreement, and the historical operation is likely to present the decision-maker with a comprehensible version of the relations among the parties, and hence of their expectations.

The Lexical Operation

If the controversy appears to hinge on semantic differences concerning particular words or phrases (lexical or grammatical differences), concentrate upon the examination of the focal agreement in the light of audience understanding of such elements at the time the agreement was made, and on problematical subsequent occasions.[26] Consider the various audiences of which both parties were members (language, dialect, special usage), taking into account audiences with relevant characteristics in terms of culture, class, interest, personality, and exposure to crisis.

If the agreement in controversy was made in the distant past, the likelihood is increased that community meanings have changed, so that present usages may not indicate the original shared expectations of the parties. It is also true that if the parties to an agreement are divided by linguistic affiliation, the probability is increased that words are understood in different senses. A common example is the

26. Popular introductions to "semantics": Hayakawa, *Language in Action* (1941); Lee, *Language Habits in Human Affairs* (1941); Johnson, *People in Quandaries* (1946). On language and the legal process: Probert, "Law and General Semantics" (unpubl. thesis, Yale Law School, 1957); "Law and Persuasion: the Language Behavior of Lawyers," 108 *U. Pa. L. Rev.* 35 (1959); Philbrick, *Language and the Law: The Semantics of Forensic English* (1949).

French word "demand" which is spelled precisely the same way that an English word is spelled. But lexical identity leads to much confusion, since the French word is much less peremptory than the English. One party may be talking about a request while the other is referring to what is in effect an ultimatum. It is notoriously true that translations may fix upon equivalents in another language whose equivalency is only partial, and which in the context are far from being interchangeable. A famous example having enormous political importance was the translation of the German word "schuld" as "guilt" in the English version of the Treaty of Versailles. German nationalists seized upon this fact to denounce the Treaty and all its works as an attempt to stigmatize as well as to impose impossible burdens upon the German people. "Schuld" could have had a much more technical connotation to the German reader, closer to the notion of "liability" or "debt." [27]

If the parties to an agreement are separated by social class differences there may be misunderstandings that must be attributed to diverse class exposures. The distinctions are often similar to the misunderstanding over the word "demand." In upper-class circles usage is generally more urbane and allusive. Lower classes are usually less given to polite and polished indirection. However, the problem is further complicated by the fact that lower-class parties may be more respectful of the upper-class party than the reverse. Hence the individual of humble origins may understate his intended meaning.[28]

Parties are also divided in many cases by close affiliation with occupational or professional interests which possess somewhat distinctive usages of the same spoken or written word.

The lexical operation requires the decision-maker to identify the audiences to which all parties belonged and the audiences in which they had separate participations relevant to the agreement. The way

27. For further development of some of the difficulties caused by linguistic differences, see Moses, "International Legal Practice," 4 *Fordham L. Rev.* 244 (1935) ; DeVries, supra note 6.

28. Striking examples of the problems involved in cross-cultural and cross-class communication are given in two special issues of the *Public Opinion Quarterly,* edited respectively by Pool and Lerner, in 1956 (volume 20, No. 1) and 1958 (volume 22, No. 3) . See also Schatzman and Strauss, "Social Class and Modes of Communication," 60 *Am. J. Soc.* 329 (1955) .

is then clear to obtain information about the usages that prevailed in these audiences.[29]

One important aspect of the problem is the degree of realism that prevails among people of various characteristics concerning the audience with which they are making agreements. For instance, the traders and consular agents for a foreign power with the benefit of special trading positions in nineteenth-century China may in good faith have had what a modern-minded man would regard as a grossly exaggerated idea of the degree to which English, or French, or some other non-Chinese tongue was known to a native (or his agent). The same point applies, perhaps, to our present view of how perfectly English was mastered by the spokesmen for the North American Indian tribes when they made treaties and other arrangements with Americans. In bi- or trilingual communities many agreements are devised with the assistance of interpreters of ascertainable reputation for a given level of competence.

Having ascertained the group audiences in terms of language, dialect, special usage to which the agreement-makers belonged, the problem is to discover the pertinent usages current at the relevant time.[30] It is not at this point a question of demonstrating that the specific parties used the terms as they were employed by their contemporaries. Unless there are excellent grounds for the view that some idiosyncratic meaning was shared by the agreement-makers, the community decision-maker is justified in adopting, preliminarily, the ordinary usages that were current in the appropriate audiences. The justification is, in fact, that agreements are not, after all, esoteric matters from the standpoint of the community as a whole. When private parties enter into arrangements that they expect to make effective in case of dispute by involving the decision-makers of the community, it is reasonable to ask that they employ words with "public" rather than esoteric significations. The "public," of course, need not

29. The significance of social context is brought out in Pickford, "American Linguistic Geography: A Sociological Appraisal," 12 *Word* 211 (1956).

30. A technical statement of current methods employed by linguists: Gudschinsky, "The ABC's of Lexico Statistics," 12 *Word* 175 (1956). For a general statement of linguistic theory see Ullmann, *The Principles of Semantics* (1951); Bloomfield, *Language* (1933). A popular introduction is Hall, *Linguistics and Your Language* (1960).

be the "man in the street" when agreement-makers share intimate acquaintance with the special usages of the stock market, the grain exchange, or the tobacco market, for example.

A less clearly defined but relevant factor in the estimation of meaning is the personality structure of the communicator, and the nature of the discount made among contemporaries for this factor.[31] When people are exposed through the years to self-assertive individuals they perceive that such persons often overstate their position, and make an appropriate discount. Timid persons, on the contrary, are more accustomed to understate their position and especially to imply a higher degree of acquiescence than they feel, or believe they have committed themselves to. Commonsense knowledge of human nature makes some allowance for this.

It is important for an interpreter to take into account the variations in communication that are connected with crisis and intercrisis situations.[32] By the term "crisis" we refer to individual or collective stresses toward action. During times of acute conflict between cultures, classes, interest groups, and personalities the tendency is to adapt words to the crisis. Insufficient attention may be given to attempting to foresee intercrisis situations; hence the terms employed may distort the expectations of the parties. During the intercrisis situation, by contrast, the words employed may reflect the expectations of the parties most ambiguously when crises must be met.

The question confronting the decision-maker can be expressed formally in these terms: If the word content of focal agreement x was expressed by participants p in circumstances c in social context k at a

31. Among linguists, especially Sapir directed attention to the interplay between personality and language: see *Cultur Language and Personality* (1949); see also Spier, Hallowell, and Newman (eds.), *Language, Culture and Personality: Essays in Memory of Edward Sapir* (1941), especially Newman's essay at 94. For attention to cultural factors, see Whorf, *Language, Thought and Reality* (1956); Holjer (ed.), *Language in Culture* (1954); Henke (ed.), *Language, Thought and Culture* (1958).

32. Crisis complicates language behavior by introducing inner conflict as well as expectations of large external change. Persuasive relations easily grade over into coercion under such circumstances. For gradations, see Schein et al., *Coercive Persuasion: A Socio-psychological Analysis of the "Brainwashing" of American Civilian Prisoners by the Chinese Communists* (1961), and the work of Lifton, Meerloo, and others.

given time t, how was the context of x understood (u) by contemporary audiences a?

The relevant contemporary audiences, we have said, are the groups in which all parties participate. Hence they are audiences with specific languages, dialects, or special usages.

In establishing contemporary usage it is now possible to call upon expert witnesses who have at their disposal the techniques of modern communication research, and who can apply these methods to the problem in hand. This problem may be exceedingly narrow since in some cases the controversy hinges upon a single word or phrase.

Not the least difficult part of interpretation is the construing of legal terms of art that are used by the parties, even though amateurs in the law, or by the professional counsel retained as agents to formulate the agreement. The usual methods of legal research can be expected to disclose the expectations attached by the bar to terms of art. But when these terms are employed by amateurs the question is less easily disposed of. The authoritative language of the law is so important in the life of the community that many of its expressions are incorporated into the speech of nonprofessionally trained publics.

In connection with the lexical operation it remains to be said that even if "public" usages promise to produce a clear-cut resolution of the problem it is still necessary to examine the usages that are distinctive of the particular parties to an agreement. These more "private" meanings can be uncovered in some cases by analyzing the terminology employed in agreements entered into by the parties during the same period in which the disputed agreement was made. Other evidence of distinctive usage may appear when the record of negotiation, for instance, is referred to.

The Logical Operation

If the controversy appears to turn upon logical (syntactic) differences in the understanding of the expressions contained in the focal agreement, a formal analysis of the agreement is required. The next step is to discover whether any contradictions, ambiguities, or gaps from the present standpoint were so regarded when the agreement was made.

Logical analysis is designed for the purpose of showing how the statements occurring in a given body of content are internally related. This branch of communication study has sometimes been called "syntactics" in order to distinguish it from "semantics," which deals with the events external to a message to which reference is made. The lexical operations described above are broadly "semantic" in the sense defined, since most of the questions are about the events to which an agreement refers, as understood by contemporaries. The logical operation, by contrast, *begins* by examining the statements comprising the focal agreement, and classifies them according to their internal relations, as understood today. As we shall see, this is preliminary to operations designed to explore original usages.

It is beyond the scope of the present undertaking to treat the operations of logical analysis in detail. Nevertheless it may be serviceable to provide some concrete indication of what is involved. Among the categories at hand for classifying the inner relationship among propositions occurring in a focal agreement, for example, are these:

1. *Implication.* This term names the relationship having the general form "If . . . then . . ."; or, as it is often put, "If *p*, then *q*". *P* is the antecedent, *q* the consequent.

2. *Conjunction.* The reference here is to two propositions joined by the symbol expressed by such a sign as "and" in a compound sentence composed of statements like: "He agrees to pay and he agrees to work"; or, more formally, "*p* and *q*".

3. *Coimplication* (often called "Equivalence"). We think of coimplication as the conjunction of two particular implications in the general form: "If *p*, then *q*, and if *q*, then *p*". For example: "He will work if and only if he is paid." This rules out such alternatives as that he will work as a matter of love or duty.

4. *Exclusive disjunction.* An exclusive disjunction is a compound statement that asserts the truth of one or the other of its subsidiary propositions, but not both. "*P* or *q*, but not both." The definition of an exclusive disjunction given above is in the form of an exclusive disjunction.

5. *Inclusive disjunction.* A disjunctive relationship is inclusive when it asserts that one or the other *or both* are true. The abbreviated definition just given of an inclusive disjunction follows this form. When a statement is transformed into possible logical expressions, the alternatives are precisely stated for decision.

6. *Negation.* We say that negation is involved when the symbol of

the kind ordinarily expressed by the sign "not" is used. Negation is more elaborately defined by saying that it is a one-place predicate representing the idea usually expressed by the word "not".[33]

It is not unusual for decision-makers to uncover what they regard as logical contradictions, ambiguities, or gaps whenever they subject the content of a focal agreement to logical analysis. But this does not solve the interpreter's problem. The question remains whether in usage contemporary to the agreement process these ambiguities were commonly regarded as unambiguous. Hence the distinctions disclosed by modern logical methods may be irrelevant to the expectations of the agreement-makers.

But this is a lexical (semantic) question, not a matter to be settled by syntactics. More precisely, the question poses a semantic query about a logical (syntactic) distinction.

The point is likely to be relevant to one of the interpreter's problems to which allusion has already been made. We called attention to the possibility that agreement-makers, though amateurs, used terms of art from legal discourse, or that professional counsel, acting as agents, used words of art. In seeking to specify the expectations current at the time, it may be necessary to investigate the authoritative statements in which the terms appeared, and to use logical analysis to disclose their probable internal relationships.

This double operation—combining the decision-maker's judgments with his estimate of other people's judgment—is among the everyday activities of decision-makers. A lower-court judge, for example, may arrive at his own *interpretation* of the statutes prescribing the response appropriate in the case before him; yet the judge may predict that the appellate bench will entertain a different view, and perhaps act accordingly.

The Operation of Assessing Gesture and Deed

If the controversy appears to depend upon differences concerning the significance of gesture and deed (course of conduct), examine the understanding of gesture and deed that prevailed during the course

33. Layman E. Allen has kindly discussed the foregoing summary with us. In this connection we note an obligation to Fitch, *Symbolic Logic: An Introduction* (1952), and Copi, *Introduction to Logic* (1953).

For studies of the informal logic of normative discourse, see Hall, *The Lan-*

of interaction among the largest groupings to which both parties belong (culture, class, interest, personality, exposure to crisis).

Controversies frequently depend upon contentions about the inferences to be drawn from gestures or deeds rather than words. Like the perspectives inferrable from words, the perspectives inferrable from deeds that prevail in a given social context at a given time are influenced by culture, class, interest, personality, and crisis factors.[34] No little confusion has been occasioned by the circumstances that the Japanese gesture for "approach" is construed by Americans as meaning "go away"; and this is but a commonplace instance of the point that body movements and postures are moulded according to the norms endorsed in a social setting. The question asked above in reference to words must be supplemented as follows: If the gesture and deed content of focal agreement x was expressed by participants p in circumstances c in social context k at a given time t, how was the content of x understood (u) by contemporary audiences a?

The Operation of Assessing Scientific Credibility

When sources that are relied upon to authenticate usage yield contradictory results, choose the source with the highest scientific credibility.

Estimates of scientific credibility are properly influenced by the degree to which a given scientist is respected for professional excellence by his colleagues. Another point is the exhaustiveness with which the most appropriate methods are applied to the problem in hand. (Obviously the results obtained by equally respected investigators may diverge according to the intensiveness with which available techniques are used). A current example of relatively new scientific instruments in the field of communication is quantitative semantics ("content analysis") which is utilized to summarize the frequency with which a given word or expression appears in a given message (content) or channel of communication during a given pe-

---

guage of Morals (1952); Toulmin, *The Place of Reason in Ethics* (1950); Hart, *The Concept of Law* (1961); Lefley, *The Language of Value* (1957); Edwards, *The Logic of Moral Discourse* (1955).

34. See Birdwhistell, *Introduction to Kinesics: An Annotation System for Analysis of Body Motion and Gesture* (1952). See also Efron, *Gesture and Environment* (1941).

riod.[35] Such quantitative methods are more dependable than the "impressions" often gained by individuals who scan the messages or materials in question. Quantitative methods are well-known means of establishing the distinctive vocabulary and style of authors and of the articulate members of any historic epoch.

The Operation of Estimating Agreement Probability

If there is a question of the probability of an agreement with specified provisions being made, investigate the frequency of similar agreements by the parties or similar parties under comparable circumstances at the time (again exploring culture, class, interest, personality, and crisis factors).

The operation to which we refer now deals with the "pragmatic" dimension of communication analysis, employing the term to refer to the "causes" and "consequences" of a communicated message. All attempts to use psychological, sociological, or other categories of explanation to account for the content of communication refer to "causes" and hence come within pragmatic analysis. In the same way all attempts to explain the social, psychological, or other "consequences" of a communicated content come within the scope of pragmatic studies of the communication process.[36]

Whenever we turn to the pragmatic dimension of analysis we are going beyond a relatively direct description of meaning to more

35. Consult Lasswell, Leites, and Associates, *Language and Politics* (1949); Pool (ed.), *Trends in Content Analysis* (1959); Berelson, "Content Analysis," 1 *Handbook of Social Psychology* 488 (Lindzey ed. 1954). See also the important volume by Philip Stone and Associates on *The General Enquirer: A Computer Approach to Content Analysis* (1966). A short summary is in North, Holsti, Zaninovich, and Zinnes, *Content Analysis: A Handbook with Applications for the Study of International Crisis* (1963). Also note Osgood, Suci, and Tannenbaum, *The Measurement of Meaning* (1957).

36. See Klapper, *The Effects of Mass Communication* (1960). The methods now available for studying communication (one-to-one, few-to-few, one to many, etc.) are described in Lindzey (ed.), 1 *Handbook of Social Psychology*, Part III (1954), and in Lerner and Lasswell, *The Policy Sciences: Recent Developments in Scope and Method* (1951), especially chapters by Shils, Lazarsfeld and Barton, Bavelas, Hyman, Katona, and Likert. See also the studies in communication and attitude change in Hovland, Janis, and Kelley, *Communication and Persuasion* (1953); and Rosenberg, Hovland, McGuire, Abelson, and Brehm, *Attitude Organization and Change* (1960).

complex chains of inference. The words or deeds uttered by agreement-makers are part of a total context of relationship between the individuals involved and the world in which they were living. Persons acquainted with the social context involved come to expect various regularities connecting antecedent factors with given responses. Or, more subtly, they come to connect these factors with a structure of expectation that makes it possible for individuals to produce a series of responses. Thus antecedent factors lead to the discovery of a variety of response phenomena that are most economically accounted for by hypotheses that describe a key symbol structure.

A modern decision-maker sometimes finds himself confronted by a focal agreement that strikes him as out of character with the individuals or the circumstances involved. It is hard for him to believe that anyone would voluntarily enter into an agreement with the expectations alleged, since they involve very heavy cost. Entertaining this doubt, as a result of what we call pragmatic considerations, the decision-maker now returns to the semantic orientation for the purpose of discovering whether contemporaries of the agreement regarded the type of arrangement as out of character or not. Sometimes the question can be disposed of very quickly since evidence is available to show that orphans, for instance, were conventionally expected to enter into agreements of a kind that shock the modern man.

Evidently the pragmatic orientation is especially pertinent to the decision-maker's problem of whether a focal agreement shall be overridden as incompatible with declared public policy. A preliminary of such a determination is to interpret the agreement; and this process can be furthered by raising the question of "proportionality" between causal factors leading up to the agreement and the expectations alleged to be shared by the parties.

The Operation of Estimating the Effects of Decision

We have underlined the point that the decision-maker who is committed to the public order of human dignity may discover questions in a given controversy which if clarified would aid in stabilizing the expectations of future agreement-makers in various contingencies. It is also pertinent to consider whether a decision of enlarged rather than narrowed scope would affect general confidence in the integrity of the decision process. In making inferences about the future, the decision-maker can take advantage of empirical procedures now existing for the study of current predispositions, and of analyzing the probable response to alternative decisions which might be made.[37]

The Operation of Examining the Self for Predispositions Incompatible with the Goals of Human Dignity

It is now feasible for the decision-maker to supplement the ordinary examination of the self by making use of newer methods of self-observation for the purpose of detecting the presence of factors tending toward interpretations incompatible with the goals of human dignity. The allusion is, for example, to the technique of free fantasy (or free association), and to the systematic scrutinizing of the factors of culture, class, interest, personality, and crisis level that have influenced one's development.[38]

37. Systematic interviewing procedures are described in Hyman, *Survey Design and Analysis* (1955), and Merton, Fiske, and Kendall, *The Focused Interview* (1956).

38. See Lasswell and McDougal, "Legal Education and Public Policy: Professional Training in the Public Interest," 52 *Yale L. J.* 203 (1943), reprinted as Ch. 2 of McDougal and Associates, *Studies in World Public Order* (1960).

3. TRENDS IN CONCEPTIONS OF GOALS AND STRATEGIES OF INTERPRETATION

Exploration of past trends in the management of principles of interpretation, for appraisal of their conformity to recommended policies, may appropriately begin with the consideration, first, of the degree of realism achieved in recognition of the necessity for interpretation; secondly, of the clarity and consistency attained in the identification and pursuit of basic community goals, and, thirdly, of the understanding and rationality exhibited in the explicit conception and employment of principles of interpretation.

RECOGNITION OF THE NECESSITY OF INTERPRETATION

An extensive sampling of contemporary decision and opinion clearly suggests that the inescapable necessity for *some* interpretation in the detailed application of *any* international agreement is today widely recognized by both authoritative decision-makers and scholars. The continuing occasional expressions of a contrary view appear to reflect only either the exaggerations of special advocacy or intermittent naïve exceptions to the main trends in decision and commentary.

The more recent discussion of the "necessity of interpretation" commonly begins, as previously noted, with Vattel's famous maxim that "it is not permissible to interpret what has no need of interpretation." [1] What Vattel intended by the phrase "no need of interpretation" he explained in this way: "When a deed is worded in clear and precise terms, when its meaning is evident and leads to no absurdity, there is no ground for refusing to accept the meaning which the deed naturally presents." [2] Until the early part of the

1. Vattel, *The Law of Nations* 199 (Fenwick transl. 1758 ed. 1916).

2. Ibid. On the basis of this explanation, a possibly equivalent formulation of the Vattel maxim would be: "It is not permissible to interpret whatever is clear

twentieth century, legal publicists after Vattel frequently affirmed a comparable principle.[3] Similarly, the decisions of international tribunals contain occasional appeals to or affirmations of the authority of such a principle, and one early decision asserts that it is "universally recognized as law." [4]

In recent years, however, publicists and decision-makers alike have rejected Vattel's principle in favor of the view that some interpretation is always required. In his work on *The Interpretation of Treaties,* Yü argues that "to interpret a treaty means to give life to dead letters as well as to complete a part of the procedure of realizing an act in the external world. Consequently, as Wigmore insists, there is an ever-ready demand for interpretation." [5] Dean Wigmore criticized the Vattel principle in a similar manner: "Instead of the fallacious notion that 'there should be interpretation only when it is needed', the fact is that there must always be interpretation." [6] The

---

. . . unless such an interpretation would lead to an absurdity." With respect to the final qualification, Vattel observes: "By the word *absurd* is meant not only what is *physically* impossible, but also what is *morally* impossible; that is to say, what is so contrary to reason that it can not be attributed to a man of good sense." Id. at 205.

3. See 2 Phillimore, *Commentaries Upon International Law* 99–100 (3d ed. 1879); Hall, *A Treatise on International Law* 334 (7th ed. 1917); Fiore, *International Law Codified* 342 (Borchard transl. 1918); Crandall, *Treaties: Their Making and Enforcement* 396–97 (2d ed. 1916).

4. *William H. Aspinwall, exec. of G. A. Howland et al. v. Venezuela,* reported sub nom *Venezuelan Bond Cases in* 4 Moore, *History & Digest of the International Arbitrations to which the United States has been a Party* 3616, 3621 (1898). See also the opinion in the *Lusitania* cases, where Umpire Parker held that the disputed provisions were "clear and unambiguous . . . Hence the fundamental maxim 'It is not allowable to interpret that which has no need of interpretation' applies." Mixed Claims Commission, United States and Germany, *Administrative Decisions* 17, 31 (1925), reprinted in 7 U.N. Rep. Int'l Arb. Awards 32, 43.

5. Yü, *The Interpretation of Treaties* 40 (1927). Yü concludes that: "words must always be taken inseparably with the sense they represent, and interpretation must be considered as involving the undertaking of finding out that sense. Hence the process of interpetation is inherently indispensable from the very nature of the problem." Id. at 45.

6. 9 Wigmore, *A Treatise on the Anglo-American System of Evidence in Trials at Common Law* 227 (3d ed. 1940). Dean Wigmore quotes from *Hartford I. M. Co. v. Cambria M. Co.,* 80 Mich. 491, 499; 45 N.W. 351, 353 (1890).

At the lexical level the dispute over whether "there must always be interpreta-

late Sir Hersch Lauterpacht, while calling Vattel's maxim "pre-eminently reasonable," also noted its "decisive drawback": "it often assumes as a fact what has still to be proved . . . it proceeds not from the starting point of the inquiry but from what is normally the result of it." [7] This trend in rejection of Vattel has been summarized in a recent arbitration decision, where the tribunal concluded that the maxim had been "repudiated by the most authoritative modern teaching of every country": "The abstract judicial norm, in order to be applied to a concrete instance, must always be interpreted in this sense, namely, the interpreter must by a process of reasoning determine its content." [8]

These reservations, expressed by most observers in recent years, stem from recognition that there are fatal flaws in Vattel's first principle. One obvious defect is that in the broadest sense it is a tautology, since the determination of what does or does not need interpretation would commonly be regarded as an *example* of interpretation. Thus to say that one should interpret only when necessary either violates the rule (discovering the absence of a need for interpretation by interpreting) or invites a redefinition of "interpretation" (e.g., in terms of the resolution of whatever is not "clear and precise"). Either alternative renders Vattel's principle useless as a guide to common expectation.[9] The more crucial defect, however, is

---

tion" is purely definitional, with one preference (Vattel's) being much narrower than the other (Wigmore's). The conflict between these views, however, cannot effectively be resolved at the lexical level, since the important issues concerning narrower or broader contextual examination in decision-making are left unresolved. When these are considered, as we explain below, a clear preference must be given to the position taken by Wigmore.

7. Lauterpacht, *The Development of International Law by the International Court* 52 (1958). The same criticism is advanced in Oppenheim, *International Law* 858 n. (Lauterpacht, 7th ed. 1948), where Vattel's maxim was admitted as a "preliminary rule," but one which "often begs the question." See also Fitzmaurice, "The Law and Procedure of the International Court of Justice," 28 *Brit. Yb. Int'l L.* 1, 5 (1951): "The conclusion that the meaning of a text is clear . . . involves itself a process of interpretation, the result of which might have been different if the records had in fact been consulted."

8. *Pertulosa Claim* (1951), reported in 18 *Int. Law Rep.* 414, 415 (1951).

9. It is more difficult to observe the shortcoming in the second alternative, since it is at least arguable that the concept of "interpretation" so defined would be useful for some purposes. The problem, however, lies in specifying what these purposes might be. It could be claimed that the requirement of ambiguity calls

that it is profoundly misleading, since the assertion that interpretation is not always required may encourage a seriously foreshortened view of what the interpreter's task involves when he genuinely accepts the goal of ascertaining the genuine shared expectations of the parties. It may lead to the belief that some decision-making situations are virtually self-executing, not worthy of a full contextual analysis. Therefore, the considerations in policy for rejecting Vattel's maxim, considerations acknowledged by most writers today, offer at least a partial recognition of the necessity for the broader kind of contextual analysis which we have recommended above.[10]

Although most contemporary writers deny that interpretation can ordinarily be mechanical, or even in some circumstances unnecessary, little clarity has been achieved in past practice or recommendation concerning the alternatives in principle and procedure likely to produce a more comprehensive approach. The caution exhibited by those who argue that interpretation is needed in *most* instances is in one sense misleading, since it leaves unexamined the assumption that some instances of interpretation may not require "giving a meaning to a text." [11] The virtue of the argument advanced by Yü, and tacitly accepted by many subsequent writers, is that the necessity

---

attention to the differences in procedure between determining the *prima facie* "ordinary" meaning of a text, on the one hand, and examining all of the features of context to determine the actual usage of the parties, on the other. But each of these operations may be less misleadingly characterized by traditional principles consistent with the common reference of "interpretation." Short of a more compelling justification for changing the reference usually accorded the term, we may reasonably conclude that such a change has no basis in policy, and therefore serves no useful function in providing either information or guidance to the decision-maker.

10. The Harvard Research in International Law, *Draft Convention on the Law of Treaties With Comment* (1935), has given the prevailing view its most familiar formulation: "The process of interpretation, rightly conceived, cannot be regarded as a mere mechanical one of drawing inevitable meanings from the words in a text. . . . In most instances, therefore, interpretation involves *giving* a meaning to a text—not just any meaning which appeals to the interpreter, to be sure, but a meaning which, in the light of the text under consideration and of all the concomitant circumstances of the particular case at hand, appears in his considered judgment to be one which is logical, reasonable, and most likely to accord with and to effectuate the larger general purpose which the parties desired the treaty to serve" (p. 946).

11. Ibid. Cf. Lauterpacht, op. cit. supra note 7, who also suggests the occurrence of *some* situations in which it would prove useful to apply Vattel's principle.

of choice in *all* situations is recognized. Thus the conclusion that some interpretation will always be necessary is, in our view, the most useful general statement afforded in past practice for suggesting the inevitable complexities and pitfalls of mediating subjectivities through signs or acts of collaboration. It focuses attention, in a preliminary fashion, upon the procedures that may be required in analyzing any communication, and more specifically upon the dangers of foreclosing recourse to any other features of the context—including even the apparently more remote characteristics of the processes of agreement, claim, and decision—prior to a thorough canvass of all potentially relevant features.

Some recent minimizations of the "necessity of interpretation" have, again building upon Vattel, derived from overemphases upon the "plain," "natural," "clear," or "ordinary" meanings of words.[12] Some writers, apparently attempting to broaden and rationalize the Vattel maxim, equate it with the plain meaning doctrine;[13] others appear to accept the insistent need for interpretation while maintaining that all interpretation proceeds (initially at least) in conformity to "ordinary" or "natural" meanings.[14] Overemphasis upon the importance of allegedly broad, community-wide meanings can of course make this well-furrowed principle serve a function comparable to that of the Vattel maxim. The more detailed exposition and criticism of this principle, however, we reserve for special emphasis and discussion below.[15]

THE GOALS OF INTERPRETATION

The recommended goal of interpreting international agreements to achieve the closest possible approximation to the genuine shared ex-

12. The plain and natural meaning doctrine, which we introduced only briefly above, is frequently stated: No recourse to other features of the context is permissible if the provision under consideration, when construed in its plain and natural meaning, provides a clear resolution to the dispute. For further discussion of this rule, see pages 216–52 below.
13. See Lauterpacht, op. cit. supra note 7, at 52; Yü, op. cit. supra note 5, at 45–49; Ehrlich, "The Interpretation of Treaties," in Ehrlich, *Interpretacja Tracktatow* 234, at 241 (1957).
14. See 1 Schwarzenberger, *International Law* 499 (3d ed. 1957); Chang, *The Interpretation of Treaties by Judicial Tribunals* 20, 22–23 (1933); Oppenheim, op. cit. supra note 7; Fiore, op. cit. supra note 3, at 342.
15. See infra, Ch. 4, pp. 216–52.

pectations of the parties, within the limits established by overriding community policies, would appear—on the level of manifest, overt acceptance—to have been given high deference in past practice and opinion. The most frequent emphasis in explicit formulation has been upon discovering the "original intent" of the participants, following the early statement of Vattel that "interpretation should have for its object merely to discover the intention of the contracting parties." [16] Lord McNair offers the most characteristic formulation of recent times: "The primary rule is that the tribunal should seek to ascertain from all the available evidence the intention of the parties in using the word or phrase being interpreted." [17]

Similar statements may be found in the works of many contemporary writers on treaty interpretation.[18] Lauterpacht, for example, has stated that "It is the intention of the authors of the legal rule in question—whether it be a contract, a treaty, or a statute—which is the starting-point and the goal of all interpretation. It is the duty of the judge to resort to all available means . . . to discover the intention of the parties." [19] Chang, in *The Interpretation of Treaties by Judicial Tribunals,* has stated the goal in this way: "the function of the interpreter is simply to discover and ascertain, with the aid of various sources of evidence, the sense in which the contracting parties actually employed particular terms." [20] In observing this trend, Sir Gerald Fitzmaurice has recently concluded that "no one seriously denies that the *aim* of treaty interpretation is to give effect to the intentions of the parties." [21]

16. Vattel, op. cit. supra note 1, at 203. A more extensive statement of the goal is set out in id. at 201.
17. McNair, *The Law of Treaties* 185 (1938). See also McNair, *The Law of Treaties* 373–82 (1961).
18. 2 Hyde, *International Law Chiefly as Interpreted and Applied By the United States* 1468–71 (2d ed. 1945); Hudson, *The Permanent Court of International Justice, 1920–1942* 643–45; Harvard Research, op. cit. supra note 10, at 937; Schwarzenberger, op. cit. supra note 14, at 491; Yü, op. cit. supra note 5, at 58–62; Brierly, *The Law of Nations* 251 (5th ed. 1955); Westlake, *International Law* 282 (1904); Fiore, op. cit. supra note 3, at 343; Crandall, op. cit. supra note 3, at 371.
19. Lauterpacht, "Restrictive Interpretation and the Principle of Effectiveness in the Interpretation of Treaties," 26 *Brit. Yb. Int'l L.* 48, 83 (1949).
20. Chang, op. cit. supra note 14, at 182.
21. Fitzmaurice, "The Law and Procedure of the International Court of Justice, 1951–54: Treaty Interpretation and Other Treaty Points," 33 *Brit. Yb. Int'l*

The policies invoked in justification of these formulations are not dissimilar to those we have identified above. After stating the overriding goal of interpretation, Vattel himself commented that unless this goal was effectively pursued, "treaties will be no more than mere words, no agreement can be safely relied upon, and it will be almost ridiculous to place any dependence upon the effect of conventions." [22] Yü has argued that if "judges of an arbitral tribunal should be given a right not only to carry out the terms of the agreement in dispute, but also to build up an edifice of their own by applying rules of construction without sufficient evidence, they . . . would be free to distort the issue even to the most unnatural shapes, and cripple where they had sought only to adjust its proportions according to their own arbitrary opinions." [23] The late Judge Hudson also cogently stated the continuing necessity of conscientiously seeking this goal:

> If Governments cannot have confidence that the instruments by which they bind themselves will not be made to serve unintended purposes, if respect is not paid to the terms and tenor of the obligations imposed by such instruments, the result may be a reluctance to assume further commitments and the progressive development of international law may be seriously retarded.[24]

The decisions of international tribunals, most importantly, contain frequent reference to and reiteration of the authority of the goal of ascertaining genuine shared expectations. In the early case concerning the *Island of Timor,* the tribunal commented: "Here again, and always, we must look for the real and harmonious intention of the parties when they bound themselves." [25] A similar position was taken by the Permanent Court in the *Chorzow Factory* [26] case when it noted that "the Court's aim is always to ascertain whether an in-

---

L. 203, 204 (1957). For the author's earlier statements on this point, see Fitzmaurice, supra note 7, at 6–8.

22. Vattel, op. cit. supra note 1, at 201.

23. Yü, op. cit. supra note 5, at 70–71.

24. Hudson, "The Integrity of International Instruments," 42 *Am. J. Int'l L.* 105, 108 (1948).

25. *The Island of Timor Case* (1914), reported in 1 Scott, *The Hague Court Reports* 354, 371 (1916).

26. *Case Concerning the Factory at Chorzow* (Jurisdiction), P.C.I.J., Ser. A, No. 9 (1927).

tention on the part of the Parties exists to confer jurisdiction upon it." [27] Here the limiting reference of the Court was to Poland's denial of the jurisdiction of the Court because of preemptory powers of other tribunals under the Treaty of Versailles and the Geneva Convention. Articles 22 and 23 of this latter agreement, especially, established the jurisdiction of the German-Polish Mixed Arbitral Tribunal for disputes arising out of the regular procedures for transferring ownership of German private property in Poland. Jurisdiction was reserved for the Permanent Court, however, in all cases where these procedures were themselves brought into issue or clearly breached.[28] In the case before it the Court thought that the procedures established had clearly not been observed, and that an irregular expropriation had occurred, which raised a question of interpretation and application of the basic provisions of the Convention (Articles 6 to 22). It concluded, therefore, that while its own competence should be conservatively construed, the intention of the drafters was to confer jurisdiction upon it in just such cases where redress from any other tribunal was precluded.

Numerous other decisions and proclamations of national and international officials affirm this goal in equally general terms.[29] The most explicit and perhaps the most comprehensive statement in recent years of the goal of interpretation was made by the International Court of Justice in the *South-West Africa* cases.[30] In summarizing its conclusions with respect to the Union argument that only "another member of the League of Nations" (of which in 1962 there were obviously none) could bring suit against the Union to en-

27. Id. at 32.

28. See the provisions of Article 23 (1), infra p. 167–68.

29. See, e.g., *Naomi Russell (U.S.) v. United Mexican States,* 4 U.N. Rep. Int'l Arb. Awards 805 (1931); *Pertulosa Claim,* supra note 8, at 420; *Re Rizzo & Others,* 19 *Int. Law Rep.* 478 (1952). For citations to earlier cases, see 5 Moore, *International Law Digest* 249–54 (1906); and see *Marryat v. Wilson,* 1 Bos. & Pul. 430, 439 (1799) and *Daniel v. Commissioners for Claims on France,* 2 Knapp 23, 49 (1825) cited in McNair (1961), op. cit. supra note 17, at 370–71 and 380, respectively. For recent English cases, see Sinclair, "The Principles of Treaty Interpretation and their Application by English Courts," 12 *Int'l & Comp. L. Q.* 508 (1963). For an excellent survey of the European Communities' Court of Justice decisions on the aims and principles of interpretation, see McMahon, "The Court of the European Communities: Judicial Interpretation and International Organization," 37 *Brit. Yb. Int'l L.* 320 (1961).

30. [1962] I.C.J. Rep. 319. The more recent decision of the Court in this same case is discussed in Ch. 6 below.

force its obligations under Article 7 of its Mandate in administering the Territory of South-West Africa, the Court stated that it must take into consideration all of the materials at its disposal "in order to ascertain the true intent and purpose of the Members of the Assembly . . ." [31] The issue to which the Court alluded in this case was the Assembly's intent in dissolving the League on April 18, 1946, with respect to the continuation of members' rights and obligations under the Mandate system. It concluded, after considering "all of the relevant facts and circumstances relating to the act of dissolution of the League," that it intended to continue these rights and obligations by vesting them in the member states regardless of their formal relations with the League.[32] For present purposes, both in its formulation of overriding goal and in its conception of appropriate methods for pursuit of that goal, the Court clearly emphasized what we have above postulated as desirable policy: the approximation of the parties' genuine shared expectations of agreement through an analysis of all of the relevant features of the context. This same goal was reiterated in the concurring opinion of Judge Jessup.[33]

Another striking recent example of judicial adoption of precisely the goal of interpretation we recommend appears in the case of *Maximov v. United States,*[34] while before the United States Court of Appeals for the Second Circuit. This case involved the interpretation of the 1945 Tax Convention between the United States and Great Britain, which provides in Article XIV that "A resident of the United Kingdom not engaged in trade or business in the United States shall be exempt from United States tax on gains from the sale or exchange of capital assets." [35] Maximov, a successor trustee under a trust established in the United States under the law of Connecticut by a resident of Great Britain, and with an American trustee,

31. Id. at 341.
32. Ibid. For a more detailed analysis of this case, see infra pp. 245–49.
33. Id. at 407.
34. 299 F.2d 565 (1962); aff'd. 373 U.S. 49 (1963), but on the ground that the terms of the treaty taken in their ordinary sense were clear: "The plain language of the Convention does not afford any support to the petitioner's argument. . . . There is no indication that application of the words of the treaty according to their obvious meaning effects a result inconsistent with the intent or expectations of its signatories." Id. at 52, 54 (opinion by then Mr. Justice Goldberg). Sharply contrasting goals and principles, in sophisticated hands, may thus be made functional equivalents.
35. 373 U.S. 49, 52.

brought suit under Article XIV for a refund on taxes paid on income from the trust. His argument was that the income was in fact income of the grantor-beneficiary who resided in England and was thus "exempted" by the express provision of the Convention. Since there was no tax in England on capital gains, the effect of such a ruling would have been to provide the grantor-beneficiary a source of tax-free income. The late Judge Clark, writing for a unanimous Court, held that under United States tax laws the income was considered income of the trust itself, and not of the beneficiary, and since the trust was established as a separate entity in the United States the income was taxable in the United States.

A principal concern of Judge Clark appeared to be to refute the notion that the case could be decided simply by looking at the literal meaning of the text. Instead he called for a broader goal:

> The basic aim of treaty interpretation is to ascertain the intent of the parties who have entered into agreement, in order to construe the document in a manner consistent with that intent . . . And to give the specific words of a treaty meaning consistent with the genuine shared expectations of the contracting parties, it is necessary to examine not only the language, but also the entire context of the agreement. We must therefore examine all available evidence of the shared expectations of the parties to this Convention in order to answer the interrelated questions [raised].[36]

Part of this "entire context" was the general purposes which the parties had hoped to achieve by the Convention, namely, the facilitation of commerce between the two countries by roughly equalizing tax burdens and particularly by eliminating double taxation. Judge Clark concluded that since this was not a case of double taxation, and since the requirement of "rough equality" did not necessitate overturning a United States tax law on the books at the time of the Convention, the trust was taxable as was any other trust established in the United States. The importance of the decision for our purposes thus rests not merely upon the Court's clear statement of the goal of interpretation but also upon its explicit willingness to examine all features of the context in implementing that goal.

Explicit rejections of the goal of interpreting international agree-

36. 299 F.2d 565, 568.

ments in accordance with the genuine shared expectations of the parties have, as noted above, been rare. Unfortunately, there are some weighty exceptions. Easily the most authoritative and potentially the most destructively influential of these is the recent (1964) International Law Commission Report on the Law of Treaties.[37] In this Report, in explicit rejection of Sir Hersch Lauterpacht's "strong advocacy of a more subjective, 'intentions of the parties' approach," the Commission takes its stand with the goal of textuality.[38] The justification offered—and twice repeated, as if repetition could make it persuasive—is that "the text [of a treaty] must be presumed to be the authentic expression of the intentions of the parties" and hence that "the starting point of interpretation is the elucidation of the meaning of the text, not an investigation *ab initio* into the intentions of the parties." [39] It is upon the basis of this arbitrary presumption that the Commission formulated its principal rule, Article 69, the first section of which reads:

> A treaty shall be interpreted in good faith in accordance with the ordinary meaning to be given to each term:
> (a) In the context of the treaty and in the light of its objects and purposes; and
> (b) In the light of the rules of general international law in force at the time of its conclusion.[40]

37. U.N. Gen. Ass. Off. Rec., 19th Sess., Supp. No. 9 (U.N. Doc. No. A/5809), p. 25 (1964). Modifications in emphasis appear minor in the Commission's final draft, Report of the International Law Commission, U.N. Gen. Ass. Off. Rec., 21st Sess., Supplement No. 9 (U.N. Doc. A/6309/Rev.1) (1966).
38. Id. at 27. The Commission notes, in invocation of support in authority, that the final formulations of the Institute of International Law, contrary to Sir Hersch Lauterpacht's recommendations, adopted the textual approach. See 46 *Annuaire de l'Institut de Droit International* 319–20 (1956). The reason given by the Institute for rejecting the "intention" of the parties' goal and accepting that of "establishing the true meaning" of the text is that "the intention of the parties is often difficult to establish" and sometimes "the parties have no common intention" (p. 321). The key concept employed by the Institute is not that of "ordinary meaning," but that of the "natural sense" of the text. It is interesting to observe that Professor Gidel suggests the substitution of "apparent" for "natural" on the ground that the latter can cause difficulties "sans nombre" (p. 352), while Judge Alfaro finds "apparent" no less ambiguous (p. 333). (Author's translations.)
39. Supra note 37, at 27.
40. Id. at 25.

Subsequent sections, articles, and commentary in the Report make clear that the Commission's primary emphasis is upon the words of texts and the "ordinary meanings" which can be ascribed to such words. The context of the agreement to which recourse is authorized is confined largely to the words of the agreement and of any other "agreement or instrument related to the treaty and reached or drawn up in connexion with its conclusion." [41]

Explicit in paragraph 1 (a) is, further, the notion that the implementation of the objects and purposes of a treaty is to be subsidiary to the implementation of its plain meaning; [42] the "objects and purposes" clause was obviously included in paragraph 1 (a) rather than in a separate paragraph, as Waldock originally recommended, as a means of de-emphasizing it as an aim in treaty interpretation.[43]

In modest recognition of the relevance of a less limited review of extrinsic factors, the Report provides in Article 70, only as "further means of interpretation," that

> Recourse may be had to further means of interpretation, including the preparatory work of the treaty and the circumstances of its conclusion, in order to verify or confirm the meaning resulting from the application of article 69, or to determine the meaning when the interpretation according to article 69:
> (a) Leaves the meaning ambiguous or obscure; or
> (b) Leads to a result which is manifestly absurd or unreasonable in the light of the objects and purposes of the treaty.[44]

Insisting that a hierarchy of rule is being established, the commentary reiterates that the "word 'further' emphasizes that Article 70 does not provide for alternative, autonomous means of interpretation but only for means to supplement an interpretation governed by the principles contained in Article 69." [45]

Similarly, though some members of the Commission doubted the need, the Report provides in Article 71, in meager generosity to par-

41. Ibid.
42. Id. esp. at 27.
43. See Sir Humphrey Waldock's Report of July 7, Supplement, 1964 in U.N. Gen. Ass. Off. Rec., 19th Sess. (U.N. Doc. No. A/CN.4/167/Add. 1–3), and the introductory commentary in the Commission's Report, supra note 37, at 3.
44. Ibid.
45. Id. at 30.

ties of unstandardized intent, that "Notwithstanding the provisions of paragraph 1 of article 69, a meaning other than its ordinary meaning may be given to a term if it is established conclusively that the parties intended the term to have that special meaning." [46] The commentary emphasizes both "that the burden of proof lies on the party invoking the special meaning of the term" and "the strictness of the proof required." [47]

It is indeed surprising, in the light of modern developments in communications analysis, to find such an authoritative body as the International Law Commission, composed of scholars and statesmen from all over the world, establishing so fragile a support as the "ordinary meaning" of words as the principal base for all its rules designed to assist in the interpretation of agreements.[48] Certainly it does not strengthen the Commission's case to argue, as it does, that its approach is commended by Max Huber's statement that "le text signe est, sauf de rares exceptions, la seule et la plus récente expression de la volonté commune des parties." [49] The questions remain of by what indices and procedures "ordinary meanings" are to be established and why such meanings are to be preferred, in a society honoring experimental enterprise and human dignity, to the individual meanings of the parties. The position of the Commission here comes perilously close to Vattel's assumption that there are plain and natural meanings which do not admit of interpretation. Similarly, the argument ascribed by the Commission to the International Court of Justice that to adopt an interpretation "counter to the clear meaning of the terms would not be to interpret but to revise the treaty" [50] both begs the question as to the goal of treaty interpretation and assumes that a failure to apply an agreement, because of some alleged verbal gap or infelicity in the text, would not in itself be a revision of the genuine shared expectations of the parties. The many, even in-

46. Supra note 37, at 25.

47. Id. at 31.

48. The self-levitation by-own-bootstraps character of the intellectual operations of the Commission become apparent when, after first justifying its choice of the textuality goal by invocation of the presumption of ordinary meaning, it later sustains the high conclusiveness of its preference for "ordinary meaning" by reference to the textuality goal. Id. at 30, 31.

49. Id. at 27. Quotation from Huber, 44 *Annuaire de l'Institut de Droit International* 199 (1952).

50. Ibid.

superable, difficulties which inhere in building a set of viable principles of interpretation about so ill-defined a goal as "ordinary meaning" will, however, become evident as we explore, principle by principle, past trends in the management of principles of interpretation.[51]

Among individual publicists, the most notable example in rejection of the goal of approximating the genuine shared expectations of the parties may be found in Sir Eric Beckett's statement to the Institute of International Law during its 1950 session: "the task of the court is to interpret the treaty and not to ascertain the intention of the parties." [52] Beckett referred to the latter aim as a "cliché . . . tending to obscure rather than illuminate the real task of the Tribunal," whereas "in fact the task of the Tribunal is that of interpreting a written document . . . and it has to proceed on the assumption that it finds the intention expressed in the words of the document which it has to interpret." [53]

Although one may find unexceptional the conclusion that a decision-maker must frequently interpret a written document, the degree of emphasis which Beckett places upon recourse to such a document must be rejected as dangerously misleading. It too greatly encourages the view, popular in times prior to the development of modern techniques of linguistic analysis, that there are fixed or "natural" meanings of words which cannot or should not be altered by the parties to the agreement, and that the task of the interpreter is simply to ascertain these meanings without recourse to the total context. The effect of such a statement may be to discourage the consideration of contextual materials which might disturb these allegedly

51. It may be amusing to note that the Commission is forced to depart from its stated goal of textuality when it confronts the problem of an agreement with several equally authoritative texts. Rather shamefacedly, it has recourse to the common intention of the parties. Id. at 32, 34.

For a brief exposition of the difficulties encountered by the Commission, see Liacouras, "The International Court of Justice and Development of Useful 'Rules of Interpretation' in the process of Treaty Interpretation," 1965 *Proc. Am. Soc. I. L.* 161.

52. 43 *Annuaire de L'Institut de Droit International* 438–39 (1950). A similar emphasis upon textuality characterizes the recent book by Bernhardt, *Die Auslegung völkerrechtlicher Verträge* (1963).

53. Id. at 438. For further support of this view, see Bernhardt, op. cit. supra note 52, at 30–39, and Degan, *L'Interprétation des Accords en Droit International* 75 ff. (1963).

"natural" meanings. Beckett himself, however, does not advocate this extreme position, as can be seen in his comment that "the court, on a study of the treaty as a whole, after hearing arguments on the circumstances which led up to the conclusion of the treaty, its relationship with other treaties which preceded it and applying all the rules of interpretation . . . is able on this basis finally to reach a definite view on the meaning of the provision." [54] Instead, his aim appears to be only that of emphasizing certain disadvantages of the policy of resolving *all* disputes by reference to the shared expectations of the parties as reflected in the framework of agreement.

Beckett calls attention to several types of situations in which such a conclusion would not be satisfactory. "As a matter of experience," he argues, "it often occurs that the difference between the parties to the treaties arises out of something which the parties never thought of when the treaty was concluded and that, therefore, they had absolutely no common intention with regard to it." [55] In other situations, he points out that "the parties may all along have had divergent intentions with regard to the actual question which is in dispute," or they may have "never had a common intention on the point which has arisen, but simply agreed on a text . . . hoping that this point would not arise in practice, or possibly expecting that if it did the text which was agreed would produce the result which it desired." [56]

In assessing Beckett's position, it should be clear that his argument, which points in a general way to features of the context which decision-makers could usefully recall, hardly supports the conclusion which he ultimately reaches rejecting the goal of interpreting according to the "intentions" of the parties. The more fitting conclusion would appear to be that under certain circumstances the application of the term "expectations" or "intention" to inferences drawn from a systematic contextual analysis is likely to be in some measure fanciful.[57] A preferable policy, as we have above recommended, would be to acknowledge that the parties were not able to project their own expectations about the specific events under consideration, and

54. Id. at 440–41.
55. Id. at 438.
56. Ibid.
57. See the related discussion of possible applications of the "intentions" doctrine in Lauterpacht, supra note 19, at 83–84.

hence that reference must be made to such features of the context as their more general aims and purposes and the relevant general principles of international law or basic policies of demanded public order.[58] The crucial defect in Beckett's position is that his injunction against ascertaining the intention of the parties does not suggest any of these alternatives. It suggests instead that a narrow textual examination will suffice even in the difficult situations where a thorough, systematic examination of the context will not yield a clear expression of the participants' expectations. The important point, in contrast, is that such an examination must be made regardless of the apparent simplicity and directness of the parties' textual expressions. If the results are equivocal, if they yield no obvious "expectation" or "intention," then recourse must of necessity be had to inferences from more general purposes or community policies.

In a passage somewhat incongruous in the context of his more general views, and susceptible to misconstruction, Charles Cheney Hyde employs language which might appear to take a position comparable to that of Beckett. After stating reasonably clearly that the goal of interpretation should be to give effect to the common design of the parties, he wrote: "It is the contract which is the subject of interpretation, rather than the volition of the parties." [59] Hyde's use of the word "volition" stemmed from his adoption of J. H. Wigmore's terminology of "sense" and "will" or "volition," which was originally employed in order to clarify the ambiguities in the concepts of "meaning" and "intention." [60] In these terms, "Interpretation as a

58. See supra, pp. 29–30, 41–42, 62–63.

59. Hyde, op. cit. supra note 18, at 1471, cited with approval in Bernhardt, op. cit. supra note 52, at 31. Bernhardt takes the anti-intentions view to its logical extreme in contending that "any search for the psyche of this or that person must be excluded" (p. 38), or otherwise one would "put into question not only [the interpretation's] own true object, but also the certainty of the law" (p. 66).

60. Wigmore, op. cit. supra note 6, at 183. By "sense" Wigmore indicates that he means the actual shared reference of any expression as opposed to the uneffected desire to communicate, which would be "volition." The distinction is explained in greater detail by Yü: "an agreement should be viewed as having been made by the negotiators in the light of what they *know* they have agreed upon rather than what they *wish* they might have agreed upon. The 'sense' in which the words have been used by the negotiator deals with the association between words and external objects, but his 'intention' deals with nothing more than his state of mind at the time of negotiation. In ascertaining the genuine standard of in-

juristic process is concerned with the Sense of the word used, and not with the Will to use that particular word." [61] Thus the shared expectations of commitment arising from the shared perspectives of the participants constitute what Hyde called the "sense" of an agreement. "Volitions" may be distinguished as referring to the parties' unilateral perspectives, or even to their shared perspectives, which are not made a part of their shared expectations of commitment.

It should be obvious that unilateral demands and expectations not shared by the party to which they are addressed provide no special difficulty, and should of course be ignored. But what of shared demands which are not made to give rise to genuine shared expectations? Shared demands with respect to another subject would of course rarely create a problem for interpreters. When the more likely claims are made, e.g. that both demands and expectations of commitment were in fact shared but inappropriately expressed, and that a solution may validly be inferred from expectations represented by more general statements of purpose or goal, the issue of whether a particular demand has created shared expectations is what is ultimately at stake. Under these conditions, to advise the decision-maker to ignore unshared and unexpressed demands is to tell him nothing more than that he must decide what the parties agreed upon. And yet this unexceptionable position nevertheless appears to be the basis of Hyde's statement that "It is the contract which is the subject of interpretation, rather than the volition of the parties." [62]

---

terpretation, therefore, the interpreter is charged with the duty to discover not what the negotiators have willed or intended to agree upon, but what is the 'sense' which they have actually attached to the terms of the agreement." Yü op. cit. supra note 5, at 62.

61. Wigmore, ibid.

62. Hyde, op. cit. supra note 18, at 1471. The approach recommended by these writers is similar in most other respects to the one which we have proposed above. In this approach the commitment to the highest-level goal of ascertaining genuine shared expectations, or of discovering the "sense" or "design" of the parties involved, in their words, a "scientific search for the sources of evidence" (Yü, op. cit. supra note 5, at 28) in order to examine "whatever sheds light on the question involved" (Hyde, ibid.). Thus, despite the difficulties of expression which we have noted, the goals which we propose have been affirmed consistently by all of these writers, without the reservations commonly made in the writings of other contemporary publicists.

In a letter to the authors Oliver Lissitzyn has suggested that Hyde often used the term "common design" with a reference very close to that of our "shared

Despite the apparent acceptance by the vast majority of writers and decision-makers in past practice of the goal of seeking the genuine shared expectations of the parties, its actual acceptance—as measured by the operations recommended by them for examining relevant features of the total context—must be seriously questioned. The extent to which various formulations of the goal of interpretation are to be read as equivalents of our preferred goal is indicated by how seriously such formulations recommend, and take, a comprehensive contextual approach. If important sources of evidence are excluded from examination, or are generally subordinated to one or several limited features of the context, the formulations put forward are not in fact equivalent to our stated goal.

Since the mediation of the subjectivities of parties to an agreement must proceed through the use of signs or by the encouragement of inferences from acts of collaboration, the most significant content of any theory of interpretation is its recommendations concerning the signs and acts of collaboration which a decision-maker is required to examine. Past attempts to exclude or order the various indices of communication have been the source of many differences among publicists and jurists alike. The positions taken have covered a wide range, varying from expressions of preference for one or a limited number of indices to outright rejection or de-emphasis of others. The issue which has most troubled recent writers has been whether any particular index can or should be consistently favored in determining expectations. Different views on this issue have generated the diverging emphases disclosed in past trends of decision, and led unhappily to no inconsiderable confusion about what is involved in the goal of giving effect to the participants' genuine shared expectations of commitment.

The most prominent attempt to inflate the importance of a single contextual detail has been the so-called "plain and natural meaning" principle. In one common formulation any reference to the wider aspects of a total context must be excluded whenever a reading of the words of a treaty in their "plain," "natural," or "ordinary" sense can

---

expectations." Where Hyde differed from the views expressed in this book was, according to Lissitzyn, not in his conception of the goal of primary interpretation but rather in his views about the helpfulness of rules of interpretation and with respect to the effect to be given to shared expectations which appear subsequently to the conclusion of the focal agreement.

be made to yield a solution to the dispute under consideration. One illustration of the way in which this principle is frequently employed is found in the famous *Lotus* case.[63] The Court, in rejecting an appeal to extrinsic evidence of the parties' expectations, said that "there is no occasion to have regard to preparatory work if the text of a convention is sufficiently clear in itself." [64] In such a formulation, the service of the principle is explicitly that of prohibiting recourse to features of the context in the name of assumed "clear" or "plain" or "ordinary" meanings deduced from the four corners of the text or a specific provision or phrase. Similar declarations in regard to nearly all other potential sources of inference about genuine expectations—which we will review in more detail below—have not infrequently been made articulate by authoritative decision-makers and publicists alike.[65]

The inadequacy of the "plain and natural" meaning principle has been recognized by the majority of writers for some time.[66] They have understood that in the process of determining the genuine shared expectations of parties to an agreement, a simple reading of the final text, while clearly indispensable, may often be of only limited assistance. Other indices of expectation, including the general features of the world social and power processes, the particular circumstances attending negotiation, the events occurring during negotiation, and the subsequent actions of the parties under the agreement, may be of much greater assistance in any given situation. The point to be stressed is that prior to a comprehensive contextual examination *no determination of the hierarchical importance or relevance of any feature of the context may be usefully made,* and any

63. *The S.S. "Lotus,"* P.C.I.J., Ser. A, No. 10 (1927).

64. Id. at 16.

65. One statement of particular importance is that of Sir Gerald Fitzmaurice, in which the reading of the text of an agreement (often referred to as the "context" of the provision being interpreted) is considered sufficient to document the parties' genuine shared expectations. Fitzmaurice calls this tendency the principle of "textuality" or "actuality." Fitzmaurice, supra note 7, at 9; Fitzmaurice, supra note 21, at 211. We make further reference to Fitzmaurice's view infra, p. 285.

66. For comments confirming this trend, see Lauterpacht, "Rapport et Projet de Resolutions" submitted to the Institute of International Law, 43 *Annuaire de l'Institut de Droit International* 366, 378–80 (1950); McNair (1938) op. cit. supra note 17, at 175.

attempt to do so must ultimately frustrate the ascertainment of genuine shared expectations. The language of the rule encourages an exaggerated assumption of clairvoyance on the part of the reader of a text, and de-emphasizes an open-eyed quest for relevant information. Although there is no reason to deny the usefulness of the common or public meanings of words as starting points in the process of interpretation, whenever a principle emphasizing such meanings threatens to become transformed into a final, exclusive procedure, it must be rejected. No acceptable justification can be given for precluding an interpreter, whose goal is to determine the shared expectations of the authors of a document, from proceeding to examine all of the relevant features of the context prior to final decision. To the degree that the plain and natural meaning rule is utilized to preclude inquiry into any relevant factor, to the degree that it proceeds in dogmatic conclusion from what should be the starting point of a sequence of interpretative activity, in such degree the recommended goal of making effective the genuine shared expectations of the parties is in fact repudiated.[67]

Other principles of interpretation, often advanced in opposition to the more strictly "textual" approaches, may also tend to defeat the primary goal. Thus overemphasis upon any phase or mode of the process of agreement in a given situation may have a distorting influence on the quest for the intentions of the parties. The most significant phase of agreement for a particular dispute may, for example, either precede or follow the culmination in commitment ceremonialized at the outcome phase. Likewise, the mode of expression that most accurately reflects the parties' genuine commitment may vary from highly specific, technical terminology to general statements of purpose or aim. It may even embrace more subtle and remote acts of acceptance or collaboration. It should be obvious that an a priori preference for any one of these factors, or a demand that any one factor be omitted from consideration entirely, will serve only to defeat the overriding goal.

67. In past trends of judicial decision, the frequency of manifest acceptance of the "plain and natural meaning" rule for this purpose has been surprisingly high, as we demonstrate below. With some exceptions, however, modern expert opinion rejects the doctrine, or seeks to restrict it, as we would prefer, to an easily rebuttable presumption with no priority. For our discussion of the present status of the doctrine, see infra, pp. 216–52.

One principle, for example, frequently recommended as preeminently reliable for determining expectations is that of "effectiveness," [68] or "major purposes." [69] This principle, as we shall see in more detail below, calls for interpretation in accordance with the more general, overriding aims or policies of the parties to an agreement. In one formulation, it calls for giving effect to such aims even in cases where they may be in conflict with specific provisions of the treaty under consideration. A more modest formulation of the principle demands merely a consideration of general aims or policies in order to *provide an understanding of* specific terms in the treaty, with the provision that in case of conflict, one or the other feature is to be effected as a general rule.[70] Too strong an initial presumption in favor of either overriding goals or specific provisions may be, in our view, detrimental to the highest-level goal which we have postulated. Only a balanced consideration of both, with final preference assigned after a systematic examination of many relevant features of the context, will insure in the total flow of cases the closest possible approximation to the genuine shared expectations of the parties.

Similarly, the view that materials prior to the outcome phase of negotiation, referred to in large part as the *travaux préparatoires* of the agreement, must be given primary effect with a view toward resolving disputes in terms of the parties' expectations at the time of commitment may in some cases make unrealistic demands upon an interpreter charged with making a contemporary assessment of the effect of an agreement. An example of obvious relevance may be noted with respect to the United Nations Charter which, like the constitutions of nation-states, has in the wake of far-reaching social changes undergone substantial changes in reference since the days of

68. Lauterpacht, supra note 19, at 67–75; Lauterpacht, op. cit. supra note 7, at 227 ff.; Fitzmaurice, supra note 7, at 9; Fitzmaurice, supra note 21, at 211.

69. Harvard Research, op. cit. supra note 10, at 947–53.

70. Lauterpacht, op. cit. supra note 7, at 228, takes the view that the overriding purposes should prevail; Fitzmaurice, supra note 7, at 8, appears to take the view that overriding aims in conflict with specific provisions of the text when taken in their ordinary meaning should not be given effect; Hexner, in his article "Teleological Interpretation of Basic Instruments of Public International Organizations," Engel (ed.), *Law, State, and International Legal Order; Essays in Honor of Hans Kelsen* (1964), makes a case for the importance of implementing general purposes as an instrument of flexibility in the interpretation of basic constitutional documents (pp. 130 ff.).

its negotiation. Under such circumstances, one could scarcely call for an interpretation which limited itself strictly to the expectations of those who drafted the basic document. The United Nations Charter and the practice in which it is applied in fact constitute a continuing, contemporary communication. Hence in the application of such an agreement, the principal aim of an interpreter should be to give effect to the continuing consensus of the parties—that is, their contemporary shared expectations concerning problems of the type being disputed.[71] In making such a determination, any index of the

71. The contemporaneity in expectation here recommended as the ultimate test in the interpretation of international agreements has its parallel in the contemporaneity demanded in the interpretation of the United States Constitution. A former Solicitor General of the United States, James M. Beck, once described the role of the Supreme Court as that of "a continuous constitutional convention." Beck, *The Constitution of the United States* 195 (Adams rev. ed. 1941). If for the Court one substitutes the whole flow of public order communications which create expectations about constitutive process in the United States, the insight is profound. The goal for interpreting the Constitution which appears to be accepted in practice is that of the closest possible approximation to the contemporary expectations created in the general community by the entire flow of past communication from all constitution makers.

An often quoted authoritative statement is that of Mr. Justice Stone in *United States v. Classic,* 313 U.S. 299, 315–16 (1941):

> We may assume that the framers of the Constitution in adopting that section [Article I, §2] did not have specifically in mind the selection and elimination of candidates for Congress by the direct primary any more than they contemplated the application of the commerce clause to interstate telephone, telegraph and wireless communication, which are concededly within it. But in determining whether a provision of the Constitution applies to a new subject matter, it is of little significance that it is one with which the framers were not familiar. For in setting up an enduring framework of government they undertook to carry out for the indefinite future and in all the vicissitudes of the changing affairs of men, those fundamental purposes which the instrument itself discloses. Hence we read its words, not as we read legislative codes which are subject to continuous revision with the changing course of events, but as the revelation of the great purposes which were intended to be achieved by the Constitution as a continuing instrument of government.

Even more eloquent are the words of the late Walton Hamilton, "The Constitution—Apropos of Crosskey," 21 *U. Chi. L. Rev.* 79 (1953):

> It is inevitable that judges should substitute doctrines of their own for those which the Fathers set down in the original document. And such a rewriting of the law—even of the enduring principles of the higher law—is as

understanding created in the contemporary audience by the whole flow of past communication, or any particular feature of such an index in terms of its explicitness, precision, and directness of application may be relevant to the solution of the dispute. Thus, as before, no advance preference for any given index is plausible in attempting to approximate most adequately the parties' genuine shared expectations of commitment.

In view of the inherent difficulty of the problem, it is not surprising to find that considerable confusion has attended past practice in the formulation of the interrelations of the several goals involved in the comprehensive application of an international agreement. These we have described in terms of making genuine inferences from relevant indices about the genuine shared expectations of the parties, of supplementing these inferences when necessary by reference to general community policies, and of appraising even genuine expectations for their compatibility with more basic constitutional community policies. The recognition of the necessity of making these shifts in goal in the processes of interpretation and application has occasioned numerous verbal formulations in past trends of decision and opinion, which have been invoked for the purpose of describing, in general terms, the various features of these processes. In direct reference to the participants' subjectivities, for example, we have referred above to the supplementation of shared expectations by reference to community policies as "filling in gaps"; in similar reference to subjectivi-

---

> necessary as it is inevitable. For the values which fix the objectives of public policy must change as the aspirations of men are broadened 'with the process of the suns'; and, even as ends endure, they must be newly instrumented amid the changing circumstances of a dynamic culture or they will be betrayed. With the fact that there is substitution we can have no legitimate quarrel. But we may object—vocally, indignantly, rightfully—at the specific substitute, at the uncritical way in which it is contrived, at the violence with which it is thrust into place, at the severity of its break with the past.

A comparable emphasis with respect to statutes may be observed in the establishment of the goal of interpretation in accordance with the contemporary expectations created by the whole legislative process (not merely the words of the statute) in the general community (see the citations supra, Ch. 1, n. 30); and, similarly, with respect to precedents, in the goal of interpreting past decisions in terms of the contemporary communication they make to the general community about the requirements of future decision (see the citations supra, Ch. 1, n. 30).

ties, some authors have suggested speaking of "inferring or implying intent" from other more general features of the agreement.[72] In relation to the specific expressions used by the parties, this process has been called an augmentation of the "open texture" of a concept.[73] The necessity of rejecting genuine expectations in favor of overriding community policies has often been alluded to in past practice as the "voiding" of an agreement in conflict with general principles of international law. This is a procedure which we have described above as the "policing" or "integrating" of an agreement.

The most informative recent discussions of the difference between ascertaining the parties' expectations of commitment and supplementing these expectations by reference to community policies are contained in the writings of Lauterpacht and Stone. As Stone has correctly observed, international tribunals in their few references to this problem have on the whole been satisfied to repeat maxims of questionable utility such as that contained in the *Peace Treaties* case that "It is the duty of the Court to interpret the Treaties, not to revise them." [74] In the absence of useful judicial guidance on this

72. Five such situations in which "implied intent" is proposed in the absence of evidence of actual expectations are described in Lauterpacht, supra note 19, at 75–82. See the more detailed discussion of this point immediately below.

73. Hart, *The Concept of Law* 121–32 (1961).

74. *Interpretation of Peace Treaties with Bulgaria, Hungary and Romania* (Second Phase), [1950] I.C.J. Rep. 221, 229. It is interesting to note that in this particular case the Court appeared to be using such a vacuous notion as a substitute for the plain meaning rule. The facts in this case are well known: after repeated violations by Bulgaria, Hungary, and Romania of civil rights guaranteed by the treaties of peace following the Second World War, the General Assembly became concerned and voted to place several questions before the Court for an advisory opinion. The first concerned treaty obligations, which the Court spelled out and affirmed. The second concerned an apparent obligation on the part of each of the countries to appoint a representative to a three-man treaty commission (one from each disputing country and one outsider) to settle the dispute, which the Court also affirmed. Upon the refusal of Bulgaria, Hungary, and Romania to so appoint, a third question arose: could the Secretary-General irrespective of this refusal appoint representatives for these countries? The relevant Treaty provision said only that "Should the two parties fail to agree . . . upon the appointment of the third [outside] member, the Secretary-General may be requested by either party to make the appointment." No mention was made of the situation in which one of the two disputing parties might fail to appoint its own representative. Thus in refusing to extend the "third-party" appointment principle, the Court appears to be relying on a doctrine of plain meaning:

point, we must turn to the more detailed treatment given the subject by publicists.

Judge Lauterpacht, perhaps more consistently than many other publicists, as we pointed out above, affirmed the goal of interpreting in accordance with the shared expectations of the parties. He no less consistently argued that this goal should be employed to limit what would otherwise be, in his terms, "an element of wide and uncontrolled discretion inconsistent with the legitimate exercise of the judicial function." [75] In order to clarify the circumstances under which the application of such a goal could be questioned, Lauterpacht described five types of situations in which it might be said that there is "an absence of an effective common intention of the parties":

> 1. There may be no common intention for the reason that the parties, although using identical language, did not intend the same result.
>
> 2. It is possible that . . . different meanings [are] attached to the same expression by . . . the deliberate design of one or more of the parties bent upon benefiting from an ambiguity surrounding the expression . . .
>
> 3. The absence of an effective common intention may be due to the circumstance that, being unable to reach an agreed solution, the parties are content to use an ambiguous or non-committal expression and to leave the divergence of views to be solved in the future by agreement or in some other way.
>
> 4. It is possible that [the treaty] affords no clue as to the solution of any particular problem or difficulty which, demonstrably, did not occur to [the negotiators] when they concluded the treaty but which falls within the purview of its general provisions.
>
> 5. There is an absence of effective common intention when two or more provisions of the same treaty are mutually inconsistent.[76]

---

the provision does not specify appointment by the Secretary-General of the country representatives, hence it cannot be done.

75. Lauterpacht, supra note 19, at 76.

76. Id. at 76–80. (The quotations here presented are sharply abbreviated.)

In all of these cases, he suggested that the terminology of shared intentions may still be legitimately employed. The procedure for its employment is uniform in the five situations: "The determination, in such cases, of the overriding—the higher—common intention of the parties, not less real because it is necessarily implied, may constitute an important aspect of the judicial function of interpretation." He argued that this function, "far from being limited to discovering the meaning of a text, may legitimately impart to it a meaning by reference to the paramount principle of the completeness and the rational development of the law and of the requirements of justice in the light of the purpose of the treaty viewed as a whole." [77] This function does not, in Lauterpacht's view, encourage the use of "uncontrolled discretion," and in fact only provides for the implementation, in any given case, of the "only one correct interpretation of the law." To believe otherwise would be to "put forward an assertion which denies the very essence of the judicial function in a society under the rule of law," and which would "obliterate the border line between the function of the judge and the powers of the legislator." [78]

Professor Stone, in his article "Fictional Elements in Treaty Interpretation," [79] has criticized Lauterpacht's view on several counts. Specifically, Stone suggests that one fictional element is contained in Lauterpacht's and others' "prejudice against judicial law making activity," which is at the center of their insistence that the terminology of "intentions" should be so widely employed. As Stone says, "the assumption that an intention must *always* be discoverable and discovered dies hard . . . To add the rider, 'by reference to . . . intention manifested by the treaty as a whole', and to talk of the discovery of the 'implied' intention, can scarcely conceal (though it undoubtedly obscures) the true nature of this analysis." [80]

The position thus taken by Stone appears to be that, under the circumstances outlined by Lauterpacht, the use of phrases such as "the discovery of intentions" is misleading, since it encourages the jurist to escape the admission of "a responsibility which will not be assumed until judicial creativeness is recognized as such." In even

77. Id. at 81.
78. Id. at 82.
79. 1 *Sydney L. Rev.* 344, 347–50 (1954).
80. Id. at 347, 349 (1954), quoting Lauterpacht, supra note 19, at 80.

stronger terms, he argues that "To conceal it behind the 'assumed' or 'implied' or 'imputed' intention of the parties is to invite the exercise of the power without the acceptance of the responsibility therefor. There is a danger, in short, of reducing 'the intention of the parties' to a 'phrase employed . . . to justify conclusions arrived at by some method other than the ascertainment of any actual intention of the parties.' " [81]

The obvious fact that, in the absence of appropriate indices of genuine shared expectations, established decision-makers must have recourse to general community policies for supplementation, is, however, fully recognized by most contemporary commentators—including both Lauterpacht and Stone. The difficulty is that this common recognition is often obscured by ambiguities and infelicities of expression similar to those which we have already seen. Thus Lauterpacht believed, consistently with his broad application of the "intentions" canon, that for the purpose of providing for all contingencies, "when the intention of the parties is not clear it must be assumed that they intended a result which is in conformity with general international law." [82] Even though Stone expresses some doubt concerning the effectiveness of such a high-level directive, he nevertheless is willing to affirm the traditional doctrine that international conventions "are to be interpreted in the light of 'the general principles of law recognized by civilized nations.' " [83]

The general acceptance of this goal is indicated by the frequency with which it has been affirmed, in differing versions, by various writers. Schwarzenberger, for example, has argued that a "prominent" aid in the interpreter's techniques of decision should be the "interpretation of a treaty . . . against the background of international customary law." [84] The American Law Institute's Restatement of the Foreign Relations Law of the United States advances much the same view in Section 130, Comment e (9) : *"Compatibility with International Law and General Principles of Law:* International agreements are to be interpreted within the general frame-

81. Id. at 349, quoting Harvard Research, op. cit. supra note 10, at 952–53.
82. Lauterpacht, op. cit. supra note 7, at 27–28.
83. Stone, supra note 79, at 360.
84. Schwarzenberger, op. cit. supra note 14, at 526. Cf., however, Schwarzenberger's "International Jus Cogens." 43 *Texas L. R.* 455 (1965), where a review of international customary law vis-à-vis *jus cogens* suggests that this "prominent" aid may be, in the author's view, relatively ineffective.

work of the international legal order. Although an international agreement could . . . displace general international law, such an interpretation would not be given in a situation of ambiguity." [85] Numerous other formulations, both by scholars and officials, might be cited which affirm the goal in equally general terms.[86]

It is unfortunate that few of these formulations proceed, beyond the preliminary invocation of customary international law, to a more detailed specification of relevant community policies. The difficulty, as we have already indicated, is that any such invocation must recall the entire context of authoritative expectations of the world community, in all their varying degrees of specificity, explicitness, and manifest acceptance. Therefore, even though some enumeration of norms is possible in a particular discussion of higher-level community goals which may, on occasion, be used to police genuine shared expectations of commitment, a more detailed examination of policies relevant for supplementing these expectations is obviously not practicable short of a general survey of international law. It should, however, be recognized that the selection of policies for any given case will require procedures which are not suggested by the general invocation of "customary international law," and that, as Stone points out,[87] the general form of acceptance should not be expected to provide, nor in fact is it able to provide, precise or detailed directives for the solution of a particular dispute.

The goal that established decision-makers must police even the genuine shared expectations of the participants in international

85. P. 136 (Tentative Draft No. 3, 1959); similar formulation carried over into final version (1965) as Section 147, paragraph h, p. 451–54.

86. See Hyde, op. cit. supra note 18, at 1374–75; Oppenheim, op. cit. supra note 7, at 808; Hall, op. cit. supra note 3, at 344; Crandall, op. cit. supra note 3, at 394; Hudson, op. cit. supra note 18, at 655; Lauterpacht, op. cit. supra note 7, at 27–28; De Visscher, *Problemes d'Interprétation Judiciaire en Droit International Public* 92 (1963). See also *Georges Pinson* case (1928), as reported in 1927–28 *Annual Digest of Public International Law Cases,* Case No. 292; *The "Kronprinz Gustaf Adolf"* (1932), in 26 *Am. J. Int'l L.* 834, 839–40 (1932), and 2 U.N. Rep. Int. Arb. Awards 1239, 1246–47; *Reparations for Injuries Suffered in the Service of the United Nations* [1949], I.C.J. Rep. 174, 178; and see the dissenting opinion of Judge Schucking, in the *Oscar Chinn* case, P.C.I.J., Ser. A/B, No. 63, p. 148, 150 (1934).

87. Stone, supra note 79, at 360. Stone argues, as we will see again below, that such formulas "leave a wide field for uninhibited creative choice by the Court." Ibid.

agreements for their compatibility with basic constitutional community policies is likewise fully accepted in contemporary authoritative opinion. The American Law Institute Draft, for example, while taking the position already mentioned, makes the following exception: "Under international law an agreement may be concluded with respect to any matter unless the agreement conflicts with . . . generally accepted standards of international conduct, as reflected in the practice of states." [88] It is obvious, as indeed is made explicit in other sections of the same work, that the conclusion must still be maintained that not *all* "generally accepted standards of international conduct" may override the parties' expectations of commitment. The problem to which attention must be drawn is that of specifying precisely what international policies have been regarded, will be regarded, and ought to be regarded as so basic that they cannot be varied even by explicit agreements between states.

88. American Law Institute, Sec. 102 (1) (a), op. cit. supra note 85, at 13.

In the final (1965) version of the Restatement, Art. 116 reads: "An international agreement may be made with respect to any matter except to the extent that the agreement conflicts with (a) the rules of international law incorporating basic standards of international conduct, or (b) the obligations of a member state under the Charter of the United Nations."

For a recent comprehensive collection of references see Verdross, *"Jus Dispositivum* and *Jus Cogens* in International Law," 60 *Am. J. Int'l L.* 55 (1966). This article offers an excellent defense of Art. 37 of the International Law Commission's draft convention on the law of treaties, which reads: "A treaty is void if it conflicts with a peremptory norm of general international law from which no derogation is permitted and which can be modified only by a subsequent norm of general international law having the same character."

One of the more eloquent statements in support of the general principle is that of Judge Radhabinod Pal, the Indian member of the International Law Commission:

> that certain principles of international law had the character of *jus cogens.* The whole perspective of United Nations policy could be characterized as a value-oriented jurisprudence, directed towards the emergence of a public order in the international community under the rule of law. The Charter sought to establish a process by which the world community could regulate the international abuse of naked force and promote a world public order embodying values of human dignity in a society dedicated to freedom and justice.

Summary record of the 683d meeting of the I.L.C., May 20, 1963, in 1 *Yearbook of the International Law Commission* 65, para. 64 (1963).

It requires but little inquiry to observe that the relatively small number of generally accepted principles of international law which have, in the past, been given such priority over the genuine shared expectations of the parties have not proved a very significant factor in the processes of interpretation and application. Nevertheless, brief mention may be made of a minimum number of frequently recommended overriding principles for the purpose of suggesting their deliberate employment in the general process of application and of encouraging the development of more adequate principles in the future course of international decision and opinion.

The most important constitutional principle of the contemporary world arena, though of relatively recent origin, is of course that of minimum order. Through the United Nations Charter, the Nuremberg Charter and Verdict, and other significant manifestations of authority, the general community of mankind has at long last established a basic distinction between impermissible and permissible coercion, with authoritative prohibition of impermissible coercion. In broadest reach, this new principle seeks to preclude all deliberate use of coercion, other than by agents of the general community, as an instrument of policy between peoples. In more precise formulation, in relation to major coercions, it seeks to prevent attacks upon the territorial integrity and political independence of peoples, and also to preclude even threats of coercion which may put their targets reasonably upon apprehension that they must use the military instrument to defend their integrity and independence.[89] It could of course only stultify this basic policy if agreements in contravention of it, however explicit, should be honored in community application. Agreements which should be denied application as contrary to this basic community policy include, for illustration, pacts to commit aggressive war against other nation-states, or to commit or encourage piracy on the high seas, or to monopolize, for the benefit of a few, strategic sharable resources hitherto held open under general community expectation for the use of all peoples. Since the objectives of the parties in agreements of this kind involve obvious threats to the overriding policy of a world community which has adopted the postulate of minimum order, it should be clear that these objectives cannot be given effect in contravention of such policy.

89. For detailed development, see McDougal and Feliciano, *Law and Minimum World Public Order,* Ch. 3 (1961).

Another basic constitutional policy may be seen in the principle, most strongly urged in recent times by Oppenheim, that "immoral obligations cannot be the object of an international treaty." [90] Although this doctrine has not received the unanimous support of Oppenheim's successors,[91] its broad direction has long been accepted as appropriate limitation upon the competence of states to make agreements. Thus Lauterpacht, who omitted his predecessor's principle from his United Nations report on the law of treaties because it could, in his view, "result in conferring upon international tribunals a measure of discretion . . . which Governments may not be willing to confer upon them and which they could exercise only with difficulty," [92] nonetheless agreed that certain more specific references of the same doctrine, such as its prohibition of agreements encouraging prostitution and slavery or other violations of human rights, may legitimately be applied to defeat the genuine shared expectations of parties who contract in violation of these prohibitions.[93]

Other overriding community policies may be found in the numerous provisions which deny clearly expressed expectations of commitment because of the range of their demanded application rather than their specific content. Examples from this area include the presumption of priority in efficacy accorded earlier commitments in the event

90. Oppenheim, op. cit. supra note 7, at 807. See also McNair, "Equality in International Law," 26 *Mich. L. Rev.* 131, 140–42 (1927), and Verdross, "Forbidden Treaties in International Law," 31 *Am. J. Int'l L.* 571, 571–77 (1937) cited in Oppenheim, ibid., in support of this position. And see Fiore, op. cit. supra note 3, at 333.

91. See Lauterpacht, "Law of Treaties," Report submitted to the International Law Commission at its 5th Session, March 24, 1953, in 2 *Yearbook of the International Law Commission* 90, 154–55 (1953).

92. Id. at 155.

93. Id. at 154–55. In the 1966 South-West Africa cases both Judge Padilla Nervo and Judge Tanaka appear willing, in dissent, to regard contemporary constitutive policies about human rights as within the ambit of *jus cogens.* [1966] I.C.J. Rep. 455. Both judges engage in powerful reasoning to this end, and Judge Tanaka puts the point quite explicitly: "If we can introduce in the international field a category of law, namely *jus cogens,* recently examined by the International Law Commission, a kind of imperative law which constitutes the contrast to the *jus dispositivum,* capable of being changed by way of agreement between States, surely the law concerning the protection of human rights may be considered to belong to the *jus cogens.*" [1966] I.C.J. Rep. 298.

of conflict with later commitments,[94] and the rules relating to the protection of third parties from the injurious application of agreements which may be otherwise valid as between the contracting states.[95] The former rule, as Professor Garner's Harvard Research draft observes, is simply one application of the principle of *pacta sunt servanda:* "It affirms in effect the principle that when a State has bound itself by a treaty with another State, it cannot thereafter relieve itself of the obligations it has thereby assumed by concluding a later treaty with another State under which it assumes obligations the performance of which would involve an impairment or repudiation of the obligations which it has already assumed *vis-à-vis* the State with which it concluded the earlier treaty." [96] The clearest formulation of the latter rule has been given by McNair: "a treaty between two States the execution of which contemplates the infliction upon a third State of what customary international law regards as a wrong is illegal and invalid *ab initio.*" [97] Thus, although two states may legally contract to change the width of their territorial waters, or to eliminate existing diplomatic immunities, or to change the present rights of their respective nationals concerning military service, confiscation of property, and so on, they are at the same time not free to apply these agreements in ways to injure nonconsenting third parties. As the development of a comprehensive world public order goes forward, it can safely be assumed that many other similar constitutional principles will become established.

It is important, finally, to point out that more is at stake in the various discussions of the interrelations between the two goals—of ascertaining the genuine expectations of the parties and of policing agreements by reference to overriding community policies—than merely determining the correct application of terms such as "intention," "expectation," "supplementing gaps" by reference to commu-

94. See Hall, op. cit. supra note 3, at 350–51; Fiore, op. cit. supra note 3, at 334; McNair (1938), op. cit. supra note 17, at 113, 116–24; see also the extensive treatment of the principle by Vattel, op. cit. supra note 1, at 218–21, and the reference in Phillimore, op. cit. supra note 3, at 78.

95. See American Law Institute, op. cit. supra note 85, at 13; Lauterpacht, supra note 91, at 154; Fiore, op. cit. supra note 3, at 334; Crandall, op. cit. supra note 3, at 402; Phillimore, op. cit. supra note 3, at 78.

96. Harvard Research, op. cit. supra note 10, at 1024.

97. McNair (1938), op. cit. supra note 17, at 113.

nity policies, and "policing." Presumably one of the more general purposes sought in employing such terms is to provide as much useful guidance to the decision-maker as possible. Another is to discourage the view that a premature "discovery" of expectations or goals, based upon the consideration of but one or a limited number of possible indices, is preferable to a rational examination and assessment of all of the relevant features of the context. Given these purposes, the utmost care must be taken to be as comprehensive and systematic as possible both in specifying the operations involved in the examination of indices of genuine expectation and in the canvass of potentially relevant community policies. Once various indices of the parties' subjectivities are specified and examined in context, and the relevant community policies are considered, no confusion need result over the "correct" description of which index is most responsible for the decision. Thus any number of sources—specific provisions of an agreement, its general purposes or aims, its preparation and subsequent enforcement, or its general historical or contemporary position in the wider context of world social and power processes—may contain material which is relevant to the solution of the dispute under consideration. Given the varying degrees of ambiguity inherent in applying any general term to a concrete case, it should be no surprise that such ambiguities can be involved not only in the employment of such terms as "intention" and "expectation," but also with terms such as "supplementing gaps" or "policing." In the view which we are recommending, however, no more useful purpose is served by disputing whether one mode of expression is the "correct" one in a given case than whether one index is "essentially" preferable to another. If the recommended procedures are employed to direct the attention of the decision-maker to all relevant features of the context, appropriate safeguards would appear to be taken against arbitrary or irrational procedure. So long as the extension or limitation in any particular case of terms, such as "intention" or "policing," does not serve to prohibit recourse to important features of the context, little point is served by debating their customary or preferred use. The same argument may be applied to any attempt to limit or extend these terms in advance of their employment in a particular case. The recommended view would be that at the levels both of general definition and of particular application, disputes over the use of such concepts may only be profitably extended to the examination of all the relevant features of the total context.

FUNCTIONS ASCRIBED TO PRINCIPLES OF INTERPRETATION

From the beginnings of contemporary international law, a most active discussion has centered upon the role of the so-called "canons," or principles, of interpretation. Conceptions of the proper function of these principles, as we have outlined above, have frequently been stated in terms of two extreme positions, both equally unacceptable. One position is characterized by an assumption that the principles of interpretation form a closed, fixed hierarchy of commands to the decision-maker which leave no doubt about their application to the individual case. One common consequence of this view has been that not only the application of the interpreter's canons, but even the specification of the general provisions of an agreement, have been thought to involve only relatively simple procedures, manifested preeminently in the traditional "plain and natural" meaning rule. At the other extreme, the view taken by several recent writers has been seen to be that the complexities of communication foreclose even the possibility that principles of interpretation might be of assistance in the process of interpretation. Among the consequences of this position have been both the discouraging of further inquiry into the nature and proper function of principles of interpretation and the adoption of an unnecessary pessimism concerning the rationality of the process of judicial decision.

The appropriate function of principles of interpretation—the more general purpose for which they may usefully and authoritatively be employed—as we have indicated above, is that of calling the attention of the decision-maker, in an orderly and economic way, to the various features of the process of commitment and its context which must be taken into account in determining the parties' genuine shared expectations and identifying relevant general community policies. The different content principles point to different factors of importance in this total context; in changing situations of controversy these factors may combine in various degrees of effectiveness to influence the outcome of interpretation. The impossibility of specifying in advance the importance of priority in application of any given principle, or of determining in any conclusive way the effect which any principle may have had in the process of decision, should be cause for neither optimism nor pessimism concerning their proper use. A realistic estimate of the potentialities of their proper use can only be made after a careful examination of what the principles can be made to accomplish, rather than by repeated insistence on their inherent shortcomings or by idealizations of their alleged past accomplishments.

In order fully to understand the origins of, and reasons for, these misconceptions, it may be helpful first to review past trends of decision and opinion in order to observe the great variety in past conception of the functions of principles of interpretation. The common practice of the earlier writers was to present lists of rules accompanied by assertions about their utility that appear to modern observers to be excessive. Vattel, for example, asserted that the rules which he advanced were "approved and prescribed by the Law of Nature" because they were "founded upon right reason." [98] Similarly, Phillimore contended that his principles were "deduced from right reason and rational equity," and proceeded to define the entire process of interpretation in these terms:

> What is meant by the term 'interpretation'? The meaning which any party may choose to affix? Or a meaning governed by settled rules and fixed principles, originally deduced from right reason and rational equity and subsequently formed into laws? Clearly the latter.[99]

This early optimism has given way in recent years to varying degrees of reluctance to affirm the traditional principles or to propose new ones. Professor Ehrlich, who among recent writers has been most receptive to the traditional principles, has nonetheless commented that "There are not recognized, and never have been, any rules as to the obligatory understanding of certain expressions or stipulations in a definitely prescribed manner." [100] Still, Ehrlich proposes "certain rules [which] have been recognized as to the admissibility of ways of

98. Vattel, op. cit. supra note 1, at 201.
99. Phillimore, op. cit. supra note 3, at 95.
100. Ehrlich, supra note 13, at 240–41.

proving the will of the parties."[101] Likewise, while Oppenheim spoke of the "questionable character of the usefulness of the rules of interpretation," he believed that nonetheless "It is of importance to enumerate some rules . . . which commend themselves on account of their suitability."[102]

Subsequent treatments of the canons of interpretation have been even more pessimistic. Judge Lauterpacht, for example, stated that "The view which is gaining increasing acceptance seems to be that some of the current rules of construction of treaties are . . . of controversial validity; that many of them are mutually exclusive and contradictory . . . and that instead of aiding what has been regarded as the principal aim of interpretation, namely, the discovery of the intention of the parties, they end by impeding that purpose."[103] Hyde likewise questioned "whether the enunciation of so-called rules of construction serves a useful purpose."[104] And Schwarzenberger, in prefacing an extensive discussion of such rules, observes that they "still require fairly full exposition if only to emphasize their limited usefulness."[105]

The most extreme position denies altogether the utility of the traditional canons. Yü has stated this position most forcefully: "It would appear . . . as futile to attempt to frame positive and fixed rules of construction as to endeavor in the same manner to set forth the mode by which the judges should draw conclusions from various species of evidence . . . [What is required is] a new system of treaty interpretation based, not on canons, but on a scientific search for the sources of evidence."[106] Yü makes it clear that in the course of this "scientific search," principles of interpretation cannot be profitably employed:

> The fundamental difficulty in prescribing a system of rules . . . lies in the imperfect nature of human language itself, through which no one can define or direct any intellectual process with perfection. How is it then expected that any artificial rules which are generally to govern the operations of human

101. Id. at 241.
102. Oppenheim, op. cit. supra note 7, at 857–58, 858 n.
103. Lauterpacht, supra note 19, at 52.
104. Hyde, op. cit. supra note 18, at 1498.
105. Schwarzenberger, op. cit. supra note 14, at 498.
106. Yü, op. cit. supra note 5, at 28.

> relationship can be of scientific value? . . . But curiously enough, no international jurists crowned with valuable experiences in international arbitrations have written any treatises, presenting the systematic procedure of tackling the problem—the procedure of invoking extrinsic evidence instead of preconceived rules.[107]

Yü's emphasis upon a broader analysis of contextual features, together with a thorough scepticism regarding the usefulness of the canons, has recently been reflected by Stone in his comment that though the "intentions," "effectiveness," "contexuality," and other such canons "appear to give *directives* to the courts, nevertheless, for the purpose of any particular decision, the directives are so wide, and the principles to which they point are so disputed, or inchoate, or self-contradictory, that the directives leave a wide field for uninhibited creative choice by the Court." [108]

It should not be surprising that in discussions which emphasize that the principles of interpretation are useless and self-contradictory, or that attempts to reformulate them are futile, the constructive function which such principles can play in the process of decision has been needlessly obscured. Stone, for example, specifies three roles which they have played in past decisions: (1) "They have . . . served as captions under which the tribunal could marshall existing precedents," (2) "given to tribunals a sense of continuity of tradition, relieving the psychological loneliness inseparable from the responsibility of policy-making," and (3) "given some support . . . to the claim of tribunals that their reasoning and the decisions arrived at had an objective validity." [109] The latter two functions, Stone asserts, involve "illusory elements" which ideally should be dispelled; only the first is "unexceptional." [110] Such a defense of principles obviously serves only to underscore the author's thorough-going skepticism and his resultant misconception of their proper place in the process of decision. Stone's emphasis upon the "libre recherche scientifique," no less than that of Hyde, Yü, and Chang upon a "scientific search for the sources of evidence," ignores the im-

107. Id. at 28–29.
108. Stone, supra note 79, at 360.
109. Id. at 364.
110. Ibid.

portant functions which principles can play both in specifying the detailed features of the "sources" of expectation and in outlining systematic and disciplined procedures for their examination.

Even those writers who have explicitly favored the use of principles of interpretation have frequently developed a misconceived notion of the purposes for which they are designed, and indeed of what they may be made to accomplish. In particular, the view has developed that their function is seriously impaired unless they can be ordered in some fixed hierarchy, which would in turn provide objectively and unambiguously for their application to each individual case. This position has been defended most forcefully in recent years by Sir Eric Beckett and Sir Gerald Fitzmaurice, as well as by other writers and jurists who have proposed so-called "master" canons. Beckett, at the Bath Session of the Institute of International Law in 1950, stated the position most clearly:

> The fundamental reason for the existence of rules of interpretation . . . is to defend the court from the charges of reaching its conclusions on arbitrary or subjective grounds. . . . Assuming, as the present writer does, that there is no good reasoning for jettisoning these rules, the problem is one of defining the application of each rule. It involves arranging them in some hierarchical order, and some further examination of the type of case to which they are respectively applicable, and studying to what extent they are mere presumptions, easily or with greater difficulty rebuttable. In the present writer's view it is probably in a study of this problem that the Institute can best assist the development of international law.[111]

Passing over Beckett's misconception of the function of principles, it is significant that he himself nowhere undertakes to order them. However, this task has been attempted—in relation to the major rules employed by the International Court of Justice—by Fitzmaurice.[112] Although the latter's "ordering" was effected by means of an analysis of past trends of the International Court, it would appear that his own recommendation is represented by the tendencies he finds. The apparent goal of the endeavor is to provide a set of "major" and "subsidiary" principles of interpretation, with indications of priori-

111. Becket, supra note 52, at 436, 439–40.
112. Fitzmaurice, supra note 7; supra note 21.

ties after the manner suggested by Beckett.[113] Although Fitzmaurice found that the establishment of a complete hierarchy was impossible (at least in terms of past trends), he nevertheless succeeded in recommending some important priorities, for example, between the principle of ordinary meaning (major) and the principles of effectiveness and of subsequent practice (subsidiary).[114]

The demand by Beckett and Fitzmaurice to reduce the principles of interpretation to an ordered hierarchy is far from unique. The literature of publicists and the opinions of judicial tribunals contain frequent attempts, as we will review in detail below, to subordinate one principle to another. The International Court has often insisted that various kinds of extrinsic evidence may not be considered if the meaning of a treaty is clear on its face.[115] Even Judge Lauterpacht contends that the principles of effectiveness and restrictive interpretation do not apply unless the intentions of the parties to an agreement are ambiguous.[116] It is significant that all of the writers who have proposed new canons, or have accepted traditional ones, have also offered some sort of hierarchy in which they are to be applied. Only those who have favored no principles at all (including Hyde, Yü, Stone, Fairman, and Chang) have, quite understandably, accepted the view that a fixed order is both unnecessary and impossible.

This demand for hierarchical ordering, it may be emphasized once again, is the result of a further misconception of what may reasonably be accomplished by the employment of principles of interpretation. The principal function of content principles is, as we have seen, to point to the many different factors which may in particular contexts affect the mediation of subjectivities between the parties and that of the principles of procedure to order the necessary examination of the context. The significance of any particular factor may in different contexts vary greatly in relation to other factors; hence no preordained significance can rationally be assigned to any particular factor. It is obviously no more possible to order in a hierarchy of importance the principles that point to the factors which may affect the

113. Fitzmaurice, supra note 7, at 9; supra note 21, at 211.

114. Ibid.

115. This doctrine, as applied to preparatory work, was first announced in the *S.S. "Lotus"* case, supra note 63, at 16. For extensions of the doctrine to other contextual features, see infra, pp. 216–52.

116. Lauterpacht, supra note 19, at 73.

mediation of subjectivities than it is to order the factors themselves. The task of interpretation, created by the necessity of making inferences from a complex of multiple, interrelated variables, requires, rather than hierarchical and dogmatic preconceptions of priority, a flexible and constant reappraisal of the importance of every detail in terms of its changing context. What those writers who do not favor the use of any principles are usually successful in demonstrating is that no one principle taken alone offers sufficient guidance for the interpreter's highly complex task. What they do not see is that a systematic, disciplined employment of all relevant principles may improve the probability of a decision-maker's achieving a closer approximation to the genuine shared expectations of the parties to an agreement.

The view we recommend thus rejects the excessive emphases of recent years both upon hierarchy as in Beckett and Fitzmaurice, and upon freedom of decision as in Hyde, Stone, and others. The choice between an ordered hierarchy of rules and the rejection of all rules is one which unnecessarily restricts the available alternatives. The disciplined, systematic use of such rules, not in precise application as justifications for apparent "objective" decisions, as has been suggested, but rather as specific directives to contextual factors and as procedures for guiding an examination of such factors, is, we suggest, the only reliable means of best approximating, in all cases, the participants' genuine expectations of commitment.[117]

It is difficult, if not impossible, to find in the various *types* of principles proposed in past practice a distinction comparable to that which we have employed in principles of content (the principles which point to features of the context to be brought to the attention of the decision-maker) and principles of procedure (principles designed to aid decision-makers in orderly and economic examination of features of the context). Hyde, for example, applied a distinction to the interpretation of agreements which was first advanced by Wigmore between the "sources of evidence" and the "standards of interpretation." [118] Though this distinction is similar in some respects to the one which we have recommended, the broad terms employed by

117. For a similar conclusion reached after a study of various administrative tribunals, see Schechter, *Interpretation of Ambiguous Documents by International Administrative Tribunals* 110–13 (1964).

118. Hyde, op. cit. supra note 18, at 1468–71; see Wigmore, op. cit. supra note 6, at 180–81.

both writers to point to such "sources of evidence" and their concern with a highly general fourfold criteria of meaning in specification of permissible interpretive standards [119] indicate neither an appreciation of the function of the principles involved, nor their separation into directives relating to features of the context and to procedures for their examination. Likewise, the distinction between specific "rules" within generic "techniques" of interpretation, introduced implicitly by Schwarzenberger and others,[120] is primarily directed, for both "rules" and "techniques," to focusing attention upon alleged hierarchies among features of the context, and thus does not parallel in any way the distinction we seek between content and procedure.[121]

It could not be surprising—in the light of all these misconceptions about the role and potentialities of principles of interpretation and of the lack of systematic elaboration of appropriate principles—that past trends in the interpretation and application of international agreements should exhibit many inequitable and impolitic decisions, unnecessarily defeating both the genuine shared expectations of the parties and basic community policies. Even the highly selective survey of past trends which follows will, we believe, too amply confirm this anticipation.

119. Wigmore, ibid. Wigmore distinguishes the following for "standards" of meaning: (1) Community meanings (the so-called "ordinary" meanings); (2) The meanings of "special classes of persons" (lawyers, diplomats, etc.); (3) The meanings of the actual parties to the dispute; and (4) The meanings of individual participants in the agreement whose views are not shared by other participants.

120. See Schwarzenberger, op. cit. supra note 14, at 491–94, 498–534. See also Fiore, op. cit. supra note 3 at 342–45; Phillimore, op. cit. supra note 3, at 97–114; Wright, "The Interpretation of Multilateral Treaties," 23 *Am. J. Int'l L.* 94, 96 (1929). Usages vary among these writers, but in general their distinctions encompass, in whole or in part, Customary, Grammatical, Logical, Historical, Functional, and Authoritative techniques of interpretation.

121. One example of a rule to which Schwarzenberger frequently returns in relation to "techniques" of interpretation is that of *jus aequum.* (See reg., id., at 491). If one were to conceive of the "techniques" as pointers to various features of the context (which is a plausible way of viewing them), it should suffice to indicate how remote the concept of procedure is from such a rule—the reference to *jus aequum* can scarcely *suggest,* much less outline, an appropriate set of procedures.

4. TRENDS IN THE MANAGEMENT OF PRINCIPLES OF CONTENT

For brief review of past trends in the management of content principles of interpretation, it is convenient to proceed systematically, principle by principle, in accordance with the outline employed above in our recommendations. We begin with the several manifestations of the principle of contextuality, and then move through the principles relating to the various phases of the process of agreement and its context to consideration, finally, of the principles relating to the process of decision. Principles relating to the different types of claims are given only occasional, indirect attention.

THE CONTEXTUALITY PRINCIPLE

Although the attention directed in past practice to relevant features of the wider context of agreement and decision has usually been limited to indications of specific sources of admissible evidence, occasional reference has been made in more general terms to the necessity of examining all significant indices of the parties' expectations of commitment, as well as the more important factors relevant to identification of overriding community policies. The American Law Institute Draft, for example, suggests that "The process of interpretation consists of ascertaining the meaning of the agreement in conformity with the intention manifest [sic] by the parties . . . determined in the light of all relevant factors bearing on such intention." [1] Hyde took much the same position in asserting that "evidence of the signification attached by the parties to the terms of their compact should not be excluded from the consideration of a tribunal

1. American Law Institute, *The Foreign Relations Law of the United States, A Restatement*, §129, at 125 (Tentative Draft No. 3, 1959).

charged with the duty of interpretation." [2] Similarly the Harvard Research urged deference by the applier to that interpretation which "in the light of the text under consideration and of the concomitant circumstances of the particular case at hand, appears in his considered judgment to be one which is logical [and] reasonable." [3]

These views are frequently specified in more detail by reference to various techniques or methods of interpretation. The American Law Institute Draft lists nine such methods, including analyses of general statements of purpose contained in the document, prior drafts submitted by the parties, and changes in the circumstances of performance—in addition to such traditional methods as considering ordinary meanings, the circumstances of negotiation, subsequent actions undertaken by the parties, and the relationship of the agreement with customary international law.[4] Chang provides a further enumeration of relevant factors in observing that

> Evidence is drawn from a variety of sources, such as the character of the language employed, historical facts relating to the subject-matter in question, kindred arrangements showing the practice of nations in using like terms in other agreements, the general purpose as deduced from the various aspects of the instrument as a whole, comparisons and contrasts drawn from other parts of the treaty or related agreements, prior negotiations, contemporary declarations, as well as practical constructions by the parties.[5]

The comprehensive provision in Article 19 (a) of the Harvard Research is perhaps the best-known modern reference to relevant contextual features:

> A treaty is to be interpreted in the light of the general purpose which it is intended to serve. The historical background of the treaty, *travaux préparatoires,* the circumstances of the par-

2. 2 Hyde, *International Law Chiefly as Interpreted and Applied by the United States* 1471 (1945).
3. Harvard Research in International Law, *Draft Convention on the Law of Treaties, With Comment* 946 (1935).
4. American Law Institute, op. cit. supra note 1, at 127–28.
5. Chang, *The Interpretation of Treaties by Judicial Tribunals* 182–83 (1933).

> ties at the time the treaty was entered into, the change in these circumstances sought to be effected, the subsequent conduct of the parties in applying the provisions of the treaty, and the conditions prevailing at the time the interpretation is being made, are to be considered in connection with the general purpose which the treaty is intended to serve.[6]

In terms of emphasis upon the importance of context, two areas of the traditional specifications have yielded and most fruitful results, and are thus separated out for special treatment here. These are: (1) the principle of *travaux préparatoires* and its correlative emphasis upon all pre-outcome features, and (2) the principle of subsequent conduct, referring to post-outcome features. The *travaux* principle, for example, has customarily been the focal point of dispute between the views supporting and rejecting recourse to *any* features of the context attending the course of negotiation. As it is most often formulated, the principle permits recourse to a wide variety of events prior to the commitment outcome, but more particularly to the official records of the conferences marking the final stages of discussion before signing and ratification. The principle of subsequent conduct, in complementary reach, authorizes the consideration of all relevant actions taken by the parties to an agreement after the outcome phase prior to the presentation of claims in a particular dispute.

It should be emphasized, however, that these discussions of both pre-outcome and post-outcome evidence usually contain far from adequate reference to the kind of contextual examination which we so emphatically recommend. Specifically, as indicated above, a number of other principles could be formulated and employed which would point in various ways to the larger context of social and power processes, and to various features of the acts of communication and collaboration which they embrace and affect. Nonetheless, the traditional references to prior and subsequent events do call attention to important "extrinsic" (i.e. nontextual) factors which are included in the principle of contextuality. Because of their extraordinary importance in past practice, each of these two traditional principles merits discussion in some detail.

6. Harvard Research, op. cit. supra note 3, at 937.

Preliminary Events

In general, the weight of decision and opinion has been in favor of the admission of evidence from the pre-outcome phase of the agreement process. This acceptance can be seen in the traditional emphasis upon the necessity of looking to the historical background of a treaty, the circumstances of the parties immediately prior to their agreement, and the values at stake for them in making it. Even in some cases where verbal limitations have been placed upon recourse to extrinsic evidence in the pre-outcome phase, in actual operation courts have examined such evidence and weighed its relevance and importance in decision. There have been occasions, however, where courts have refused to consider the relevance of preliminary events.

One early position, for example, deriving primarily from European publicists and decision-makers, employed various rules seeking to restrict the examination or use of *travaux préparatoires* for ascertaining genuine shared expectations. Under influence of this position, the trend of decision and opinion until very recently was on the whole opposed—at least in verbal statement—to examining preparatory work as a regular feature of the process of interpretation. Various rules thus emerged, particularly in the jurisprudence of the Permanent Court, which restricted the use of such evidence. These included the already mentioned Vattel maxim concerning instances where no interpretation was deemed to be necessary, the "plain and natural meaning" rule prohibiting recourse to preparatory work when the issues are allegedly clear and the dispute resolvable *prima facie,* and the rule of textuality which has been used to emphasize the value of verbal analyses over more thoroughgoing contextual ones. One traditional version of the principle of restrictive interpretation also served the same purpose in favor of a spurious "protection" of state sovereignty.

Despite the echoes of these views in the jurisprudence of the present International Court and the writings of some publicists, the current trend is decidedly against such restrictions even on the admission of preparatory work and in favor of more systematic, empirical surveys of relevant features of the context of agreements. Even during the time of the Permanent Court, some publicists—particularly those in the United States led by Hyde and his students Yü and

Chang—called for greater use of contextual materials than was then regarded as appropriate. This emphasis soon appeared in other writings and, after World War II, with increasing frequency in international arbitral and court decisions. Thus today it is fair to say that the majority of writers and decision-makers reject the restrictions of earlier years—even if in somewhat indirect ways—and favor instead a thorough contextual analysis within the limitations of time and resources available in any given case.

The highest-level formulation authorizing recourse to data prior to the outcome of an agreement may be illustrated by an early case, *Maltass v. Maltass,*[7] in which the tribunal concluded that "in construing . . . treaties, we ought to look at all the historical circumstances attending them, in order to ascertain what was the true intention of the contracting parties, and to give the widest scope to the language of the treaties in order to embrace within it all the objects intended to be included." [8] Similar formulations calling for recourse to preliminary events in general terms are contained, as we indicated briefly above, in both the Harvard Research and American Law Institute drafts. The latter, in fact, states more specifically that

7. 1 Rob. Ecc. 67 (1844), reported in Lauterpacht, "Some Observations on Preparatory Work in the Interpretation of Treaties," 48 *Harv. L. Rev.* 549, 563–64 (1935). This case involved the contested will of John Maltass, a businessman born and raised in Turkey of British parents. The principal issue was whether the British-Turkish agreement of 1809—providing that upon the death of "any Englishman" in Turkey a will disposing of his Turkish property was to be honored despite the Turkish custom not to recognize wills—should apply to a native-born permanent resident of Turkey such as Maltass. The tribunal decided that (1) as the son of British parents, Maltass, who had never renounced his British ties, was still an Englishman; and (2) that the historical circumstances which attended the conclusion of the agreement of 1809 left it clear that Englishmen permanently residing in Turkey, as well as visitors, came within the compass of the British wills specified in Article 26 of that agreement. Historically it was clear, the tribunal concluded, that British subjects did not reside permanently in Turkey prior to or at the time of the agreement; it saw in this fact the probable reason why direct reference to domicile was not included in Article 26. Nevertheless, it was equally clear that in 1809 the parties were attempting to encourage the development of British business interests in Turkey, an aim which would scarcely be enhanced by excluding from protection those businessmen who decided to remain. In deference to these conditions, the tribunal concluded that domicile, even if conclusively established, did not disqualify Maltass from protection under the agreement.

8. 1 Rob. Ecc. 67, 76; Lauterpacht, id., at 564.

"Among the factors to be taken fairly into account in the interpretative process are . . . The background of, and the circumstances attending, the negotiation of the agreement . . . Drafts submitted for consideration, action taken on them, and the official record of deliberations during the course of the negotiation." [9]

Among the publicists and decision-makers who have called attention to the necessity of recourse to pre-outcome evidence in this manner, most if not all have emphasized the basis in community policy by which such a requirement must inevitably be justified. The trend of this support is suggested in the *Maltass* case by the tribunal's reference to the additional indices which such evidence may produce of the "objects intended to be included" in the scope of the agreement by the participants. This view is articulated in greater detail by the Harvard Research Draft.

> A treaty is not concluded *in vacuo;* it has its definite place in the unending flow of events, their causes and effects, which we know as history. As a result of past developments, certain circumstances came into existence which the parties desired in some manner to regulate or alter, and to accomplish this end they chose to enter into a treaty. The treaty, in short, stands, therefore, as a related part of the general setting in which the parties acted, and that setting must be taken into account if the purpose which the treaty was intended to serve is to be fully comprehended and effectuated.[10]

Similar recognition of the potential indices provided by preliminary materials of the parties' shared expectations of agreement appear in the ALI Draft [11] and elsewhere.[12]

9. American Law Institute, op. cit. supra note 1, §130 (3) and (4), at 127–28; other factors are elaborated in Comment (e) (4), at 133–34.
10. Harvard Research, op. cit. supra note 3, at 953.
11. American Law Institute, op. cit. supra note 1 §129, at 125–27; §130, at 127–28.
12. Cf. Hudson, *The Permanent Court of International Justice, 1920–1942* 656–57 (1943); 1 Schwarzenberger, *International Law* 514–17 (3d ed. 1957); 1 Hambro, *The Case Law of the International Court* 43–51 (1952); Yü, *The Interpretation of Treaties* 192–202 (1927); Fitzmaurice, "The Law and Procedure at the International Court of Justice 1951–54: Treaty Interpretation and Other Treaty Points," 33 *Brit. Yb. Int'l L.* 203, 219 (1957); De Visscher, *Problems d'Interprétation Judiciaire en Droit International Public* 115–21 (1963).

Other commentators have noted the degree to which past decision-makers have accepted the employment of historical evidence as a means of determining the parties' genuine shared expectations. Hyde, for example, generalized that the judges of the Permanent Court had made a "faithful effort to ascertain and take full cognizance of the historical and other backgrounds revealing the position in which the parties found themselves when they undertook to agree, as a helpful means of ascertaining their exact design when they did so." [13] Despite this effort, which can be discerned in the decisions of the present International Court as well,[14] the major area of explicit concern for its usefulness has been directed to the long-standing problem presented by a limited, although highly significant, feature of the total context, namely, the official records of the conference of negotiators, i.e., the *travaux préparatoires.*

As noted above, the earliest tendency in the use of *travaux préparatoires* is expressed in the well-known rule laid down in the *Lotus* case [15] that "there is no occasion to have regard to preparatory work if the text of a convention is sufficiently clear in itself." [16] In this instance, preparatory work of the Lausanne Conference of 1923 had been relied upon by France in its claim that Turkish jurisdiction over the French captain of the *Lotus* contravened "principles of international law," designated by Article 15 of the Lausanne Convention as being decisive of jurisdiction in cases of the type in contro-

13. Hyde, op. cit. supra note 2, at 1495.
14. The Court in the *South-West Africa Cases* (Preliminary Objections), [1962] I.C.J. Rep. 319, while giving only passing mention to the need to "take into consideration all of the relevant acts and circumstances" relating to the dissolution of the League of Nations in order to determine the intentions of its members, clearly and repeatedly made use of preliminary work. In deciding that South Africa's Mandate agreement was a "treaty . . . still in force" it referred to documents and exchanges at the trial of the transfer of the League authority to the United Nations, id. at 332–35, and in deciding that the term "members of the League of Nations" did not apply solely to membership during the actual existence of the League, it referred to discussions of the First Committee, of its Assembly, and of other circumstances surrounding the founding of the United Nations, id. at 335–42. In addition, Judge Jessup, in his separate opinion, made extensive use of preliminary events in support of the Court's decision, id. at 387 ff. See also Hogg, "The International Court: Rules of Treaty Interpretation II," 44 *Minn. L. Rev.* 5, 28–40 (1959), for other related cases.
15. *The S.S. "Lotus,"* P.C.I.J., Ser. A, No. 10 (1927).
16. Id. at 16.

versy. At the Conference, the Turkish proposal to extend local jurisdiction to crimes committed abroad had been rejected in favor of Article 15; France argued that this rejection was thus an affirmation of a customary international law restriction of jurisdiction to crimes committed locally. The Court rejected the French contention, taking the view indicated above, while at the same time noting the content of the *travaux* which France had relied on. This action, as we shall see in greater detail below, established a pattern frequently affirmed by later decisions of various international courts.[17]

In more recent years, however, this doctrine which presumes against the introduction of *travaux préparatoires* when a text is allegedly clear has come under attack from many commentators, and to a lesser extent from officials as well. The late Judge Lauterpacht, for example, argued that the earlier practices of scholars and decision-makers had already been reversed as early as 1935: "The first and principal lesson which can be deduced from [the work of international tribunals] is that in no circumstances ought preparatory work to be excluded on the ground that the treaty is clear in itself." [18] Lauterpacht attempted to show that past international judicial practice permits recourse to preparatory work under all circumstances, even when the text is thought to be *prima facie* clear.[19] Although this conclusion may well be questioned, it is certain that in recent years the doctrine limiting recourse to the *travaux* has been less frequently applied. Nevertheless, the highest tribunals have not yet explicitly rejected the *Lotus* doctrine. As a result it would appear that a more accurate description of past decision is contained in the Har-

17. Cf. *The S.S. "Wimbledon,"* P.C.I.J., Ser. A, No. 1, p. 22; *The Payment of Various Serbian Loans Issued in France,* P.C.I.J., Ser. A, No. 20, p. 30 (1929); *Polish Postal Service in Danzig,* P.C.I.J., Ser. B, No. 11, p. 39 (1925); *Jurisdiction of the European Commission of the Danube,* P.C.I.J., Ser. B, No. 14, pp. 28–41 (1927); *Interpretation of the Statute of the Memel Territory,* P.C.I.J., Ser. A/B, No. 47, p. 249 (1932); *Employment of Women During the Night,* P.C.I.J., Ser. A/B, No. 50, p. 378 (1932). For the attitude of the present International Court, see *Competence of the General Assembly for the Admission of a State to the United Nations* [1950] I.C.J. Rep. 4, 8, and *Constitution of the Maritime Safety Committee of the Inter-Governmental Maritime Consultative Organization* [1960], I.C.J. Rep. 150, 159–60.

18. Lauterpacht, supra note 7, at 571.

19. Id. at 571–73. See also Lauterpacht, "Restrictive Interpretation and the Principle of Effectiveness in the Interpretation of Treaties," 26 *Brit. Yb. Int'l L.* 61–75 (1949).

vard Research Draft, prepared in 1933 but equally confirmed by more recent trends:

> The Permanent Court has frankly had recourse to *travaux préparatoires* when called upon to interpret a text the meaning of which it has considered to be doubtful. On the other hand, in cases in which it has been confronted with a text which it has regarded as "clear" or "sufficiently clear", it has repeatedly asserted that *travaux préparatoires* were not then to be taken into account.[20]

In most recent times the great majority of publicists reject the requirement that a text be unclear before *travaux* can be admitted, but the notion still persists in some scholarly writings. Thus Fitzmaurice recently concluded that although "there is probably no school of thought that rejects recourse to *travaux préparatoires* in all circumstances . . . the real issue lies between those who consider that such recourse should be quasi-habitual (even where the text is apparently clear) and those who consider that it should be resorted to only in case of patent ambiguity or obscurity." [21] Trends among decision-

20. Harvard Research, op. cit. supra note 3, at 964.

21. Fitzmaurice, "The Law and Procedure of the International Court of Justice: Treaty Interpretation and Certain Other Treaty Points," 28 *Brit. Yb. Int'l L.* 1, 5 (1951). Support for the view that recourse to *travaux préparatoires* must be limited to situations of "patent ambiguity" has been given most forcefully by recent British writers, including McNair, Beckett, and Fitzmaurice. McNair, for example, stated at the 1950 Session of the Institute of International Law that "the more we encourage advocates to delve into the mass of *travaux préparatoires,* the more we weaken the terms of the treaty." 43 *Annuaire de l'Institut de Droit International* [I] 450 (1950) (author's transl.). The feeling that examination of preparatory work necessarily encourages a lack of concern for the treaty itself is also reflected in Beckett's statement of the conditions which permit a decision-maker to consult the treaty text: "if the Tribunal cannot reach a conclusion that the treaty is unambiguous, and, when properly interpreted results in only one possible conclusion, recourse must be had to the *travaux préparatoires.*" Id. at 442. Clearly this view is not designed to encourage examination of even a limited aspect of the total context, as Beckett himself emphasizes in the same statement. Despite this crippling consequence, the same position has received support, with greater or lesser degrees of explicitness, from others, including Fitzmaurice, id. at 15–17; Schwarzenberger, op. cit. supra note 12, at 514; Bernhardt, *Die Auslegung volkerrechticher vertrage* 109 (1963). Cf. also Judge Alvarez in *Admissions to the United Nations,* supra note 17, at 18, and Azevedo, id. at 23.

One notable exception to the policy proposed by British writers was provided

makers and publicists alike in the last two decades show that, despite a small minority to the contrary, most insist upon constant or "quasi-habitual" recourse to the materials of negotiation.[22]

Several attempts have been made by publicists in recent years to reconcile the continued manifest acceptance by international tribunals of the *Lotus* doctrine with their actual practices and with the perspectives of contemporary writers. The approach adopted by

---

by Lauterpacht. In 1935 he criticized the prevailing doctrine in these terms: "While it is inadmissible to depart from the absolutely clear meaning of a treaty, there ought to be the greatest reluctance to assume, without exhaustively examining the available sources, that the meaning is absolutely clear. . . . The statement that the meaning is absolutely clear is—or ought to be—the result of the process of interpretation, not the starting point." Lauterpacht, supra note 7, at 593. Although he remained unwilling to reject the "clear meaning" doctrine altogether, Lauterpacht was among the first to insist that recourse to features of the context—and here he spoke primarily of *travaux préparatoires*—should not be limited by a preconceived notion of the "clear" or "ordinary" uses of words. See Lauterpacht, *The Development of International Law by the International Court* 52–60 (1958). In this he led in expressing what has now come to be the predominant view, which permits "habitual" recourse to the materials of negotiation, as well as other features of the context.

22. Recent supporters of "quasi-habitual" recourse to *travaux préparatoires* include Lauterpacht, Hambro, Schwarzenberger, Hyde, Yü, Chang, Hudson, Ehrlich, Hogg, and Stone. Particularly in the United States, the "quasi-habitual" view has received support even in the absence of any presumption in favor of "clear" or "ordinary" meanings. Hyde for example, stated that "Declarations on the part of the negotiators of a treaty at the time of its conclusion . . . should not be disregarded," least of all in the name of textual plain meanings. (Hyde, op. cit. supra note 2, at 1497.) Similarly, Hudson argued that "the construction of the text cannot be arrived at without a consideration of its setting, and the development of the negotiations forms a part of the history which constitutes that setting. Where a dispute revolves about issues connected with the preparation of a text . . . it seems merely stultifying to say that *travaux préparatoires* cannot be examined." Hudson, op. cit. supra note 12, at 652. And Yü concludes:

> It is the function of the interpreter to ascertain the genuine sense in which the negotiators have employed the words rather than to ascertain the bare meaning of the words themselves. If the document is approached from the provisions *per se,* it is not rightly approached, because in dealing with the erroneous terms of the agreement, the words causing the mistake cannot be overthrown from within, so to speak. For this reason, the wide range of freedom in searching for extrinsic evidence is imperative for scientific interpretation.

Yü, op. cit. supra note 12, at 67.

some, notably Hyde, is to deny that the doctrine is still being applied, or to predict that it will presently decline in application because of a "growing appreciation of the embarrassing implications necessarily involved in the acknowledgment or assertion that linguistic clearness is to be regarded as a decisive token of design." [23] However, despite the best efforts of these writers, such an appreciation does not seem to have developed as predicted. In the recent *Admissions* case, for example, the International Court was convinced that "the text is sufficiently clear; consequently, it does not feel that it should deviate from the consistent practice of the Permanent Court of International Justice, according to which there is no occasion to resort to preparatory work if the text of a convention is clear in itself." [24] The Court has reaffirmed this position on other occasions.[25]

Faced with the frequent reiteration of this limiting perspective, observers have emphasized the difficulties which tribunals have encountered in applying it. Lauterpacht, for example, pointed to the *Asylum* case as an example of the absurd results to which the doctrine may lead.[26] In this case [27] the majority of the Court held that any alternative interpretation of the crucial provision of the Havana Convention other than that resulting from the ordinary meanings of the terms employed was "inconceivable." [28] Judge Read, in dissent, thought that his own alternative interpretation was not only conceivable but also more in conformity with the actual usages of the parties involved.[29] Thus the majority application of the *Lotus* doctrine did not have the support even of all members of the Court that the meaning was "clear" and any other alternative "inconceivable." Other examples will be shown below of disagreements over provisions appearing "clear" to some justices but not to others, or of

23. Hyde, op. cit. supra note 2, at 1488.
24. *Conditions of Admission of a State to Membership in the United Nations,* [1948] I.C.J. Rep. 57, 61.
25. For further treatment by the Court, and for further elaboration of past decision and opinion concerning the relationship of the "clarity" and *"travaux préparatoires"* doctrines, see infra, pp. 225–50, and for citations see note 403 at p. 235 and notes 440–41 at p. 245.
26. Lauterpacht, cited in Fitzmaurice, supra note 21, at 11 n.
27. *Asylum Case* (Colombia v. Peru) [1950] I.C.J. Rep. 266.
28. Id. at 284.
29. Id. at 316, 321–22.

incompatible alternative interpretations appearing "clear" to different judges.[30]

A related approach to the problem, which on the whole has been inadequately developed in past opinion, has been to focus attention upon the actual operations which are customarily carried out, or omitted, as a result of the use of the *Lotus* restriction. A characteristic example of this approach is provided by Fitzmaurice:

> There is a certain element of unreality in much of the discussion about recourse to *travaux préparatoires,* since in fact the parties to the dispute, in their arguments, invariably draw the attention of the Court to anything material which the records may contain. In that sense the Court always *looks* at the *travaux préparatoires.* The question is, however, not whether the Court will notice the *travaux,* but whether it will *take account* of them in arriving at its conclusions, whether in other words it will or will not base its findings in whole or in part on them.[31]

Other writers, including Hyde, Lauterpacht, and Beckett, have made a similar point, based, in some instances, upon evidence provided by explicit statements of international tribunals themselves.[32] The importance of this point cannot be overemphasized. It promises, if correct, to shift the focus of past discussions from the operations of merely examining the materials of negotiation offered by counsel during a trial to the operation of explicitly discussing and weighing the significance of these materials in the court opinion resolving the dispute. It offers, at least, a clarification of the ambiguous terms "recourse to" and "consideration of" in terms of this distinction. In consequence, one is encouraged to view the statements of decision-makers in past practice as preferences, exhibited by the refusal to *discuss* other evidence, for the expressions contained in the outcome

30. For further examples and discussion of these trends, see the subsequent discussion of the plain and natural meaning doctrine, infra at pp. 216–52.
31. Fitzmaurice, supra note 21, at 13 n.
32. See Hyde, "The Interpretation of Treaties by the Permanent Court of International Justice," 24 *Am. J. Int'l L.* 1, 4–7 (1930), but see Hyde, op. cit. supra note 2, at 1486–1502, for modifications of this view; Lauterpacht, op. cit. supra note 21, at 116–27, 130–34; Beckett, "Comments on the Report of Lauterpacht," 43 *Annuaire de l'Institut de Droit International* 435, 441–42 (1950); Hogg, "The International Court: Rules of Treaty Interpretation," 43 *Minn. L. Rev.* 369, 383–84 (1958).

phase of the agreement process after a consideration of all of the relevant features of the total context.[33]

Even if one could thus be assured, however, that all relevant preparatory work would be examined in each case, the unfortunate fact still remains that the authoritative doctrine establishes a set of priorities which demands the consistent de-emphasis of an important source of evidence of the genuine shared expectations of the parties. This de-emphasis obviously occurs whenever a text is said to be so clear in its plain and natural meaning that this meaning cannot be qualified by reference to the *travaux*. The greatest danger in this approach lies, however, precisely in the initial determination of what is allegedly "clear," since the outcome of a case may well depend entirely upon such a determination without the benefit of a full contextual analysis.

In recent years, much emphasis has been given to demonstrating possible shortcomings in the *travaux préparatoires* as reflections of the parties' genuine shared expectations of agreement. Schwarzenberger, for example, has remarked that *travaux préparatoires* are "largely equivocal" and thus of "limited value" under most circumstances.[34] Beckett, while also noting the equivocality of preparatory work, was especially concerned—at the 1950 session of the Institute of International Law—to point out that such material often does not represent the genuine expectations of the participants because it omits what he calls the "compromise behind the scenes," or "the intervention in private meeting of the Heads of Delegations." [35] The agreement reached at these meetings, Beckett argues, is often not reflected in the official *travaux préparatoires*. Beckett makes the further point that "The text of the treaty, when once signed, assumes . . . a sort of life of its own. It is soon found that half the points which trouble people during negotiation are of little importance but a whole lot of new points which were hardly thought of then are those which seem to matter . . . To hark back to the

33. One notable exception to the assumption that *travaux préparatoires* are always admitted in evidence even if not discussed in the opinion is the well-known *Case Relating to the Territorial Jurisdiction of the International Commission of the River Oder,* P.C.I.J., Ser. A, No. 23 (1929), where the Permanent Court refused to admit *travaux* into evidence vis-à-vis three of the parties to the cause who had not participated in the negotiations.

34. Schwarzenberger, op. cit. supra note 12, at 514.

35. Beckett, supra note 32, at 443.

travaux préparatoires for the purposes of interpretation may operate like bringing a dead hand from the grave or subjecting a grown mature man to the paternal injunctions of his boyhood." [36]

It is important to observe that these writers do not recommend that, as a result of such difficulties, *travaux préparatoires* should not be initially examined. Schwarzenberger, for example, states that "a court or tribunal should take into consideration 'all the materials' at its disposal," and that therefore, "no reason exists why [preparatory work] should be excluded altogether." [37] If one could assume this basic position is widely shared, the conclusion could only be that such cautionary analyses, especially those of Beckett and Fitzmaurice, are beneficial. Attention should of course be paid to whether the *travaux* are indeed representative of the genuine intentions of the participants during negotiations, or are in fact secondary in importance to unrecorded personal conversations or other features of the context. In addition, if records of negotiation *are* equivocal, this result should be taken into consideration, as well as the role of anticipated and unanticipated contingencies. The most constructive conclusion would therefore seem to be that these cautionary remarks are themselves attempts to point to relevant features of the context which ought to be taken into consideration in the process of decision. The only practices which must be rejected, and which the large majority of writers today do appear to reject, are either (1) the attempts to use such warnings as a means of avoiding the examination of preparatory work altogether, or (2) the attempts to provide invariable orderings (irreversible standards of de-emphasis) for preparatory work. With respect to potential specific weightings in particular cases, the suggestions which these writers have offered may be valuable guides to a decision-maker in determining how important one feature, in this case the written record of negotiation, should be considered in relation to other features in achieving an appropriate interpretation in the case before him.

Subsequent Conduct

The examination of events subsequent to the outcome of commitment in an international agreement has traditionally been under-

36. Id. at 444. Cf. also Fitzmaurice, supra note 21, at 14–17.
37. Schwarzenberger, op. cit. supra note 12, at 514.

taken in various ways, differing with the type of event which has given rise to claims for interpretation. The two types most frequently encountered in past practice relate to courses of conduct which vary in the degree of explicitness with which they purport to supplement or alter the original expectations of commitment. The first type, commonly the sole referent of the so-called "principle of subsequent conduct," [38] refers to any behavior subsequent to the outcome phase of the process of agreement which appears to be relevant or useful in determining the continuing consensus of the parties. In traditional doctrine, the examination by decision-makers of this type of event in response to a claim for interpretation is most frequently called "practical" or "conventional" interpretation. The second type refers to subsequent events in a much narrower sense, embracing only explicit interpretations or revisions by the parties of an earlier agreement by a later one which specifically calls attention to the change. The technique of interpretation associated with this type of event is often referred to as "authentic" or "authoritative" interpretation, and is reserved for making inferences from expressions of commitment which are communicated in a formal manner, i.e., not left to be inferred from a subsequent course of conduct as in practical or conventional interpretation.[39]

The traditional statement of the rule of "authoritative" interpretation is given by Schwarzenberger: "authoritative interpretation is interpretation of the treaty by the parties themselves . . . In this sense, 'the right of giving authoritative interpretation of a legal rule belongs solely to the person or body who has the power to modify or suppress it.' " [40] He distinguishes this type of interpretation both

38. See generally 5 Hackworth, *Digest of International Law* 263–65 (1943); Hyde, op. cit. supra note 2, at 1496–98; Hudson, op. cit. supra note 12, at 658–59; McNair, *The Law of Treaties* 252–55 (1938); Fitzmaurice, supra note 21, at 20–22; Fitzmaurice, supra note 12, at 223–25. Cf. also Hambro, op. cit. supra note 12, at 55–56, and 2 Hambro, *The Case Law of the International Court* 41 (1960) for citations of court dicta concerning subsequent conduct.

39. For discussions of past practices in the application of 'authentic' or 'authoritative' interpretation see Schwarzenberger, op. cit. supra note 12, at 531–32; Harvard Research, op. cit. supra note 3, at 968–70; Hudson, op. cit. supra note 12, at 643; Ehrlich, "De l'Interprétation des Traités," 24 *Recueil des Cours* 5, 36 (1928); 2 Phillimore, *Commentaries upon International Law* 97–98 (3d ed. 1882).

40. Schwarzenberger, op. cit. supra note 12, at 531, quoting from the *Jaworzina Boundary Case,* P.C.I.J., Ser. B, No. 8, at 37.

from the explicit, formal *revision* of treaties and from inferences made from the subsequent behavior of the contracting parties. While such inferences may, he asserts, only be considered "for the purpose of strengthening its conclusions on the common intention of the parties," authoritative interpretation may presumably be considered for other purposes as well, even to the point of altering the original commitment.[41]

The formulation in the Harvard Research states the most familiar version of the principle of subsequent conduct, or of "practical" interpretation: "In interpreting a treaty, the conduct or action of the parties thereto cannot be ignored. If all the parties to a treaty execute it, or permit its execution, in a particular manner, that fact may reasonably be taken into account as indicative of the real intention of the parties or of the purpose which the instrument was designed to serve."[42] The limitation implicit in this framing of the rule, namely, that subsequent behavior may be considered only in order to confirm or supplement the parties' orginal expectations, has not always been imposed. A different and more acceptable alternative is indicated by Lord McNair: "The contracting parties may themselves have attached a particular meaning to the terms of a treaty either impliedly by a long course of conduct or by express agreement, and in either case this agreed meaning may be either a *bona fide* interpretation of an obscure term or an attempt to substitute a new stipulation for the original one."[43]

The policies underlying the emphasis on subsequent conduct have often been partially expressed, as in the Harvard Research, in the statement of the rule itself. In general, a major purpose in examining the subsequent actions of the parties is that of canvassing an exceptionally reliable source for determining their genuine shared expectations. In the case of "authoritative" interpretation, the goal is more specifically to provide as much freedom as possible to the parties to interpret or revise their agreement as they see fit. For any instance of the authoritative application of an agreement the events subsequent to the outcome phase may take on an importance greater than the

41. Id. at 532.
42. Harvard Research, op. cit. supra note 3, at 966. See also Bernhardt, op. cit. supra note 21, at 124, 168, where even a strict textual approach admits of pre-emptory evidence from subsequent conduct.
43. McNair, op. cit. supra note 38, at 252.

initial participants anticipated. As Judge Hudson commented: "With the lapse of time, intentions entertained by the draftsmen of an instrument may lose some of their importance, and a course of action by those who must live with and under the provisions of the instrument may assume a correspondingly greater significance." [44] Whether we say, however, that the aim of considering subsequent acts is to defer to the expectations of "those who must live with" a treaty, or as *Harvard Research* implies, to determine the original intentions of the participants, the thrust in policy is clear: the admission of post-outcome evidence is designed to make available a feature of the broader context of the agreement process for the purpose of maximizing the probability that the interpreter will correctly determine the participants' genuine expectations. To be sure, the degree to which this feature may vary in terms of compatibility with alleged initial subjectivities, or be explicitly and unambiguously communicated, will affect the weight which should be given to it in each individual case. Such variability in modality and degree of relevance can, however, hardly be considered a valid basis for failing to accord subsequent events the most careful consideration.

The trends in decision among national and international tribunals have long been favorable to the admission of evidence from subsequent conduct. In the manner indicated above, they have dealt with formal communications under the rubrics of "authentic" and "authoritative" interpretation. The Permanent Court on several occasions indicated its willingness to defer to the authority of explicit, official interpretations by the parties. In the *Polish Postal Service in Danzig* case,[45] for example, the Court commented that if it were presented with such a situation, "a so-called authentic interpretation . . . is in effect a new decision" and must be considered binding.[46] Upon the facts before it, however, the Court thought that no such interpretation had been made. Under the Treaty of Versailles, Poland was granted, inter alia, rights to establish and operate a Polish Postal Service in Danzig.[47] Under a subsequent convention between

44. Hudson, op. cit. supra note 12, at 659. See also De Visscher, op. cit. supra note 12, at 121–27.
45. P.C.I.J., Ser. B, No. 11 (1925).
46. Id. at 31.
47. The central article in the dispute, Article 29, holds in part that "Poland shall have the right to establish in the port of Danzig a post, telegraph, and telephone

Poland and Danzig, the League of Nations High Commissioner in Danzig had been given powers, subject to specified judicial procedures, to settle disputes between Poland and Danzig concerning the postwar administration of the city.[48] Pursuant to these powers and procedures, the High Commissioner rendered two decisions during 1922 concerning the Polish Postal Service in Danzig. On January 6, 1923, he informally interpreted these decisions in a letter to the Commissioner-General of Poland, narrowly interpreting Poland's rights, claiming—in the Court's words—that "Poland had no right to establish a postal service extending in any respect outside the premises allotted to it." [49] When subsequently Poland attempted to set up letter boxes on the streets of Danzig, a dispute arose which in due course was submitted to the permanent Court. The Court held that the January letter could not be considered as an authoritative interpretation of these decisions because it "cannot be regarded as, and by its very terms was not intended to be, a decision . . . he [the High Commissioner] cannot give a decision, within the meaning of Article 39 of the Paris Convention, unless the essentials of a judicial procedure have been complied with." [50] The Court held that since these essentials had been in no way fulfilled, the letter could only be considered as expressing the Commissioner's "personal opinion . . . an opinion which, as the Court has already stated, cannot alter the proper meaning of a decision." [51] It then proceeded to examine the dispute on its merits and decided in favor of Poland.[52]

---

service communicating directly with Poland." Subsequently articles provided for sale and lease of "all the facilities necessary" for these operations. Id. at 33.

48. Article 39 of this Convention provides that "Any differences arising between Poland and the Free City of Danzig in regard to the present Treaty . . . or to any matter affecting the relations between Poland and the Free City, shall be submitted by one or the other Party to the decision of the High Commissioner." Id. at 24.

49. Id. at 16.

50. Id. at 31.

51. Ibid.

52. Apparently on "plain meaning" grounds: "It will be seen that there is no trace of any provision confining the operation of the Polish postal authorities to the inside of its postal building. The postal service which Poland is entitled to establish in the port of Danzig must be interpreted in its ordinary sense so as to include the normal functions of a postal service as regards the collection and distribution of postal matter outside the post-office. Indeed, any limitations or restrictions in this respect would be of so exceptional a character that they can-

In two subsequent cases the Court also affirmed the right of any participants to give authoritative interpretations of their agreements, while at the same time denying that the case in point presented an example of an official authorized to give such interpretations. In the *Jaworzina Boundary* case,[53] a subsequent opinion by the President of the Conference of Ambassadors which had been responsible for setting the Jaworzina boundary, stating that the boundary "was not defined in the decision" of the Conference, was rejected by the Court in favor of the plain meaning of the text indicating that such a decision had been made. While agreeing that "it is an established principle that the right of giving an authoritative interpretation of a legal rule belongs solely to the person who has the power to modify or suppress it," [54] the Court held that such powers of the Conference of Ambassadors were terminated with the filing of its initial decision. In the absence of such authority, the Court concluded that "it is obvious that the opinion of the authors of a document cannot be endowed with a decisive value when that opinion has been formulated after the drafting of that document and conflicts with the opinion which they expressed at that time." [55] Somewhat less sweeping language, but a similar argument based upon the expiration of authority for decision, was also used by the Court in the *Danube Commission* case [56] to deny that a later interpretative protocol could "prevail against the Definitive Statute" in determining the extent of judicial powers over the disputed sector of the Danube.

The Permanent Court also admitted evidence of "practical" interpretation, under a restricted version of the familiar principle of subsequent conduct, on several occasions. In the *Brazilian Loans* case,[57] the Court authorized "resort . . . to the manner of performance in order to ascertain the intention of the Parties." [58] It added, however, that this authorization only applied "where a contract is ambiguous,"

---

not, in the absence of express reservations, be read into the text of treaty stipulations." Id. at 37.

53. *The Delimitation of the Czechoslovak-Polish Frontier* (Question of Jaworzina), P.C.I.J. Ser. B, No. 8, p. 6 (1923).

54. Id. at 37.

55. Id. at 38.

56. Supra note 17, at 34–35.

57. *Payment in Gold of Brazilian Federal Loans Contracted in France,* P.C.I.J. Ser. A, No. 21 (1929).

58. Id. at 119.

and it held that the French-Brazilian loan agreements of 1910 and 1911 contained no such legitimizing ambiguity. These agreements provided that payment of interest on the Brazilian bonds was to be made in "gold francs." In subsequent years, however, payment was made in French paper francs at their current rate of exchange. Several years after the devaluation of the paper franc in 1919, French bondholders and ultimately the French government began to complain that the more stable and well-established standard of the 'gold franc' should be used for payment of interest on the bonds (the gold franc being the equivalent of approximately one-third gram of gold at current market prices). In the meantime, from 1919 to the initiation of negotiations in 1924, the devalued paper franc was used by Brazil and accepted by the bondholders. The Court held that this course of conduct could not be invoked for the purpose of changing the plain meaning of the text: the text itself stipulated the use of the 'gold franc,' which was a well-known and clearly defined monetary standard, and any behavior of either party in conflict with this stipulation was contrary to the agreement.[59]

An analogous, and somewhat broader, invocation of the doctrine of subsequent conduct is to be found in the *International Labor Organization* (*Employers*) case,[60] where the Court sought to give effect to "a contemporaneous practical interpretation made by the High Contracting Parties of the scope of the competence which they had conferred upon the [Organization]."[61] Here the question was whether the ILO was authorized to adopt, as it did on July 5, 1924, a draft convention prohibiting night work in bakeries, such prohibition applying to all persons involved, "including proprietors as well as workers." The Court held that both the terms of Part XIII of the Treaty of Versailles and the actions of the parties taken under it since 1919 suggested that incidental regulation of proprietors was within the intentions of the High Contracting Parties. The Court observed that "before as well as since the Treaty of Versailles, it has been a common thing to require the closing of shops, factories and places of business within certain hours of the day, or on certain days of the week, thus suspending and regulating the particular kind of

59. Id. at 118–20.
60. *Competence of the International Labour Organization to Regulate, Incidentally, the Personal Work of the Employer*, P.C.I.J., Ser. B, No. 13 (1926).
61. Id. at 19.

work, whether performed by the employer or by the employed." [62] That this course of action was foreseen by the drafters of the Treaty was shown by their inclusion, in the agenda for the first meeting of the first ILO Conference provided for in Article 426, of just such a dual regulation of employer and employed in "the use of white phosphorus in the manufacture of matches." [63]

In the early *Chamizal Arbitration* [64] the tribunal took account of the subsequent behavior of the participants in these terms: "it appears to be impossible to come to any other conclusion than that the two nations have, by their subsequent treaties and their consistent course of conduct in connection with all cases arising thereunder, put . . . an authoritative interpretation upon the language of the Treaties of 1848 and 1853." [65] These treaties had established the center of the Rio Grande as the border between Mexico and the United States along most of its course. The principal disputes that began to arise concerned the disposition of lands on either side of the river when it shifted course: did the boundary also shift or did it remain the original river bed? As most of the important changes had cut into Mexican territory, the Mexican government urged the "fixed line" theory, while the United States argued that the boundary changed with the movements of the river. Subsequent to the original treaties, in 1884 and thereafter, the parties signed a further agreement and established a Boundary Commission to settle all boundary disputes. The 1884 agreement clarified the boundary in favor of a modified version of the "shifting boundary" theory relied on by the United States:

> The dividing line shall forever . . . follow the centre of the normal channel of the rivers named, notwithstanding any alterations in the banks or in the course of those rivers, provided that such alterations be effected by natural causes through . . . slow and gradual erosion.[66]

Although the disposition of the *Chamizal* claim eventually turned on whether the changes involved were the result of "slow and gradual

62. Id. at 18–19.
63. Id. at 19.
64. *The Chamizal Arbitration Between the United States and Mexico* (1911), reported in 5 *Am. J. Int'l L.* 782 (1911).
65. Id. at 805.
66. Boundary Convention Rio Grande and Rio Colorado, Article I, id. at 798.

erosion" as defined by the treaty, the prior determination—for which the tribunal invoked the doctrine of subsequent conduct—concerned the application of the 1884 treaty to claims arising between 1848 and 1884. The Mexican government argued that the 1884 agreement was not retroactive. However, the evidence of the government's subsequent conduct through its representative on the Boundary Commission was taken by the tribunal as conclusive of its acceptance of the contrary view. Many of the disputes which had been litigated under the later agreement, and heard by the authorized Mexican representative on the Commission, had arisen prior to 1884. Thus, by its implicit course of conduct through its representative on the Boundary Commission, the Mexican government had accepted, in the view of the tribunal, the shifting line theory of the boundary since its inception in 1848.

Recent support has been given to the principle of subsequent conduct by the International Court and other international tribunals. In the *Corfu Channel* case,[67] for example, the claim of Albania was that the Court was not empowered (by the Special Agreement submitting the dispute) to determine the amount of compensation due. At no point in the proceedings, however, had Albania questioned this right until, apparently, it appeared that the Court would decide to impose liability upon Albania. No objection had been raised to the consistent claim of Britain for damages amounting to £875,000, and in one reply Albania had expressly stated that this claim "should obviously form the subject of an expert opinion." [68] As Britain had naturally continued to support the right of the tribunal to render an opinion on this subject, it was concluded that "The subsequent attitude of the Parties shows that it was not their intention, by entering into the Special Agreement, to preclude the Court from fixing the amount of the compensation." [69]

Similarly, in the case concerning the *International Status of South-West Africa*,[70] the Court, declaring that "Interpretations placed upon legal instruments by the Parties to them, though not conclusive as to their meaning, have considerable probative value when they

67. *The Corfu Channel Case* (Merits), [1949] I.C.J. Rep. 4.
68. Id. at 28.
69. Id. at 25.
70. [1950] I.C.J. Rep. 128.

contain recognition by a party of its own obligations under an instrument,"[71] held that statements of the Union of South Africa subsequent to the dissolution of the League of Nations indicated that it continued to recognize its Mandate obligations. The Union's argument before the Court was that, with the dissolution of the League with the advent of the Second World War, all obligations which it had incurred in administering its mandate over the territory of South-West Africa ceased. The Court reviewed, however, several statements of the South African government between April 1946 and July 1947, indicating that it would "continue to administer the Territory scrupulously in accordance with the obligations of the Mandate," which, despite the disappearance of the League, the Union believed to be "necessarily inalienable."[72] The majority concluded that subsequent actions "constitute a recognition by the Union Government of its obligations under the Mandate and not a mere indication of [its] future conduct."[73] It thus held the Union responsible for all prior League commitments under the Mandate system.

Recent contributions by publicists have generally favored the admissibility of evidence from subsequent conduct. Fitzmaurice has included the "principle of subsequent practice" as a "major principle of interpretation" in two important articles.[74] He goes so far as to say that "In interpreting a text, recourse to the subsequent practice of the parties, as evidenced in rules of procedure they have formulated, or in other ways, is not only permissible but desirable; in brief, the way in which the treaty has actually been interpreted in practice is evidence (sometimes the best evidence) of what its correct interpretation is."[75] Hudson also commented on previous practice by suggesting that courts "cannot ignore action which may have been taken by the parties to an instrument . . . Subsequent action taken by the parties may also furnish some indication of the purpose with which an instrument was concluded."[76] In fact no respected commentator on interpretation has failed to endorse the principle of sub-

71. Id. at 135–36.
72. Id. at 135.
73. Ibid.
74. Fitzmaurice, supra note 21, at 9; see also Fitzmaurice, supra note 12, at 211.
75. Fitzmaurice, supra note 21, at 9.
76. Hudson, op. cit. supra note 12, at 658.

sequent conduct, although some have cautioned against placing too much emphasis upon the evidence obtained from it in particular situations of possible conflict with initial expectations.

The most serious objection raised to the employment of evidence from subsequent conduct was stated in surprisingly strong terms by Hyde:

> the action of the parties long subsequent to the negotiation of a treaty is not necessarily probative of the sense in which the terms were used at the time when the agreement was made; and . . . if such action is to be respected it is attributable to reasons that do not grow out of the requirements of interpretation. The Court may find convenient confirmation of its conclusions in the action of the parties, and it may even regard itself in a particular case as obliged to defer thereto. Such deference, save when the action of the parties is contemporaneous with the consummation of their agreement, marks an avoidance of the task of interpretation.[77]

The reasons that may have induced Hyde to regard the consideration of subsequent events as "an avoidance of the task of interpretation" are not at all clear. Furthermore, his preference for fixing the meaning of a treaty solely at the time of the outcome phase is similarly unsupported, except by his reiteration of his general goal of deference to the genuine shared expectations of the parties at the time of commitment.[78]

77. Hyde, op. cit. supra note 2, at 1496–97.

78. Much the same position has been taken, for similar reasons, by Schwarzenberger, op. cit. supra note 12, at 532: "The attitudes adopted by the parties to a treaty subsequent to its conclusion are evidence which an international judicial institution may take into account in its interpretative work, but only for the purpose of strengthening its conclusions on the common intention of the parties or the meaning of the treaty at the time of its conclusion."

The issues raised by these writers may perhaps be clarified in the following way: (1) deference must be given to explicit interpretations or revisions of treaties by the contracting nations, and (2) some reluctance should be shown by international tribunals in inferring "revisions" of treaties from implicit courses of conduct (i.e., conduct which does not clearly and explicitly indicate that a revision was intended to be made). Nevertheless, such conduct may be considered in order to determine the degree of continuing consensus of the parties at the time of commitment and down to the time of the dispute (the word "interpretation" would thus be reserved for this latter process). It is important to note

A position similar to Hyde's was taken by the Permanent Court in the *Treaty of Lausanne* (border between Iraq and Turkey) case,[79] where it was concluded that "facts subsequent to the conclusion of the Treaty of Lausanne can only concern the Court in so far as they are calculated to throw light on the intention of the Parties at the time of the conclusion of that Treaty." [80] Under this rubric, the Court examined the discussions between Turkish and British representatives in the League of Nations Council less than a year before the dispute, and concluded that they confirmed the conclusion, taken from the *prima facie* meaning of Article 3 of the Treaty of Lausanne, that both parties intended to make the Council settlement of the border between Turkey and Iraq final and binding.[81] Similar assumptions concerning the function of subsequent events in interpretation may be found in the *ILO* (*Agriculture*) case,[82] as well as the *Brazilian Loans* case described above.[83]

Attempts such as these to provide in advance for the preferred weighting of an interpretative principle in particular context can, as we indicated above, only serve ultimately to defeat the genuine shared expectations of the parties to agreements. In a given case any factor, including the subsequent actions of the parties, may be of paramount importance in determining the relevant expectations. In our recommended goals, evidence of the parties' expectations at the time of commitment should of course be given an initial presump-

---

that (a) Hyde is not arguing against the *admissibility* of evidence from subsequent conduct—its authorization in this respect is complete; and (b) he is willing to recommend that under all circumstances the expectations of the framers of a document should be conclusive in determining the meaning to be attached to an agreement. Hyde's position thus relates to the weighting of subsequent events, which he would subordinate to the original expectations of commitment as a general rule.

For recent expression of a strong preference for the interpretation of treaties in accordance with contemporary, rather than original, expectations, see *Eck v. United Arab Airlines, Inc.* 15 N.Y. 2d. 53, 203 N.E. 2d 640 (1964).

79. *Article 3, Paragraph 2, of the Treaty of Lausanne (Frontier Between Turkey and Iraq)*, P.C.I.J., Ser. B, No. 12 (1925).

80. Id. at 24.

81. Id. at 24–25. See further discussion, infra p. 278–79.

82. P.C.I.J., Ser. B, No. 2, p. 39 (1922).

83. Supra note 57, at 119. Note particularly the stipulation that an ambiguity must be found in the text taken in its plain and natural meaning in order to include and weigh subsequent events in decision.

tion which would hold in the absence of persuasive indices that such expectations had been altered by subsequent explicit communications or implicit acts of collaboration. If such evidence is produced, however, the parties' contemporary expectations should be respected. It seems of little value to say as a matter of policy that such a choice by a decision-maker marks an "avoidance of the act of interpretation" when in fact it constitutes an effort to determine the parties' genuine shared expectations, though as of the time at which the claims are presented for resolution.

PRINCIPLES RELATING TO THE PROCESS OF AGREEMENT

Participants

The Principle of Involvement

Occasional reference has been made in past practice to differences in the degree of involvement of the parties to an agreement, especially in those situations where the total number of parties was large and the degree of involvement varied. Several recent commentators have called attention to the conditions which have necessitated the weighing of such differences, especially in relation to the increasing number and significance of modern multilateral agreements affecting the total value position of all participants in the world social process. H. J. Tobin, for example, has pointed out that earlier agreements, limited both in participation and the range of values affected, required decision-makers only to examine contexts in which the probable degrees of involvement were relatively less complicated:

> When Grotius published his great work, the treaties available for consideration were for the most part bipartite instruments of commerce, of dynasty, of alliance, or of peace at the close of a war, and generally of indefinite duration. In the course of the succeeding centuries, however, the treaty field was broadened to cover international guaranties, the setting up of the Concert of Europe, and the whole field of international legislation including such varied subjects as the conduct of war, the setting up of international unions, the protection of labor and the financial reconstruction of states.[84]

84. Tobin, *The Termination of Multipartite Treaties* 15 (1933).

The differing features of earlier bipartite agreements as contrasted with more recent multilateral ones have led some writers, most notably McNair, to conclude that a separate set of goals and methods of interpretation should be adopted to deal with each class of agreements. As he noted in 1930, "the seed-bed of the traditional rules . . . was sown at a time when the old conception of a treaty as a compact . . . was exclusively predominant and the dawn of the new multilateral treaty had not begun." [85] The recommended solution was to "free ourselves from the traditional notion that the instrument known as the treaty is governed by a single set of rules, however inadequate, and set ourselves to study the greatly differing legal character of the several kinds of treaties and to frame rules appropriate to the character of each kind." [86]

It is significant that McNair, despite this recommendation, did not attempt to formulate alternative sets of rules for interpreting these differing types of agreements. Instead he restricted his analysis to the likely effects of actions taken under two types of treaties, traditionally called "law-making" and "contract" treaties.[87] Other writers have generally followed this practice, while excepting one rule which McNair himself had briefly alluded to concerning the relevance of *travaux préparatoires* in the interpretation of the two types of agreement. Briefly stated, this rule restricts the use of *travaux* for multilateral law-making treaties to explicit reservations incorporated in the treaties themselves. Professor Wright has summarized its past application most clearly. While admitting that "The line between contractual treaties and law-making treaties is not a sharp one," Wright argued that one important difference was that "With respect to multilateral law-making treaties . . . it is not common to utilize preliminary materials except in so far as incorporated in reservations formally attached to the instrument on signature or ratification, and accepted by the other parties to the convention." [88]

The trend of recent commentary fortunately rejects this distinc-

85. McNair, "The Functions and Differing Legal Character of Treaties," 11 *Brit. Yb. Int'l L.* 100, 106 (1930).

86. Id. at 118.

87. Id. at 105–16.

88. Wright, "The Interpretation of Multilateral Treaties," 23 *Am. J. Int'l L.* 94, at 101, 103 (1929). McNair, while questioning the accuracy of Wright's summary of past trends, calls the position "intrinsically reasonable." McNair, supra note 85, at 107.

tion between *traités-lois* and *traités-contrats* for determining appropriate principles of interpretation. In terms of our preferences, a leading justification for this rejection is precisely the employment of the distinction, as proposed by both McNair and Wright, to restrict recourse to significant features of the context of agreement.[89] As we have emphasized above, no divergence in the degree of involvement or the number of participants to a treaty can rationally be allowed to affect the requirement that the interpreter systematically examine all of the relevant features of the context. Any materials, whether incorporated in the official records of the process of negotiation or not, may be relevant to the determination of the genuine shared expectations of the participants, and should not be disregarded under any conditions, least of all those in which the number of participants and breadth of values affected has significantly increased.

The more rational import of a distinction between "law-making" and "contract" treaties becomes obvious when its function is conceived as that of pointing to features of the context relating to the varying degrees of involvement which parties may assume in the processes of negotiation, commitment, and termination of commitment. As Tobin has so aptly pointed out with regard to the termination of "law-making" treaties, the effects of events such as reservations, denunciations, international coercion, or subsequent agreements may be entirely different depending upon the characterization of a treaty as "law-making" or "contract." [90] It may be important, for example, to place less emphasis upon preliminary materials in cases where the claimants did not participate in the negotiation of the agreement, and only ratified after the outcome crystallization.

International tribunals, and especially the International Court of Justice, have occasionally referred to the varying degrees of interest and participation manifested in multipartite conventions. In the case concerning the *Competence of the International Labor Organization (Agriculture)* [91] the Permanent Court took cognizance of the contention that "Powers who took no part in the preparatory work were

89. The assumption of such practice appears to be that subsequently acceding parties could not have shared expectations arising out of the preparatory work. It should be clear, however, that this may not be the case. In any event, whether such expectations were or were not established is an empirical question to be answered in each instance and should not be determined in advance by a policy decision which is allegedly a principle of interpretation.

90. Tobin, op. cit. supra note 84, at 7–9, 280–88.

91. P.C.I.J., Ser. B, No. 2 (1922).

invited to accede to the Treaty as it stood, and did so accede," in assessing the relevance of preparatory work concerning Part XIII of the Treaty of Versailles.[92] This part of the Treaty established the International Labor Organization as a "permanent organization" to combat conditions of labor which involved "such injustice, hardship and privation to large numbers of persons as to produce unrest so great that the peace and harmony of the world are imperilled." [93] Since no provision was included specifically extending the authority of the Organization over agricultural labor, a few nations which were not desirous of such an extension questioned its competence in this area and initiated a request to the Court for an advisory opinion. During the hearings held by the Court on this matter, evidence from the preparatory work for this part of the Treaty was adduced attempting to show that agricultural labor had in fact been included in the general terms ("travailleurs," "conditions du travailleurs et régime du travail," etc.). The government of France, by then the sole party wishing to restrict the Organization's competence, argued that such evidence should not be received because of the implicit burdens which it placed upon acceding nations. While the Court did "not think it necessary to discuss these contentions" to decide the case (concluding that the terms of the Treaty were *prima facie* clear in their grant of authority to the ILO over agricultural labor), it nonetheless examined the evidence and concluded that "there is certainly nothing in the preparatory work to disturb this conclusion." [94] Similar considerations moved the Court to reject contentions based upon statements in *travaux préparatoires* in the *Tunis and Morocco Nationality Decrees* case,[95] in which evidence from Conference discussion of Article 15, paragraph 8, of the League of Nations Covenant was rejected, and in the case concerning the *Jurisdiction of the European Commission of the Danube*,[96] in which the Court rejected *travaux* relating to the Statute of the Danube with the well-known and highly controversial argument that "preparatory work should not be used for the purpose of changing the plain meaning of a text." [97]

92. Id. at 41.
93. Id. at 25.
94. Id. at 41
95. P.C.I.J., Ser. B, No. 4, p. 23 (1923).
96. P.C.I.J., Ser. B, No. 14 (1927).
97. Id. at 31.

With the exceptions noted, most contemporary observers agree that evidence of the participants' varying degrees of involvement in preliminary negotiations should be considered in relation to their actual degree of participation and their awareness of the *travaux*. Also, the prevailing view has been that subsequently acceding states should be held responsible for obligations spelled out in *travaux* if these were common knowledge or were informally communicated to them, taking into consideration the intensity of value involvement motivating parties to examine all features of the context before acceding. The position taken by Wright in this connection, that "the acceding states are usually officially cognizant only of the text and formal reservations and cannot be supposed to have accepted interpretations suggested in the preliminary conversations of the original negotiators," [98] is, we believe, contrary to the expectations of most parties, acceding or other, and should be rejected. Under certain circumstances also, such as those involving crucial benefits and burdens to the respective participants, or involving easy access to the preliminary negotiations, or more especially involving the creation of expectations in other participants as a result of their purported acceptance of the agreement, the acceding parties may reasonably be required to accept the responsibility of having known what the records of the preliminary negotiations contain. In any case, the possibility of relatively minor degrees of involvement by some of the parties should provide no reason for failing to consult preparatory work altogether.

The Relevance of Characteristics

GROUP

Account has frequently been taken, though in a largely unsatisfactory manner, of the different characteristics of various group participants, especially in cases where at least one participant was not a nation-state. The view that only nation-states may be "subjects of international law" has led to numerous disputes before international tribunals in which the claim of the non-nation-state (private association, individual) has been assumed and supported by the state of its nationality. Numerous other disputes have involved claims by, or against, international organizations. Under such circumstances, tribunals have been faced with the question whether the initiation of

98. Wright, supra note 88, at 104.

the claim by a non-nation-state participant, or the interest of such a participant, should affect the outcome of the process of interpretation.

The most frequent response to this problem has been to admit that group differences may be relevant to an interpretation but to deny that the peculiar characteristics of non-nation-state participants call for the automatic application of doctrines favoring state sovereignty. Many precedents have established that the doctrine of restrictive interpretation, as protecting state sovereignty, cannot overcome a clear grant of competence to an international authority, and that the doctrine can be given effect "only in cases where ordinary methods of interpretation have failed." [99] Conversely, very high deference has been given to the competence granted by nation-states to international organizations by interpreting organizational charters extensively.[100]

Similarly, tribunals have been willing to consider the relevance of special characteristics of private associations and individuals to interpretation without attempting to establish an all-embracing rule about such differences or characteristics. The differences may, of course, on occasion be found to have been within the expectations of the parties. In the *Anglo-Iranian Oil Co.* case,[101] for example, the International Court considered the question of whether the 1933 agreement between the Anglo-Iranian Oil Company and Iran constituted a "treaty" in the light of Great Britain's interest in the Oil Company's case. If it were a treaty it would thus come within Iran's 1932 declaration of its acceptance of the compulsory jurisdiction of the Court with respect to disputes involving treaties signed subsequently. The Court held that the agreement did not qualify as a treaty, since it did not involve relations between two states. At no time, the majority argued, could Iran have called upon Great Britain to perform any obligation to Iran as a result of the concession agreement, and since "treaties" were limited to relations between states, the 1933 agreement could not be considered under the declaration.[102]

The problem more frequently faced by international tribunals,

99. The terms used by the Permanent Court in *Polish Postal Service in Danzig,* supra note 45, at 39.

100. See the authorities cited in Lauterpacht, op. cit. supra note 21, at 267–81; see also id. at 243–56, 319–33, and Lauterpacht, supra note 19, at 67–82.

101. (Preliminary Objection), [1952] I.C.J. Rep. 93.

102. Id. at 112.

however, relates to whether standards different from those applied between states should be created for agreements between states and private associations or individuals. The most interesting recent discussion of this problem is in the *Saudi Arabia-Aramco* arbitration,[103] where the tribunal specifically rejected the view that the principle of restrictive interpretation should be applied in favor of Saudi Arabia on the ground that Aramco was a private association. It insisted that "the rights of the Parties must be evaluated and examined in a spirit of complete equality" and that such evaluation "cannot be founded only upon the quality of the subjects involved in a contractual relationship."[104] In justifying this conclusion, the tribunal commented that "the rights of one Party are increased as a result of restrictive interpretation to the extent that the rights of the other Party are restricted . . . The restrictions of its powers, which a State accepts by contract, are a manifestation of its sovereignty and States are bound to fulfill their obligations to the same extent as private persons."[105]

One possible way of viewing some issues of standing before courts is to regard them as problems concerning the characteristics of the participants. Most of these cases, of course, are related to the parties' degree of material or other involvement in the values at stake. But occasionally they also involve the prerequisite of some kind of status or class characteristic before the respective parties are permitted to bring suit. A paradigm example for such an analysis was provided in the recent *South-West Africa* cases (Preliminary Objection).[106] Here one of the questions was whether or not Liberia and Ethiopia must qualify as "members of the League of Nations" in order to have standing before the Court to press their claims against South Africa with respect to the latter's obligations under the Mandate system. The Union government argued that they did not have requisite standing, and in fact that no nation did, because of the dissolution of the League. Thus the issue was whether the characteristic of being a current "member of the League" was necessary in order to bring suit, or whether a renewal of that status in the United Nations, to-

103. Award of August 23, 1958; reported, sub nom. *Saudi Arabia v. Arabian American Oil Co.* (1958), in 27 *Int. Law Rep.* 117 (1963).
104. Id. at 86–87; 27 *Int. Law Rep.* 117, 191.
105. Id. at 87; 27 *Int. Law Rep.* 117, 191–92.
106. [1962] I.C.J. Rep. 319.

gether with whatever rights vested in individual nations survived the League's dissolution, was sufficient. The Court ruled that the characteristic of being a current member of the League was not a prerequisite to invoking the jurisdiction of the Court. Its argument, which we examine in greater detail below, was in essence that such a clearly established and continuing system of rights and obligations as those which were vested in South Africa could not, in order to fulfill the purposes of the Mandate system, be left unenforceable because of the technical absence of "members of the League." The Court concluded that these purposes could easily be effected by assuming that such rights were given to individual nations while the League endured, and that they survived as rights of those nations after the League's dissolution. The only characteristic which was ultimately required of Ethiopia and Liberia was this original grant and their continuation as independent states. No further class memberships were necessary.

INDIVIDUAL

The attention which past decision-makers have accorded such factors as the culture, class, group affiliations, personality, and previous exposure to crisis of the individuals who participate in the process of international agreement-making has been largely brief and unsystematic. Discussions of cultural differences, for example, have largely been restricted to the problems of translation, and to other problems presented by the interpretation of texts in different languages.[107] Attempts have been made by some past decision-makers, however, to account for specific cultural factors, such as attitudes in the United States toward prohibition in the 1920s, whenever they were relevant.[108]

Analyses of perspectives about class differences and their influence on agreements have most frequently, indeed virtually exclusively, been mentioned by Soviet writers on interpretation. V. M. Shurshalov, in his book *Basic Questions of the Theory of the Interna-*

107. For discussion of the traditional problem of versions in different languages, see infra, pp. 324–30.

108. See *Ford v. United States,* 273 U.S. 593 (1927). Cf. the *Treaty of Lausanne* case, supra note 79, at 29, where the "political position" of the parties was considered; and other cases involving cultural affinities and alignments, e.g., *Faber v. United States,* 221 U.S. 649 (1910); *Universal Adjustment Corp. v. Midland Bank, Ltd. of London,* 281 Mass. 303 (1933).

tional Treaty, comments on the tendency of Western legal positivists (referred to as "normativists") to divorce the process of interpretation from class and other political problems: "Soviet international scholars without a doubt reject the theoretical constructs of the normativistic school, which divorces legal norms from real relations, castrates their class essence, and repudiates the political character of legal relations." [109] Shurshalov also extends the notion of "class" difference to relations between nation-states in his insistence that all previous "imperialistic" agreements between "unequal" nations are illegal: "When interpreting a treaty, it is necessary to bear in mind that the parties are equals. Conclusions of interpretation which stand in contradiction with the demands of equality may not be considered acceptable and ought to be repudiated." [110] Beyond such general calls for the repudiation of "unequal" treaties, Soviet and other writers have not exhibited a genuine interest in an empirical examination of the effects of class differences upon the perspectives of parties to agreements.

References to personality factors have usually been limited in past practice to statements indicating in a most general way the possible relevance of such factors. At times they have involved little more than an oblique notation of the relevance of motivational factors in the agreement process. In the *Free Zones* case,[111] for example, Judges Hurst and Altamira commented that "human psychology and more particularly . . . governmental psychology" should be taken into account in determining the extent of the Court's functions as imposed by the claimants, France and Switzerland, in their Special Agreement to arbitrate. This agreement came after two failures by these nations to negotiate a new agreement with respect to the free zones of Savoy and Gex; it also contained a directive to the Court: "Failing the conclusion and ratification of a convention between the two Parties," to "settle for a period to be fixed by it and having regard to present conditions, all the questions involved by the execution of paragraph 2 of Article 435 of the Treaty of Versailles." [112] This article had established the machinery for settling the Savoy-Gex dispute as soon as possible after the Versailles Treaty "consistent

109. P. 32 (Jakaboski transl., unpubl. Yale Law School, 1961).
110. Id. at 26.
111. P.C.I.J. Ser. A/B, No. 46 (1932).
112. Id. at 57.

with present conditions." Judges Hurst and Altamira concluded that, in petitioning the Court after two failures to agree, the parties had recognized their own failures in requesting it to resolve the dispute once and for all; otherwise the provisions for decision "failing . . . a convention" between them would make no sense.[113]

Situations in which an international tribunal has been called upon to assess specific characteristics of the negotiators of an agreement appear to have been infrequent. Occasional reference has been made, however, as in the *Maninat* case, in which the tribunal considered the "skilled and erudite diplomatists" who had drafted the agreement involved, and who had "weighed [every word] and its force and significance" in determining the appropriate words to mediate the subjectivities of the contracting parties.[114] This awareness permitted them, in drafting an agreement relating to the claims of French nationals for wrongs committed in Venezuela, to select words of frequent and well-defined usage in international diplomacy. Thus in the eyes of the tribunal their limitation of claims to those "entered *by* Frenchmen" specifically excluded those entered *for* Frenchmen by persons of another nationality. Thus the requirement was imposed that one of the heirs of Jean Maninat, the deceased for whose wrongful death the action was initiated, had to be able to prove that he or she was a French citizen.[115] Similarly, the tribunal in the *Tacna-Arica* arbitration indicated its willingness to take notice of the relatively small exposure which the negotiators of the agreement, settling the Tacna-Arica boundary, had to the region, and that their "little exact knowledge of the geography" of the area could easily have led to technical errors in their final expression of commitment.[116]

An approximation in reference to past exposure to crisis is contained in those cases which concern treaties signed by participants affected by recent or immanent coercion. Thus in the *Customs*

113. Id. at 182–83.
114. *Heirs of Jean Maninat* (1905), in Ralston, *Report of French Venezuelan Mixed Claims Commission of 1902* 44, 72 (1906), and 10 U.N. Rep. Int'l Arb. Awards 55, 77.
115. Ibid.
116. *Tacna-Arica Question* (1925), 17; 2 U.N. Rep. Int'l Arb. Awards 921, 954. See also *United States v. Texas,* 162 U.S. 1, 36–38 (1896), and Lord Halsbury's comments on the effectiveness of participants in understanding and construing their own agreements, in *Hilder and Others v. Dexter,* [1902] A.C. 474, 477–78.

Union case, the Court took notice of "the profound political changes resulting from the late war," which the drafters of the Peace Treaty of Saint-Germain had lived through and in part helped resolve by prohibiting Austria from committing "any act which might . . . directly or indirectly . . . compromise her independence." [117] (The Court concluded that the proposed Austro-German Customs Union did so violate this prohibition.) Similarly, in the case concerning *German Interests in Upper Silesia (Merits)*, the Court referred to the fact that the treaty under consideration was essentially "war-time legislation" and should be interpreted in light of the assumed level of crisis at that time.[118]

Objectives

The Relevance of Value Range

Little consideration has been given in past practice to the range of values involved in the processes of agreement and claim. Only minimal effort has been made to separate out all values specifically sought in or affected by an agreement, to relate such values to a comprehensive spectrum (such as that of power, wealth, enlightenment, skill, well-being, respect, rectitude, and affection), or to suggest the probable importance for interpretation of the predominance of one or several values among expectations in any given instance. The closest approximation to an adequate examination of the relevance of values affected has been made by scholars and decision-makers concerned with the breadth of values involved in modern bilateral and multilateral agreements. Notice has been taken, in this respect, of the high correlation between multilateral agreements and agreements generalized to all values, and conversely of the coincidence of bilateral and single-valued agreements.[119] Despite the obvious fact that these correlations are frequently far from complete, the simul-

117. *Customs Regime Between Germany and Austria,* P.C.I.J., Ser. A/B, No. 41, at 42, 53 (1931).

118. P.C.I.J., Ser. A, No. 7, p. 74. See also the general reference to wartime and postwar expectations in the *Free Zones* case, supra note 111, at 148 ff.

119. See Tobin, op. cit. supra note 84, outlining "categories" of multilateral treaties, at 5–8, and carrying the analysis of political, economic, etc. treaties through each category in Chs. 1–2; Wright, supra note 88, at 98–102; and McNair, op. cit. supra note 38, at 112–18.

taneous increase in the importance of multilateral and value-general agreements have at least caused observers to give passing notice to the relevance of value range in their examinations of the great modern constitutive instruments.

Occasional general reference to the range of values at stake—usually without mention of the specific values—may be found in past decision. An example is the *Case Concerning the Barcelona Traction, Light & Power Co., Ltd.* (Preliminary Objections),[120] where the International Court of Justice took into consideration the multiplicity and range of agreements affected by the automatic substitution of the new Court—through Article 37 of its Statute—for its predecessor, the Permanent Court, in all existing agreements naming the Permanent Court as the arbitral tribunal.[121] Spain and Belgium in this case had such an agreement, but Spain claimed that the arbitration clause lapsed in 1946 with the end of the Permanent Court and was only transferred, if at all, to the states ratifying the Statute at that time.[122] Spain relied on the Court's holding in *Israel v. Bulgaria,* where a unilateral declaration by Bulgaria was held to lapse in 1946 when Bulgaria did not join the United Nations and thus did not accept the obligations of the Statute. In distinguishing its earlier holding, the Court stated that in contrast to its virtually *sui generis* character,

> any decision of the Court, relative to Article 37, must affect a considerable number of surviving treaties and conventions providing for recourse to the Permanent Court . . . It is thus clear that the decision of the Court in the present case, whatever it might be, would be liable to have far-reaching effects.[123]

Despite its admonition that "This is in no way a factor which should be allowed to influence the legal character of that decision," the

120. [1964] I.C.J. Rep. 6.

121. The relevant portion of Article 37 reads: "Whenever a treaty or convention in force provides for reference of a matter . . . to the Permanent Court of International Justice, the matter shall, as between the parties to the present Statute, be referred to the International Court of Justice." Id. at 27.

122. The clause was contained in the Hispano-Belgian Treaty of Conciliation, Judicial Settlement and Arbitration of 1927, and provides, in relevant part, that "either party may . . . bring the question direct [sic] before the Permanent Court of International Justice by means of an application." Ibid.

123. Id. at 29.

Court also commented that "it does constitute a reason why the decision should not be regarded as already predetermined" by *Israel v. Bulgaria.*[124] Thus it took into full consideration the differences in range of values affected—even if in an entirely unspecific manner—in distinguishing the otherwise quite similar facts in *Israel v. Bulgaria* and in establishing its jurisdiction.[125]

The Principle of Projecting Genuine Expectations

Under the traditional rubrics of "effectiveness" and "restrictive interpretation," the principle of projecting genuine expectations has been most influential in affecting past decisions.[126] This principle, considered in terms of the complementarities of its component parts, has had the attention of nearly all modern publicists and decision-makers, and would appear to have been the most widely accepted interpretive standard in the traditional repertoire.

The principle of effectiveness, often called the principle of "major purposes" or of "extensive interpretation," has been formulated in numerous ways in past practice. In commenting on the primary aim of interpretation—that of effecting the shared expectations of the parties—Lauterpacht stated this "hardly less important principle" very simply, namely, "the treaty must remain effective rather than ineffective." [127] In the Harvard Research, Garner and his associates

124. Id. at 29–30.

125. See, generally, *Reparations for Injuries Suffered in the Service of the United Nations,* [1949] I.C.J. Rep. 174. *Reservations to the Convention on the Prevention and Punishment of the Crime of Genocide,* [1951] I.C.J. Rep. 15; *Right of Nationals of the United States of America in Morocco,* [1952] I.C.J. Rep. 176; and the *Anglo-Iranian Oil Co.* case, supra note 101, for further examples of the relevance of value range.

An appropriate emphasis with respect to statutory interpretation is offered by Friedmann, "The Interpretation of Statutes in Modern British Law," 3 *Vand. L. Rev.* 544, 556 (1950) : "It is therefore submitted that different principles of interpretation should apply to statutes carrying out a definite social or legal reform, to penal statutes, taxation acts, and predominantly technical statutes."

126. For general characterizations of these trends, see Lauterpacht, supra note 19, at 56–75; Hyde, op. cit. supra note 2, at 1478–81; Harvard Research, op. cit. supra note 3, at 948–53; Fitzmaurice, supra note 21, at 18–20; Fitzmaurice, supra note 12, at 220–23.

127. Lauterpacht, op. cit. supra note 21, at 227–28. The author goes on to caution that "the maximum effectiveness should be given to [a treaty] consistently

proposed another version of the principle: "A treaty is to be interpreted in the light of the general purpose which it is intended to serve." [128]

Similarly, the principle of restrictive interpretation has received various formulations in past opinion. One version frequently invoked is that of McNair: "the interpretation should be adopted which is favourable to the freedom of states and places the lesser restriction on its liberty of action." [129] More recently, Sir Gerald Fitzmaurice has generalized the doctrine in these terms: "Definite rights and obligations, or specific derogations therefrom, cannot be read into treaty provisions by a process of inference, unless this is a *necessary* and not merely a *possible* consequence of the language used." [130]

Despite apparent agreement among scholars and decision-makers concerning the high-level formulation of the rules both of effectiveness and restrictive interpretation, little consensus has been achieved with respect to their appropriate specification and application. The most difficult problem has been to clarify the operations involved in these rules which distinguish them from other more specific standards or from the more general goals of interpretation. The different views which have arisen concerning performance of this task may be best demonstrated by some further examples from the many discussions of the principle of effectiveness.

---

with the intention—the common intention—of the parties," keeping in mind the contingency that "there may have been no intention to render the treaty fully effective." Id. at 228, 229. With respect to the relationship of "clear meanings" to the doctrine of effectiveness, Lauterpacht initially took the view that the principle of effectiveness was "a major principle, in the light of which the intention of the parties must be interpreted even to the extent of disregarding the letter of the instrument and of reading into it something which, on the face of it, it does not contain." *The Development of International Law* 69–70 (1930). In the revised edition, however, Lauterpacht added "so long as that 'something' is not contradicted by available and permissible evidence of the intention of the parties." Op. cit. supra note 21, at 228.

128. Harvard Research, op. cit. supra note 3, at 937.

129. McNair, op. cit. supra note 38, at 211.

130. Fitzmaurice, supra note 21, at 22. These alternative emphases have been usefully combined by Hall: "Whenever, or in so far as a state does not contract itself out of its fundamental legal rights by express language a treaty must be so construed as to give effect to those rights. . . . Any restriction of such rights must be effected in a clear and distinct manner." *A Treatise on International Law* 348 (7th ed. 1917).

In modern times, discussions of the doctrine of effectiveness date back to the writings of Grotius, Vattel, and Pufendorf. Of these authors, Grotius and Pufendorf spoke in terms of "extending" or "broadening" the ordinary, community-wide meanings of words, thus founding the modern tradition of "extensive" or "liberal" interpretation.[131] Only Vattel considered explicitly the role of major purposes, and it is his formulation that has affected the greater number of recent commentators on the doctrine of effectiveness:

> *The motive of the law, or of the treaty,* that is to say, the purpose which the parties had in mind, is one of the surest means of fixing its true sense, and careful attention should be paid to it whenever there is question either of explaining an obscure, equivocal, or undetermined passage in a law or treaty, or of applying it to a particular case. *When once the purpose which has led the speaker to act is clearly known his words must be interpreted and applied in the light of that purpose only. Otherwise he would be made to speak and act contrary to his intention and to the object he had in view.*[132]

Vattel's insistence that to disregard the "purpose which has led the speaker to act" would be "contrary to his intention" has been reproduced in numerous later writings, with the consequence that his choice of terms has not always been rendered in any consistent fashion. The Harvard Research, for example, suggests that "the 'purpose' of a treaty is closely connected with what is often referred to as the 'intention of the parties.' "[133] Conversely, Lauterpacht argued that the principle of major purposes, or of effectiveness, is "applicable only when the intention of the parties is doubtful."[134] Despite the caution of the Harvard statement, the context makes clear that in its

131. Grotius, *The Law of War and Peace* 413, 421–26 (Kelsey transl. 1646 ed., 1925); 2 Pufendorf, *De Jure Naturae et Gentium Libri Octo* 805–06, 810–16 (Oldfathers transl. 1688 ed. 1934). See also 2 Phillimore, op. cit. supra note 39, at 110–14; Fiore, *International Law Codified* 345 (Borchard transl. 1918); Crandall, *Treaties, Their Making and Enforcement* 371–77 (2d ed. 1916). For a survey of the United States Supreme Court's tradition of "liberal" interpretation, see Chang, op. cit. supra note 5, at 159–81; Hyde, op. cit. supra note 2, at 1478–81; Lauterpacht, supra note 19, at 67–68; and citations below at note 149.

132. Vattel, *The Law of Nations* 207 (Fenwick transl. 1758 ed. 1916).

133. Harvard Research, supra note 3, at 952.

134. Lauterpacht, supra note 19, at 73.

view no distinction whatever remains between "purpose" and "intent," thus equating the two concepts and bringing their usage in apparent contrast with that of Judge Lauterpacht. This verbal difference would be of little importance if the operations referred to were clearly specified, and if the terminology used was not misleading to subsequent commentators. Unfortunately, such has not been the case. The operation most frequently referred to requires postulating that whenever a systematic, contextual survey fails to yield a specific anticipation by the parties of the dispute under consideration, doubt may be removed by referring to the more general aims or purposes of the parties.[135] What is usually excluded in this view are other possible comparisons and weightings among the various strata of objectives. Higher-level purposes, for example, may conflict with specific statements, ambiguities in the general aims of an agreement may be resolved by reference to unambiguous grants in individual provisions, etc. In addition, numerous other sources of evidence may throw light upon the significance which the parties attach to any one of the several levels of statement.

References to the principle of effectiveness by national and international tribunals have been even more diverse than those of recent publicists. The most frequently invoked formulation of the principle is, for example, that of Judge Anzilotti in the case concerning the *Employment of Women During the Night:*

> I do not see how it is possible to say that an article of a convention is clear until the subject and aim of the convention have been ascertained, for the article only assumes its true import in this convention and in relation thereto. Only when it is known what the Contracting Parties intended to do and the aim they had in view is it possible to say that the natural meaning of the terms used in a particular article corresponds with the real intention of the Parties.[136]

With this statement, however, Anzilotti was dissenting from the Court's finding that the restriction on the employment of women under the disputed agreement was "free from ambiguity or ob-

135. For relevant commentary, see De Visscher, op. cit. supra note 12, at 62–66. Degan, *L'Interprétation des Accords en Droit International* (1963), also assumes this restriction in his survey of cases relevant to this point. See id. at 102–06.
136. P.C.I.J., Ser. A/B, No. 50, p. 383 (1932).

scurity" when "considered by itself" in accordance with the "natural sense of the words." [137] Under circumstances so assumed, the majority saw no need to upset the "clear" meaning of the provision by considerations such as those urged by Anzilotti.[138] This same restriction on the application of the principle of effectiveness was repeated in the *Free Zones* case,[139] and again in the case concerning *Postal Service in Danzig.*[140]

137. Id. at 373; the relevant provision, Article 3 of the 1919 Convention on the Employment of Women During the Night adopted by the International Labor Conference, reads as follows: "Women without distinction of age shall not be employed during the night in any public or private industrial undertaking, or in any branch thereof, other than an undertaking in which only members of the same family are employed." Id. at 370.

138. Id. at 378.

139. Supra note 111, at 13.

140. P.C.I.J., Ser. B, No. 11, p. 39 (1925). In the *Free Zones* case, supra note 108, the Court held that "in case of doubt the clauses of a special agreement by which a dispute is referred to the Court must, if it does not involve doing violence to their terms, be construed in a manner enabling the clauses themselves to have appropriate effects." Id. at 13. In the *Postal Service* case, P.C.I.J., Ser. B, No. 11, the Court stated its restriction upon the total effect of projecting expectations in its most extreme form: "the rules as to a strict or liberal construction of treaty stipulations can be applied only in cases where ordinary methods of interpretation have failed" (p. 39). In actual application, this latter restriction was not as broad as it appears, nor was its employment in the decision to limit the principle of effectiveness. The issue facing the Court was whether Poland's establishment of letter boxes in the City of Danzig was acceptable within the provisions of Article 29 of the Paris Convention of 1929 between Poland and Danzig: "Poland shall have the right to establish in the port of Danzig a post, telegraph and telephone service communicating directly with Poland. Postal and telegraphic communications via the port of Danzig between Poland and foreign countries, as also communications between Poland and the port of Danzig, shall be dealt with by this service" (p. 33). Counsel for Danzig had argued that the Polish Postal Service should be limited to operations which could be carried out within the central building which the Polish Post Office occupied, in consequence of the restrictive interpretation of Article 29 made necessary by the derogation of Danzig's sovereignty implied in the grant of postal rights to Poland. Despite the way it was introduced, the principle was in fact employed by the Court to deny Danzig's demand for a restriction on Poland's mail-gathering activities. Having granted Poland the right to "establish a postal service" in Danzig, the Court concluded that an integral part of that service must be the establishment of letter boxes. The partly ironic result is that, after stating an apparently extreme limitation upon the principle of effectiveness, the Court in reality applied it in a rather straightforward and conventional manner.

On other occasions, however, the Permanent Court indicated its willingness to apply the principle of effectiveness in less equivocal and restrictive terms. In the *Greco-Bulgarian "Communities"* case,[141] the Court commented that it "considers it necessary to recall the general purpose which the Greco-Bulgarian Convention . . . was designed to fulfill." [142] Article 6 of that Convention had granted reciprocal rights to persons in Greek and Bulgarian communities who desired to emigrate across the established national boundaries. The principal task of the Court was to define the concept of a "community" under this provision. Roughly stated, Bulgaria argued that "community" meant *juridical* community under municipal law, while Greece argued that the term referred to a *cultural* community "united by . . . identity of race, religion, language and traditions." [143] In affirming the Greek view by invoking the general purposes of the Convention, the Court argued that

> the aim and object of the Convention, its connection with the measures relating to minorities, the desire of the signatory Powers, to which the whole Convention bears witness, that the individuals forming the communities should respectively make their homes permanently among their own race, the very mentality of the population concerned—everything leads to the conclusion that the Convention regards the conception of a "community" from the point of view of this exclusively minority character which it has had for centuries past.[144]

The Permanent Court frequently carried out an operation similar to that involved in the *Communities* case, without offering explicit discussion of the principle of effectiveness. In the cases relating to the application of the Minorities Treaty in Poland, for example, it asserted that "The main object of the Minorities Treaty is to assure respect for the rights of Minorities and to prevent discrimination against them by any act whatsoever of the Polish State." [145] Similarly, in the dispute concerning the *Acquisition of Polish National-*

141. P.C.I.J., Ser. B, No. 17 (1930).
142. Id. at 19.
143. Id. at 21.
144. Id. at 21–22.
145. *Certain Questions Relating to Settlers of German Origin in the Territory ceded by Germany to Poland,* P.C.I.J., Ser. B, No. 6, p. 25 (1923).

ity,[146] the Court held that the refusal of Poland to grant nationality to resident minorities came within the Treaty's prohibition of harmful discrimination to such groups, since "if this were not the case, the value and sphere of application of the Treaty would be greatly diminished." [147] Such a result would be contrary to the purpose of the Treaty with respect to persons of non-Polish origin, since "the Principal Allied and Associated Powers desired to create a sure guarantee in favour of these persons; with this object in view they inserted stipulations on the subject in the Minorities Treaty, thus indicating their intention that these persons should benefit by the protection provided for." [148]

Numerous other examples might be cited in which the Permanent Court, as well as other national and international tribunals, affirmed the doctrine of major purposes.[149]

In the case of *Reparations for Injuries Suffered in the Service of the United Nations*,[150] the present International Court was called

146. P.C.I.J., Ser. B, No. 7 (1923).
147. Id. at 16.
148. Ibid.
149. *Case Concerning the Factory at Chorow (Jurisdiction)*, P.C.I.J., Ser. A, No. 9, p. 25 (1927); the *Jaworzina Boundary* case, supra note 53, at 40; the *ILO (Employers)* case, supra note 60, at 18. For confirmation by the present Court, see *Corfu Channel* case, supra note 67, at 24; *Effect of Awards of Compensation Made by the United Nations Administrative Tribunal,* [1954] I.C.J. Rep. 47, 57; *Maritime Safety Committee* case, supra note 17, at 170–71. For similar expressions of acceptance of the general purposes doctrine by other tribunals, see the discussion of effectiveness vis-à-vis the doctrines of plain and natural meaning and of "textuality" below; and see *Gold Looted by Germany from Rome in 1943* (1953), reported in 1953 *Int. Law Rep.* 441, 474; *Statute of the Saar Territory,* (1955), 1955 id. 630, 631; *Kozuh v. Uff. Stato Civile de Milano* (1952), 1952 id. 322, 1324. For cases determined in a similar manner under the United States Supreme Court's doctrine of "liberal" construction, see *Shanks v. DuPont,* 3 Pet. 242 (1830), *Hauenstein v. Lynham,* 100 U.S. 483 (1879); *Geofroy v. Riggs,* 133 U.S. 258 (1890); *In Re Ross,* 140 U.S. 453 (1891); *Tucker v. Alexandroff,* 183 424 (1902). *Terrace v. Thompson,* 263 U.S. 197 (1923); *Asakura v. Seattle,* 265 U.S. 332 (1924); *Jordan v. Tashiro,* 278 U.S. 123 (1928); *Nielsen v. Johnson,* 279 U.S. 47 (1929); *Santovincenzo v. Egan,* 284 U.S. 30 (1931); *Factor v. Laubenheimer,* 290 U.S. 276 (1933); *Valentine v. U.S. ex rel. Neidecker,* 290 U.S. 5 (1936); *Choctaw Nation v. U.S.,* 318 U.S. 423 (1943); *Shoshone Indians v U.S.,* 324 U.S. 335 (1945); *Warren v. U.S.,* 340 U.S. 523 (1951).
150. [1949] I.C.J. Rep. 174.

upon to apply the effectiveness principle in a very direct way. The issue presented in this case was whether the organization had competence under the Charter to bring a claim against a government for reparation of injuries to United Nations agents in the course of their duties. Article 104 provides that "The Organization shall enjoy in the territory of each of its Members such legal capacity as may be necessary for the exercise of its functions and the fulfillment of its purposes." The well-known events which led to the request by the General Assembly for an advisory opinion from the Court involved the assassination of Count Bernadotte and others serving the United Nations in Palestine. In the principal part of its request, the General Assembly asked the Court the following question:

> In the event of an agent of the United Nations in the performance of his duties suffering injury in circumstances involving the responsibility of a State, has the United Nations, as an Organization, the capacity to bring an international claim against the responsible *de jure* or *de facto* government with a view to obtaining the reparation due in respect of the damage caused (a) to the United Nations, (b) to the victim or to persons entitled through him? [151]

In attributing to the organization what it considered the necessary "international personality" to carry out the general purposes of "the maintenance of international peace and security, the development of friendly relations among nations, and the achievement of international co-operation in the solution of problems of an economic, social, cultural or humanitarian nature," the Court concluded that

> the Organization was intended to exercise and enjoy, and is in fact exercising and enjoying, functions and rights which can only be explained on the basis of the possession of a large measure of international personality and the capacity to operate upon an international plane. It is at present the supreme type of international organization, and it could not carry out the intentions of its founders if it was devoid of international personality. It must be acknowledged that its Members, by entrusting certain functions to it, with the attendant duties and responsibili-

151. Id. at 174, 175.

> ties, have clothed it with the competence required to enable those functions to be effectively discharged.[152]

In specifically answering part (a) of the above question posed by the General Assembly, the Court concluded that it was "clear that the Organization has the capacity to bring a claim for this damage," for "it is impossible to see how it can obtain reparation unless it possesses capacity to bring an international claim." [153] In answering part (b) of the question, the Court admitted that "The Charter does not expressly confer upon the Organization the capacity to include, in its claim for reparation, damage caused to the victim or to persons entitled through him." [154] Nevertheless, in direct application of the doctrine of effectiveness, the Court concluded that "the Organization must be deemed to have those powers which, though not expressly provided in the Charter, are conferred upon it by necessary implication as being essential to the performance of its duties." [155] In this instance, "to ensure the efficient and independent performance of these missions and to afford effective support to its agents, the Organization must provide them with adequate protection," [156] including, in the Court's view, reparations for damages suffered by the victim. In claiming for the victim, however, the Court insisted that the organization still must intend only effectively to serve its own major purposes: "[In such claims] the Organization does not represent the agent, but is asserting its own right, the right to secure respect for undertakings entered into towards the Organization." [157]

152. Id. at 179.
153. Id. at 180.
154. Id. at 182.
155. Ibid.
156. Id. at 183.
157. Id. at 184. See also the case concerning the *Effect of Awards of Compensation,* supra note 149, where the Court considered the necessity of administrative dispute settlement in authorizing the Administrative Tribunal despite the fact that "there is no express provision for the establishment of judicial bodies or organs and no indication to the contrary." The majority nonetheless concluded that "It would . . . hardly be consistent with the expressed aim of the Charter to promote freedom and justice for individuals, and with the constant preoccupation of the United Nations Organization to promote this aim that it should afford no judicial or arbitral remedy to its own staff for the settlement of any disputes which may arise between it and them. . . . Capacity to do this arises by necessary intendment out of the Charter." Id. at 57.

In the famous *Certain Expenses of the United Nations* case,[158] in confirming the competence of the General Assembly with respect to the budgeting and apportioning of expenses in relation to the Suez and Congo peace-keeping operations (a decision which we will review in more detail below), the International Court of Justice made reference to both the specific purposes of Article 17 of the United Nations Charter and the more general purposes of the whole organization. The question of interpretation directly posed was whether the Assembly's asserted competence could be brought within Article 17, which confers upon the Assembly the authority to "consider and approve the budget" of the United Nations and to apportion "the expenses of the Organization" among the various members.

In its first reference to "purposes" in aid of its interpretation, the Court focused explicitly upon Article 17:

> The general purposes of Article 17 are the vesting of control over the finances of the Organization, and the levying of apportioned amounts of the expenses of the Organization in order to enable it to carry out the functions of the Organization as a whole acting through its principal organs and such subsidiary organs as may be established.[159]

From this perspective, the Court then proceeded to refute the argument that expenses relating to the maintenance of international peace and security constitute an exception, as being allegedly within the exclusive competence of the Security Council.

One of the more important reasons given by the Court for its conclusion, rejecting an exclusive competence in the Security Council and confirming the competence of the Assembly to approve and apportion expenditures for peace-keeping operations, was its concern for the general purposes of the organization. It was agreed by the Court that if expenditures were to be brought within the compass of

158. [1962] I.C.J. Rep. 151. Some of the subsequent history of this famous case is indicated in Nathanson, "Constitutional Crisis at the United Nations: The Price of Peace-Keeping," 32 *U. Chi. L. Rev.* 621 (1965), 33 *U. Chi. L. Rev.* 249 (1966). The dramatic change of position by the United States government upon the constitutional issues was announced by Ambassador Goldberg in his first speech to the Assembly, U.S. Mission to the U.N., Press Release No. 4615, Aug. 16, 1965. The more basic issues appear still unresolved. See "U.N. Fund Formula Remains Elusive," *N.Y. Times,* June 12, 1966, p. 20, col. 1.

159. Id. at 162.

Article 17 (2) such expenditures had to be "tested by their relationship to the purposes of the United Nations in the sense that if an expenditure were made for a purpose which is not one of the purposes of the United Nations, it could not be considered an 'expense of the Organization.' "[160] The relevant purposes for this test were, however, the broad purposes as stated in Article 1 of the Charter:

> The first two purposes as stated in paragraphs 1 and 2, may be summarily described as pointing to the goal of international peace and security and friendly relations. The third purpose is the achievement of economic, social, cultural and humanitarian goals and respect for human rights. The fourth and last purpose is: "To be a center for harmonizing the actions of nations in the attainment of these common ends."[161]

As broad as these purposes are, the Court insisted that "when the Organization takes action which warrants the assertion that it was appropriate for the fulfillment of one of the stated purposes of the United Nations, the presumption is that such action is not *ultra vires* the Organization."[162] An especial importance must be ascribed, the Court also noted, "to international peace and security" since "the fulfillment of the other purposes will be dependent upon that basic condition." The Court had, hence, little difficulty in ultimately concluding that the operations in question "were undertaken to fulfill a prime purpose of the United Nations, that is, to promote and maintain a peaceful settlement of the situation," and were thus within the compass of Article 17 (2).[163]

Decision-makers have, on several occasions, commented on the relative priority of the major purposes doctrine in relation to other

160. Id. at 167.
161. Id. at 167–68.
162. Id. at 168.
163. Id. at 171–72. In his article "Expenses of the United Nations Peace-Keeping Operations: The Advisory Opinion of the International Court of Justice," 17 *Int'l Org.* 1 (1963), Professor Leo Gross spells out in some detail the Court's emphasis upon purposes and regrets that the Court did not see fit to apply the principle of restrictive interpretation. Limitations upon the principle of effectiveness are, of course, stressed by some of the dissenting judges in its *Certain Expenses of the United Nations* case. See, e.g., Judge Winiarski's dissenting opinion, 1962 I.C.J. Rep. 227, 230.

principles of interpretation. These comments have, on the whole, been limited to comparisons of major purposes and the plain meaning doctrines. For example, in the *Chorzow Factory* case (Jurisdiction),[164] the Permanent Court proposed that its holding in favor of jurisdiction was "deduced from the object" of the 1922 German-Polish Convention of Geneva and "could only be defeated . . . by the employment of terms sufficiently clear to show a contrary intention on the part of the contracting Parties." [165] The question in this instance was whether the Court had jurisdiction under Article 23 (1) of the Geneva Convention for the purpose of determining reparations claimed by Germany. This article provided that all disputes arising under Articles 6–22 of the Convention "shall be submitted to the Permanent Court of International Justice." Poland contended that 23 (1) applied, if at all, only to determinations of liability and not to the determination of reparations. The Court concluded that:

> An interpretation which would confine the Court simply to recording that the Convention had been incorrectly applied or that it had not been applied, without being able to lay down the

164. P.C.I.J., Ser. A, No. 9 (1927).

165. Id. at 25. One danger in the Court's formulation of such a comparison between major purposes and "plain and natural" meanings is that it might encourage the assumption that the determination of major purposes does not require a thoroughgoing contextual analysis. Such an assumption could be made from the Court's choice of words, that it had "deduced" the "natural object" of the convention *"prima facie."* Id. at 25. It is clear from the context of the opinion, however, that the Court did, in fact, take many other factors into consideration, including "the historical development of . . . such treaties, and of the grammatical and logical meaning of the words used, but also and more especially of the function which, in the intention of the contracting Parties, is to be attributed to this provision" (p. 24). Similarly, cf. the *ILO (Employers)* case (supra note 60, at 19) where it was said somewhat misleadingly under very specific circumstances that "the Court, in determining the nature and scope of a measure, must look to its practical effect rather than to the predominant motive that may be conjectured to have inspired it." Far from attempting to discourage contextual examination, the Court was only saying that one set of aims in establishing the ILO—that of improving safety conditions for workers—was irrelevant in deciding whether the ILO could incidentally regulate the work of employers. The "practical effect" of safety regulations fell incidentally upon employers as well as workers, and were thus precedents for the present dispute regardless of their original "predominant motive."

> conditions for the re-establishment of the treaty rights affected, would be contrary to what would, *prima facie,* be the natural object of the clause; for a jurisdiction of this kind, instead of settling a dispute once and for all, would leave open the possibility of further disputes.[166]

Since it was unable to find any "contrary intention" to that plainly expressed in the arbitral clause, the Court held that it had jurisdiction under that clause. Thus, far from having to apply the priority it had set up in favor of the plain meaning doctrine, it found that the plain meaning of Article 23 (1) and the major purposes of the Convention complemented one another.

The doctrine laid down in the *Chorzow* case, however, found a more direct application much later in the *Peace Treaties* case (second phase).[167] In this case a dispute had arisen when the Secretary-General of the United Nations attempted to persuade Bulgaria, Hungary, and Romania to settle alleged civil liberties violations by arbitration under the provisions of Article 36 of the Treaty. Article 36 stipulated that in certain disputes each party was to appoint one arbitrator and agree upon a third; upon a failure of the parties to agree, the article provided that "The Secretary General . . . may be requested by either party to make the appointment" of the third arbitrator.[168] After the failure of the accused nations to appoint their own representatives, the Secretary-General appointed the neutral member and subsequently petitioned the Court to determine whether or not the decisions of such a tribunal, in the absence of the third member, would be binding. The Court held that the Secretary-General did not have the power to appoint the third member in the absence of either of the other two, even though the result of such a decision would be to defeat the application of Article 36 whenever either party refused to act. The Court said:

> The principle of interpretation expressed in the maxim: *Ut res magis valeat quam pereat,* often referred to as the rule of effectiveness, cannot justify the Court in attributing to the provisions for the settlement of disputes in the Peace Treaties a

166. Ibid.

167. *Interpretation of Peace Treaties With Bulgaria, Hungary and Romania* (Second Phase), [1950] I.C.J. Rep. 221.

168. Id. at 226.

> meaning which . . . would be contrary to their letter and spirit.[169]

The difficulty involved in balancing the "letter and spirit" of particular provisions with the higher-level objectives of the parties is a superficially distinguishing feature of the *Peace Treaties* case in relation to the previous International Court cases cited. A more pronounced conceptual problem, both for jurists and publicists, has resulted in situations such as this, when both general goals and specific means are articulated. Even in this situation, however, it should be clear that the formulation of a general rule regulating the relation of these indices of expectation cannot be recommended. Thus specific directions about means which appear to be derogations from the more general purposes may or may not, in the expectations of the parties, be of greater significance; the parties may expect that their higher purposes should prevail even in cases of direct conflict with specific provisions read with alleged literality. All that can be usefully stated in advance is that no conclusion should be reached in balancing the various indices of expectation until all factors are taken into account, including any evidence of the parties' expectations regarding the relative importance of their specific or general purposes. Final choice here, as upon other conflicts, must depend on the whole constellation of indices of interpretation.

A peculiarly complex problem in applying the principle of effectiveness may of course arise, even in situations in which its overriding significance is not questioned, when it is difficult to determine which of proposed alternatives most adequately represents the major objectives of the parties. It has been argued by Stone that frequently under these circumstances "the principle of maximum effectiveness in itself gives no decisive guidance." [170] The example he gives chiding Hambro [171] involves the alleged dilemma presented by the absence of a permanent member from a vote of the Security Council. In ringing peroration, he demands: "Would it . . . maximize *'the* effect' of the Charter to restrict the power of the Security Council by

169. Id. at 229. Contrast this statement with that of Lauterpacht cited above, note 134.

170. Stone, "Fictional Elements in Treaty Interpretation—A Study in the International Judicial Process," 1 *Sydney L. Rev.* 334, 353 (1954).

171. "Pollux," "The Interpretation of the Charter," 28 *Brit. Yb. Int'l L.* 54, 70 (1946).

holding that absence of a Permanent Member makes decisions of substance impossible? Or contrarily to restrict sovereign prerogatives of States by holding that absence is equivalent to abstention, and that mere abstention does not imply non-concurrence in the decision? . . . Either course would 'maximize the effect' of the Charter, according to which was chosen as 'the effect.' "[172] With respect to this particular dilemma, the argument has been fully developed elsewhere that it is a false one, easily resolvable by reference to the Charter's major purposes of promoting international peace and security, as indeed by its words, history, and reinforcing practice.[173] It is, however, deserving of attention that situations may occur in which both parties involved may contend that the acceptance of their claim would maximize the effectiveness of an agreement, and it is in fact difficult to choose between them on this ground. In such instances the interpreter's recourse must of necessity be to other features of the context and to the basic public order goals of the community he represents.

An excellent recent example of a case in which each party plausibly argued that its interpretation was compatible with the principle of effectiveness is found in the *Saudi Arabia-Aramco* arbitration.[174] The principal grant requiring interpretation in this case was Article I of the parties' 1933 Concession Agreement, which read in part:

> The Government hereby grants to the Company . . . the *exclusive right,* for a period of sixty years from the effective date hereof, to explore, prospect, drill for, extract, treat, manufacture, transport, deal with, carry away and export petroleum, asphalt, naphtha, natural greases, ozokerite and other hydrocarbons, and the derivatives of all such products.[175]

Aramco contended that in order to make this stipulation fully effective it had to be interpreted to confer upon the company the exclusive right to transport all of the specified products by sea to European and other markets, since without such right the general purpose of

172. Stone, supra note 170, at 353.

173. See McDougal and Gardner, "The Veto and the Charter: An Interpretation for Survival," 60 *Yale L. J.* 258 (1951), reprinted in McDougal's *Studies in World Public Order,* Ch. 7, p. 718, especially at 736 et seq. (1961).

174. Award of August 23, 1958; also reported sub nom. *Saudi Arabia v. Arabian American Oil Co.,* 27 *Int. Law Rep.* 117 (1963).

175. Id. at 76; 27 *Int. Law Rep.* 117, 175.

both parties—to enhance their own economic well-being—would be defeated. The government, on the other hand, argued that external transport by Aramco was in no way essential to the establishment of foreign markets, since such transport could be effected, as indeed it always had been, by others. That such an exclusive right was not envisioned by the parties in 1933 was supported, moreover, by (1) the fact that no mention of it was made either in the preamble or body of the agreement, (2) the fact that long after 1933 Aramco possessed no shipping fleet capable of such transport, and (3) the obvious fact of the government's continuing interest in maintaining as much control over the total operations as possible in order to take advantage of every opportunity to promote the welfare of its people.

The tribunal held that an appropriate teleological interpretation of the agreement supported Aramco's position. In sweeping conclusion, it said: "The common aim was thus, ever since the conclusion of the contract, to obtain the greatest reward possible from the operation of the enterprise and, to this end, to give to the concessionaire the complete direction of the enterprise so that it could engage in all the operations deemed by it advisable or necessary for this common purpose." [176] The tribunal added that such a "teleological interpretation, i.e., by the analysis of the purpose of the contract, fully corroborates the interpretation already arrived at" by other interpretative principles.[177] Since, however, the tribunal alluded only in passing to determinate features of the context which it thought indicated a purpose of the parties to include within their common aim of economic gain the further investing of "complete direction" of all operations in Aramco,[178] the observer is left to speculate upon what single feature or combination of features distinguished its "teleological" interpretation from its operations in employment of other relevant principles.[179]

The principle of restrictive interpretation, sometimes referred to as "narrow" or "strict" interpretation, has been employed for many diverse purposes in past practice, and with varying degrees of recog-

176. Id. at 84; 27 *Int. Law Rep.* 117, 189.
177. Id. at 84–85; 27 *Int. Law Rep.* 117, 189–90.
178. Id. at 85; 27 *Int. Law Rep.* 117, 190.
179. Candor perhaps requires the notation that one of the authors, McDougal, was of losing counsel in this case. From defeat in advocacy books are sometimes born.

nition and explicit acceptance in its application to particular disputes. In earlier writings, for example, restrictive interpretation was contrasted with "extensive" or "liberal" interpretation:

> Just as a provision is extended to cases which, although not included within the meaning of the terms, are included within the intention of the provision and are embraced by the motive which gave rise to it; so also a law or a promise may be restricted by following out the motive of the law or promise, contrary to the literal meaning of the terms.[180]

Thus restrictive interpretation was defined in terms of changes in the ordinary or "literal" application of specific provisions to conform with the more "restricted" intentions of the parties. At its inception, this version of the rule received its justification in policy from Vattel:

> We resort to restrictive interpretation in order to avoid falling into absurdities . . . When a case arises in which it would be too severe upon and too injurious to anyone to take a law or promise strictly according to its terms, the principle of restrictive interpretation is applied, and an exception is made of the case, agreeably to the intention of the legislator or of the person who has made the promise.[181]

More recent formulations of the rule have usually not been limited to alterations of "ordinary" meanings, but at the same time have frequently taken on, as we saw above, the limitation of being employed only for the purpose of protecting state sovereignty, or as McNair put it, protecting the "freedom of states." One recent writer has insisted that "The main explanation of the prominence of the rule of restrictive interpretation in the international sphere is that it has been resorted to by reference to and on account of the sovereignty of independent states." [182]

This view has won far from unanimous approval in contemporary writings. A late formulation of the rule by Sir Gerald Fitzmaurice,

180. Vattel, op. cit. supra note 132, at 210.
181. Ibid.
182. Lauterpacht, supra note 19, at 57–58.

for example, makes no stipulation whatever with respect to its employment in protecting state sovereignty:

> All those concerned with the interpretation of texts know how difficult is the type of case where something is neither included nor excluded, or where it is a possible but not a necessary inference from the text. In such cases there are two modes of approach. According to one, if the matter in question is not actually excluded, and if a useful purpose would be served by inferring it, and the text affords a possible basis for drawing such an inference, then it may legitimately be drawn. According to the other approach, if a thing is not expressed, it is not, generally speaking, permissible to infer it as merely not being inconsistent; it must *follow* from the language used, as a necessary consequence of the terms of the treaty.[183]

The implicit recognition by Fitzmaurice that the principle of restrictive interpretation may be seen as limiting the excessive application of its complement, the principle of effectiveness, is more directly expressed in other recent writings, most notably those of Hyde. In commenting that "The reference in terms of liberality to the character of commitments which a contracting State assumes is believed . . . to be of doubtful value as a means of ascertaining the exact design of the interested parties," Hyde observes that, in the United States at least, courts have been "respectful of the freedom of such States to attach to the words of an agreement any signification that might be desired by them. Hence it has not been prone to invoke or to heed rules of construction subversive of the consequences of such freedom. In a word, the conclusions of the Court as to the designs of contracting states have been expressed in terms revealing deference for what the evidence established rather than for any other consideration." [184]

The authoritative character of the principle of restrictive interpretation has seldom been questioned. Even Lauterpacht, perhaps the most consistent opponent of the principle in the form in which he conceived it, nonetheless agreed that "a substantial part of the pleadings before international tribunals has been conducted in terms of the argument of restrictive interpretation." [185] Lauterpacht stated

183. Fitzmaurice, supra note 21, at 23–24.
184. Hyde, op. cit. supra note 2, at 1481. See also Hogg, supra note 14, at 19–28.
185. Lauterpacht, supra note 19, at 58.

his belief that not only is the rule, in the version he understood, of "questionable value" but also that "there seems to be no case on record in which the [International] Court decided the issue exclusively on the basis of the principle of restrictive interpretation." [186] Elsewhere he urged that it has been so severely limited in possible range of application in past practice that it has been virtually abandoned, and that whatever is left of its vitality will in all probability disappear in the near future:

> there is reason to believe that the appeals to restrictive interpretation of limitations of State sovereignty will disappear from the pleadings of the parties and that it will be found practicable to dispense with the soothing concession of restrictive interpretation in "doubtful cases". As already stated, reliance upon that particular argument has been disappearing in fact; that process may be regarded as well-nigh completed.[187]

Needless to say, numerous publicists and decision-makers, to whose work we will presently turn, have questioned Lauterpacht's conclusion and have, in direct opposition, affirmed that the principle of restrictive interpretation has received "equally authoritative support" to that accorded the principle of effectiveness.[188] Lauterpacht himself on occasion gave hesitating acknowledgment to its consistent reception in past practice, while insisting upon several shortcomings which make the rule's effective application unlikely. Its inherent shortcoming, he urged, is that "A restrictive interpretation of the obligations of one party implies a restrictive interpretation of the rights of the other party. Undue regard for the sovereignty of one State implies undue disregard of the sovereignty of another." [189]

186. Id. at 61–62.

187. Lauterpacht, op. cit. supra note 21, at 305.

188. See, e.g., Schwarzenberger, op. cit. supra note 12, at 509–10; Fitzmaurice, supra note 21, at 22–23; Hyde, op. cit. supra note 2, at 1494–95; Hudson, op. cit. supra note 12, at 660–61; Hogg, supra note 14, at 19–28; McNair, op. cit. supra note 28, at 211–16; Fiore, op. cit. supra note 131, at 345; Phillimore, op. cit. supra note 39, at 113–22; Vattel, op. cit. supra note 132, at 210–11; Grotius, op. cit. supra note 131, at 414–21. See also citations to decisions of international courts below, and the collection of statements of the Permanent and International Courts in Hambro, op. cit. supra note 12, at 51–53, and Hambro, op. cit. supra note 38, at 41.

189. Lauterpacht, op. cit. supra note 29, at 306.

Based upon the version of the principle which Lauterpacht proposed, one which gains some support from the trend of decision among international tribunals, we would agree that this is indeed an important feature that should be called to the attention of any interpreter. Features such as these, in fact, provide additional justification for considering the principle in the broader sense which we reviewed above, in which the recommended formulation would be specified in terms of the expectations of the parties concerning the importance of objectives at various levels of intensity in demand—thus taking into consideration their natural concern with protecting state sovereignty, as well as in promoting the wider shaping and sharing of all values across state boundaries.

Earlier support of the principle of restrictive interpretation given by national and international tribunals reflects, despite the emphasis of writers such as Vattel and Grotius, an almost total concern with the policy of protecting sovereignty by restricting inferences in favor of state obligations. Thus in the *North Atlantic Coast Fisheries* case,[190] the tribunal commented that "a line which would limit the exercise of sovereignty of a state within the limits of its own territory, can be drawn only on the ground of expressed stipulation, and not by implication from stipulations concerning a different subject matter." [191] The facts which gave rise to this conclusion are well known. An 1818 agreement between Great Britain and the United States provided, inter alia, that "inhabitants of the said United States shall have forever, in common with the subjects of His Britannic Majesty, the liberty to take fish of every kind" from specified areas of the coasts of Newfoundland and Labrador, and that in all other areas "the United States hereby renounce forever any liberty heretofore enjoyed or claimed by the inhabitants thereof, to take, dry, or cure fish on, or within three marine miles of any of the coasts, bays, creeks, or harbors of His Britannic Majesty's dominions in America." [192] Of the several differences which had arisen between the two parties over the appropriate interpretation of these provisions, the initial one (presented in a joint question to the tribunal) related to the extent of legitimate regulation which Great Britain could exercise over the rights exercisable within the specified "open" area. Issues were

190. (1910), reported in 1 Scott, *Hague Court Reports* 141 (1916).
191. Id. at 169.
192. Id. at 147.

raised, for example, over whether Britain should be allowed to restrict the hours and seasons of fishing, the implements to be used, and other similar regulations. While the United States agreed that some legislation, if reasonably related to the preservation of common interests and nondiscriminatory as between Canadian and American fishermen, was desirable, it objected to the specific measures enacted and enforced by Great Britain. It also argued that any such legislation should be *bilateral,* i.e., that all questions of "appropriateness, necessity, reasonableness, and fairness be determined by the United States and Great Britain by common accord and the United States concurs in their enforcement." [193] Rejecting both contentions, the Court, as quoted above, invoked the doctrine of restrictive interpretation to find that Great Britain could impair its sovereignty only by grants of "express stipulation." The ultimate effect of this attitude was to shift to the United States the burden of disproving the presumption in favor of sovereignty, a burden which the Court subsequently concluded had not been upheld.[194]

The customary statement of the situation authorizing the use of the principle of restrictive interpretation was given at an early date in *The "Kronprinz Gustaf Adolf"* case,[195] where the tribunal was called upon to assess the legality—under Swedish-American commercial agreements—of the wartime (1917) emergency detention of Swedish ships in New York:

> considering the natural state of liberty and independence which is inherent in sovereign States, they are not to be presumed to have abandoned any part thereof, the consequence being that the high contracting Parties to a Treaty are to be considered as bound only within the limits of what can be clearly and unequivocally found in the provisions agreed to and that those provisions, in case of doubt, are to be interpreted in favor of the natural liberty and independence of the Party concerned.

This principle was subsequently reaffirmed in the well-known case concerning the *Radio Corporation of America v. The National*

193. Id. at 149.

194. Id. at 169–72.

195. (1932), reported in 2 U.N. Rep. Int'l Arb. Awards 1239, 1254. See also the formulation and application of the rule in relation to the question of jurisdiction in the *Colombian Bond* cases, 4 Moore, *International Arbitrations* 3612, 3614 (1898).

Government of the Republic of China.[196] In this case, R.C.A. claimed that it had been granted the exclusive right to establish U.S.–Chinese radio communications, inter alia, under paragraph 3 of their agreement of November 10, 1928. The paragraph stipulated, in relevant part, that "The Council (the Chinese Government) shall transmit every message within its control destined to the United States of America or intended for transit through the United States unless routed otherwise by sender." [197] Shortly after the conclusion of this agreement, the Chinese government authorized an additional, parallel service by a different company. The tribunal admitted, somewhat paradoxically, that paragraph 3 had "established for the Radio Corporation a privileged position with regard to other possible circuits" but that such a privilege was limited to the fact that R.C.A. was to be "given all the radio traffic which is not being routed otherwise." [198]

In denying R.C.A.'s claim, the tribunal applied what it called the "correct rule, known and recognized in common law as well as in international law," namely, "that any restriction of a contracting government's rights must be effected in a clear and distinct manner." [199] The tribunal conceded that while "The Chinese Government can certainly sign away a part of its liberty of action" nevertheless "as a sovereign government, on principle free in its action for the public interest as it sees it, it cannot be presumed to have accepted such a restriction of its freedom of action, unless the acceptance of such a restriction can be ascertained distinctly and beyond reasonable doubt." [200] It held in consequence that since R.C.A. had failed to demonstrate its exclusive authorization "beyond reasonable doubt," its claim must be denied. It relied therefore upon a restrictive interpretation of paragraph 3 in protection of China's alleged interest of sovereignty.

The Permanent Court of International Justice, on a number of occasions, affirmed the continuing authority of the principle of restrictive interpretation. In its initial contentious case, the famous *Wim-*

196. (1935); reported in 30 *Am. J. Int'l L.* 535 (1936); also in 3 U.N. Rep. Int'l Arb. Awards, 1621; and 1935–37 *Annual Digest of International Law Cases* 26.

197. Id. at 545.

198. Id. at 543, 546.

199. Id. at 540.

200. Ibid.

bledon[201] decision, it laid down the rule that when the fulfillment of one obligation resulted in a derogation of state sovereignty, "This fact constitutes a sufficient reason for the restrictive interpretation, in case of doubt, of the clause which produces such a limitation."[202] In this instance, the "clause" referred to was contained in Article 380 of the Treaty of Versailles, and provided that "The Kiel Canal and its approaches shall be maintained free and open to the vessels of commerce and of war of all nations at peace with Germany on terms of entire equality."[203] The incident which gave rise to the dispute under this article occurred when the S.S. *Wimbledon,* a munitions-carrying British steamship under French charter and destined for Poland, was refused passage through the Kiel Canal. The reason given by Germany was that she wished to maintain her position of strict neutrality in the Russo-Polish War, and that by allowing Polish arms to be shipped through the Kiel Canal she would lose this position. In deciding that the *Wimbledon* should have been allowed to pass—pursuant to Germany's obligations under Article 380 since she was not at war with either Poland or Russia—the Court laid down the above rule and observed that there could be no doubt that in this case "Germany has to submit to an important limitation of the exercise of the sovereign rights which no one disputes that she possesses over the Kiel Canal."[204] Nevertheless, the Court concluded that this limitation had been clearly stated in Article 380, and must not be allowed to be preempted by Germany's present concern over her neutrality: "the Court feels obliged to stop at the point where the so-called restrictive interpretation would be contrary to the plain terms of the article and would destroy what has been clearly granted."[205]

Similarly, in the *Treaty of Lausanne* (Frontier Between Turkey and Iraq) case,[206] the Court spelled out what was involved in the content of the traditional rule: "if the wording of a treaty provision is not clear, in choosing between several admissible interpretations, the one which involves the minimum of obligations for the Parties should be adopted."[207] In this case, Turkey argued that the princi-

201. *The S.S. "Wimbledon,"* P.C.I.J., Ser. A, No. 1 (1923).
202. Id. at 24.
203. Id. at 21.
204. Id. at 24.
205. Id. at 24–25.
206. P.C.I.J., Ser. B, No. 12 (1925).
207. Id. at 25.

ple of restrictive interpretation should be applied, in the absence of a clear text, to deny final and binding status to the League Council determination of the Iraq-Turkey frontier under Article 3 (2) of the Treaty of Lausanne. The Court, however, rejected this argument, while affirming the Turkish formulation of the principle in general terms: "This principle [of restrictive interpretation] may be admitted to be sound. In the present case, however, the argument is valueless, because, in the Court's opinion, the wording of Article 3 is clear." [208]

In other cases, the Permanent Court indicated, though without explicit discussion, its willingness to apply this version of the principle of restrictive interpretation. Thus in the case concerning *Polish War Vessels in the Port of Danzig,*[209] the Court interpreted Part III, Section XI, of the Treaty of Versailles and concluded that it made "no mention of Polish war vessels in connection with Danzig." There was, to be sure, evidence that the matter had been discussed in the preliminary negotiations at Versailles, at least to the extent that Poland had been guaranteed "free and secure access to the sea," [210] but the Court saw no license in this fact to go beyond the "natural interpretation" of the provisions ultimately inserted in the Treaty. The crucial provision, Article 104, only granted unrestricted access to Polish ships in Danzig which were "necessary for Polish exports and imports." Since war vessels were obviously not covered by Article 104, and no mention of them was made elsewhere, the Court did not believe that the parties left any reliable index of their intention to extend the class of ships given free access. Following its ruling that since "the rights claimed by Poland would be exercised in derogation of the rights of the Free City . . . [and] must therefore be established on a clear basis" the Court held that unrestricted access to Polish war vessels must be denied.[211]

208. Ibid.
209. *Access to, or Anchorage in, the Port of Danzig of Polish War Vessels,* P.C.I.J., Ser. A/B, No. 43 (1931).
210. Id. at 142.
211. Ibid. See also *The S.S. "Lotus"* case, P.C.I.J., Ser. A, No. 10 (1927), and the case of *Phosphates in Morocco* (Preliminary Objections), P.C.I.J., Ser. A/B, No. 74 (1938), where international jurisdiction was not asserted under contradictory formulations of the restrictiveness doctrine. In the *Lotus* case, Turkish domestic jurisdiction was upheld in part directly through the principle that "restrictions on the independence of the states cannot be presumed" (p. 18). In the *Morocco*

The most extreme limitation, in general terms, sought to be placed upon the application of the principle of restrictive interpretation was proposed by Professor Verzijl as President of the Court in the *Georges Pinson* case.[212] He there asserted that the principle of restrictive interpretation, while a recognized interpretative canon in international law, should be applied only "in the case of the absolute impossibility of ascertaining the exact meaning" of the provision under consideration.[213] More recently, in the *Saudi Arabia-Aramco* arbitration,[214] the tribunal, while also observing that "the principle of restrictive interpretation should [not] be considered as abandoned" took a considerably more expansive view of its legitimate scope:

> As soon as one of the Parties has a doubt regarding the meaning and scope of the contract, in good faith . . . all the rules of legal interpretation may be resorted to. The jurist's art consists in choosing one or other of these rules, while taking into account all the peculiarities of a given case. The principle of restrictive interpretation aims at discovering the true limits of the obligations undertaken by the parties to a contract, and at maintaining the integrity of this contract by eliminating obligations which are not necessary to the common purpose of the contracting parties. Since it has this function, it is a necessary corrective of the principle of teleological interpretation.[215]

---

case, however, the Permanent Court denied jurisdiction in the dispute between Italy and France by a manifestly restrictive interpretation of the French declaration of acceptance of the compulsory jurisdiction of the Court while commenting that there was "no occasion" to resort to the principle (p. 23).

212. (1928); reported in *Annual Digest of Public International Law Cases* 1927–28.

213. Id. at 427. The Permanent Court supported this limitation in the *Polish Postal Service in Danzig* case, supra note 140, at 39, when it urged that "the rules as to a strict or liberal construction of treaty stipulations can only be applied in cases where ordinary methods of interpretation have failed," and again in the *River Oder* case, supra note 33, at 26, where it proposed that "only when, in spite of all pertinent considerations, the intention of the parties still remains doubtful, that interpretation should be adopted which is most favorable to the freedom of States."

214. Supra note 174.

215. Id. at 86. 27 *Int. Law Rep.* 117, 191 (1963). For detailed analysis of the principle as stated to the facts of the case, see pp. 87–91, 27 id. 190–95. For a statement of the facts of the case see supra p. 170.

What emerges from this statement is a clearly broadened notion of the principle of restrictive interpretation, one no longer invoked in blind subservience to the freedom of states, but instead employed as a helpful tool in ascertaining the genuine shared expectations of the parties.

A similar tendency to enlarge the scope of the principle, to view it as a "necessary corrective" to the excessive application of the effectiveness doctrine, may be discerned in the jurisprudence of the International Court.[216] In the *Peace Treaties* case,[217] for example, in interpreting the arbitration provisions in the peace treaties with Bulgaria, Hungary, and Romania, the Court held that the obligation to arbitrate, and especially the procedures authorized to bring it about, must be interpreted restrictively. Specifically, it held that the power given the United Nations Secretary-General to appoint a third, neutral arbitrator must be restricted so as to deny him authority to appoint the third arbitrator prior to the selection of the various participants' representatives on the arbitral commission.[218] The Court observed that "The Secretary-General's power to appoint a third member is derived solely from the agreement of the parties as expressed in the disputed clause of the Treaties; by its very nature such a clause must be strictly construed and can be applied only in the case expressly provided for therein." [219] As a result, the Court concluded that "The power conferred upon the Secretary-General to help the parties out of the difficulty of agreeing upon a third member cannot be extended to the situation which now exists," e.g., one in which a "complete refusal of co-operation" had been tendered by one of the participants.[220]

It should not be surprising, in light of the reluctance expressed in these decisions to apply the principle, that Lauterpacht and others have relied strongly upon such formulations in their rejection of its

216. Fitzmaurice, supra note 201 at 22–24; Hogg, supra note 14, at 27–28.
217. Supra note 167.
218. Id. at 230.
219. Id. at 227.
220. Ibid. See also, in this respect, the majority opinion in the *Case of Certain Norwegian Loans,* [1957] I.C.J. Rep. 9, esp. at 23–27. Cf. the joint dissenting opinion of Judges McNair, Basdevant, Klaestad, and Read in the *Ambatielos* case, [1953] I.C.J. Rep. 25, 33–34, and the dissenting opinion of Judge Read in the *Anglo-Iranian Oil Co.* case, supra note 101, at 143.

authority.[221] For this purpose, however, some characteristics of the range of operations which the courts are apparently attempting to circumscribe should be noted. It is not unfair to say that the objection to the principle most commonly expressed relates to a type of operation which results in arbitrarily limiting the obligations of states in those cases where all of the ordinary techniques of interpretation, when directed to specific provisions of an agreement, have failed to yield unambiguous indices of expectation. A policy designed to achieve such a limitation would, as Lauterpacht insisted, hardly be satisfactory, since the parties' more general goals, as well as the maintenance of appropriate world public order, may clearly demand the opposite. Therefore this version of the principle of restrictive interpretation, seen as an absolute prohibition of further analysis of the parties' more intensely demanded objectives, is as unsatisfactory as any other method of limiting recourse to relevant features of the context. Unless one is willing to argue, as none have to date, that the parties' expectations of giving effect to objectives at all levels of generality should be defeated by an absence of foresight and clarity at one level, the only consistent conclusion is that such a version of the principle of restrictive interpretation must be rejected as being incompatible with the fundamental community goal of ascertaining all genuine shared expectations of commitment.

A less circumscribed application of the principle, such as that first suggested by Vattel and Grotius and supplemented in recent times by Fitzmaurice and Hyde, has not been entirely overlooked in past trends of decision. The Permanent Court in the *Mavrommatis* case,[222] for example, held that Article 6 of the disputed protocol, which excepted prewar concession "readaptation" guarantees if the beneficiaries had not begun operations by the time the protocol was signed, must be interpreted restrictively since such an interpretation was "the only one which is in harmony with the system of the Protocol." [223] In this instance the employment of the principle was neither attached solely to considerations of sovereignty nor limited

221. Lauterpacht, supra note 19, at 56–67; Hyde, op. cit. supra note 2, at 1494–95.

222. *The Mavrommatis Jerusalem Concessions,* P.C.I.J., Ser. A, No. 5 (1924).

223. Id. at 49. Cf. the majority opinion in the *Nationality Decrees Issued in Tunis and Morocco (French Zone)* case, P.C.I.J., Ser. B, No. 4, pp. 24–25 (1923).

by adaptations of the plain and natural meaning rule; instead the Court utilized it after a consideration of the entire context of Article 3 and indicated that the expectations of the drafters of the protocol were that exceptions to the general rule—that prior concessions should be carried over into the postwar regime—should be interpreted restrictively to ensure the protection of the concessions involved.

The several instances which we have examined of applications of the principles of effectiveness and restrictive interpretation to situations of conflict among objectives of varying levels of generality, degrees of explicitness, and clarity of reference must not be interpreted, after the fashion of some writers, as reflecting general shortcomings of the principles themselves. The task of projecting the participants' genuine shared expectations by the rational employment of the principles of effective and restrictive interpretation, in the broad formulations which we recommend, is one of the interpreter's most difficult, but nonetheless most important functions in a world community committed to the policy of deference, within limits, to freely concluded agreements among participants as a primary instrument of order. It is essential, therefore, to gain an adequate perspective of the valid function of the complementary principles which are necessarily involved in this task, in order to avoid the mistaken conclusion that such principles are merely methods of obscuring the more vital, higher-level goals of the process of interpretation.

From an appropriate perspective of the tasks of an interpreter it is not difficult to identify the rational functions of the principles of effectiveness and of restrictive interpretation. The functions of these principles, as of other principles of interpretation, are twofold; first, to guide the attention of the interpreter to the various factors in the total context which experience has shown to be reliable indices of the major expectations which parties create in each other, and secondly, to articulate in convenient form the relevant established policies of the public order relating to the balancing of these demands and expectations at various levels of generality, abstraction, and explicit reference.

The complementarity in form of the principles of effective and restrictive interpretation—the fact that they are commonly conceived of and applied as logical opposites—need be no cause for doubting their utility, nor for doubting the ultimate rationality of the techniques of interpretation. Such complementarity in form, required for comprehensiveness of reference to the world of events, is, on the contrary, an indispensable aid to rationality in the search for expectations and policies. The total context of events, including the making of agreements and controversy as to their application, presents itself to an interpreter not in terms of neatly ordered logical isolates, but rather in terms of gradations and shadings in the processes of interaction. The complementarity in form and range of reference of these principles serves both to guide an interpreter to all relevant factors and policies in the context and to assist him in considering and ordering these factors and policies in relation to each other for the better securing of the expectations of the parties and other established policies of the public order.

The principle of effectiveness, it may be emphasized, need not be regarded as a mere truism that "clauses should be allowed to have their appropriate effects." Likewise, it contains something more than a vague reference to "liberal" interpretation or *pacta sunt servanda.* Everyone accepting a public order honoring agreement, as opposed to coercion, as a primary instrument of order is committed to the policy that agreements should be made effective: the difficulty is to ascertain the specific content of the agreement that is to be made effective. It is the special function of the principle of effectiveness both to direct an interpreter's attention to the more general, "essential" purposes of the parties in making the agreement and to prescribe that, when unfolding events inevitably lay bare ambiguities or contradictions of reference in the agreement and, hence, alternatives of interpretation with respect to the detailed practices by which essential purposes are to be achieved, such deficiencies in the expression of the agreement should be remedied and completed by an interpretation designed best to promote the essential purposes of the parties. The fundamental import of the principle is, in other words, to prescribe that the various detailed provisions of an agreement, whatever their apparent precision or imprecision of reference, are best interpreted in light of the essential purposes of the parties as determined in relation to all of the significant features of the context.

The principle of restrictive interpretation, as we have suggested, may be employed by interpreters as an indispensable complement to the principle of effectiveness. It too embodies more than a preference for so-called "narrow" or "strict" interpretations, or for the fundamental policy that in a free society agreements should not be made for or imposed upon the parties. It is the special function of the principle of restrictive interpretation both to point to the factors in the context of an agreement, such as the varying responsibilities of the parties as governments or private associations, which experience has established as valid indices of limits upon the expectations of the parties as to the extent of commitment, and to prescribe that the implementing inferences of an interpreter in remedying ambiguities or contradictions in the agreement should be confined to what is necessary to achieving the essential purposes of the parties, and should not be extended to imposing new purposes and unnecessarily detailed obligations upon the parties. The authoritative role of the principle is, in other words, to preserve the integrity of agreements as an instrument for ordering human affairs. Without such a limit upon interpretative inference it would be impossible for parties to enjoy any stability in their expectations from agreement, and a social order purportedly built on their expectations would be utterly subverted.

The principles of effectiveness and of restrictive interpretation are therefore two different sides of the same fundamental policy—that of securing and preserving the integrity of agreements by reference to the major objectives of the parties. The one principle is a positive formulation that ambiguities and contradictions in specific provisions should be completed and remedied in a way to promote the essential purposes of the parties; the other principle is a negative formulation that implementing inferences should be made to stop short of defeating these purposes, and of imposing unassumed burdens either of general or detailed obligation. "*Restrictive* [interpretation] is," as Lord Phillimore wrote, "the reverse of *Extensive Interpretation,* but founded upon the same principle of making the language correspond with the intention of the parties to the convention." [224] Although the reference which Phillimore makes to "restrictive" and "extensive" interpretation is linked with the community-wide or "ordinary" significations of terms, the policy which he outlines, applied to the recommended emphasis on participants' objectives at varying levels of generality, is of fundamental importance for a rational conception of the proper function of these complementary principles. For only when viewed as necessary alternatives in method for a thorough examination of the possible range

224. Phillimore, op. cit. supra note 39, at 113.

and intensity of objectives in the process of agreement do these principles become indispensable strategies to the decision-maker in his attempts to approximate the parties' genuine shared expectations in the context of world community policies.

The Principle of the Anticipated Solution

Detailed references to solutions anticipated by the parties to an agreement, but not explicitly mentioned by them in the agreed text, appear infrequently in past practice. Publicists have, in recent years, called attention to various factors which may affect the negotiators' decision to include or omit in the final text matters which were anticipated with varying degrees of explicitness in the preliminary phases of the agreement process. Authoritative decision-makers who might, however, be expected to weigh such factors in the settlement of disputes over the parties' ultimate expectations have on the whole failed explicitly to assess such considerations.

Hudson, in his discussion of the Permanent Court's treatment of the goal of ascertaining genuine shared expectations, commented that in relation to preliminary negotiations, "The parties seldom proclaim their intention in unmistakable terms . . . More often, the problem raised before the Court was not foreseen when the instrument in question was being drafted, neither the particular problem nor the general class to which it belongs; or if it was foreseen its solution was not definitely agreed upon." [225] Hudson recalled from his own experience in drafting international conventions that frequently "The conferences . . . did not have their attention drawn to the precise problems presented to the Court in the cases which have called for their interpretation and application." [226] The deter-

225. Hudson, op. cit. supra note 12, at 644.

226. Id. at 644 n. See also Hudson's further discussion of purposive omissions and ambiguities in texts of agreements, id. at 644.

Recently Sir Eric Beckett has pointed to one explanation of the difficulties, described by Hudson, of examining the materials of negotiation for the purpose of providing a reliable index of the participants' anticipated solutions. He suggests in the following manner the way in which this limitation may be discovered:

> often, a person reading the *travaux préparatoires* will come across something which, if he studies them in detail, he finds completely baffling. Something appears to have happened but there is no record of it at all . . . What, of course, has happened is that as the conference was making heavy

mination of the precise degree to which the contracting parties anticipated the dispute being considered, and of the limits of the proper scope and effect of such evidence in settling the dispute, is, as Hudson emphasizes, a highly relevant and important task which the interpreter may only carry out by means of a thorough examination of all relevant contextual features. To the degree to which such an examination reveals a specific anticipated solution, it should obviously be effected. More frequently, however, an adequate analysis of the parties' anticipated solutions reveals a gap in their expectations which must be resolved in terms of the established constitutional policies of the community.[227]

As one might expect, the International Court has on several occasions dealt with cases—especially those involving large, multilateral agreements—where the parties' anticipations of difficulties subsequently arising under an agreement were vague or otherwise inconclusive. In the *Genocide* case,[228] for example, the Court explained the omission of a special provision for reservations to the Convention on the grounds of its "desire not to invite a multiplicity of reservations." [229] In this case, the Court was called upon to determine whether reservations to the Genocide Convention were permissible,

---

> weather, some private meeting was called . . . That private meeting probably results in the adoption of a text, and the text is a compromise, but what people said about it at the time they agreed to it is not on record anywhere. Beckett, supra note 32, at 443.

The expectations of the parties in including or omitting any given solution to an envisioned conflict must therefore, in Beckett's view, be inferred primarily from the words of the text ultimately agreed on. Thus what promises to be, and unintentionally is an excellent reminder by Beckett of a repeatedly important feature of the context of agreement—the private conference—ends up as still another excuse for ignoring *travaux.* For what Beckett fails to consider is the possibility of determining, by an analysis of *travaux,* just what issues were deadlocked and what anticipated conflicts were resolved or left unresolved by such a conference. Obviously it is only by an examination of *travaux* that such a discovery of possible anticipated solutions could be made.

227. For an excellent recent treatment of this point, see Hexner, "Teleological Interpretation of Basic International Charters," in Engel (ed.), *Law, State, and International Legal Order; Essays in Honor of Hans Kelsen* (1964).

228. *Reservations to the Convention on the Prevention and Punishment of the Crime of Genocide,* [1951] I.C.J. Rep. 15.

229. Id. at 22.

and if so, what kinds of reservations were authorized. The Court concluded, after an analysis of the negotiations leading up to the Convention, that "Although it was decided during the preparatory work not to insert a special article on reservations, it is none the less true that the faculty for States to make reservations was contemplated at successive stages of the drafting of the Convention." [230] The Court thus concluded that reservations would be acceptable which, in its words, were "compatible with the object and purpose of the Convention" as determined by the parties themselves.[231]

It should not be surprising that more extensive references by decision-makers to explicit anticipated solutions of subsequent disputes are seldom found, since in the degree to which solutions are spelled out either in the text or in preparatory work the probability of the dispute reaching the level of community decision obviously decreases. However, the increasing diversity in the various indices of expectations in modern multilateral agreements, as indicated by recent holdings of the International Court, may serve to encourage litigation even in cases where one of these indices clearly outlines an anticipated solution. In addition, as Beckett has pointed out, participants may be induced to present claims, for various reasons of prestige or diplomatic advantage, even in the presence of explicitly communicated anticipations of present contingencies.

Situations

The Principle of Assessing the Particular Interactions of the Parties in Reference to the General Pattern of the Setting

Characteristics of the setting in which the parties commit themselves have been given some consideration by scholars and decision-makers, though usually in brief and general terms. An example may be found in the Harvard Research insistence that an agreement occurs "as a related part of the general setting in which the parties acted, and that setting must be taken into account if the purpose which the treaty was intended to serve is to be fully comprehended and effectuated." [232] More specific references to situational features such as spa-

230. Ibid.
231. Id. at 29–30.
232. Harvard Research, op. cit. supra note 3, at 953.

tial and time elements, degrees of institutionalization, and levels of crisis in the process of commitment are not often found in past practice. The few notable exceptions deserve more detailed examination.

SPATIAL POSITION

The degree of direct interaction among the parties in the process of agreement has frequently been considered in relation to the justification (or lack of justification) for ascribing to states which did not participate directly in the negotiation of an agreement responsibility for interpretations and commitments contained in the preliminary materials.[233] Although similar concern could be exhibited in relation to expectations of commitment based upon the parties' understanding of the final text, no explicit reference to this possibility has been found in past discussion.

TIME FACTORS

The duration of communication has commonly been considered relevant because of the light which it throws upon the evolution of the various parties' demands in relation to their degree of qualification and compromise in the ultimate agreement. Thus in the *Island of Timor* case,[234] the tribunal traced the successive reductions over time in the claims made by Portugal in her dispute with the Netherlands about their respective possessions on the island. The record of these claims was reproduced during the negotiations of 1902–04: "throughout the negotiations, [Portugal] found compensations deemed sufficient by her for abandoning the line . . . that she claimed. She finally accepted the line . . . claimed by the Netherlands *sine qua non*. Thus it is certain that this line . . . should be considered, in the intention of the parties, as a *concession* made by Portugal to the Netherlands." [235] The effect of this concession, viewed in terms of the historical sequence of claims, was the abandonment by Portugal of traditional claims of sovereignty over parts of the island expressed by boundary lines affixed to a map accom-

233. See the *River Oder* case, supra note 33, at 42, and other cases collected in Wright, supra note 88, at 103–07. See also supra, p. 146.
234. (1914), reported in 9 *Am. J. Int'l L.* 240 (1915).
235. Id. at 253.

panying the treaty. Portugal's concessions through time, formulated in terms of these lines, were held to be the determining indices of the parties' expectations even in the presence of some confusion in the various descriptions of the natural boundaries involved.[236] Other instances may be pointed to in which particular time sequences, usually in relation to the parties' successive assertions and withdrawals of claims in the process of agreement, have been considered by international tribunals.[237]

INSTITUTIONALIZATION

On several occasions international tribunals have examined relevant institutional patterns as contributing to the parties' shared expectations. In the case concerning *German Interests in Upper Silesia,*[238] the Permanent Court held that "liability to expropriation of rural property constitutes, under the Geneva Convention, an exception" to the institutional practices and procedures which the Convention established precisely in order to safeguard such property against unreasonable seizure, and that such exception must as a result be interpreted with great caution: "in case of doubt as to the scope of this exception, its terms must therefore be strictly construed." [239] The authorization of institutional practices by the terms of any agreement has long established a presumption that the parties thereby intended to carry out the agreement in the manner prescribed by the procedures of the institution. In the case concerning the *Jurisdiction of the Courts of Danzig,*[240] for example, the Court observed that the agreement (*Beamtenabkommen*) between Poland and Danzig must be considered as a contract of service between the Polish Railways Administration and its Danzig employees, enforceable in the Danzig courts, in large measure because of the change in institutional prac-

236. Id. at 267–68.

237. See *Treatment of Polish Nationals in Danzig,* P.C.I.J., Ser. A/B, No. 44, pp. 32–35 (1932); The *Mavrommatis Palestine Concessions,* P.C.I.J., Ser. A, No. 2, pp. 13 ff. (1924); (cf. also the decision in *The Mavrommatis Jerusalem Concessions,* supra note 222, at 9 passim); *Interpretation of Peace Treaties,* supra note 167, at 221, 226–29; and *The Minquiers and Ecrehos* case, [1953] I.C.J. Rep. 47, 71–72.

238. Supra note 118.

239. Id. at 76.

240. P.C.I.J., Ser. B, No. 15 (1928).

tices which it effected. Although the Court took judicial notice of the fact that "according to a well established principle of international law, the *Beamtenabkommen,* being an international agreement, cannot, as such, create direct rights and obligations for private individuals," [241] it nevertheless held that this rule need not apply when a special regime had been established to deal directly with contract rights of Danzig nationals:

> According to its contents, the object of the *Beamtenabkommen* is to create a special legal regime governing the relations between the Polish Railways Administration and the Danzig officials, workmen and employees who have passed into the permanent service of the Polish Administration. That this special regime . . . is to be governed by the very provisions of the *Beamtenabkommen,* may be seen for instance from an analysis of Article 4 . . . This article (No. 2) stipulates that Danzig officials are subject to the disciplinary laws of Poland . . . But No. 5 expressly stipulates that [if subsequent Polish legislation is enacted] 'these provisions' (i.e., the provisions of the *Beamtenabkommen* concerning discipline) 'shall be amended and brought into harmony with the Polish disciplinary law' . . . The necessity of resorting to this additional procedure . . . shows . . . that . . . in so far as the matters regulated by its provisions are concerned, the *Beamtenabkommen* constitutes a legal document governing the relations between the Polish Railways Administration and the Danzig officials.[242]

Since the relations of the Administration and its officials were to be regulated directly through the provisions of that agreement, the Court concluded that it therefore constituted a contract of service between them which could legitimately be enforced by Danzig courts. In so doing, it took appropriate notice of the fact that the *Beamtenabkommen* had in fact established an institution which controlled the contracts of Danzig nationals and which should in consequence be reviewable by domestic courts in the absence of an express stipulation to the contrary, or in the absence of any other specified recourse to adjudication under the agreement.

A paradigm example of the consideration of institutional practices

241. Id. at 17.
242. Id. at 18–19.

occurred in the recent *Inter-Governmental Maritime Consultative Organization* case.[243] In this case, which we review in great detail below, the principal issue concerned the institutional practice of determining the total seagoing tonnage of nations. Liberia and Panama, which were third and eighth in total registered tonnage, claimed election to the Maritime Service Committee of IMCO under Article 28 (a) of the IMCO convention stating that the members of this committee should be comprised of the "8 largest shipowning nations." Several other nations claimed that registered tonnage was not the best criterion for ownership, since most of the "owners" of Liberian and Panamanian ships did not reside or conduct much business in these countries and only used their respective flags for tax and other commercial advantages. While the Court's principal discussion was in terms of the plain and natural meaning of "largest shipowning nations," they did examine in some detail the institutional practices surrounding the wide usage of Liberian and Panamanian flags. A number of the indices which they considered, including Lloyd's of London's periodic listings of the largest shipowning nations and their total tonnage, were thought by the Court to carry more than mere paper significance. In light of the respect and other value consequences attributed by the shipping industry to these institutional practices, the Court upheld the right of Liberia and Panama to serve on the Committee.[244]

CRISIS LEVEL

Little explicit reference to varying expectations of crisis during the process of agreement is found in past practice. Consideration has occasionally been given in more general terms to the effect of high intensities of past crises upon subsequent agreements, as in the *Customs Regime* case, where the Permanent Court commented that "profound political changes resulting from the late war" made the political solution of the status of Austria "a sensitive point in the European system," in light of which the conclusion of the treaty establishing the Customs Union had to be viewed.[245] More specific refer-

243. [1960] I.C.J. Rep. 150.

244. Id. at 171–72. See particularly the Court's survey of the context of Article 28 (a), id. at 161–71.

245. *Customs Regime Between Germany and Austria,* P.C.I.J., Ser. A/B, No. 41, p. 42 (1931).

ences to the effect of successive levels of crisis upon the process of agreement are, however, rare and oblique in the few relevant discussions offered in past decision.[246]

Base Values

The Principle of Assessing the Value Positions of the Parties

The relative value positions of the parties appear to have been considered relevant to the determination of the parties' shared expectations on few occasions, and only a small number of publicists give attention to the problem. The few references which occur have been made in highly general terms to the concatenation of all values, rather than to any specific values directly affecting the parties' expectations of agreement.

Among publicists the most frequent insistence upon the examination of relevant differences in control over base values has come from Soviet writers. Shurshalov, for example, in arguing for the "repudiation" of all "imperialistic" treaties, contends that the "equality" of nation-states should be a necessary precondition for all valid agreements:

> It [the principle of equality] is especially important for treaty relations between states. Juridical equality of the parties to a treaty is looked upon in contemporary international law as one of the most important foundations for the validity and effectiveness of an agreement. Unequal treaties are justly condemned by the world democratic community and are considered to be either a relic of the past or a result of the imperialistic practice of the present. The institution of interpretation may not ignore this circumstance.[247]

The precise reference of "juridical equality" is not made clear. In addition, it appears that Shurshalov envisions that the principle will be applied to *override* shared expectations rather than merely to aid the interpreter in determining them. In light of these considerations

246. See, e.g., *Polish War Vessels in the Port of Danzig,* supra note 209, at 143–44; *Treatment of Polish Nationals in Danzig,* supra note 237, at 27–28. Cf. *The Free Zones* case, supra note 111, at 148.

247. Shurshalov, op. cit. supra note 109, at 26.

it seems unlikely that the principle as Shurshalov conceives it will provide any useful guidance to decision-makers in their primary task of interpretation. It does, however, offer some recognition of the relevance of differences in control over base values. Such an emphasis, misleading as it may be, is to be preferred to the total absence of reference by Western publicists to the role of base values in the making and performance of agreements.

The International Court of Justice, in the *Reparations* case, made a passing reference to the possible effect of differences in control over base values upon the expectations of the parties about the relevant sections of the United Nations Charter.[248] The majority, in holding that the United Nations possessed the requisite "international personality" to collect damages for injury to Count Bernadotte, commented that nations whose control over persons, resources, etc., was relatively less substantial, the "smaller and weaker nations," might be less able to promote effective claims for such damages: "it is essential that—whether the agent belongs to a powerful or to a weak State; to one more affected or less affected by the complications of international life . . . he should know that in the performance of his duties he is under the protection of the [United Nations] Organization." [249] Consequently, the inference was made that the expectations of the member nations, including not only nations predominantly "less affected by the complications of international life" but also nations of a higher degree of involvement, had been in favor of eliminating any likely inequalities in claim resulting from this type of difference in control over base values.

STRATEGIES

The Principle of Including All Strategic Acts

The total sequence of acts and deeds which constitute the process of agreement has been, as our discussion above demonstrates, regarded as relevant and subject to examination by various methods and principles in past practice. These methods and principles include emphasis upon signs of varying degrees of generality, abstraction, and ex-

248. For a more complete discussion of this case see p. 162 above.
249. *Reparations for Injuries Suffered,* supra note 150, at 183–84.

plicitness in the principles of plain meaning and of effectiveness, upon signs from different sources and in varying sequences through time in the principles of contextuality and *travaux préparatoires,* and upon acts of collaboration in the principle of subsequent conduct. Explicit reference, however, to the possible roles of signs and deeds in any given interaction and to the importance of taking into account all signs and deeds occurs infrequently in either past decision or writings of publicists.

One rather indirect emphasis on the importance of recognizing all strategic acts which has received increased attention in recent years requires brief examination. This emphasis was best formulated in the jurisprudence of the Permanent Court by Judge Anzilotti in the *Lighthouses* case when he said that "it is a fundamental rule in interpreting legal texts that one should not lightly admit that they contain superfluous words: the right course, whenever possible, is to seek for an interpretation which allows a reason and a meaning to every word in the text." [250] Judge De Visscher has reformulated the same rule for the International Court of Justice in his dissent in the first *South-West Africa* case: "treaty clauses must not only be considered as a whole, but must also be interpreted so as to avoid as much as possible depriving one of them of practical effect for the benefit of others." [251]

In the version proposed by De Visscher, such a rule is difficult to distinguish in operation from various others we have examined previously. Furthermore, it is safe to assume if any unique operation has been consistently invoked in past practice, it is the one most clearly expressed by Anzilotti, insisting that no interpretation should be adopted which leaves "superfluous" or "surplus" words in a document.[252] However, even this formulation of the rule leaves some doubt concerning its standard application. One alleged application of the "superfluous" or "surplus" words rule occurred in the *Anglo-Iranian Oil Co.* case [253] in relation to the declaration of acceptance

250. *Lighthouses Case Between France and Greece,* P.C.I.J., Ser. A/B, No. 62, p. 31 (1934).

251. *International Status of South-West Africa,* [1950] I.C.J. Rep. 186, 187.

252. See the discussion of past trends on this point in Schwarzenberger, op. cit. supra note 12, at 501–05; Lauterpacht, supra note 19, at 68–73, 77–80; Hogg, supra note 14, at 6–13.

253. (Preliminary Objection), [1952] I.C.J. Rep. 93.

of the compulsory jurisdiction of the International Court by Iran. This declaration reads in part as follows:

> [Iran] recognizes as compulsory *ipso facto* and without special agreement in relation to any other state accepting the same obligation . . . the jurisdiction of the Permanent Court of International Justice . . . in any disputes arising after the ratification of the present declaration with regard to situations or facts relating directly or indirectly to the application of treaties or conventions accepted by [Iran] and subsequent to the ratification of this declaration.[254]

Iran argued that this declaration, made in 1932, applied only to "treaties or conventions" accepted subsequently, and not to any subsequent "situations or facts" arising out of treaties or conventions signed at any time. Great Britain, in supporting the latter alternative, contended that Iran's interpretation would result in leaving superfluous terms, presumably the expression "after the ratification of the present declaration," while its own would not.[255] This argument is difficult to understand in light of the fact that an alternative statement of Great Britain's interpretation could be made as follows: "Iran accepts jurisdiction in any dispute subsequent to ratification which arises from treaty obligations accepted at any time." The claim that the words rendered surplus by Great Britain's version were less significant than those similarly ignored by Iran is thus hardly supportable. The provision, to be sure, was apparently drafted, as the Court preferred to put it, *ex abundante cautela.* In some cases, speculation with regard to specific wordings in clauses of this sort might yield useful results in excess of the policy of abundant caution. But such speculation would have to be supported by the demonstration that the alternatives were relevant to the presence or absence of superfluous words, and that some further justification could be found for *not* considering that they were inserted *ex abundante cautela.*

The very manner in which contracts, statutes, treaties, and the like are drafted should give doubt to the frequency with which the so-called doctrine of superfluous words is helpful in the process of decision. In the form in which it is presently stated, however, it is even

254. Id. at 103.
255. Id. at 97–101.

potentially misleading. Surely it is not a wise policy to favor the interpretation which gives effect to all terms "whenever possible." A better formulation might read "whenever the parties themselves intended the terms to be given effect." For this determination, all relevant evidence from the total context would of course be admissible to indicate whether or not they did in fact have a specific justification for the inclusion of provisions which may appear, *prima facie,* to be superfluous.[256]

Other references to the importance of giving appropriate weight to all strategic acts are contained in the familiar insistence upon construing agreements as a whole, as well as in the frequent demand that an entire course of pre-outcome and post-outcome behavior be considered by decision-makers in resolving disputes. Reference may be made to our treatment of these topics elsewhere.[257]

The Principle of the Preferred Mode of Expression

Nearly all past scholars and decision-makers have focused attention upon the various modalities of expression to which the parties show preference in expressing their ultimate expectations of commitment, but by far the greatest emphasis has been placed upon the examination of different features of the text of the agreement itself. In general, words—as opposed to gestures or deeds—have been seen as the preferred mode of expression in the agreement-making process, and more specifically words formalized at the outcome phase of that process. A few scant references can, however, be found to the consideration by decision-makers of the impact of gestures—if only grossly detected ones—and deeds upon the agreement process.

Emphasis upon careful consideration of the concatenation of relevant words in an agreement is of course ubiquitous, while at the same time being almost entirely confounded with the various phases of the process of agreement. Thus no explicit consideration of the effects of one mode of expression as opposed to another can easily be found in past decision. What one finds very frequently instead is an emphasis upon one part of the text or another, or upon preferring the present text to prior ones, or to preparatory work, etc. These ap-

256. For further discussion of the development of this rule in the jurisprudence of the International Court, see Hogg, supra note 14, at 6–10.

257. See (d) below, this section, and chapter 5, part 1.

proaches, treated in the traditional literature under the rubrics of "plain and natural meaning" and the principle of textuality, are discussed in detail elsewhere in this volume and need not be here repeated.[258]

Of the various modalities, gesture has been least frequently mentioned in the traditional literature. While one can hardly imagine that gestures have not played an important role in many agreements, for reasons that are not entirely clear (perhaps related to the difficulty in recording them unless they appear at the time to be crucial to the continuing consensus of the parties), they have virtually never been discussed in judicial decisions. One exception to this trend, in the *Eastern Greenland* case[259] before the Permanent Court, has been commented upon by several publicists. The facts in this case are well known; it involved a dispute between Denmark and Norway to sovereignty over portions of Greenland. While much of the case involved the presentation of evidence about various assertions of sovereignty over Eastern Greenland by both parties, two alleged "gestures" on the part of Norwegian officials were of particular importance. One involved the raising of the Norwegian flag in Mackenzie Bay by a group of hunters, which was adduced in evidence despite an apparent denial by the Norwegian government of its political importance at that time. This was, in our terms, more clearly a gesture than the example more frequently cited, which involved a response by Norway's foreign minister to a Danish claim of sovereignty over the whole of Greenland. In a private meeting with his Danish counterpart, he was alleged to have said in an offhand manner that Norway "will not make any difficulties" for a crucial Danish claim to sovereignty.[260] While gesture appears to have been involved in this transaction, and may well have been responsible for the somewhat different version adduced by the Danish minister, it is clear that this was primarily a verbal transaction. The Court, in holding for Denmark on a number of grounds, relied heavily upon this transaction, while implicitly discounting the Norwegian gesture toward sovereignty over Mackenzie Bay in Eastern Greenland as a purely private act unrelated to the continuing claims of the two governments.[261]

Comments by decision-makers upon the deeds of parties to agree-

258. See below, p. 216.
259. *Legal Status of Eastern Greenland,* P.C.I.J., Ser. A/B, No. 53 (1933).
260. Id. at 70.
261. Id. at 72–73.

ments as expressing their genuine shared expectations have appeared largely in their treatment of preparatory work and subsequent conduct, both of which have been discussed extensively in reference to the principle of contextuality.[262]

The Principle of Logical Relationships

Numerous problems in logic and syntax have in past practice received the attention of publicists and decision-makers alike, with the result that several allegedly logical rules have been developed in order to facilitate the analysis and, hopefully, the resolution of difficulties in interpretation. Extensive claims have been made for the relevance of these rules for the solution of disputes arising from logical or syntactic ambiguities. As we point out in some detail in the next chapter, these claims are frequently ill founded, not only because of the inability of the particular rules to deal effectively with syntactic ambiguities, but also because of their more fundamental inability to qualify at all as rules of logic or syntax. As a result, the inquiry prescribed by our recommended principle of logical relationship has received largely unsatisfactory treatment in past trends of decision and opinion.[263]

For purposes of our present analysis, what is perhaps most surprising is the absence of any general recognition on the part of decision-makers of the relevance or importance of examining syntactical ambiguities in the search for genuine shared expectations of agreement. While cases requiring detailed examination of such ambiguities are indeed somewhat rare, a much more satisfactory explanation of this absence would appear to be found in the relative directness and completeness of our inherited general vocabulary for describing logical operations. Its application in appropriate cases tends, it would seem, to be taken for granted and as a result directly carried out in quest of the actual shared subjectivities of the particular parties about possible logical relations. Thus there is very little discussion of the appropriateness or of the necessity of such inquiry, and one must conclude from this silence that its authorization is unquestioned.[264]

262. See above, p. 119; also cf. procedural contextuality discussed at 273 below.
263. For recent restatement of traditional views, see De Visscher, op. cit. supra note 12, at 113.
264. For an apparent exception see Bernhardt, op. cit. supra note 21, at 178–82, where traditional pseudo-logical rules are said to be "largely unnecessary."

Since, however, logical operations are commonly ancillary to other procedures, we have thought it more appropriate to discuss them in the next chapter.

Preliminary mention may be made of the efforts of decision-makers to locate their logical analyses, as we have recommended in the principle of logical relationship, in the larger context of their inquiry in order to maximize the probability of correctly determining the genuine shared expectations of the parties. On the whole, decision-makers have been extremely careful to engage in logical analysis not as an end in itself nor in final resolution of a given dispute, but rather as one of many means toward achieving the overall goals of interpretation. Various courts have engaged in syntactical or quasi-syntactical analyses in relation to preparatory work,[265] the features of the text or agreement taken as a whole,[266] the general purposes of the parties,[267] and the meanings of texts in other languages.[268]

The Principle of Adapting the Level of Generality or Particularity to the Other Features of the Context

Without direct recognition of the problem, past decision-makers have on numerous occasions sought to assess the level of generality of specific words or phrases in relation to features of the larger context. While the determination of level of generality is not often explicitly discussed, it is clear that the ascription of "meanings" to specific provisions is frequently based upon an analysis of the level of generality to be attached to such provisions in the light of the text taken as a whole or in light of other features of the total processes of agreement, claim, and decision.

265. Cf. *Guillemot-Jacquemin Claim,* reported in 1951 *Int. Law Rep.* 403. See also various statements by British officials on the relationship of the rule of *ejusdem generis* to the pre-outcome context of agreement collected in McNair, op. cit. supra note 38, at 207–10.
266. See the early case of *Factor v. Laubenheimer,* 290 U.S. 276 (1933). See also, the *Anglo-Iranian Oil Co.* case, supra note 253.
267. See the *Palumbo Claim* (1956), reported in 1956 *Int. Law Rep.* 499, 501. See also the report by J. D. Harding, Queens Advocate, commenting on the interpretation to be given an early British-Turkish commercial treaty, in McNair, op. cit. supra note 38, at 397–99.
268. See *In Re Esau* (1949), reported in 1949 *Int. Law Rep.* 482.

Indications of the level of generality given greatest emphasis in the communications of the participants—including position, repetition, elaboration, explicitness, degree of ambiguity, and many others—have received infrequent attention from publicists and decision-makers. Concerning position, for example, attention has usually been limited to discussions of the role of preambles in determining the parties' genuine shared expectations, especially in relation to their general aims and purposes.[269] Repetition and elaboration have not often been explicitly considered as indices of the parties' emphasis, but at least one attempt has been made to confer special significance on both, following the assumption that the parties had no intention to include superfluous passages in their agreement.[270] Explicitness and ambiguity have been considered, in an indirect way, in several of the traditional principles.

Direct invocations of the principle of adapting the level of generality to the context are rare. To be sure, recent trends toward an analysis of larger portions of the context, which we discuss under the rubric of the principle of contextuality, give general guidance in application of this principle. But more precise references to the use of such analyses in establishing the generality of individual provisions of an agreement are very infrequent. What instead more often turns up is a call for the interpretation of individual provisions in light of a much more limited feature of the total context, namely, the four corners of the text of agreement.

One of the traditional rules does appear to be directly addressed to the question of levels of generality. This is the rule of *ejusdem generis,* also referred to as the rule of *generalia specialibus non derogant.* The most familiar statement of this rule is that given by McNair, who presented it as "a useful doctrine or presumption, well recognized and frequently applied in English, Scots, and American law, to the effect that general words when following (and sometimes when preceding) special words are limited to the *genus,* if any, indicated by the special words."[271] Other writers, while restating the

269. For discussions of this problem and its past trends of judicial decision, see Hackworth, op. cit. supra note 38, at 245–46; Fitzmaurice, supra note 21, at 24–25; and Fitzmaurice, supra note 12, at 227–29.

270. Cf. Hogg, supra note 14, at 6–13. And see the further discussion of this problem, supra, pp. 195–97.

271. McNair, *The Law of Treaties* 393 (1961).

rule in similar terms, have been less hesitant to include the doctrine as an established canon of international law. Fitzmaurice, for example, has recently referred to it as an "ancillary" principle in the jurisprudence of the International Court of Justice.[272] His version of the doctrine, which he calls *generalia specialibus non derogant,* is somewhat more detailed than that given by McNair:

> It does not merely involve that general provisions do not *derogate* from specific ones, but also, or perhaps as an alternative method of statement, that a matter governed by a specific provision, dealing with it as such, is thereby taken out of the scope of a general provision dealing with the *category* of subject to which that matter belongs, and which therefore might otherwise govern it as part of that category.[273]

In addition to differences in detail, Fitzmaurice's formulation differs in an important way from that of McNair. Whereas the latter had focused attention primarily upon concepts ("words"), Fitzmaurice calls attention to comparisons of the relative generality of complete expressions, even entire paragraphs ("provisions"). This distinction, although not articulated by either author, may be usefully employed for the purpose of discussing the problems relating to levels of generality which have hitherto been brought to the attention of community interpreters.

The Permanent Court, in the *Serbian Loans* case,[274] advanced one formulation of the *ejusdem* rule which has been frequently reiterated in subsequent decisions. It asserted that "special words, according to elementary principles of interpretation, control the general expressions."[275] France, which had petitioned the Court on behalf of its nationals holding Serbian bonds, claimed that its nationals had an enforceable right against Serbia to be paid interest in gold francs as the bonds announced. Although Serbia did not deny that in most references to payment the terms "gold francs" had been used, it called attention to a few instances in which only the

272. Fitzmaurice, supra note 12, at 227.
273. Id. at 236.
274. *The Payment of Various Serbian Loans Issued in France,* P.C.I.J., Ser. A, No. 20 (1929).
275. Id. at 30.

term "francs" had been employed. In response to this claim, the Court invoked the *ejusdem generis* rule: "It is argued that there is ambiguity because in other parts of the bonds, respectively, and in the documents preceding the several issues, mention is made of francs without specification of gold. As to this, it is sufficient to say that the mention of francs generally cannot be considered as detracting from the force of the specific provision for gold francs . . . The bond must be taken as a whole, and it cannot be so taken if the stipulation as to gold francs is disregarded." [276]

In several early cases reported by McNair, applications were made of the *ejusdem* rule which indicate the way it has been conceived in past practice in Great Britain. What are more often shown are the limitations placed on it in application. A British Prize Court, in interpreting Article 11 of the Treaty of 1661 between Britain and Sweden providing "that no goods called goods of contraband, and particularly that no money, provisions, weapons, fire arms" and other munitions could be furnished to an enemy of either party, held that a Swedish cargo of pitch and tar fell within the provision. It observed that "those [items] enumerated were mentioned rather for example than by way of exclusion, and . . . there are other contraband goods than what are mentioned in that article." [277] Similarly, the British government argued in a dispute with Turkey over Article 2 of their 1838 treaty which abolished "all monopolies of agricultural produce or of any other articles whatsoever" that *rags* came within the provision, since the contracting parties clearly did not intend to limit the application of "any other articles" by specifically mentioning "agricultural produce." [278] These two instances, it should be recalled, are the central examples provided by McNair in his presentation of the *ejusdem* rule. This indicates, inter alia, that the rule has to be documented by instances which were predominantly exceptions or rejections of it. Thus the standard application of the rule would have produced the opposite result in the Turkish case, as British counsel admitted: "according to the most strict and legal construction, it might be fairly contended that the words 'any other Articles whatsoever' coming after 'agricultural produce,' ought to be limited by construc-

276. Ibid.
277. *The Med Guds Hielpe,* 1 Eng. Prize Cases 1 (1745), cited in McNair, op. cit. supra note 271, at 399.
278. Reported in McNair, op. cit. supra note 271, at 397–99.

tion to other "articles *ejusdem generis.*" [279] However, in the Swedish case the exception is not as obvious, since it is by no means certain that the class of items enumerated forms a subclass under "goods of contraband." The two could easily have been synonymous, which is what the Court appears to have found.

Still other conceptions of the rule may be found in American cases. Thus in the well-known case of *Factor v. Laubenheimer,*[280] the Supreme Court held that extradition could be granted of an alien who accepted money obtained by fraud, under a treaty which authorized extradition only if the accused knew that it had been "stolen or unlawfully obtained," since the word "stolen" could not be interpreted to restrict the latter phrase by *ejusdem generis.* The Court observed that: "the words of the treaty present no opportunity for so narrow and strict an application of the rule of *ejusdem generis.* The rule is at most one of construction, to be resorted to as an aid only when words or phrases are of doubtful meaning." [281] Similarly, in *Goldsmith v. United States,*[282] the Court held that the *ejusdem* rule could not be applied whenever the context manifests a contrary intention, i.e., whenever "the intention of the statute is clear." Restrictions such as these—in terms of the relative clarity of the provisions and more generally in terms of the whole concatenation of factors which comprise the parties' emphasis on one level of generality as opposed to another—are quite obviously attempts to modify the policy prescribed in the more unqualified statements of the doctrine. If the doctrine is to be retained as an aid in the interpreter's search for the genuine shared expectations of the parties, it would appear desirable that any unlimited rule such as "special words control general expressions" be qualified so as not to defeat the shared expectations of the parties to the contrary. Nevertheless, it is obvious that reference to the entire context in an undifferentiated way, as in the *Goldsmith* case, could be supplemented by more specific reference to features such as position and elaboration, to the overriding aims of the agreement, to specific elements in the pre-outcome and post-outcome interactions of the parties, and to degrees of explicitness,

279. Id. at 398.
280. 290 U.S. 276 (1933).
281. Id. at 303.
282. 42 F.2d 133, 137 (1930).

vagueness, and ambiguity in all phases of their communication.[283]

The broader formulation of the *ejusdem* doctrine, to include reference to whole provisions in varying degrees of generality, has frequently been invoked under the rubric of "effective interpretation." [284] More detailed consideration of varying levels of generality among particular provisions has become customary only in recent years, especially in the precedents of the International Court of Justice. In the *First Admissions* case,[285] for example, the Court concluded that Article 4 of the Charter, which dealt with the conditions for United Nations membership, could not be upset in its effect by Article 24, which dealt with the functions and powers of the Security Council, in determining, inter alia, the states that would be admitted as members. It argued that "Article 24, owing to the very general nature of its terms, cannot, in the absence of any provision, affect the special rules for admission which emerge from Article 4." [286] The Court's view that Article 24 is "very general" and Article 4 is "special" raises an issue with respect to the suitability of adapting these terms to the comparison of entire provisions, since a close reading of the respective articles would lead one to conclude that *both* could justifiably be called "general" in their terminology. Thus Article 4 speaks of admitting only "peace-loving States" which "accept the obligations contained in the present Charter," while Article 24 speaks equally generally of the Security Council's "responsibility for the maintenance of international peace and security" under the "Purposes and Principles of the United Nations." The Court's decision to call Article 4 "special" indicates its unwillingness to contrast it with Article 24 in the degrees of generality of its particular concepts. "Special" could thus be equally well contrasted with "less directly

283. See above, p. 156–86. See also *Ships Taken at Genoa,* 4 C. Rob. 388 (1803) and other cases cited in McNair, op. cit. supra note 271, at 397–99; *German Interests in Polish Upper Silesia,* supra note 118, at 33–34; *Aleksich v. Industrial Accident Fund,* 116 Mont. 127, 139; 151 P.2d 1016, 1021 (1944); *State v. Western Union Telegraph Co.,* 196 Ala. 570, 572–73; 72 So. 99, 100 (1916); and other United States cases collected in *Goldsmith v. United States,* supra note 278, at 137–38.

284. See this chapter pp. 156–86.

285. *Conditions of Admission of a State to Membership in the United Nations,* [1948] I.C.J. Rep. 57.

286. Id. at 64.

concerned in subject matter." Still, the *significance* of the two kinds of provisions is not a matter that can be legislated in advance of an examination of all relevant indices of the parties' preferences.

It is equally fruitless to reformulate the traditional doctrine, as Judge Hsu Mo did in the *Ambatielos* case, that "a specific provision prevails over a general provision." [287] Even if such an injunction is understood in terms of possible relevance in subject matter, it can hardly be supported as a general rule. It would be better, if somewhat less economic, to say that specific (central) provisions prevail over general (peripheral) ones only if all other indices both of the parties' expectations and of relevant community policies so require. Such a formulation would at least have the advantage of not misleading the decision-maker into thinking that he is relying on a general rule of unexceptional authority in justifying his final preference, but rather upon an indicator of the importance of all contextual factors in his final selection of the appropriate aspects of directness of concern, specificity, and generality.

Outcomes

The Principle of the Distinctive Phase of Agreements

The importance, in responsible search for the shared subjectivities of the parties, of placing special emphasis upon the outcome phase of the process of agreement has been widely recognized. This has been true even to the extent, as we saw above, of restricting recourse to important features of the context. The varying degrees of emphasis —from injunctions to ignore both pre-outcome and post-outcome evidence to more moderate suggestions that greater emphasis should, under most circumstances, be placed on evidence from the outcome phase—have been expressed in two different ways by past decision-makers. One urges greatest emphasis upon the *text* produced at the outcome, even to the extent of ignoring all else. The other urges that special attention be given to the phase itself, that is, to all the distinctive subjectivities common to the parties at this phase of the agreement process. These two emphases have caused past writers to recommend quite different operations, as well as different suggested weightings to be given to these operations.

287. Supra note 220, at 88.

The especial importance of the text accepted by the parties has been emphasized under a number of rubrics, including the principle of plain and natural meaning, the doctrine of merger,[288] the principle of "actuality" or "textuality,"[289] and many others. The aims of these principles have varied in a manner corresponding to their author's view of the operations required to indicate high deference to the outcome document. The principle of plain and natural meaning, as we will see in detail below, is most often employed to limit recourse to wider features of the context whenever the document is found to be *prima facie* unambiguous.[290] The other doctrines, as Lauterpacht and Fitzmaurice have shown, have also been used for various purposes, including limitations on contextual analysis, weightings of the various factors, and even widening of the view of the amount of the context which may be considered part of the distinctive phase of the agreement.

Lauterpacht, in his early discussion of the relationship of *travaux préparatoires* to the ultimate text of a treaty, provided the classic analysis of the doctrine of merger in its context of possible alternative effects:

> it is this final expression of will [in the final text itself], and not anything which may have preceded it, that reveals with decisive effect the legally relevant intention of the parties. It is of little importance whether we clothe this principle in the garb of a substantive or procedural doctrine; whether we give it the name of the principle of merger, or of integration of legal acts, or of "best evidence," or of exclusion of parol evidence. The result is the same. The principle that the final instrument supersedes the former conflicting expressions of intention is not a rigid principle of legal formalism but a necessary requirement of legal certainty, justice, and convenience. In this sense the principle of merger must be constantly kept in mind as a summons to caution whenever preparatory work is resorted to for the purpose of interpretation.[291]

The examples which Lauterpacht cites are said to be characteristic of the legitimate functions of the merger principle. Thus in the

288. Cf. Lauterpacht, supra note 7, at 586–90.

289. Fitzmaurice, supra note 21, at 9; supra note 12, at 211.

290. See infra, p. 216.

291. Lauterpacht, supra note 7, at 586.

Polish War Vessels in the Port of Danzig case,[292] the Permanent Court rejected Poland's plea that the assurance of open access to the sea allegedly given by the Allied Powers in pre-outcome communications be granted precedence over the specific solutions adopted in the final Treaty: "The Court is not prepared to adopt the view that the text of the Treaty of Versailles can be enlarged by reading into it stipulations which are said to result from the proclaimed intention of the authors of the Treaty, but for which no provision is made in the text itself." [293] Similarly, in the earlier *North Atlantic Coast Fisheries* case [294] the tribunal rejected the United States' contention that in negotiating the Treaty of 1818 Great Britain had implicitly disclaimed the right to exclusive regulation of the fisheries: "The tribunal . . . considers that such conflicting or inconsistent expressions as have been exposed on either side are sufficiently explained by their relations to ephemeral phases of a controversy of almost secular duration, and should be held to be without direct effect on the principal and present issues." [295]

These examples of the application of the doctrine of merger may, as Lauterpacht points out, be described in terms of the tribunal's response to the argument of counsel that extrinsic evidence is *incompatible* with evidence from the most distinctive phase of agreement. On this basis its relatively infrequent use is said to be explained: "it is only by way of exception that parties admittedly oppose preparatory work to the clear wording of the treaty; as a rule they invoke it to confirm their own interpretation." [296] In the latter event the usual restrictions upon recourse to extrinsic evidence are applied, as we have observed above; however, in the event of alleged *contradictions* of pre-outcome and outcome evidence it must be agreed that frequently the justification for preferring the outcome phase will be clearer. It is still doubtful, however, that more than a preliminary presumption in favor of the outcome phase should be established, since conceivably what appears to be the outcome may not actually be the climactic phase in the expectations of the parties. Such a situation is most likely to arise whenever, as in the *Polish Ships* case, gen-

292. Supra note 209.
293. Id. at 144.
294. Supra note 190.
295. Id. at 166.
296. Lauterpacht, supra note 7, at 588.

eral assurances are made in negotiation followed by a text drawn up by only one of the parties, in which the original assurances are purportedly incompletely provided for.[297] Under such circumstances, the factors to be weighed include the recipient's probable expectations from such assurances, as well as his more specific expectations from signing the outcome document. A principle ascribing a general, dogmatic preference to the outcome phase is not likely to be either useful or desirable under such circumstances. Lauterpacht recognizes this in his final comment on the principle of merger: "There is all the difference between using declarations made in the course of negotiations for the purpose of interpreting a final agreement and regarding them as the agreement itself . . . What ultimately matters in the process of interpretation is the common intention of the parties, not the intention of one of them as expressed in his drafts or declarations—except when there is evidence to show that the point of view there expressed has been accepted by the other party." [298] Once it is added that even unilateral expectations included in the outcome document will be defeated by genuine shared expectations based upon other indices, the doctrine of merger may be affirmed as a useful indicator of possible weightings of the phases of agreement in order to approximate the more exact expectations of the participants.

The only formulation of the principle of "actuality" or "textuality" that points to features of the context we have not emphasized previously is that of Fitzmaurice. He argues in favor of the presumptive importance of the entire outcome document in interpreting the various indices of genuine shared expectation. All too often, as we have observed above, the effect of principles of this kind has been to prohibit examination of important features of the context. The likelihood of such an effect may be seen in his very statement of the principle of textuality: "texts must be interpreted as they stand, and, *prima facie,* without reference to extraneous factors." [299]

297. For a discussion of the subsidiary doctrine of contra proferentem (infer against the draftor) which has been invoked in past decision and opinion, see Vattel, op. cit. supra note 132, at 199–200; Fiore, op. cit. supra note 131, at 343; 1 Oppenheim, *International Law* 860 (Lauterpacht, 7th ed. 1948); Hudson, op. cit. supra note 12, at 661; Lauterpacht, commenting that "the rule has not been prominent in international practice," collects some applications of it in his article cited above note 19, at 63–64.

298. Lauterpacht, supra note 7, at 590.

299. Fitzmaurice, supra note 12, at 212.

It is not surprising that Fitzmaurice finds support for such a rule in the announced perspectives of the International Court of Justice.[300] A number of maxims have been adopted by the Court to indicate its preference for the outcome text. In the second *Peace Treaties* case, for example, it stated that "It is the duty of the Court to interpret the Treaties, not to revise them."[301] The Court also decreed—somewhat more specifically—in the *Anglo-Iranian Oil* case that Iran's declaration of acceptance of its compulsory jurisdiction "must be interpreted as it stands, having regard to the words actually used."[302] And again in the *United States Nationals in Morocco* case, the Court said of the Act of Algeciras that it (the Court) "can not . . . derive from the Act a general rule . . . which it does not contain . . . [and similarly it] can not disregard particular provisions . . . which are, in fact, contained in the Act."[303]

As Fitzmaurice's formulation of the principle might indicate, such apparently unexceptionable dicta—when seen in their actual function and effect in the decisions of the Court—have become controversial and ultimately unsatisfactory. In the *Peace Treaties* case,[304] for example, the alternative which presumably would have led to a "revision" of the treaty was that which would have allowed the United Nations Secretary-General to appoint the neutral member of a three-member arbitration commission authorized by the peace treaties between Bulgaria, Hungary, and Romania and the Allied Powers despite the failure of Communist-bloc nations to appoint their own representative. The Court concluded that "The case envisaged in the Treaties is exclusively that of the failure of the parties to agree upon the selection of a third member and by no means the much more serious case of a complete refusal of co-operation by one of them."[305] Any discussion of likely policy bases for "extending" or restricting the anticipated solutions in the event of "more serious" conflicts, which one would expect in light of the Court's admission that the present conflict was not "envisaged," was not undertaken by the Court. It appeared to assume that a "strict" interpretation of the

300. Id. at 212–13; Fitzmaurice, supra note 21, at 10–17.
301. Supra note 167, at 229.
302. Supra note 101, at 105.
303. Supra note 125, at 199.
304. Supra note 167, at 228–29.
305. Id. at 227.

provision, based upon community policies the content of which was not specified, was within its competence, but a supplementation of gaps in whatever the parties "envisaged" in order to enlarge the powers granted was not. To "interpret" treaties, therefore, meant presumably to exclude the application of community policies for any purpose—even in the absence of explicit expectations of commitment on the part of the participants in relation to the point in dispute. The Court unfortunately did not have the effective power to preclude its decision from having inevitable consequences for general community policies.

In the *United States Nationals in Morocco* case,[306] the Court took the position that the United States' claim to full consular jurisdiction under the Act of Algeciras of 1906 was not justified under any of the fourteen provisions cited in litigation. It argued that no reference was made in the Act to *general* acceptance of existing rights which had accrued to France and Britain during the prior "regime of Capitulations" which the Act in its preamble purported to supersede. Thus the Court in effect held that the claim to full consular jurisdiction was not supportable on the basis of the existing rights of some of the parties: "An interpretation . . . establishing or confirming consular jurisdiction would involve a transformation of the then existing treaty rights of most of the twelve Powers into new and autonomous rights based upon the Act." [307] The Court also concluded that, solely from the "clear" indications of the text, the United States had been granted consular jurisdiction over *some* disputes in addition to, or in specification of, rights existing at the signing of the Act. In attempting to characterize the nature of these grants it pointed to Article 102, which stipulated that with regard to acts of fraud or smuggling "every confiscation, fine, or penalty must be imposed on foreigners by consular jurisdiction." [308] Although all of its conclusions in favor of limited jurisdiction were made on the basis of textual considerations, the Court, in one sentence, registered its belief that "Neither the preparatory work nor the Preamble gives the least indication of any such [contrary] intention." [309]

Although, as we will see below, the Court also invoked the

306. [1952] I.C.J. Rep. 176.
307. Id. at 198.
308. Id. at 197.
309. Id. at 198.

analogous doctrine of plain and natural meaning in both the *Peace Treaties* and *Iranian Oil* cases in order to further emphasize its preference for the outcome text,[310] the distinguishing feature of its more general preference in these instances is that it did not insist on applying only the "ordinary" or community-wide meanings of the concepts involved. The possible advantages of the formulations which the Court advanced, however, are attenuated in those cases in which the plain and natural meaning doctrine is subsequently applied, or in the larger number of cases in which the allegedly "contextual" operation is limited entirely to the document itself.[311] When the application of "plain" meanings is made a primary goal, the recommended use of the textuality principle—to focus attention upon possible weightings of various indices in determining the parties' conception of the distinctive phase of their agreement—has obviously been discarded.

The second emphasis in past practice upon the distinctive phase of agreement—relating to the expectations of the contracting parties at the moment of final commitment as opposed to the signs adopted in the outcome document—has received relatively little treatment either from publicists or decision-makers. Among publicists, Hyde most consistently supported the view that the parties' expectations at the time of final commitment should be effected as a general, and unexceptionable rule:

> Inasmuch as it is not the function of the interpreter to revise a treaty, as by putting himself in the place of the parties in order to produce a fresh accord, the need of ascertaining the sense in which they used the terms employed, or more broadly, of getting at their design at the time of contracting, is an unceasing burden. It is only through such an achievement that the interpreter is able to determine whether an alleged undertaking was as-

310. See below, p. 244.

311. The *Polish War Vessels in Danzig* case, supra note 178, at 209; *North Atlantic Coast Fisheries* case, supra note 190, at 187; The *Anglo-Iranian Oil Co.* case, supra note 101, at 104; the *Maritime Safety Committee* case, supra note 17, at 150. Discussions of the subsidiary question concerning what documents should constitute the "document itself" may be found in Beckett, supra note 32, at 440–43; and in the *Autonomy of Eastern Carelia* case, P.C.I.J., Ser. B, No. 5, p. 26 ff. (1923), and the *European Commission of the Danube* case, supra note 96, at 34.

> sumed or imposed by the agreement. The same test is invariably applicable regardless of the length of the interval between the date of the consummation of a treaty and that of an interpretative adjudication. In every case the interpreter must satisfy himself whether the contracting parties are to be deemed to have bound themselves to confer or withhold the particular privilege that is claimed by virtue of the arrangement.[312]

Lauterpacht appears to have taken the same position when he stated that "what is decisive [for interpretation] is not only the common intention of the parties, but their common intention at the time of signature, namely, their intention as expressed in the treaty." [313]

References by past decision-makers to the time at which the shared expectations of the parties is to be ascertained are contained largely in general and oblique descriptions of conditions prevailing at the time of alleged agreement. In the *Ambatielos Claim* case,[314] the Arbitration Commission referred to the fact that "Their [the parties'] wording was influenced by the customs of the period, and they must obviously be interpreted in the light of this fact." Similarly, in the *Morocco* case,[315] the International Court, in interpreting the scope of the term "dispute" in the Treaty of 1836 between the United States and Morocco, observed that "at the times of these two treaties, the clear-cut distinction between civil and criminal matters had not yet been developed in Morocco. Accordingly, it is necessary to construe the word 'dispute,' as used in Article 20, as referring both to civil disputes and to criminal disputes." [316] Such instances do not of course add up to adequate consideration of the pertinence of the parties' subjectivities at the outcome phase in the process of agreement.

Although specific applications of the concept of contemporary usage, such as those in the *Morocco* case, have not gone unchallenged in past practice, the generality with which the supporters of the concept have advanced it has given rise to dispute among writers as to the importance of changing conditions in relation to the goal of

312. Hyde, op. cit. supra note 2, at 1472.
313. Lauterpacht, supra note 7 at 590. See also Fitzmaurice, supra note 21, at 9–18.
314. (1956), reported in 1956 *Int. Law Rep.* 306, 321.
315. Supra note 306.
316. Id. at 189.

ascertaining the genuine shared expectations of the parties. The most vivid, if not the most characteristic, argument in support of giving effect to changed conditions in the process of interpretation is that of Judge Azevedo in the *Second Admissions* case: [317]

> interpretation of the San Francisco instruments will always have to present a teleological character if they are to meet the requirements of world peace, cooperation between men, individual freedom and social progress . . . To comply with [the United Nations Charter's] aims one must seek the methods of interpretation most likely to serve the natural evolution of the needs of mankind . . . Even more than in the applications of municipal law, the meaning and the scope of international texts must continually be perfected, even if the terms remain unchanged.

A similar feeling was expressed by Judge Alvarez in the same case when he commented that "a treaty or a text that has once been established acquires a life of its own. Consequently, in interpreting it we must have regard to the exigencies of contemporary life, rather than to the intentions of those who framed it." [318] Putting aside for the moment the difficulties of describing the integrations of community policies into the interpretative process raised in these comments by both Azevedo and Alvarez, we may distinguish two elements in the current preference for "teleological" interpretation. One is that, in speaking of the "natural evolution of the needs of mankind" and the "exigencies of contemporary life," obvious reference is made to changes in community policy and to the necessity of applying current policies even in the absence of changes in the expectations of agreement. This emphasis has earned for Azevedo and Alvarez the accolade that they would "involve tribunals in legislative instead of judicial or interpretive functions." [319] But a second emphasis may be discerned. Since changes in social, economic, or political conditions customarily bring with them equivalent changes in the parties' expectations, one may see in the position of Azevedo and Alvarez a call for the implementation of the parties' continuing consensus whenever it can be discovered. Such an emphasis would accord

317. [1950] I.C.J. Rep. 4, 23.
318. Id. at 18.
319. Fitzmaurice, supra note 21, at 8.

with more recent insistence on the importance of participants' authoritative or practical interpretations of their agreements, especially of the multilateral variety upon which Azevedo and Alvarez formulated their own positions.[320] But it is equally clear that, whether the agreement is multilateral or bilateral, "law-making" or "contractual," the discovery of the continuing consensus of the parties to an agreement is a goal of overriding significance in light of the commitment, accepted by all writers, to respect the integrity of agreements within the limits established by general community policies. The relatively greater degree of difficulty in identifying such a consensus in multilateral agreements is reason neither for ignoring entirely the possible relevance of such consensus, nor for insisting upon tying the parties' expectations to the time of initial approval. Neither does it provide any ground for refusing to implement relevant contemporary goals. To effect the current genuine shared expectations of the parties to an agreement—when such expectations do not conflict with more important constitutional policies of the community—should, as we have recommended above, be regarded as a highest-level goal of interpretation.[321]

Post-Outcomes

The consideration of evidence subsequent to the outcome phase of agreement has been undertaken, as we have seen above, mainly un-

320. See the discussion of authoritative and practical interpretation, supra, pp. 135–42. Note also the discussion of the relevance of contemporary expectation in Ch. 3, p. 98 ff.

321. Cf. Kelsen, *Recent Trends in the Law of the United Nations* 911 (1951):

> The author, however, is fully aware of the fact that the law of a community —national or international—and especially its constitution or constituent treaty, may be changed not only by formal amendments carried out in accordance with the procedure laid down for this purpose in the law itself. It may be modified also by its actual application based on an interpretation which, more or less consistent with the letter of the law, is not in conformity with the ascertainable intention of its authors. This is the way the law adapts itself to changing circumstances if it is too difficult or impossible to put in operation the amendment procedure. This is the case with the amendment procedure prescribed in the Charter of the United Nations. Since the rule of unanimity among the five great Powers having permanent seats in the Security Council applies to this procedure, amendments to the Charter are practically impossible.

der the rubrics of subsequent conduct and of authentic interpretation. Our detailed examination of the treatment accorded post-outcome evidence in earlier sections may be recalled and incorporated in entirety here.[322] The point requiring especial emphasis is of course the high deference given in virtually all past decisions to subsequent courses of action and explicit perspectives of modification on the part of the participants or their successors, as well as to changes in community policy in the lapse of time since the initial commitment.

Principles Relating to the Context of Factors Affecting the Process of Agreement

THE PRINCIPLE OF THE LARGEST SHARED AUDIENCE

Direct references to the relevance of shared audiences comprehending the parties to agreements have been made primarily in terms of linguistic usages shared in the different communities of the parties. Presumptions have been established in various ways, but in general the consideration of community usage has been limited to studying expressions found in the outcome phase of the agreement process. The principle which has traditionally dealt with such usages has been described by numerous titles, as in the various statements of preference for the "plain," "ordinary," "clear," or "natural" meanings of words in the outcome text.

The earlier versions of this doctrine, such as in the writings of Grotius and Vattel, noted briefly in prior sections, were frequently less extreme than versions employed in the decisions of national and international tribunals. Grotius, for example, commented that *"If there is no implication which suggests a different meaning,* words are to be understood in their natural sense, not according to the grammatical sense which comes from derivation, but according to current usage" [323] (emphasis added). Vattel, despite his unfortunately influential doctrine that a "clear" meaning need not be interpreted,[324] also held that if proportionate evidence was adduced to

322. See above, pp. 132–44.

323. Grotius, op. cit. supra note 131, at 409.

324. Vattel, op. cit. supra note 132, at 199.

prove that a contrary meaning was intended by the participants it should be adopted.[325] Pufendorf endorsed the "natural" meaning doctrine of Grotius; [326] and Suarez, who observed that "the law-maker is presumed to employ words according to their common usage," also believed that such a presumption "should necessitate some forcing of the strict meaning of the words of the law, because the law must be adapted to the customs of the [men who are bound by it]." [327]

Later publicists have favored the plain and natural meaning doctrine in a form more nearly approximating the prohibition of contextual analysis found in the past utterances of some community decision-makers. Phillimore, for example, lists as the "principal rule" of interpretation that one must "follow the ordinary and usual acceptation, the plain and obvious meaning of the language employed . . . If the meaning be evident, and the conclusion not absurd, you have no right to look beyond or beneath it, to alter or add to it by conjecture." [328] Hall, placing the same relatively insignificant restrictions on its application, presents the doctrine in this form: "When the language of a treaty, taken in the ordinary meaning of the words, yields a plain and reasonable sense, it must be taken as intended to be read in that sense." [329] And Fiore, placing no restrictions on his generalized version of the rule, argues that "The meaning of words used must be fixed and determined according to common usage, rather than according to elegant language with all literary niceties." [330]

325. Id. at 202–03: "All these wretched subtleties are overthrown by this rule, the justice of which can not be questioned: *When it is clearly seen what meaning agrees with the intention of the contracting parties it is not permissible to twist their words so as to make them give a contrary meaning.* It is the intention, sufficiently made known, which constitutes the real subject of the agreement, the promises that are made and accepted, the terms asked and granted. To act contrary to the clear intent of the parties is what constitutes a violation of the treaty rather than to disclaim the terms in which it is drawn up; for the terms count for nothing apart from the intention they express."

326. Pufendorf, op. cit. supra note 131, at 794.

327. Suarez, *De Legibus, Ac Deo Legislatore* 589, 587 (Williams et al. transl. ed. of 1612, 1944).

328. Phillimore, op. cit. supra note 39, at 99.

329. Hall, op. cit. supra note 130, at 344.

330. Fiore, op. cit. supra note 131, at 342.

More recent commentators have taken two noticeably different views of the plain and natural meaning doctrine. One group, reacting strongly to the traditional acceptance of the doctrine by jurists (and by publicists such as Hall and Fiore), reject the doctrine altogether, taking the view that it has been, or should have been, outmoded by the contemporary sciences of linguistic analysis.[331] Others, while rejecting the presumption against a full contextual analysis whenever a dispute may be solved by "plain" meanings, still see a useful function for the doctrine in the absence of evidence that the parties have used their expressions in a manner contrary to an apparent ordinary meaning in the total context of agreement.

Several American writers, following Wigmore, Holmes, and others,[332] have bluntly rejected the plain meaning doctrine, calling it, in the words of T. C. Yü, a "relic" of "primitive formalism," outmoded in the present century by "scientific rationalism":

> The mischievous nature of the rule lies obviously on the surface. It is . . . based on the false premise that language can be perfectly identical with human thought. That one term may be very plain under certain circumstances, but very obscure when those circumstances no longer exist; or that certain provisions in a contract may be very plain to one party, but ambiguous to the

331. For the most extreme statements of this view, see Yü, op. cit. supra note 12, at 79–85; Hyde, op. cit. supra note 2, at 1470; Stone, supra note 170, at 355–57; Cheshire and Fifoot, *The Law of Contract* 105–06 (3d ed. 1952); Schwarzenberger, op. cit. supra note 12, at 499–501.

332. See 9 Wigmore, *A Treatise on the Anglo-American System of Evidence in Trials at Common Law* 191–92 (3d ed. 1940): "There can be, in the nature of things, no absoluteness of standard interpretation . . . The fallacy consists in assuming that there is or ever can be *some one real* or absolute meaning. In truth, there can be only *some person's* meaning"; Holmes, "The Theory of Legal Interpretation," 12 *Harv. L. Rev.* 417 (1899): "It is not true that in practice . . . a given word or even a given collection of words has one meaning and no other. A word generally has several meanings, even in the dictionary. You have to consider the sentence in which it stands to decide which of those meanings it bears in the particular case, and very likely will see that there was a shaded significance more refined than any given in the word-book." And cf. Anzelotti, in the *Employment of Women During the Night* case, supra note 17, at 383, cited with favorable comment in Harvard Research, op. cit. supra note 3, at 947–48. For further discussion and documentation see McDougal and Gardner, in McDougal, op. cit. supra note 173, at 723–28.

> other, is almost a truism which no scientific mind will fail to recognize.[333]

Support for the position taken by the American writers, even in its most extreme form, may be found in other sources. Lauterpacht, who spoke at one time in terms of "undeveloped law" exhibiting "formalism and rigidity" through rules such as that of plain and natural meaning,[334] shortly before his death restated his dislike of the rule in these terms:

333. Yü, op. cit. supra note 12, at 55. Professor Hyde, the originator of this revolt as expressed in the field of international law, stated the position in somewhat more moderate terms:

> one must reject as an unhelpful and unscientific procedure the endeavor to test the significance of the words employed in a treaty by reference to their so-called "natural meaning" or any other linguistic standard, and then to attempt to reconcile therewith the thought or conduct of the contracting parties. Such a method involves the implication that those parties must be deemed to have employed words in a sense that usage may have decreed, even though contrary to their common design. It transforms the function of the interpreter from a fact-probing endeavor to ascertain the actual sense in which the parties used the words of their choice, to an effort to find what usage appears to decree as to the significance of those words, and thereupon to reconcile the conduct of the parties therewith. In so far as the interpreter essays to make that effort he is diverted from the task of ascertaining the truth concerning the design of the parties as exemplified by the text of their agreement, and endangers the success of such an attainment. Hyde, op. cit. supra note 2, at 1470.

Other American writers have taken the more moderate view that appropriate warnings against the possible misapplications of the doctrine should suffice. Hudson, for example, while commenting that its invocation by the Permanent Court was "soothing" on certain occasions, observed that "there may be some danger in allowing the 'natural' meaning to overcome the results of other investigations" of the total context of agreement. Op. cit. supra note 12, at 645. Chang suggested that the doctrine may not be applicable whenever "the precise sense in which the words were employed by the parties cannot be deduced from a mere analysis of the text." Op. cit. supra note 5, at 61.

See also Pound, "Spurious Interpretation," *Col. L. Rev.* 371, 381–82 (1907); 365; Hackworth, op. cit. supra note 38, at 246–255; see also Holmes in *Towne v. Eisner,* 245 U.S. 418, 425 (1918): "A word is not a crystal, transparent and unchanged, it is the skin of a living thought and may vary greatly in color and content according to the circumstances and the time in which it is used."

334. Lauterpacht, supra note 7, at 551.

> Upon analysis, there may be found to be little substance in the statement that there is no need to have recourse to preparatory work when the meaning of the treaty is "clear". As in other respects, so also here the doctrine of "plain meaning" may result in actual disregard of the true function of interpretation. What is meant by saying that the meaning of the treaty is "clear"? A phrase or word is seldom, if ever, "clear" in itself. A term is clear by reference to the mind of the judge.[335]

Other recent British works have provided strong rejections of the plain and natural meaning doctrine.[336]

The dominant trend of opinion among contemporary publicists would appear, however, to reject the notion that the plain and natural meaning principle expresses only "primitive formalism" and to find important functions for the principle. The view most commonly taken is similar to that initially taken by Grotius and more recently stated by Chang: "if there is no evidence to the contrary, it is natural to assume that the parties have followed the 'popular sense' in using words in a treaty. But if there is specific evidence to the contrary, the reason for following this 'clear meaning' in treaty interpretation seems no longer to exist." [337]

335. Lauterpacht, op. cit. supra note 21, at 138–39.
336. See, e.g., Cheshire and Fifoot, op. cit. supra note 331, at 106:

> It has sometimes been said, with a touching ingenuousness, that a written contract is to be construed according to . . . 'the plain, natural meaning'. In truth, the 'meaning' of a word is an elusive quality, the implications of which have in recent years been recognized by the development of a "science of language", baptized under the name of Semantics. The authors of the leading work upon the subject give sixteen main definitions of 'meaning', together with nine sub-varieties . . . Few words, it may safely be said, have a 'plain' meaning; and, indeed, if they had, disputes upon them would seldom arise. It is just because they are inherently ambiguous and well have been understood in different senses by the two parties to a contract that the Courts are required to interpret them.

And Schwarzenberg, op. cit. supra note 12, at 501:

> The most unsatisfactory features of this technique [of interpreting texts by the plain and natural meaning rule] are its presumptuousness, inarticulateness, and illogicality . . . it is hard to believe that the vision of the 'clear,' 'natural' or 'ordinary' meaning of a clause has descended on a supernaturally enlightened majority.

337. Chang, op. cit. supra note 5, at 56.

The latest important statement of this position is provided in the 1956 Resolution of the Institute of International Law concerning the interpretation of agreements.[338] The Institute's attempt to mediate the "natural and ordinary meaning" principle with other considerations is indicated in Article 1, in which, following the traditional statement of the principle, it is stipulated that if "it is established that the terms used should be understood in another sense, the natural and ordinary meaning of these terms will be displaced." [339] To be sure, the Institute's insistence that interpreters should "consider whether and to what extent there are grounds for making use of other means of interpretation" in addition to the plain meaning rule is hardly productive of clarity when Article 1 insists that the rule itself requires that "provisions of the treaty should be interpreted in their context as a whole." [340] But by "context" one may assume that the Institute refers only to the entire *text*.[341] The puzzling question is how extraordinary senses could be "established" (an allowance for

338. Reported in 46 *Annuaire de l'Institut de Droit International* 364–65 (1956). The Resolution is as follows:

Article 1

1. The agreement of the parties having been embodied in the text of the treaty, it is necessary to take the natural and ordinary meaning of the terms of this text as the basis of interpretation. The terms of the provisions of the treaty should be interpreted in their context as a whole, in accordance with good faith and in the light of the principles of international law.

2. If, however, it is established that the terms used should be understood in another sense, the natural and ordinary meaning of these terms will be displaced.

Article 2

1. In the case of a dispute brought before an international tribunal it will be for the tribunal, while bearing in mind the provisions of the first article, to consider whether and to what extent there are grounds for making use of other means of interpretation.

2. Amongst the legitimate means of interpretation are the following:
   a) Recourse to preparatory work;
   b) The practice followed in the actual application of the treaty;
   c) The consideration of the objects of the treaty.

339. Id. at 365.

340. Ibid.

341. The customary invocations of "context" have not been unambiguous on this point. Some writers use the word to refer to the *total* range of relevant verbal and nonverbal behavior: Harvard Research, op. cit. supra note 3, at 948, 953–56; Stone, supra note 170 at 357–58; Hambro, op. cit. supra note 12, at 68;

which is demanded by Article 1) without "making use of other means of interpretation" which the tribunal is granted the authority to deny. The Institute's wording unfortunately cannot be given a natural and ordinary construction on this point, for surely "making use of . . . recourse to preparatory work, the practice followed in the actual application of the treaty . . . [and] the objects of the treaty" [342] would ordinarily mean *consulting* or *examining* or *considering* such extrinsic factors.

To the extent to which a court accepted extrinsic evidence in attempting to establish a special meaning under Article 1(2), it would be *a priori* consulting, examining, or considering the very factors which it is asked to weigh and authorized to reject in virtue of Article 2 of the Institute Resolution. One possible construction of the Resolution would be that in which the terms "making use of . . ." would be interpreted as making use of (a), (b), or (c) in the tribunal's written *opinion* to justify its conclusion that the claimant's attempt to establish his extraordinary interpretation had failed. One might, however, question whether the authors intended only to comment on what items the decision-maker should include in his opinion, and whether perhaps a stronger statement, though unarticulated, was intended.[343]

Several recent commentators have indeed taken stronger, and on

---

Fiore, op. cit. supra note 109, at 343; McNair, op. cit. supra note 35, at 185–97. Others appear to refer solely to the entire text of an agreement or of related agreements: Hudson, op. cit. supra note 112, at 646–48; Fitzmaurice, supra note 20, at 11; supra note 12, at 209–10; American Law Institute, op. cit. supra note 1, at 131. The more consistent trend in international decision appears to favor the latter usage: *The Postal Service in Danzig* case, P.C.I.J., Ser. B, No. 11, p. 39, frequently cited in subsequent decisions; the *Second Admissions* case, supra note 283, at 8; and the *Maritime Safety Committee,* supra note 16, at 158–60.

342. Supra note 338.

343. For the reasons stated, the Resolution is not likely to provide very clear-sighted direction to interpreters who wish to obtain an adequate understanding of the proper role of the plain meaning rule. The major difficulty, of course, stems from the Institute's attempts, hesitating as they were, to provide a hierarchy among the various indices of the parties' expectations. We have urged above that the abandonment of this attempt, especially in relation to the plain meaning doctrine, is essential if a meaningful conception of the principles of interpretation is to be achieved. For further discussion of this point and the views concerning it by one of the Institute's members, Sir Eric Beckett, see supra note 21, p. 127.

the whole clearer, positions with respect to the plain and natural meaning doctrine. Stone has taken the position that since "the particular parties to a particular treaty may not use the general standard of meaning, but some regional or technical standard, or some standard peculiar even to them alone . . . it is that standard which must be applied, notwithstanding the canon of the 'plain' meaning." [344] The legitimate application of the canon, according to Stone, must be made under these conditions: "It is only insofar as no other common intention is to be found, and yet the words do have some relevant meaning by the ordinary standard, that a tribunal can fix the parties with that 'ordinary' meaning." [345] In commenting on the treatment of the canon by the International Court of Justice, a recent commentator, J. F. Hogg, has suggested that it has been most usefully applied in the absence of any other clear index of the parties' expectations concerning the resolution of their dispute: "The rule of ordinary meaning is an acknowledgment that where the thought and the understanding coincide, effect must be given to that agreement. Yet it is an acknowledgment also that where some or all of the parties could reasonably understand the words in a particular sense, effect must likewise be given to that constructive agreement." [346]

One noteworthy exception to the trend among recent publicists toward insistence on a thorough contextual approach is that of the International Law Commission. In its Report,[347] the Commission urges a carefully qualified reversion to earlier emphases on the exclusive priority of the agreement text and upon its "ordinary" meanings. The principal canon proposed is in fact that "A treaty should be interpreted in good faith in accordance with the ordinary meaning to be given each term" in its overall context.[348] This approach, which its authors call the "textual" approach, is given in its "very essence" as follows: "The parties are to be presumed to have that intention which appears from the ordinary meaning of the terms used by them." [349] This is indeed the only "autonomous" mode of inter-

344. Stone, supra note 170, at 356.
345. Ibid.
346. Hogg, supra note 32, at 401–02.
347. "Report of the International Law Commission on the Law of Treaties," U.N. Gen. Ass. Off. Rec., 19th Sess., Supp. No. 9 (A/5809) (1964).
348. Id. at 25.
349. Id. at 27.

pretation authorized by the Commission, all other modes being subordinated to a determination that the text is not clear in its ordinary meaning.

The members of the Commission insist that there is nothing novel in their recommendations and that, on the contrary, they merely codify a viewpoint that is "established law." [350] It is extremely doubtful, however, as our survey should demonstrate, that their formulation represents an accurate summary of past practice; on the contrary, the trend would appear to be decidedly against such a formulation both in decision and in the opinions of publicists. The Commission thus places itself in the awkward position of recommending a return to antiquated principles—principles never entirely accepted and increasingly rejected in recent years. It would be unfortunate if the highly authoritative character of the Commission's work should have the effect of rejuvenating the increasingly anachronistic Vattel tradition.

Some publicists have joined the ILC in disputing that any decline has in fact occurred in the International Court's application of the plain meaning rule. Fitzmaurice, for example, argues that the version of the rule emphasizing the primacy of the "plain" text over extrinsic evidence is "part of the settled jurisprudence of the Court." [351] Degan even goes so far as to assert that its application by the courts has been "unanimous." [352] The implications of the Court's jurisprudence were spelled out by Sir Eric Beckett in the 1950 session of the International Law Institute:

> The learned Rapporteur [Lauterpacht] argues that the Tribunals which have asserted this rule with regard to the plain sense of the words have tended rather to pay mere lip service to it . . . This criticism does not take account of the fact that the State litigants before the court naturally plead in the alternative. They first make their case on the wording of the treaty as a whole and . . . They then in the alternative go into the *travaux préparatoires* . . . The judgments of the Hague Court have frequently followed the parties in this course by adopting alternative grounds for the conclusion. They first give the meaning

350. Ibid.

351. Fitzmaurice, supra note 21, at 10. Similarly Bernhardt, op. cit. supra note 21, at 64–66.

352. Degan, op. cit. supra note 135, at 79.

> according to the plain sense of the words and declare that this really settles the matter, but then, since the parties have gone into the *travaux préparatoires,* they declare without prejudice to the main ground of their decision, and as an alternative ground supporting it that the *travaux préparatoires* when examined, only support the view that they had independently arrived at.[353]

The rule then, as Beckett conceives it, is one which prescribes the priority to be given textual expressions in relation to extrinsic evidence under procedural conditions in which all factors have been brought to the Court's attention.[354] The ultimate issue that can only be resolved by a careful examination of the conditions under which the Court has applied the principle—an examination which Beckett does not undertake—is whether such an operation can be successfully subsumed under the formulation of the rule usually given. For light upon this issue, we now turn to the decisions of courts and tribunals, both international and national.

The most influential formulation, in general terms, of the plain meaning doctrine was made by the Permanent Court in the *Polish Postal Service in Danzig* case: "It is a cardinal principle of interpretation that words must be interpreted in the sense which they would normally have in their context, unless such interpretation would lead to something unreasonable or absurd." [355] Since the Court made no attempt, in this particular expression, to give priority to its "cardinal principle" over other possible principles of interpretation, it should not be surprising that its position has been widely cited and approved.[356] Unfortunately, however, in most instances in which tribunals have applied the doctrine, such hierarchical relationships have in fact been established, with the result that it has customarily been employed to restrict the scope or effect of other principles or techniques of interpretation. The most frequent confrontations relate to (1) the examination of *travaux préparatoires,* and (2) the use of the principles of effective and restrictive interpretation.

353. Beckett, supra note 32, at 441–42.
354. For a similar conception, see De Visscher, op. cit. supra note 12, at 52–58.
355. P.C.I.J., Ser. B, No. 11, p. 39 (1925).
356. Cf. Stone, supra note 170, at 355–56; Chang, op. cit. supra note 5, at 56–60; Hyde, op. cit. supra note 2, at 1486–88; and Hudson, op. cit. supra note 12, at 645–46.

The immediate aim of the Court's statement in the *Postal Service* case was to deny the application of the principle of restrictive interpretation. In the sentence preceding that quoted above, it said that "In the opinion of the Court, the rules as to a strict or liberal construction of treaty stipulations can be applied only in cases where ordinary methods of interpretation have failed." [357] Since the reference to "ordinary methods" must be taken to mean the application of the principle of plain meaning, the Court here employed the principle to defeat Danzig's claim that the treaty stipulations granting postal rights to Poland in Danzig's territory be restrictively interpreted in its (Danzig's) favor.[358] Similar applications of the principle vis-à-vis "effective" interpretation may be cited.[359]

The more frequent use of the plain meaning principle, however, has been, as we have previously noted, to limit recourse to *travaux préparatoires*. The most familiar formulation of this doctrine is found in the *Lotus* case, where the Court said: "there is no occasion to have regard to preparatory work if the convention is sufficiently clear in itself." [360] The doctrine in this version has been invoked in nearly all discussions by the Permanent Court and its successor of the legitimacy of recourse to *travaux préparatoires*, and thus in a substantial number of the total applications of the doctrine itself.[361] In examining these applications, the matters of interest are (a) what standards, if any, have been invoked by the Court to determine what is, or is not, "clear," "plain," "natural," or "ordinary," and (b) what uniformities in effect, if any, have been achieved in restricting the employment of other methods of interpretation by means of the principle of plain and natural meaning.[362]

357. Supra note 355, at 39.

358. For a more complete statement of the facts of this case see above, p. 135.

359. Cf. the *Free Zones* case, supra note 111, at 13; the *Employment of Women* case, supra note 17, at 377; the *Peace Treaties* case, supra note 167, at 229.

360. P.C.I.J., Ser. A, No. 10, p. 16 (1927).

361. For a collection of precedents in the Permanent Court, see Hudson, op. cit. supra note 12, at 652 n.; for later decisions, see Fitzmaurice, supra note 21, at 10–11; Hogg, supra note 14, at 28–40.

362. In the discussion to follow, although emphasis is placed upon the decisions of the International Court, it should be obvious that in light of the early development of the plain meaning rule numerous other tribunals have appealed to its authority in a variety of contexts. A representative sample of such earlier cases may be found in Chang, op. cit. supra note 5, at 40–60; Yü, op. cit. supra note 12, at 81–137, passim; and Hyde, op. cit. supra note 2, at 1473–85.

The Permanent Court first applied the principle of plain meaning in its decision in the S.S. *Wimbledon* case.[363] In interpreting Article 380 of the Treaty of Versailles it stated that "the terms . . . are categorical and give rise to no doubt," and that they are "clear" and "self-contained." [364] The Court referred in these statements to the well-known provision in Article 380 that "The Kiel Canal and its approaches shall be maintained free and open to the vessels of commerce and of war of all nations at peace with Germany on terms of entire equality." [365] As we have seen, the S.S. *Wimbledon,* a British steamship under French charter carrying munitions destined to Poland, was denied access to the Canal on the grounds that its cargo was to be used by Poland in its conflict with Russia and that the cargo's shipment through the Kiel Canal would violate Germany's policy of neutrality as expressed in its 1920 Neutrality Orders. German representatives argued that Article 380 should be interpreted restrictively so as to allow Germany to protect its right to remain neutral.[366] The Court held that "the Kiel Canal must be open, on a footing of equality, to all vessels . . . of commerce, but on one express condition, namely, that these vessels must belong to nations at peace with Germany . . . If the conditions of access to the canal were also to be modified in the event of a conflict between two Powers remaining at peace with the German Empire, the Treaty would not have failed to say so." [367] Thus, manifestly, the Court invoked the plain and natural meaning doctrine to justify its conclusion that the Allied Powers, in drawing up the Versailles Treaty, had intended to confine Germany's right to deny access to the Canal to instances directly involving its own belligerency and that as a result the principle of restrictive interpretation urged by Germany could not be applied:

> the fact remains that Germany has to submit to an important limitation of the exercise of [her] sovereign rights which . . . constitutes a sufficient reason for the restrictive interpretation, in case of doubt, of the clause which produces such a limitation. But the Court feels obliged to stop at the point where the so-

363. P.C.I.J., Ser. A, No. 1 (1923). See discussion, supra p. 178.
364. Id. at 22, 24.
365. Id. at 21.
366. Id. at 17–18.
367. Id. at 22–23.

> called restrictive interpretation would be contrary to the plain terms of the article and would destroy what has been clearly granted.[368]

Again, in the *Acquisition of Polish Nationality* case,[369] the Court was called upon to interpret a provision, Article 4 of the Minorities Treaty of 1919, which it considered *prima facie* clear:

> Poland admits and declares to be Polish nationals *ipso facto* and without the requirement of any formality persons of German, Austrian, Hungarian or Russian nationality who were born in the [annexed] territory of parents habitually resident there, even if at the date of the coming into force of the present treaty they are not themselves habitually resident there.[370]

Before the Court, counsel contended that Poland's attempt to deny nationality to Germans whose parents did not reside in the annexed territory at the conclusion of the Treaty was authorized by Article 4 which applied only to qualified "persons . . . born" in the territory but who subsequently left. The Court rejected this argument, commenting that Poland's contention would amount to "an addition to the text," which would go "beyond its terms." If the persons themselves were not, by the "natural meaning of the words," required to reside in the territory at the time the Treaty was concluded, to require their parents to do so would be to impose a "useless" condition which was "not provided for in the Treaty" and which "would be equivalent, not to interpreting the Treaty, but to reconstructing it." [371] The Court added that its task in this instance was "clearly defined": "Having before it a clause which leaves little to be desired in the nature of clearness, it is bound to apply this clause as it stands, without considering whether other provisions might with advantage have been added to or substituted for it." [372]

In the *Exchange of Greek and Turkish Populations* case,[373] the Court relied on the "natural meaning" of the term "established" in Article 2 of the Lausanne Convention of 1923, which excepted and

368. Id. at 24–25.
369. P.C.I.J., Ser. B, No. 7 (1923).
370. Id. at 13.
371. Id. at 18–19.
372. Id. at 20.
373. P.C.I.J., Ser. B, No. 10 (1925).

forbid the compulsory exchange of "The Greek inhabitants of Constantinople [and] the Moslem inhabitants of Western Thrace . . . who were already established before the 30th of October, 1918" in these respective cities.[374] The Turkish government contended that "established" must be interpreted as understood in Turkish law, on the assumption that it would not have permitted the abrogation of a municipal law by international agreement in the absence of a specific provision to the contrary. The Greek contention was that "established" meant only, in the understanding of both parties, physical residence and the expectation of retaining it. The Court accepted the Greek position, commenting that while it was not required to offer an "abstract interpretation" of the term, "In the present case, the word 'established' . . . naturally embraces those inhabitants who, on October 30, 1918, were already residing at Constantinople with the intention of remaining there for an extended period." [375] With respect to the invocation by Turkey of the principle of restrictive interpretation, the Court said: "the obligations of the contracting States are absolutely equal and reciprocal. It is therefore impossible to admit that a convention which creates obligations of this kind, construed according to its natural meaning, infringes the rights of the High Contracting Parties." [376]

The Permanent Court's most widely discussed invocation of the plain meaning doctrine in relation to alleged overriding objectives—in consequence of the vigorous dissent it elicited from Judge Anzilotti—was made in its case concerning the *Employment of Women During the Night.*[377] In interpreting Article 3 of the 1919 Convention Relating to the Employment of Women, the Court referred to its terms as being "in themselves clear and free from ambiguity." [378] The central issue was whether the term "women" in Article 3 applied only to female manual workers (*ouvriers*) or to other female industrial employees as well. Article 3 required that "Women without distinction of age shall not be employed during the night in any public or private industrial undertaking, or in any branch thereof, other than an undertaking in which only members of the

374. Id. at 10.
375. Id. at 19.
376. Id. at 21.
377. P.C.I.J., Ser. A/B, No. 50 (1922).
378. Id. at 373.

same family are employed." [379] Although the Court indicated its willingness "to find some valid ground for interpreting the provision otherwise than in accordance with the natural sense of the words," [380] it could find none in the evidence presented by the parties. The majority held that the plain and natural meaning was consistent with "the title . . . the Preamble, or with any other provisions of the Convention" as well as its general aims and purposes as expressed in the treaty and in negotiation: "The grounds considered above upon which it has been suggested that the natural meaning of the text of the Convention can be displaced, do not appear to the Court to be well founded." [381]

Judge Anzilotti, after considering the same sources, reached the conclusion that the scope of Article 3 extended solely, in the intention of its authors, to women manual workers and not to women employees of managerial rank. The only conceptual objection which Anzilotti voiced to the Court's decision was embodied in his statement cited above.[382] He spelled out this objection as follows: "In my view . . . Article 3 should not be taken by itself and considered separately; it should be construed in relation to the Convention of which it forms a part and which, by its nature, concerns the employment of women manual workers." [383] Despite the vagueness of Anzilotti's warning against considering the provision by itself and in favor of relating it to the entire convention, it is still doubtful that he is pointing to any operations which the majority had not already undertaken. Instead he rejects the Court's manifest procedures in establishing the "natural" meaning of Article 3, claiming that they omitted reference to the Convention's general aims and purposes. The significance in Anzilotti's attack is precisely in its calling attention to the possibility that the Court employed the plain meaning doctrine to camouflage its decision to enlarge the scope of the Convention with respect to the employment of women during the night. From the evidence adduced in both opinions it would appear that his point is well taken—although his documentation leaves something to be desired—that indeed the general aims of the Convention centered

379. Ibid.
380. Ibid.
381. Id. at 373, 378.
382. See above, pp. 159–60.
383. Id. at 387.

upon the rights of manual workers. While the Court may have been justified in enlarging this scope—either because of an altered consensus of the parties or because an overriding community policy was at stake—it clearly chose, as Anzilotti usefully points out, obscurantist grounds for so holding. What both opinions left unanswered, of course, was whether in fact such a continuing consensus had developed with respect to nonmanual laborers or whether contemporary community policy demanded it.

The Court's employment of the principle of plain and natural meaning to preclude examination of *travaux préparatoires* has, as we have already indicated, been subjected to extensive analysis by a number of recent publicists.[384] Judge Lauterpacht, for example, in his Report to the Institute of International Law called attention to the instances, exemplified by the *Lotus* case, in which the stated function of the principle was to foreclose recourse to *travaux;* and to the apparently puzzling instances in which the Court announced, under the *Lotus* doctrine, that *travaux* would be examined despite the clarity of the text.[385] Other observations have been made of the Court's infrequent willingness to employ *travaux* after finding the text ambiguous, or, more frequently, after making no finding whatever with respect to the *prima facie* clarity of the text taken in its "ordinary" or "natural" sense.[386]

In the *Lotus* case [387] the Court was asked to interpret a provision, from Article 15 of the Treaty of Lausanne (1923), which would not appear on first observation to be a very likely candidate for the application of the plain meaning doctrine: "all questions of jurisdiction shall, as between Turkey and the other contracting Powers, be de-

384. Cf. Hyde, "The Interpretation of Treaties by the Permanent Court of International Justice," 24 *Am. J. Int'l L.* 1 (1930); Hyde "Judge Anzilotti on the Interpretation of Treaties," 27 id. 502 (1933); Chang, op. cit. supra note 5, at 95–120; Yü, op. cit. supra note 12, at 138–202; Hudson, op. cit. supra note 12, at 652–55; Schwarzenberger, op. cit. supra note 12, at 514–17; Lauterpacht, op. cit. supra note 21, at 49–60, 116–27; Stone, supra note 170, at 350–52, 357–59; for discussion of later developments, see Hogg, supra note 14, at 28–40.

385. Lauterpacht, "De l'Interpretation des Traités," 44 *Annuaire de l'Institut de Droit International* 366, 377–402 (1950).

386. See Hudson, op. cit. supra note 12, at 652–53; Harvard Research, op. cit. supra note 3, at 956–66; Hyde, op. cit. supra note 2, at 1488–92; see also Fitzmaurice, supra note 21, at 10–17.

387. P.C.I.J., Ser. A, No. 10 (1927).

cided in accordance with the principles of international law." [388] France contended that the phrase "principles of international law," construed in light of the preparatory work of the Lausanne conference, should be extended to exclude Turkish jurisdiction over incidents on the oceans such as that in which the *Lotus* was involved. This well-known incident involved the collision of the French ship *Lotus* and the Turkish ship *Boz-Kourt*. The Turkish ship sank, and after rescue operations the *Lotus* proceeded on its journey to Constantinople. Upon arrival, M. Demons, the *Lotus'* first officer and officer of the watch at the time of the collision, was arrested by Turkish authorities and charged with manslaughter. He was tried and convicted despite French complaints that international law forbade the prosecution by municipal courts of extraterritorial offenses by non-nationals. France also argued that the rejection by the Drafting Committee for the Treaty of Lausanne of a Turkish proposal for domestic jurisdiction over crimes committed within the boundaries of third states, especially, supported this view. The Court, in rejecting the argument by invoking the maxim cited above, commented specifically that "the words 'principles of international law,' as ordinarily used, can only mean international law as it is applied between all nations belonging to the community of States. This interpretation is borne out by the context of the article itself . . . In these circumstances it is impossible—except in pursuance of a definite stipulation—to construe the expression . . . otherwise." [389] Despite the Court's apparently final rejection of recourse to extrinsic evidence, it did in fact make reference to such evidence in the next sentence: "The records of preparation of the Convention respecting conditions of residence and business and jurisdiction would not furnish anything calculated to overrule the construction indicated by the actual terms of Article 15." [390] In response to France's assertion that the present Turkish position had been explicitly rejected in the course of negotiations, the Court agreed that

> It is true that the representatives of France, Great Britain and Italy rejected the Turkish amendment already mentioned. But only the British delegate . . . stated the reasons for his opposition to the Turkish amendment; the reasons for the French and

388. Id. at 16.
389. Id. at 16–17.
390. Id. at 17.

> Italian reservations . . . are unknown and might have been unconnected with the arguments now advanced by France.[391]

Although it must be admitted as plausible that the connection urged by France between its preliminary rejection of the Turkish amendment and its contention before the Court that municipal jurisdiction over accidents upon the oceans had been foreclosed by the Lausanne Convention was inapt, it is equally likely that the same goal—to insure disinterested settlement of disputes occurring beyond national boundaries—motivated all assertions. However, as the Court pointed out, an amendment restricting jurisdiction of Turkish courts to crimes committed within Turkey was also discarded by the Drafting Committee in favor of Article 15. Having usefully noted the equivocality of evidence from the records of negotiation, it is unfortunate that the Court reverted to its "plain text" argument to resolve an apparent conflict of intention which was scarcely enlightened by the words ultimately adopted. If, as one writer has suggested, a thorough contextual analysis would "point . . . conclusively to the different views held by Turkey and France in the matter," [392] in the absence of a more explicit final text the approach would be open to the Court to discuss and solve the dispute on more direct policy grounds. The Court's unwillingness to do this, as has frequently been observed, is perhaps the most notable feature of the *Lotus* decision.[393]

On at least one occasion the Permanent Court explicitly held that a provision under consideration was not clear and that as a result the materials produced in the course of negotiation could be legitimately examined. In the *Polish Nationals in Danzig* case,[394] the Court concluded that the terms of Article 33 of the treaty regulating Polish rights in Danzig were not "absolutely clear," and that in consequence "it may be useful, in order to ascertain its precise meaning, to recall here somewhat in detail the various drafts which existed prior to the adoption of the text now in force." [395] The Court then proceeded to analyze several of the important changes made by the Con-

391. Ibid.
392. Lauterpacht, op. cit. supra note 29, at 55.
393. Id. at 55–56. See also Schwarzenberger, op. cit. supra note 12, at 515; Chang, op. cit. supra note 5, at 99–102; Fairman, "The Interpretation of Treaties," 20 *Trans. Grotius Soc.* 123, 128–29 (1934).
394. P.C.I.J., Ser. A/B, No. 44 (1932).
395. Id. at 33.

ference of Ambassadors at Paris, including especially the ambassadors' memorandum to the Danzig delegation and the numerous drafts through which the final provision was processed.[396]

On another occasion the Court made an oblique reference to the failure of, inter alia, a textual examination and the resultant necessity of recourse to *travaux préparatoires*. In interpreting the Special Agreement between France and Greece in the *Lighthouses* case,[397] it commented that "where the context does not suffice to show the precise sense in which the Parties to the dispute have employed these words . . . the Court, in accordance with its practice, has to consult the documents preparatory to the Special Agreement, in order to satisfy itself as to the true intention of the Parties."[398] The dispute which had arisen between France and Greece, and which under the Special Agreement they had agreed to arbitrate, concerned a 1913 concession agreement between a French firm and the Ottoman government which renewed the firm's concession to maintain a system of coastal lighthouses around the Ottoman Empire. Shortly thereafter, however, as a result of successive military defeats, the Empire lost a considerable amount of the land on which the lighthouses stood. In various treaties, Greece obtained sovereignty over some of the land. The present dispute arose when Greece claimed control over some of the lighthouses operated by the French firm which were allegedly on its soil. Near the end of a long and complex series of disagreements, France (representing its nationals) and Greece signed the Special Agreement to have the Permanent Court determine whether the agreement of 1913 "was duly entered into and is accordingly operative as regards the Greek Government." The Court, laying down the principle cited above, said that it "cannot regard the expression 'duly entered into' as a technical term, invariably possessing the same signification" and that from its reading of the whole text "the precise import of the question put in Article 1 of the Special Agreement . . . is not clear."[399] Consequently, an examination of extrinsic evidence became necessary. After a thorough examination of this evidence, the Court concluded that indeed the 1913 contract was "duly entered into" and from further evidence that it was enforceable against the Greek government.

396. Id. at 33–39.
397. P.C.I.J., Ser. A/B, No. 62 (1934).
398. Id. at 13.
399. Id. at 13, 14.

The approach to the mediation of plain or natural meanings and preparatory work which has most troubled past commentators, as we mentioned above, is that in which the *Lotus* formula is applied *in addition to* a subsequent examination and discussion of the preliminary negotiations. This approach may be illustrated by the Permanent Court's decision in the *Employment of Women During the Night* case.[400] Although the majority held that the term "women" in Article 3 of the Convention of 1919 was "clear and free from ambiguity," and that the Court did not intend to "derogate in any way from the rule . . . that there is no occasion to have regard to preparatory work if the text of a convention is sufficiently clear in itself," it nevertheless found itself "so struck with the confident opinions expressed" in the preliminary negotiations that it did in fact examine extensively the relevant portions of the available records.[401] The Court concluded that these records confirmed its interpretation of the "natural" meaning of the article, namely, that no restriction to manual laborers should be inferred: "The preparatory work thus confirms the conclusion reached on a study of the text of the Convention that there is no good reason for interpreting Article 3 otherwise than in accordance with the natural meaning of the words." [402] The Court repeated this procedure on other occasions.[403]

Attention has also been called to cases in the two international courts, as well as those in other tribunals, in which yet another approach has been taken to the admission of evidence from *travaux préparatoires*. In these cases, the tribunals did not establish either that the text was *prima facie* clear *or* that it was ambiguous; neither did they discuss the propriety of examining and discussing the records of preliminary negotiations. Their approach was characterized by the employment of evidence from these records without com-

400. Supra note 377.

401. Id. at 373, 378.

402. Id. at 380.

403. In the *Treaty of Lausanne* case, supra note 206, for example, where the dispute considered by the Court related specifically to the successive steps of the negotiators in preparing the Treaty, the Court held that the text was "sufficiently clear," and yet at the same time proceeded to consider it "in light of the negotiations" leading up to the final commitment (p. 22). See also the *ILO (Agriculture)* case, supra note 91, at 41; *The Payment of Various Serbian Loans Issued in France,* P.C.I.J., Ser. A, No. 20, p. 30 (1929); *Interpretation of the Statute of Memel Territory* (Preliminary Objection), P.C.I.J., Ser. A/B, No. 47, p. 249 (1932).

ment, except for appropriate weightings of the relevance of this evidence to the genuine shared expectations of the parties.[404]

The treatment of the plain and natural meaning principle by the International Court of Justice had been similar, at least in broad perspective, to that of its predecessor. It has, in fact, relied explicitly upon the precedents established in the prewar period, especially with respect to the alleged need for recourse to *travaux préparatoires*. As the Court said in the *First Admissions* case,[405] in interpreting Article 4 of the United Nations Charter: "The Court considers that the text is sufficiently clear; consequently, it does not feel that it should deviate from the consistent practice of the Permanent Court of International Justice, according to which there is no occasion to resort to preparatory work if the text of a convention is sufficiently clear in itself." [406]

In this case, the Court affirmed the "natural meaning of the words used" in Article 4 (1) : "Membership in the United Nations is open to all . . . peace-loving States which accept the obligations contained in the present Charter and, in the judgment of the Organization, are able and willing to carry out these obligations." [407] The issue before the Court was whether a member state could condition its acceptance of a state petitioning for membership on grounds other than those stated in 4 (1) . Four members of the Court, in a minority opinion, discussed evidence from the preparatory work of the San Francisco Conference which they thought indicated conclusively that other standards of admission were anticipated by the contracting parties.[408] In declining to discuss this evidence, the Court in effect invoked the plain meaning doctrine in its strictest form to reject ex-

404. See Hudson, op. cit. supra note 12, at 653 n.; for later developments see Hogg, supra note 14, at 28–40.

405. [1948] I.C.J. Rep. 57.

406. Id. at 63.

407. Id. at 62.

408. Id. at 87–90. The central evidence discussed was taken from the minutes of Commission I, Committee 2, which drafted Article 4 (1) : "It was clearly stated that the admission of a new Member would be subject to study, but the Committee did not feel it should recommend the enumeration of the elements which were to be taken into consideration. It considered the difficulties which would arise in evaluating the political institutions of States and feared that the mention in the Charter of a study of such a nature would be a breach of the principles of non-intervention, or if preferred, of non-interference. This does not im-

trinsic evidence of the participants' intentions in the absence of either a very detailed, specific provision or agreement among the members of the Court that the provision, read in its natural or ordinary sense, was clear. As it observed in relation to 4 (1): "The natural meaning of the words used leads to the conclusion that these conditions constitute an exhaustive enumeration and are not merely stated by way of guidance or example. The provision would lose its significance and weight, if other conditions, unconnected with those laid down, could be demanded." [409] The Court did not refuse entirely to go beyond the "natural meaning" of the terms, as it cited evidence from the interpretation of 4 (1) in Rule 60 of the Provisional Rules of Procedure of the Security Council. The rule stipulated that "The Security Council shall decide whether in its judgment the applicant is a peace-loving State and is able and willing to carry out the obligations contained in the Charter, and accordingly whether to recommend the applicant state for membership." [410] The Court did not comment either upon the persuasiveness of this provision in relation to its decision (the assumption being that the term "accordingly" indicates the exhaustiveness of the conditions specified) or upon its authority for judicial decision. It was "observed" solely as further support for the disputed provision's "natural meaning." This "observation" by the Court followed immediately upon its rejection of recourse to *travaux préparatoires,* raising the question as to why one factor was legitimately "observed" and the other not. Even more important, however, was the Court's refusal to discuss any policy basis adopted by the drafters of the provision, or by subsequent interpreters, or by the Court itself, for the view that the provision "would lose its significance" if construed in a manner which made other alternative conditions of membership possible. If seen in the light of extrinsic evidence which, as the minority contended, would demonstrate the drafters' *intention* that the conditions be necessary but not sufficient, the provision would "lose its significance" under the Court's interpretation. The use of the plain meaning doctrine in this way, to avoid a realistic examination and discussion either of indices of the participants' expectations or of

---

ply, however, that in passing upon the admission of a new Member, considerations of all kinds cannot be brought into account." Id. at 88.

409. Id. at 62.

410. Id. at 63.

relevant overriding community policies can scarcely be justified by any standard short, perhaps, of the necessity of adjusting available time and resources to the importance of the issues presented. In light of the importance, especially in 1948, of admission standards to the United Nations, and the notably light workload of the Court at that time, its refusal to consider all relevant indices of expectation or of policy cannot be regarded as in the common interest.

The Court also invoked the plain meaning doctrine in the *Second Admissions* case.[411] In this case, the provision under consideration was paragraph 2 of Article 4: "The admission of any . . . State to membership in the United Nations will be effected by a decision of the General Assembly upon the recommendation of the Security Council." [412] The Court commented that it found "no difficulty in ascertaining the natural and ordinary meaning of the words in question and no difficulty in giving effect to them." [413] Although preparatory work had been adduced in order to show a contrary meaning, the majority held that "Having regard . . . to the considerations above stated, the Court is of the opinion that it is not permissible, in this case, to resort to *travaux préparatoires.*" [414] The conclusion of the Court is given particular significance by its description of the operational priority established in favor of the "natural" meaning doctrine:

> The Court considers it necessary to say that the first duty of a tribunal which is called upon to interpret and apply the provisions of a treaty, is to endeavor to give effect to them in their natural and ordinary meaning in the context in which they occur. If the relevant words in their natural and ordinary meaning make sense in their context, that is an end of the matter. If, on the other hand, the words in their natural and ordinary meaning are ambiguous or lead to an unreasonable result, then, and then only, must the Court, by resort to other methods of interpretation, seek to ascertain what the parties really did mean when they used these words . . . When the Court can give effect to a provision of a treaty by giving to the words used in it

411. [1950] I.C.J. Rep. 4.
412. Id. at 7.
413. Id. at 8.
414. Ibid.

> their natural and ordinary meaning, it may not interpret the words by seeking to give them some other meaning.[415]

An interesting feature of this case is that the dissenting judges, especially Alvarez and Azevedo, affirmed in equally vivid terms the majority's refusal to consider the preparatory work for the Charter, while at the same time arriving at the opposite conclusion as to what effect the "clear" text was to be given.[416] Although both Alvarez and Azevedo insisted on interpreting the Charter in the light of its general purposes, and, as we saw above, in the light of the "new international law" conforming to the "exigencies of contemporary life," there is unfortunately no real evidence either that the majority included or excluded such considerations. To be sure, the indices of its efforts to ascertain ordinary meanings in their *context* are too scarce to permit an adequate assessment of the operations which were actually undertaken. Nevertheless, the Court's references to the "context as a whole" on other occasions have served as operational equivalents of an examination of the higher-level purposes of the parties, and the likelihood of such a reference in this case should not be overlooked. Part of the verbal difficulties incurred by both the majority of the Court and the dissenters, however, derives from their failure to specify what operational differences, if any, are involved in construing the treaty's "natural meaning in context" and its "general purposes under current conditions." If none are involved, the more subtle differences in weightings of the various features of the context, including overriding community policies, should be more adequately spelled out. In relation to the central phrase, "upon the recommendation of . . . ," a more adequate policy would be, after considering all relevant indices of the negotiating parties' expectations, to admit its probable logical and lexical ambiguity and discuss the consequences for comprehensive public order of the two major alternative interpretations. In this respect, the dissenting opinions of Alvarez and Azevedo may be preferred for having raised the ultimate issue of the authority granted by the Charter to the various branches of the United Nations in relation to their respective rights and obligations concerning admission.

Other cases before the Court have elicited similar responses in

415. Ibid.
416. Id. at 18, 30.

favor of the plain and natural meaning principle, often in both majority opinion and dissent. The restriction put forward in the *Lotus* case on the use of preparatory work was, for example, affirmed in the *Ambatielos* case (Preliminary Objection).[417] Here the Court was asked by the British government, in one of its allegations, to consider evidence extrinsic to the Declaration of July 16, 1926, between Greece and Great Britain. It responsed that "where, as here, the text to be interpreted is clear, there is no occasion to resort to preparatory work."[418] The text of the declaration formed an integral part of the two central instruments which the Court considered. Together these were: (1) the Treaty of Commerce and Navigation of 1886, which in an appended protocol provided for arbitration of "any controversies which may arise respecting the interpretation or the execution of the present Treaty"; (2) the Treaty of Commerce and Navigation of 1926, which superseded the earlier treaty, but referred all disputes to the Permanent Court as arbiter; and (3) the declaration of 1926, carrying the same date as the Treaty, and providing that "the Treaty of Commerce and Navigation . . . does not prejudice claims on behalf of private persons based on the provisions of the Anglo-Greek Commercial Treaty of 1886, and that any differences which may arise between our two Governments as to the validity of such claims shall, at the request of either Government, be referred to arbitration in accordance with the provisions of the Protocol of November 10, 1886, annexed to the said Treaty."[419] The principal issue before the Court was whether these three instruments granted it jurisdiction to determine whether Britain was under an obligation to arbitrate its dispute with Greece over the *Ambatielos* claim. In concluding that it did have jurisdiction, the Court applied the *Lotus* doctrine to Britain's contention that an examination of the negotiation records of the 1926 agreement would show the parties' intention to deny any claim arising subsequent to that time (the Greek claim for Ambatielos had been formulated in 1933). Even though the Court, in stating the doctrine, insisted that the text of the declaration established no date-of-claim requirement and that "the only requirement is that they should be based on the Treaty of 1886," it nonetheless referred to the preliminary records and concluded that they "do not

417. [1952] I.C.J. Rep. 28.
418. Id. at 45.
419. Id. at 35, 36.

support the [British] contention. They show that although the Hellenic Government originally suggested a draft of the Declaration referring to *'anterior* claims . . . deriving from the . . . Treaty of 1886,' this draft was ultimately not accepted, and both Parties adopted, instead, the text of the Declaration as it now appears" (emphasis added).[420] The Court also invoked the plain meaning rule to deny the Greek allegation that since the 1929 treaty adopted many of the clauses of its predecessor, that the declaration conferred jurisdiction on the Court to adjudicate all claims based on the earlier treaty whose clauses had been retained. The Court held that this allegation "introduces a distinction for which the Court sees no justification in the plain language of the Declaration . . . The language of the Declaration makes no distinction between claims based upon one class of provisions of the 1886 Treaty and those based on another class." [421] Thus the Court concluded that it lacked authorization to adjudicate any claims based upon the earlier agreement.

In the *Corfu Channel* case (Preliminary Objection),[422] the plain meaning rule was invoked both to justify and to dissent from the Court's interpretation of its own jurisdiction under Article 36 (1) of its Statute, which reads: "[The jurisdiction of the Court] comprises all cases which the parties refer to it and all matters specially provided for in the Charter of the United Nations or in treaties and conventions in force." [423] The issue finally determined by the Court rested upon the first clause of the article ("all cases which the parties refer"). Albania had submitted a memorandum to the Court, following Britain's unilateral application, in which it indicated that it was willing, "notwithstanding this irregularity in the action taken by the Government of the United Kingdom, to appear before the Court." [424] The memorandum referred explicitly to "its [Albania's] acceptance of the Court's jurisdiction for this case." [425] It later objected that it had at no time submitted to the jurisdiction of the Court free of the prior determination of the legitimacy of Britain's application procedure. To the question of whether, by this declara-

420. Id. at 45.
421. Id. at 41.
422. [1948] I.C.J. Rep. 15.
423. Id. at 21.
424. Id. at 19.
425. Ibid.

tion, Albania had accepted the jurisdiction of the Court under 36 (1), the Court answered that the document "removes all difficulties" because the "language used by the Albanian Government cannot be understood otherwise than as a waiver of the right subsequently to raise an objection directed against the admissibility of the Application founded on the alleged procedural irregularity of that instrument." [426] Although Albania's commitment to "appear before the Court" would scarcely support the Court's assertion that the government had accepted its jurisdiction without reservation, it would appear abnormal, to say the least, for Albania to refer to its "acceptance of the Court's jurisdiction" if it intended to communicate that it wished, at a later time, to dispute it. What is perhaps more important, Albania was unable to point to any other indices of its intention, at the time the memorandum was conveyed to the Court on July 2, 1947, to dispute the jurisdictional issue. The sole remaining index, in the memorandum itself, gave every reason to believe that Albania was prepared to argue the merits of the case.[427] On this basis, the Court retained its conclusion that the *prima facie* expression of Albania's "acceptance" was its genuine intention at the time of the commitment.[428]

A more complicated conflict in the application of the plain meaning rule occurred in the *Inter-Governmental Maritime Consultative Organization* case.[429] In this case the Court was called upon to interpret Article 28 (a) of the IMCO Convention:

> The Maritime Service Committee shall consist of fourteen Members elected by the Assembly from the Members, governments of those nations having an important interest in maritime safety, of which not less than eight shall be the largest ship owning nations, and the remainder shall be elected so as to ensure adequate representation of Members, governments of other nations with an important interest in maritime safety, such as

426. Id. at 26–27.

427. The Memorandum stated that Albania "fully accepts the recommendation of the Security Council" which urged that the two governments "immediately refer the dispute to the International Court of Justice," and that it was "Profoundly convinced of the justice of its case, [and] resolved to neglect no opportunity of giving evidence of its devotion to the principles of friendly collaboration between nations and of the pacific settlement of disputes." Id. at 19.

428. Id. at 27.

429. [1960] I.C.J. Rep. 150.

> nations interested in the supply of large numbers of crews, or in the carriage of large numbers of berthed and unberthed passengers, and of major geographical areas.[430]

The principal question referred to the Court, it may be recalled, was whether Liberia and Panama, third and eighth in total world tonnage, should be "elected" to the Committee as members of the "eight largest ship owning nations."[431] Great Britain, among others, argued that registered tonnage should not be the sole criterion of the "largest" shipowning nations, since both Liberia and Panama's registered tonnage was largely composed of "flags of convenience" whose actual owners were citizens of other nations. It was insisted, therefore, that Liberia and Panama did not have the requisite interest in maritime safety, which was the Assembly's principal purpose in establishing the Committee. In addition, it was argued that to determine membership solely upon registered tonnage would be to deny any reasonable meaning to the term "elect," since the choice would be automatic, and would in no sense constitute an "election."[432]

The Court rejected the British argument, upholding the right of Liberia and Panama, as well as of any other nation meeting the tonnage requirement, to serve on the Committee. In dealing with the crucial terms in Article 28, the Court commented that "The words . . . must be read in their natural and ordinary meaning, in the sense which they would normally have in their context. It is only if, when this is done, the words of the Article are ambiguous in any way that resort need be had to any other methods of construction."[433] Even though the Court concluded that the provisions were "perfectly clear," it did, nevertheless, resort to numerous other methods of interpretation, including comparison of Article 23 with other articles in the Convention and with similar articles in other agreements, examination of preparatory work, and consideration of the Convention's general aims and purposes. These methods, the Court contended, only served to confirm its conclusions based upon the ordinary and natural meanings of the terms in their context.[434]

430. Id. at 154.
431. Id. at 153.
432. Id. at 155.
433. Id. at 159–60.
434. These methods included reading the specific terms of 28 (a) "in the context of the whole provision," id. at 161–62, in relation to "the history of the article and the debate which took place" over various proposals (pp. 163–64) and the

The increasing insistence of the International Court on relating plain meanings to the whole agreement is made explicit by the majority in its discussion of the term "elected" in 23 (a). The consideration proposed in dissent by Judge Klaestad, that "elected" taken in its natural sense precluded an "automatic" choice based on total tonnage,[435] had apparently been advanced by counsel and was answered by the Court in this way:

> The meaning of the word "elected" in the Article cannot be determined in isolation by recourse to its usual or common meaning and attaching that meaning to the word where used in the Article. The word obtains its meaning from the context in which it is used. If the context requires a meaning which connotes a wide choice, it must be construed accordingly, just as it must be given a restrictive meaning if the context in which it is used so requires.[436]

Thus the ordinary and natural meaning of the term "elected," inferred from its context, was one which did not demand an open choice of alternatives, but could be consistently used to describe the formal act of acceptance on the part of the Assembly of the eight nations having the greatest registered tonnage.

A similar point was made in the *Anglo-Iranian Oil Co.* case[437] when the Court commented on its interpretation of the central terms of the Iranian declaration: "the Court cannot base itself on a purely grammatical interpretation of the text. It must seek the interpretation which is in harmony with the natural and reasonable way of reading the text, having due regard to the intention of the Government of Iran at the time when it accepted the compulsory jurisdiction of the Court."[438]

In the *Second Peace Treaties* case,[439] the Court likewise refused to interpret the text solely "in its literal sense" but insisted more broadly, in its view, upon an interpretation based upon the "natural

"general purpose of the convention" (p. 170). The Court decided in turn that all of these methods yielded results which confirmed the ordinary and natural meaning of the provision.

435. Id. at 173–76.

436. Id. at 158.

437. [1952] I.C.J. Rep. 93.

438. Id. at 104.

439. [1930] I.C.J. Rep. 221, 227.

and ordinary meaning of the terms." Distinctions such as these, to be sure, are neither very precise, nor, to the extent to which they are understandable, are they entirely uniform in their emphasis. They do, however, indicate a tendency on the part of the Court to broaden its application of the rule to meet the criticisms leveled against the plain meaning method in the jurisprudence of the Permanent Court.[440] In another sense, this tendency is an extension of precedents set by the Permanent Court in favor of interpreting terms according to their ordinary *technical* meaning when the context so indicates.[441] It should be clear, however, that the new Court's emphasis goes beyond that of its predecessor in referring to matters beyond solely "technical" settings.

An example of what is potentially a more reasonable use of the plain meaning canon may be found in the majority opinion in the recent *South-West Africa* cases (Preliminary Objections).[442] Here the Court did not by its silence on the issue merely implicitly reject the hierarchical structuring of the canon in relation to an examination of the context, but instead stated explicitly for the first time that it could not be bound by such a limiting rule:

> this rule of interpretation is not an absolute one. Where such a method of interpretation results in a meaning incompatible with the spirit, purpose and context of the clause or instrument in which the words are contained, no reliance can be validly placed on it.[443]

The Court at this point was dealing with the second of four objections raised by the Union of South Africa to its jurisdiction in the case. The principal dispute, as we have mentioned, related to the administration by the Union of the territory of South-West Africa, which had been mandated to its prior Empire representatives by the

440. See, especially, Anzilotti in *Employment of Women During the Night,* supra note 400, at 383; *The Legal Status of Eastern Greenland,* P.C.I.J., Ser. A/B, No. 53, p. 82 (1933); and Anzilotti and Haber in *The S.S. "Wimbledon,"* supra note 363, at 35.

441. Cf. *Certain German Interests in Polish Upper Silesia,* P.C.I.J., Ser. A, No. 6, p. 14 (1925); *Exchange of Greek and Turkish Populations,* supra note 373, at 18–21; *Interpretation of the Greco-Turkish Agreement of December 1st, 1926,* P.C.I.J., Ser. B, No. 16, p. 22 ff. (1928); *Lighthouses* case, supra note 397, at 13.

442. [1962] I.C.J. 319.

443. Id. at 336.

League. Upon the failure of the Union to submit to the Trusteeship System of the United Nations, various attempts were instituted in the General Assembly and the Court to require protection of the rights allegedly granted to the inhabitants of the territory by both the Covenant and the Charter. Since the Union had explicitly refused to assume these obligations under the Charter, the principal issue in the case was whether similar obligations still persisted from the Union's participation in the Mandate system under the Covenant. In the 1952 case the Union had also objected to the jurisdiction of the Court and had lost the point. Many of the same objections were raised in the present case. The second of these was that the Court had no jurisdiction to deal with the dispute because the Covenant obligations for judicial settlement of disputes, even if still in force—which the Union had denied in its initial objection—extended under Article 7 of the Mandate only to "Members of the League of Nations." Since the League had ceased to exist after 1946, the Union's argument was that no parties, i.e. no "Members of the League," remained to enforce whatever rights such parties may once have held. In so arguing the Union relied on the "natural and ordinary meaning of the words employed in the provision." [444]

The Court denied this contention by reference to the general purposes for which the League Mandate system had been established. The purpose of this system, the Court argued, was to place in the hands of a major power the right to administer the non-self-governing territories as a "sacred trust of civilization." While the "faithful discharge of the trust" was left to the mandatory power, "the duty and the right of ensuring the performance of this trust were given to the League with its Council, the Assembly, the Permanent Mandates Commission and all its Members within the limits of their respective authority." [445] In light of the fact that the members of the League fully expected their rights and obligations to persist while being transferred to the United Nations in 1946, the Court concluded that unless there was specific evidence to the contrary it was to be assumed that both the right of South Africa to administer the Territory and its obligations to serve the best interests of its inhabitants were preserved, as was the right of the members to bring suit to enforce the observance of these interests under Article 7 of the Mandate.

444. Ibid.
445. Ibid.

There was specific evidence that South Africa had accepted a continuation of both its rights (it continued to administer the territory) and its obligations; on April 9, 1946, nine days before the dissolution of the League, its representative stated:

> The Union Government will nevertheless regard the dissolution of the League as in no way diminishing its obligations under the Mandate, which it will continue to discharge with the full and proper appreciation of its responsibilities until such time as other arrangements are agreed upon concerning the future status of the territory.[446]

The Court took this declaration into consideration in deciding that indeed the *Union's* rights and obligations postdated the League; that they complemented the purpose of the Mandate system in upholding the "sacred trust"; and that in line with this purpose they would refuse to recognize the anomalous situation in which such a system of obligations would exist with no parties qualified to enforce them. Thus the rights of the member nations of the League to bring suit to ensure the observance of these obligations also postdated the League and were brought under the jurisdiction of the International Court by Article 37 of its Statute.[447]

In denying South Africa's assertion of the plain and natural meaning rule, and in invoking the purposes of the Mandate system as well as the behavior of the Union government itself, the Court obviously did not intend to deny the importance of the rule in all instances. In fact, in dealing with the third preliminary objection, which asserted that Liberia and Ethiopia had no "dispute" with South Africa according to the Article 7 requirement that "any *dispute* whatever" (emphasis added) which "cannot be settled by negotiation" be submitted to the Court, it invoked the rule itself. Speaking of South Africa's contention, the Court commented that it

> runs counter to the natural and ordinary meaning of the provisions of Article 7 of the Mandate, which mentions "any dispute whatever". . . The language used is broad, clear and precise: it gives rise to no ambiguity and it permits of no exception . . . the manifest scope and purport of the provisions of this Article

446. Id. at 340.
447. Id. at 341–42.

> indicate that the Members of the League were understood to have a legal right or interest in the observance by the Mandatory of its obligations both toward the inhabitants of the Mandated Territory, and toward the League of Nations and its Members.[448]

It is important to note for present purposes that the Court did not invoke the natural and ordinary meaning rule in order to preclude an analysis of the context; it did in fact allude to such evidence, although in characteristic lack of detail.[449] Even though it may have employed the rule as a means of emphasizing the text over extrinsic matters, it eliminated the absurd notion perpetrated in previous opinions that contextual information could or should be ignored.

The dissenting opinion of Judges Spender and Fitzmaurice provides an interesting contrast to the Court opinion in both the rejection and application of the plain meaning rule. With respect to the second objection, where the Court refused to apply the rule, Spender and Fitzmaurice applied it; and with respect to the third objection, where the Court applied the rule, these dissenters rejected it and appealed to the *travaux préparatoires.* The first of these two conflicts we have considered above, for in nearly all respects the Spender-Fitzmaurice opinion accepts the South African argument that the rights granted to "Members of the League" *prima facie* lapsed with the League's dissolution, and "that little more should be necessary to be said on this part of the case." [450] The second conflict presents a much more interesting dilemma, since the dissenters engage in a rather extensive examination of the *travaux préparatoires* in support of their argument that the intention of the drafters of Article 7 was to protect their own commercial and other related rights in case of "disputes" with other members of the League, and not to protect the interests of the inhabitants through "disputes" of the present kind in which no direct or *material* interest was at stake.[451] Although the evidence which they adduce does not appear entirely conclusive on the issue, the search did yield convincing proof that one major goal of the parties was self-protection and that this was a dominant motive

448. Id. at 343.
449. Id. at 344.
450. Id. at 505.
451. Id. at 554.

inspiring the insertion of the arbitral clause of Article 7. That such presumption might have been rebutted is clear even from the material presented by the dissenters; but that the Court chose to ignore this material, and did not bother to cite any of its own, weakens the Court's position, and from our point of view represents an entirely inadequate performance of the task of interpretation. Needless to say, the same considerations hold as against the dissenter's invocation of the plain meaning concept in relation to the first and second objections.[452] Their contention that "provisions are *prima facie* to be interpreted and applied according to their terms where these are clear and unambiguous in their expression of the intention of the parties" is very similar to the familiar myth associated with Vattel. It is also important to note, in this regard, the modification of this doctrine announced by Spender and Fitzmaurice prior to their own disregard of the rule: "such terms can only be ignored or overridden (if at all) on the basis of some demonstrably applicable legal principle of superior authority." [453]

The direction in which the present tendency will lead the Court cannot easily be predicted. Over thirty years ago Hyde forecast that the Court would be increasingly urged both to look beyond plain and natural meanings to materials outside the four corners of the focal agreement and—simultaneously—to refuse to do so.[454] His prediction appears to have been borne out by subsequent events: as we have seen, alongside the International Court's attempts to broaden the base of application of the plain meaning rule stands the simultaneous use of the rule to limit recourse to *travaux préparatoires*—a restriction the Court has by no means abandoned or sufficiently liberalized. In sum, neither the continuing authority of the rule in general terms nor its application in specific restriction upon the examination of relevant features of the context has in explicit terms as yet been successfully challenged. Within its traditional realm of operation, however, its use has been significantly broadened to include a larger portion of the interpreter's methods in assessing the text itself.

It should be clear by this time that our examination of past trends in the application of the plain and natural meaning rule does not

452. Id. at 490, 505.
453. Id. at 468.
454. Hyde, supra note 384, at 19.

establish that the rule has been used without exception, or even in a majority of cases, to limit recourse to important features of the context. To be sure, examples have been cited such as in the *Lotus* and *Admissions* cases, in which it apparently has been so employed with respect to preparatory work. But this practice has had numerous exceptions. As we have seen, courts have been willing to examine preparatory work under appropriate circumstances whether the text was found to be clear in its ordinary meaning, or not clear, or undetermined, even though the results have in every case been held to confirm an alleged ordinary meaning of the text.[455] Thus in relation to the *travaux* doctrine, past decision-makers have, in formal reiteration of the *Lotus* formula, appeared to accept a much stronger restriction on inquiry than they have actually been willing to observe. The operational basis for this discrepancy, in the presentation and receipt of claims from preliminary records in the course of litigation, has been outlined, as we saw above, by Beckett.[456] In calling attention to the procedures by which claimants present evidence from relevant contextual materials, Beckett has pointed to the ambiguity which we previously discussed in relation to the restriction upon "recourse to" preparatory work.[457] Decision-makers, in being urged to prefer this feature of the context, are in actuality *weighing* the various features in favor of the outcome text of the agreement. In light of our recommendations above that no such presumption can be rationally established in advance of an explicit, systematic analysis of all relevant features of the context, it should be clear that a preference established by refusing to consider the claims advanced in litigation is, for similar reasons, entirely unacceptable.

The relation of the plain and natural meaning principle to that of major purposes has also presented special problems to past decision-makers. One of these problems arises simply from the difficulties involved in specifying a distinct set of operations for determining the parties' general purposes, as, for example, could be established in re-

455. For discussion of past trends in the examination of *travaux préparatoires,* especially in relation to the later condition, see supra page 122, and Hudson, op. cit. supra note 12, at 652–55; Lauterpacht, op. cit. supra note 21, at 116–41; Chang, op. cit. supra note 5, at 95–140; Fitzmaurice, supra note 21, at 10–18; Hogg, supra note 14, at 28–40.

456. Beckett, supra note 32, at 440–44.

457. See supra, pages 130–31.

lation to the examination of preparatory work. The result is that an observer cannot be certain that a court did not consider the parties' major purposes in determining the "plain meaning" of their agreement. The least that is called for is a more explicit discussion of whatever competing or complementary operations are involved in each case. What is perhaps more important is that this clarity in discussion be used to avoid the pitfall of ignoring general purposes in the name of the plain meaning rule, or of establishing an *a priori* preference for the alleged plain meaning of specific terms over the more general inferences of aim to be drawn from the context taken as a whole.

Another problem arises from the unique nature of one formulation of the principle complementary to the major purposes doctrine, namely, the principle of restrictive interpretation. In one traditional statement, the principle of restrictive interpretation calls attention only to a very limited feature of the context in the assumed demands of participants to protect their rights of sovereignty. It is often applied, as we have seen, as an overriding community policy to be employed in order to limit the obligations of states whenever the terms of their agreements are not clear in asserted natural meaning. To apply the principle of plain and natural meaning in rejecting a "restrictive" interpretation, therefore, would only rarely run the risk of defeating the genuine shared expectations of the participants, and would at the same time limit the scope of a highly questionable community policy. In this limited respect, the employment of the plain and natural meaning doctrine might serve a modest useful purpose.[458]

Aside from general considerations of the formulation and employment of the plain meaning rule in relation to other principles in past decision, an important criticism is often made of its application to specific cases. It has been argued, both by publicists and by dissenting judges, that the rule has been misapplied, and that *in reality* the provision declared by a tribunal to be "clear" in its ordinary meaning is not clear or, more appropriately applied, would lead to quite different results. In many instances in which the claim has been made that the provision is not clear in its ordinary sense, the view is also proposed that the tribunal has used the plain meaning rule to "cover up

458. Cf. Lauterpacht, op. cit. supra note 21, at 300–06, supra note 19, at 61–67, for statements of this same view.

a decision arrived at by other means."[459] If these "other means" can be specified—as Anzilotti attempted to do in the *Employment of Women* case—a valuable service is performed in making more explicit the actual strategies or policies of the decision-maker. It is also obvious that this task ought to be undertaken by decision-makers themselves, rather than by dissenters or publicists who do not have direct access either to the subjectivities of such decision-makers or in many cases even to the evidence they employ.

From the observer's viewpoint, it must of course always be somewhat a matter of speculation as to whether or not "other means" were the *real* grounds of decision. This speculation is particularly noticeable when the observer attempts to claim that a provision under dispute is not clear in its ordinary sense, or that some other ordinary meaning is equally clear. The commentator who makes such a claim must be willing to speculate in the same degree as the decision-maker whom he is criticizing. It would be pointless to deny that a general consensus can on occasion be achieved as to "plain" meanings—in fact this happens in one form or another much of the time in human communication. Yet there would appear to be a limit to the usefulness of speculative hunches in areas of disagreement as to the "real" plain or ordinary meanings. A more constructive alternative would be for decision-makers to adopt a more thorough, systematic examination of all relevant indices of the parties' expectations and of the significant community policies at stake in a particular application, and to weigh these factors explicitly in decision. Such a practice might both block claims of obfuscation or "cloaking" of the actual grounds of decision and promote decisions more in accord with the genuine shared expectations of the parties and basic community policies.

THE PRINCIPLE OF THE PROBABILITY OF AGREEMENT

Publicists and decision-makers have frequently considered the relevance of prior agreements and declarations to disputed provisions

459. This view has been expressed by Lauterpacht, supra note 19, at 53, op. cit. supra note 21, at 52–60; Fairman, supra note 393, at 132–34; Verzijl, "Fifteen Years of International Law" cited in F. Andreae, *An Important Chapter from the History of Legal Interpretation* 75 (1948); Yü, op. cit. supra note 12, at 27–39, passim; Stone, supra note 170, at esp. 355–57.

of a treaty similar in content and scope. Earlier opinion focused mainly on analogous treaties employed among the participants themselves. Thus Fiore suggested that

> It is reasonable to presume that parties which, in manifesting their will, have left some uncertainty as to the meaning of the words used to express it, have employed those words in the sense deducible clearly and without ambiguity from another agreement between them. There is no reason why it should not be conceded that the contracting parties have probably entertained the same thought as in other analogous cases.[460]

Later writers have broadened Fiore's emphasis to include *any* agreements with similar provisions which the parties themselves might have been expected to duplicate.[461] Most recently, two commentators on the jurisprudence of the international courts, Fitzmaurice and Degan, have observed a similar tendency in past trends of decision to consider other agreements, often of diverse participation, as a unit for purposes of interpretation.[462] As Hudson said in describing a situation frequently faced by the Permanent Court: "Two or more instruments may be so related, or so interdependent, that the text of one must be construed with reference to that of the other." [463]

The employment of evidence from instruments other than that embodying the focal agreement was an established custom prior to the precedents established by the Permanent Court. One of the earliest cases as reported by McNair, is that of the *Vryheid (No. 1)*.[464] In this case the tribunal laid down the general rule that all contemporary treaties of commerce between two parties "are to be taken as one contract . . . so that no one treaty, or article of the treaty, is to be taken substantive, or standing alone and single from the rest." [465]

460. Fiore, op. cit. supra note 131, at 343.
461. See Oppenheim, op. cit. supra note 297, at 859–60; Schwarzenberger, op. cit. supra note 12, at 528–29; Lauterpacht, op. cit. supra note 21, at 368–81.
462. See Fitzmaurice, supra note 21, at 18–20, supra note 12, at 220; Degan, op. cit. supra note 135, at 100–02. See also Hudson, op. cit. supra note 12, at 649–50.
463. Hudson, id. at 649.
464. Hay and Marriott 188, 192 (1778), cited in McNair, op. cit. supra note 38, at 198.
465. Hay and Marriott 188, 192; McNair, ibid. See also other cases collected by McNair, ibid.; and *The "Franciska,"* in 2 Spinks, *Ecclesiastical and Admiralty Reports* 113 (1855).

Later cases have consistently upheld this rule. In the *Reserved Fisheries* arbitration,[466] for example, in interpreting a treaty of commerce between the United States and Great Britain, the Umpire accepted an argument that the traditional designations of river, bay, and sea fisheries as revealed in previous treaties between the United States and Great Britain should be considered in resolving the dispute which had arisen: "[It may be assumed that] the definitions previously used, and adopted, would be mutually binding in interpreting the treaty, and that the two countries had consented to use the terms in the sense in which each had before treated them in their public instruments, and to apply them as they had been previously applied." [467] Similarly, in the *Elton* case, the United States-Mexican Claims Commission commented, in interpreting its own jurisdiction under the U.S.-Mexican Treaty of 1923, that "it is proper to consider stipulations of earlier or later treaties in relation to subjects similar to those treated in the treaty under consideration." [468]

The Permanent Court was called upon in numerous situations to compare treaty provisions with earlier ones of a similar kind, especially when the treaties were complementary in their general aims and purposes. In the *Danube Commission* case [469] the Court argued that although "the first source to be consulted" was the agreement establishing the Definitive Statute of the Danube Commission, the Statute was "not complete in itself; on the contrary, many of its articles refer to previous international engagements, and Article 41 expressly provides that all treaties . . . are maintained in all their stipulations not abrogated or modified by the Statute itself." [470] In light of these conditions, the Court felt obliged to examine "the whole system of the international acts applicable before the war to the maritime Danube." [471] Even though it admitted that some of these acts appeared to cast doubt upon the jurisdiction of the Danube Commission in the contested area, it concluded that such "manifest and regrettable inconsistencies" could not suffice to overrule the overall impression that these acts taken together conferred

466. (1858), in 1 Moore, *International Arbitrations* 449 (1898).
467. Id. at 458.
468. *G. L. Elton (U.S.) v. United Mexican States* (1929), 4 U.N. Rep. Int'l Arb. Awards 529, 533. *Naomi Russell (U.S.) v. United Mexican States* (1931), 4 id. 805, 815 (1931).
469. P.C.I.J., Ser. B, No. 14 (1927).
470. Id. at 23.
471. Id. at 55.

jurisdiction in the prewar era, and were thus taken over into the present Statute explicitly through Article 41.[472] In broader application in the *Oder River* case,[473] the Court, for determining the jurisdiction of the Oder Commission under the Treaty of Versailles, laid down the similar requirement that it must "go back to the principles governing international fluvial law in general and consider what position was adopted by the Treaty . . . in regard to these principles." [474] The principal issue which the Court faced in this case was whether the jurisdiction of the Commission extended to parts of tributaries of the Oder which were solely within the territorial boundaries of Poland. Article 331 of the Treaty of Versailles established international control over all international rivers and "all navigable parts of these river systems which naturally provide more than one State with access to the sea." [475] The Court, in looking to previous agreements to determine whether "all navigable parts" included solely internal parts of the Oder's tributaries, concluded that the drafters of the Treaty of Versailles explicitly departed from earlier tendencies to restrict international fluvial control to principal international waterways and international portions of tributaries: "In contradistinction to most previous treaties which limit the common legal right to riparian States, the Treaty of Versailles . . . adopted the position of complete internationalization, that is to say, the free use of the river for all States, whether riparian or not." [476] As a result, the Court concluded that "all navigable parts" referred to parts of tributaries *the whole of which* were international, thus conferring jurisdiction on the Commission over the disputed portions of the Netze and Warthe rivers which, considered in their entirety, were international tributaries of the Oder.[477] Numerous other cases may be cited in which the Court compared various families of agreements to resolve a particular dispute, especially in relation to the minorities treaties, but under other circumstances as well.[478] On at least two occasions, the Court concluded that agree-

472. Ibid.
473. P.C.I.J., Ser. A, No. 23 (1929).
474. Id. at 26. See also the *Greco-Turkish Agreement* case, supra note 441, at 19.
475. Id. at 24.
476. Id. at 28.
477. Id. at 28–29, 31–32.
478. Cf. the *Greco-Bulgarian "Communities"* case, P.C.I.J., Ser. B, No. 17, pp. 19–22 (1930); *Certain German Interests in Polish Upper Silesia,* supra note 451,

ments which were related *prima facie* were in fact "entirely independent," and could not be relied on to resolve disputed claims arising from the provision under consideration.[479]

The International Court of Justice has also relied on interlocking or related agreements in its constructions of the parties' focal agreement. In the *United States Nationals in Morocco* case,[480] the Court referred to previous treaties on two occasions. In the first, it interpreted the U.S.-Morocco Treaty of 1836 in light of previous treaties between the parties and with other nations. In relation to the contention that the central term "dispute" in Article 20 of the Treaty[481] applied only to civil disputes, the Court commented that

> it is necessary to take into account the meaning of the word "dispute" at the times when the . . . treaties were concluded. For this purpose it is possible to look at the way in which the word "dispute" or its French counterpart was used in the different treaties concluded by Morocco: e.g., with France in 1631 and 1682, with Great Britain in 1721, 1750, 1751, 1760, and 1801. It is clear that in these instances the word was used to cover both civil and criminal disputes.[482]

Likewise on the second occasion the Court construed the French-Spanish declaration of 1914, presented as evidence of the intention of the French government to abandon permanently all consular jurisdiction in the French Zone of Morocco, in light of other similar declarations made at the same time: "The Declaration . . . was one of a series of agreements negotiated by France with more than twenty foreign States . . . At least seventeen of these agreements used the

at 8; *Minority Schools in Upper Silesia,* P.C.I.J., Ser. A, No. 15, p. 33 (1928); *Acquisition of Polish Nationality,* supra note 369, at 20. Also cf. the *Chorzow Factory* case, supra note 148, at 22; the *Jaworzina Boundary* case, supra note 53, at 38.

479. *Treaty of Neuilly, Article 179 (Interpretation)*, P.C.I.J., Ser. A, No. 3, p. 9 (1924); *The Diversion of Water from the Meuse,* P.C.I.J., Ser. A/B, No. 70, p. 13 (1937).

480. [1952] I.C.J. Rep. 176.

481. Article 20 provides that "If any of the citizens of the United States, or any persons under their protection, shall have any dispute with each other, the Consul shall decide between the parties; and whenever the Consul shall require any aid, or assistance from our government, to enforce his decisions, it shall be immediately granted to him." Id. at 188–89.

482. Id. at 189.

expression *'renonce a reclamer'* as a means of bringing about a complete abrogation of all rights and privileges arising out of the regime of Capitulations."[483] Since the effect of all of the remaining agreements was to renounce all consular jurisdiction, the Court held that the French declaration could provide no exception in the absence of special evidence to the contrary.

In other cases the Court has relied less extensively upon prior agreements. In the *Genocide* case,[484] it referred in general terms to the context of agreements in determining the legitimacy of reservations to the Genocide Convention in the absence of a provision by which they were specifically authorized.[485] The majority held that such reservations were permissible, even in the absence of specific provision, in light of the tendency notable in modern multilateral conventions to allow reservations without requiring unanimous consent of all participants. As it said: "More general resort to reservations, very great allowance made for tacit assent to reservations, the existence of practices which go so far as to admit that the author of reservations which have been rejected by certain contracting parties is nevertheless to be regarded as a party to the convention in relation to those contracting parties that have accepted the reservations—all these factors are manifestations of a new need for flexibility in the operation of multilateral conventions."[486] While referring to the "great number of reservations which have been made of recent years to multilateral conventions," the Court concluded that "In this state of international practice, it could certainly not be inferred from the absence of an article providing for reservations . . . that the contracting States are prohibited from making certain reservations."[487] In the *Anglo-Iranian Oil Co.* case,[488] the Court, in interpreting the declaration of Iran, referred to similar declarations by other nations accepting its jurisdiction.[489] Although it admitted that some of the other declarations were not ambiguous in the same way as the

483. Id. at 195.
484. [1951] I.C.J. Rep. 15.
485. Id. at 20 ff.
486. Id. at 21–22.
487. Id. at 22.
488. (Preliminary Objection), [1952] I.C.J. Rep. 93.
489. Id. at 104. In particular, Britain relied upon the 1925 Belgian declaration which accepted compulsory jurisdiction "au sujet de situations ou de faits posterieurs à cette ratification."

Iranian declaration, it concluded that such declarations could not be given decisive weight since they were "so much altered that it is impossible to seek [the meaning of] the Iranian Declaration" through such comparisons.[490]

PRINCIPLES RELATING TO THE DECISION PROCESS

Officials

The Principle of Impartiality

Remarkably little systematic attention to deviations from impartiality has been given by decision-makers themselves or by publicists who characterize the process from various perspectives and attempt to account for the actual flow of decision. Our presentation of the principle of impartiality drew attention to the distortions that may arise unless appropriate measures are adopted to nullify the influence of culture, class, interest, personality, and level of crisis. It appears to be a belated discovery among those who specialize in theories *about* law that those who participate in the legal process, whether as claimants or decision-makers, share the frailties of mankind. No doubt practical wisdom of this kind has been commonplace in the arenas of national and transnational life. It has, however, been perceived as a kind of guilty knowledge, more suitable to intimate conversation or embittered polemic than to candid self-examination of decision-makers or careful evaluation by commentators. The prevailing silence is not to be commended if, as may eventually be demonstrated, silence discourages disciplined insight and understanding.

Occasional recognition has been given to one or more of the factors that militate against an impartial approach by decision-makers. The most obvious point has been to impugn the impartiality of municipal courts when they are called upon to resolve disputes between their own nationals and the nationals of other countries.[491] Such issues have been implicitly raised in relation to many well-

490. Id. at 105.
491. Cf. the treatment given this point by McNair, op. cit. supra note 38, at 163–64; Briggs, *The Law of Nations: Cases, Documents and Notes* 896–97 (2d. ed. 1952); Harvard Research, op. cit. supra note 3, at 973–77.

known jurisdictional problems such as those discussed in the *Nationality Decrees* and *The David J. Adams* cases.[492] Occasional comments by publicists may be found in relation to such difficulties, even though the issue of impartiality is seldom explicitly raised.[493] Where the issue has been raised, the treatment has been relatively cursory; hence a broad allegation of "national" bias has not been critically evaluated to clarify the identity of the predisposition involved. Is it a simple matter of exposure to a national culture, or is the response to be attributed to class biases—upper, middle, lower—or to exposure to and current expectations from an interest group related to rival political ideologies and organizations, or to competing economic blocs (and so on through the value-institution list that is available for use in thinking about the social process)? No assessment of factors affecting impartiality can fail to reckon with the intensity of the internal conflicts existing in the personality structure of decision-makers, which may modify the mind's openness to new points of view. The trend of decision cannot plausibly be accounted for without taking note of the crisis level, whether intense or moderate, in each category of the factors referred to above (culture, class, interest, personality).

Some pertinent points have occasionally been scored in connection with the discussion by publicists of the International Court of Justice and, to a lesser extent, its predecessor, the Permanent Court of International Justice. Elementary studies of judicial response have shown widespread adherence by national judges to the position advocated by their own state in a current dispute. Allowing for some disparity in the results reported, it can nonetheless be said that national judges appear to have voted for the position championed by their own country about 80 percent of the time.[494] As might be anticipated, the figure is somewhat higher for ad hoc judges. Some studies bring into the open the important observation that ideological lines are often blurred[495]—as socialists, for example, join with nonsocialist coalitions in the deciding phase of no inconsiderable number of

492. *Nationality Decrees Issued in Tunis and Morocco,* supra note 223, at 28–30; *In the Matter of the David J. Adams* (1921), reported in 16 *Am. J. Int'l L.* 315, 318 (1922). Cf. others cited in McNair, id. at 163–74; and in Briggs, ibid.
493. Cf. Briggs, ibid; McNair, ibid.
494. Cf. 2 Liacouras, *The International Court of Justice* 527 (preliminary ed. 1962).
495. See Grzybowski, "Socialist Judges in the International Court of Justice," 1964 *Duke L. J.* 536.

issues.[496] Investigations have yielded no evidence of a consistent bias separating either the developed–underdeveloped or the major–minor powers from one another.[497]

The tantalizing results thus far made public by competent inquirers amply vindicate the rising degree of attention now being given by publicists and decision-makers to the complex of factors whose disturbing impact on impartiality have often been noted.[498] With appropriate study it may now be possible both to appraise the role of culture, class, interest, personality, and crisis factors in decision trends and to clarify the countervailing principles necessary to facilitate the pursuit of impartiality.

Objectives

The Principle of Primary Interpretation

By far the vast majority of past decisions appear, despite some notorious retrogressions, to reflect a continuing concern on the part of appropriate officials to ascertain and effectuate the genuine shared expectations of the parties. In the search for sound bases of inference regarding these expectations, decision-makers have ordinarily relied on a number of ancillary aims and strategies that harmonize with the inclusive principle recommended here. We refer, for example, to the thoroughness with which the component parts of the context of agreement are explored and to not infrequent deliberate efforts to achieve explicitness about the actual grounds of decision.

The Principle of Supplementing Expectations by Public Order Goals

It is not to be assumed that the inquiries conducted by the world's most competent and conscientious decision-makers invariably result in a relatively certain, unambiguous, and complete image of the genuine shared expectations of the parties. Hence it is incumbent on the

496. Liacouras, op. cit. supra note 494, Part IV, Table 3, at p. 453a.

497. Cf. Anand, *International Courts and Contemporary Conflicts* 375–76 (JSD thesis, Yale Law School, 1964).

498. See Samore, "National Origins v. Impartial Decisions: A Study of World Court Holdings," 34 *Chi-Kent L. Rev.* 193 (1956); Liacouras, op. cit. supra note 494; and Anand, ibid.

community's authorities to take responsibility for filling gaps by supplementing the known elements in the pattern of expectation in the light of public order goals, thus reducing the disruptions in society which may be generated by frustrating the effects typically and permissibly sought to be realized through the agreement process. Our review of the record definitely confirms the fact that community decision-makers are accustomed to take the initiative required in many of the controversies before them. Nevertheless, they are often reluctant to acknowledge what they have done or to set forth in detail the chain of inference on which they have relied. Hence it can be said that international decision-makers are on occasion willing to explain themselves only in highly cryptic terms, a practice that lays them open to the types of criticism reviewed earlier, particularly to the alleged "cloaking" of the actual grounds on which results are based.[499]

It is, of course, an unavoidable obligation of decision-makers to decide how far they can go in concrete circumstances in disclosing their genuine perspectives and strategies, since the costs of disclosure may appear to be disproportionately high.[500] In view of the doubts about the candor and hence the trustworthiness of many international decision-makers, it is not implausible to insist that unwillingness to deal openly with numerous acts of supplementation has intensified rather than evaporated the fog of suspicion that so often envelops the decision process.

The Principle of Constitutive Priority

Insofar as this principle is concerned, any competent review of the trend of decision can come to but one conclusion: there is a growing consensus that when the shared expectations of the parties to an agreement are in conflict with general community expectations about the approved features of public order the decision-maker has no alternative other than to act for the purpose of frustrating rather than of giving effect to such expectations. The public order takes priority over particular agreements that contravene its fundamental values and institutions.

499. See supra, pp. 9, 113.

500. See the brief discussion of the effectiveness of decisions, this section pp. 263–65.

This increasing degree of concurrence about the basic principle does not, of course, carry with it a corresponding agreement in regard to the norms that are actually to be defended and fulfilled in particular controversies. Though the community's voice does indeed deserve deference there are still great uncertainties and dissenting views about what the voice says. Latent in these debates is, however, the assumption that an inclusive set of overriding goals can in fact be made articulate at some phase of world political evolution.

The Principle of Stable Future Expectations

On the whole, past decision-makers have been thoroughly committed to the goal of stabilizing the future expectations of the parties to an agreement. This commitment has frequently been expressed, as we have seen in detail above, as the highest-level goal of interpretation.[501] Many commentators have affirmed that, both in general perspectives and in more detailed procedures designed to effect these perspectives, past decision-makers have attempted to promote stability in the agreement-making process. Publicists have differed concerning the most appropriate words and acts to carry out this goal, and, as a result, considerable disagreement over the relative success of past efforts. Hudson, for example, in reviewing the emerging trends in the International Court, concluded that "a tendency now seems to prevail in some quarters to undermine . . . [the integrity of agreements] by torturing the meaning of great international instruments and by forcing them to serve purposes for which they were never designed, purposes at variance with the desires entertained by Governments when the instruments were brought into force." [502]

A gratuitous source of confusion is occasionally introduced by jurists and commentators who play down the significance of *continuing consensus* among the parties and advocate the wisdom of ignoring the "intentions of the parties" in favor of a "new international law" which is alleged to promote stability in the future expectations of participants. The most economic method of stabilizing the relevant expectations would be to give effect to the continuing consen-

501. See supra, p. 82 ff.

502. Hudson, "Integrity of International Instruments," 42 *Am. J. Int'l L.* 105 (1948).

sus, within the limits established by overriding contemporary community policy. The point applies even in situations in which the parties have modified the pattern of shared expectations with which they originally entered the agreement process. We emphasize most emphatically the disruptive impact on stable expectations when any attempt is made to give effect to outmoded assumptions among the parties at the very moment when particular topics of dispute are brought before community decision-makers. Hence in commenting on the various dissents of Judges Azevado and Alvarez we have reaffirmed the significance of the principle of stable future expectations and underlined the importance of striving to overcome the difficulties connected with attempts to ascertain the contemporary shared expectations of agreement among the parties.

Base Values

The Principle of Making Decisions Effective

Among the relatively unacknowledged principles of interpretation, whether on the part of decision-makers or commentators, the principle of making decisions effective deserves prominent mention. It belongs to the category of perspectives that would appear to be regarded as faintly scandalous, even though informal conversation among experienced observers cannot fail to provide evidence of its currency. After all, it is commonly understood that great power at the disposal of a participant in the political process is a factor that confers weight on his commitments. Similarly, a poverty of power leads to further deprivation if the impoverished one seeks to rule beyond his means.

In the world arena few facts are more evident than the difference in the assets available to national tribunals, on the one hand, and to international tribunals on the other; they enjoy contrasting degrees of authority and control over values relevant to the management of sanctions. The most explicit recognition of this feature has been offered by Judge Lauterpacht, who saw as a "reason for restraint and caution" by international tribunals the fact that "Government . . . will not be prepared to entrust with legislative functions bodies composed of their authorized representatives . . . will not be willing to allow or tolerate the exercise of such activity by a tribunal enjoined by its Statute to apply the existing law." [503] Lauterpacht also observed that:

> With this is connected a further reason for restraint and caution in the international sphere, namely, the fact of the voluntary nature of the jurisdiction of international tribunals. An international court which yields conspicuously to the urge to modify the existing law . . . may bring about a drastic curtailment of its activity. Governments may refuse to submit disputes to it or to renew obligations of compulsory judicial settlement already in existence. There is [also] to be considered the fact that in the international sphere there is no certainty of compulsory execution of the judgments rendered by an international court—a circumstance which imposes a duty of particular restraint in order to remove any justification of the plausible, although rightly discredited, allegation that there has taken place an excess of jurisdiction and a usurpation of powers.[504]

In commenting on the same problem, Professor Stone interprets the fact of voluntary jurisdiction and uncertainty of execution not as suggestions for restraint but as justifications for the use of "fictions" to conceal the legislative function at the international level: "The international judiciary has not yet achieved that institutional stability which has in many municipal societies permitted judges to assume openly and with impunity the role of final reviewing authority of the common weal . . . There is room, therefore, for the view that the fictions which combine to conceal judicial creativeness in international law serve the proper social function of protecting the growing judicial arm against premature strains." [505]

If the positions thus taken by Stone and Lauterpacht are construed as calls for apparent and genuine restraints, respectively, in applying overriding community policies at the international level, it should be clear that Lauterpacht's position must be preferred. It is highly unlikely that international tribunals will be adequately protected against "premature strains" by "fictions"; neither the participants in processes of decision nor scholarly observers are likely to be tranquilized by attempts to "conceal judicial creativeness" by such evasions,

503. Lauterpacht, op. cit. supra note 21, at 76.
504. Ibid.
505. Stone, supra note 170, at 367.

even if skillful. On the other hand, the necessity of restraint *in actual operation* in international judicial decision, as Lauterpacht recognized, may for several reasons be an important factor in the deliberation of international jurists. In addition to the international tribunal's relatively minor degree of control over base values for assuming jurisdiction and enforcing decision, there are also the factors of cultural, class, and interest differences between the parties, and perhaps between the parties and the tribunal, which reduce the probability that the tribunal will be able to identify and establish a continuing consensus in its selection of policies. To this extent, the tribunal should be modestly hesitant to impose new policies, especially in derogation of apparently expressed genuine shared expectations. Too deliberate an assertion of control, with doubtful authority, could have a potentially harmful effect both upon the parties and upon the development of the jurisdiction of international tribunals.

STRATEGIES

The Principle of Explicit Rationality

It seems obvious to observers of the highly expert dialectic of argument before decision-makers, and of the care that judges bestow on justification of their commitments, that decision-makers demand of themselves and of one another the most punctilious conformity to the requirements of explicit rationality. If, however, by rationality is meant the practice of resorting to the use of the most appropriate procedures in problem solving, it is not possible to ascertain from the language of opinion what assumptions are current among responsible officials about the character of the actual problem solving that occurs at the several phases of decision. Nor is it possible to discover the degree to which distinctions are made and followed that are explicitly parallel, for example, to the principles of content and procedure outlined in our present analysis. Similarly, it is outside the manifest content of the published opinions to establish the conceptions of logic that are regarded as rational in the deliberations of the tribunals involved. We cannot clearly demonstrate, for example, that modern developments in the field of mathematical logic have affected the frame of reference of the judges, lawyers, and other officials involved in the total process. As indicated by the considerations reported earlier, the "either-or" logic of tradition continues to exercise a persistent suction on minds which are operating in a world of "more or less."

Even when principles are mentioned, there are, as we have seen, a number of dangers in assuming that they have been applied in the manner asserted. In the numerous decisions in which principles of interpretation are not mentioned at all or only casually, a presumption could be raised that explicit rationality is not in fact accepted as a strategy of decision. This presumption would, however, overlook the fact that institutionalized decision frequently transpires in at least two arenas: a cameral or closed arena, in which the direct participants arrive at a final characterization and formulation, and an open or promulgative arena, in which the direct participants communicate their decision in ideological terms that they seek to make acceptable to a considerably broader audience. Decision-makers may sometimes find compelling reasons for suppressing the actual considerations upon which their cameral deliberations were based. In given contexts, the suppression may be justifiable on policy grounds that no serious observer can deny. For example, it may be expedient as an aid to common action to indicate, by mild sanction, that a state's behavior is unlawful, without saying this in so many words or divulging the reasons for the finding. The absence of indicia of explicit rationality in the promulgative arena need not, thus, necessarily indicate that explicit rationality was not employed in the cameral arena. The enormous volume of literature on interpretation seems to suggest that only the most insular decision-maker could embark on an interpretative enterprise without realizing that he was doing so and appreciating the myriad complexities involved. It is important to note in this regard, however, that recent trends increasingly favor the explicit use of principles of interpretation and application in total surveys of relevant indices of expectation and policy. The International Court of Justice,[506] and other international tribunals,[507] have with increasing frequency canvassed an entire range of contextual factors by employment of appropriate principles.

506. See particularly our survey of decisions whose procedures merit special consideration, Ch. 5 at p. 283.

507. See especially the *Saudi Arabia-Aramco Arbitration,* supra note 174; see also the *Flegenheimer Claim* (1958), reported in 1958 *Int. Law Rep.* [I] 91.

OUTCOMES

The Principle of Comprehensive Mobilization of Authority Functions

No decision phase, when fully and competently examined, can be found that lives alone, wholly cut off from interaction with every other phase of the total decision process. No conventionally recognized organ of commitment can fail to perceive itself and to be perceived by others as part of a total system concerning whose interdependences complex expectations are current throughout the relevant arenas. So far as the task of interpretation is concerned the officials who are especially charged with the application function give little evidence of understanding that a problem of interpretation provides an occasion for mobilizing all the assets available in the decision process as a whole. Lacking a comprehensive explicit conception of all that is involved, official appliers perform the interpretative act in haphazard fashion, accepting some forms of assistance from other organs but overlooking or rejecting others.

The intelligence arm of official and semi-official organs of government is the principal reliance of appliers who are engaged in interpretation. While international tribunals rely in general upon counsel for most of their supply of information, there is a growing tendency, particularly in areas of continuing administrative concern, to turn to other perhaps less biased sources of evidence.[508] International tribunals generally retain for themselves the right to visit a relevant locale (*descente sur les lieux*). Through a process of judicial notice and the principle of *iura curia novit*, courts can introduce relevant facts and policies which the litigants have not pleaded. In addition to these self-help intelligence measures, courts turn to other participants for aid. Although there is no *amicus curiae* institution in international law comparable to that in the national arena, interested states which perceive themselves as likely to be affected by a pending decision often are accorded a right to plead. Insofar as in-

508. For a survey of judicial response, see Alford, "Fact Finding by the World Court," 4 *Vill. L. Rev.* 37 (1958). For a survey of intelligence in the Security Council, see Kerby, "The Powers of Investigation of the United Nations Security Council," 55 *Am. J. Int'l L.* 892 (1961).

ternational organizations enjoy this right—as for example in the advisory jurisdiction of the International Court—a new source of intelligence is introduced whose perspective differs from that of a nation-state. In less organized applicative arenas, participation in the intelligence function is even broader. In indirect relation to the interpretative process, data gathering of course proceeds at many levels and among many types of intelligence organizations—whether among states or private groups or among scientists and diplomats.[509]

In the process of interpretation, many of the participants in intelligence also fulfill a recommending function. We would emphasize that the increase of communication channels probably portends an increase in the number of participants who play a recommending role. In some cases very considerable promotional activity is necessary before a dispute in which important issues of interpretation are raised can reach an official agency of invocation or application. Legal experts may cross the line between intelligence and promotion by influencing the pronouncements of political parties or pressure associations.

Before controversies that turn on questions of interpretation can receive definitive consideration, the function of invocation must be exercised. In transnational judicial arenas, the capacity to invoke decision has traditionally been narrow. In the wake of the most recent South-West Africa decision, it appears to have been attenuated even further. This situation is mitigated somewhat by doctrines of diplomatic protection, which assure nationals some opportunity for stimulating, though indirectly, international tribunals. In certain regional experiments, formal invocative capacity is somewhat broader. The optimum measure of invocative competence is of course dependent upon context. In certain circumstances, there may be compelling reasons for a restriction of competence to invoke. However that may be, the situation which currently prevails is anachronistic and a barrier to the full contribution to world public order which international tribunals are capable of making. Access to the International Court and its predecessors is restricted to representatives of nation-states.[510]

509. See generally the discussion of the intelligence, recommending, and other functions in McDougal, Lasswell, and Vlasic, *Law and Public Order in Space* 113–27 (1963).

510. This restriction is not found, of course, in the multiple complex of national arenas and other specially constituted international arenas.

Despite the self-awareness that is presumably induced by public prominence, and especially by perpetual appraisals conducted by members of a learned profession, it cannot be unequivocally demonstrated that international decision-makers recognize the advantages to them of a systematic exercise of the appraisal function. There are few if any analyses designed to bring into the open the past consequences of the modes of interpretation previously employed. Occasional aphorisms and maxims—embellished by linguistic esotericism—do not warrant the assertion that the efficacy of earlier modalities of interpretation have been critically reviewed by those most involved and concerned with the choice of interpretative principles. The manifest content of what must be brought to mind in the search for sound interpretative results remains fragmentary, obscure, and perhaps deliberately in shadow.

The greatest possible opportunity to participate in the process of interpretation is, however, offered in the appraisal function. Anyone—official or private—to whose notice a decision is brought may take it upon himself to offer an appraisal. These individuals may go further and recommend either structural or functional changes in the authoritative process in order to improve future decision. The increase in the number of nation-states has brought a concomitant increase in effective elites who may introduce a degree of authority into their appraisals. Since such elites are generally served by a coterie of professional advisers who can bring a measure of expertise to bear, participation in appraisal and the quality of that participation may come to be improved.

5. TRENDS IN THE MANAGEMENT OF PRINCIPLES OF PROCEDURE

For brief survey of past trends in the employment and management of principles of procedure it will be convenient, again, to follow the outline of these principles which we adopted in our recommendations. The appropriate function of principles of procedure, it may be recalled, is to assist the decision-maker or other interpreter in examining the subject matter designated as pertinent by the content principles. They assist both by suggesting an economic order or agenda of inquiry and by specifying the detailed techniques or operations necessary to the effective application of the content principles. The principles that guide or order inquiry indicate how the focus of attention of a decision-maker can be directed successively toward the larger, or smaller, features of the configuration of events whose pertinence has been prefigured by the principles of content. The principles specifying detailed operations offer certain specialized modes of assessing whether an alleged content, proffered by a particular source, measures up to the requirements made explicit in the criteria of relevance.

In our examination of past practice in relation to content principles we noted that decision-makers characteristically avoided a careful and explicit statement of the principles which they were in fact employing and, even in instances in which their identification of relevant principles was relatively more explicit, often refrained from giving the operational indices to their formulations which would permit others to understand and appraise their decisions. These same two tendencies are, unfortunately, even more pronounced in the past procedural operations of decision-makers; hence inference from relatively implicit features of the context must in considerable measure replace direct observation as a basis for our survey and appraisal. It would appear, however, that in relation to no aspect of the process of responsible decision has the default of decision-makers and scholars been greater than in their failure to articulate and apply appropriate principles of procedure. It is only in a few relatively recent cases, especially in the International Court of Justice, that we begin to get indications that an appropriate conception of a comprehensive, orderly, and economic inquiry is beginning to emerge.

A dim awareness of the potential relevance of procedural principles may underlie some of the content principles, such as the various unfortunate formulations with respect to the admissibility of *travaux préparatoires,* which limit recourse to significant features of the process of communication upon the ground that, under certain loosely prescribed conditions, one feature of the context is to be preferred to another. Explicit principles have been used less frequently to describe more specific operations by which decision-makers may be assisted in examining features of the context to which general, and often multiple, reference is made in the traditional principles of content. Since in our previous survey the proposed hierarchies of content principles have been analyzed and criticized in some detail, it remains in succeeding sections to call attention to the occasional references by scholars and jurists to the procedures which have been developed in past practice to establish the order best adapted to exhibit the relevance of the traditional principles of content and to note the degree to which the findings of modern science have, or have not, been brought to bear in employment of the other recommended principles.

In the few discernible procedural guidelines offered either by decision-makers or by publicists, several trends may be noted in *types* of approaches preferred. One approach adopted by some judges and arbitrators involves simply deferring to the order of presentation offered by the parties themselves. Another approach, occasionally preferred, employs procedures for examining context in a relatively systematic widening of the decision-maker's focus of attention. A third requires an implicit, if not more fully articulated, canvass of all the traditional content principles. While none of these approaches had been fully spelled out in past decision and opinion, the tentative deference accorded each deserves emphasis as at least an initial step toward the recommended goal of systematic employment of explicit procedural principles.

The practical considerations of securing competence and expeditiously hearing claims are doubtless responsible for the frequent deference given to the procedural operations proposed by the parties. For most international disputes the tribunal's competence is carefully limited by the parties in their specifications of the issues open for hearing. Frequently these specifications are detailed enough to be adopted by the parties as the outline of their own series of arguments before the tribunal, with corresponding limitations upon the information provided the tribunal and the sources invoked in support of particular arguments. In such cases, the tribunal may be easily tempted to follow a line of least resistance both in review for decision and in formulating its opinion.

Recommendations have frequently been made by both publicists and decision-makers in support of the second alternative, the "expanding focus" viewpoint. Even decision-makers who have apparently concentrated on the plain meanings of a text have often commented that one should begin with particular words and phrases, and should continue, when particular words are ambiguous, to enlarge the focus of attention to other phrases, sentences, or paragraphs. More recently, some writers have recommended this procedural approach as a regular matter—not simply as a stopgap measure when particular words or phrases are regarded as ambiguous. The recent emphasis upon looking at the "whole text" also contains in some versions an "expanding focus" viewpoint, albeit the extent of the focus is severely limited. As we will see shortly in discussing the contextual principle, increasing insistence has also been placed upon the inclusion of broader, nontextual features of the context in a systematic enlargement of the decision-maker's focus of attention.

Finally, it is only in very recent decisions that a systematic, comprehensive canvass of principles of interpretation has come to be taken for granted. For reasons not yet clearly articulated, in a number of contemporary cases recourse has been made to the whole repertoire of principles in attempting—through an appropriately contextual approach—to determine the parties' genuine shared expectations. Even the initial deliberations and opinions of the present International Court of Justice gave little advance warning of so revolutionary a development. In its more recent cases, however, the Court has appeared willing to employ a wide range of traditional principles in the course of reaching and explaining its decision.

While the order of these principle-by-principle examinations still too frequently remains anecdotal or obscure, we will presently see that there is much to applaud in such pathfinding efforts to evolve a workable set of principles of procedure.

THE CONTEXTUALITY PRINCIPLE

The principle of contextuality—which provides in its procedural version that the decision-maker should employ techniques designed to bring all potentially relevant content to the focus of his attention in the order best adopted to exhibiting actual relevance, meanwhile suspending final commitment—gets little clear articulation in the inherited literature. While an observer may assume that numerous attempts have been made to follow the procedures most likely to bring the entire context of an agreement to the attention of the decision-maker, very little explicit recognition can be found of the potential operations involved in such a task. International tribunals have, of course, invoked various maxims designed to indicate the necessity of considering all elements of the context prior to final decision. The Permanent Court, for example, commented on various occasions that its task in interpreting an agreement was to "interpret the text as it stands, taking into consideration all of the materials at [its] disposal," and that the assessment of these materials was the most significant task of the interpreter since "the context is the final test" of the participants' genuine shared expectations of commitment.[1] In some instances, this "context" is spelled out in greater detail, as in the *Chorzow Factory* case where the Court emphasized that "account must be taken not only of the historical development of arbitration treaties, as well as of the terminology of such treaties, and of the grammatical and logical meaning of the words used, but also and more especially of the function which, in the intention of the contracting Parties, is to be attributed to this provision." [2] Beyond such general injunctions as these, however, until very recently decision-makers failed, for the most part, to elaborate even minimally ac-

1. *Treatment of Polish Nationals and Other Persons of Polish Origin or Speech in the Danzig Territory,* P.C.I.J., Ser. A/B, No. 44, p. 40 (1932); *International Labor Organization (Agriculture)*, P.C.I.J., Ser. B., No. 2, p. 35 (1922).
2. *Case Concerning the Factory at Chorzow* (Jurisdiction), P.C.I.J., Ser. A, No. 9, p. 24 (1927).

ceptable procedural suggestions which would facilitate a thorough, systematic examination of the contextual materials at their disposal.

What we have characterized as an "expanding focus" approach, that of describing the increasingly broader features of the context which a decision-maker should examine with respect to any particular agreement, had a notably strong proponent in Judge Hudson. In outlining a simple version of this approach, Hudson wrote:

> The context is not simply the particular sentence, or the particular paragraph in which the term to be construed occurs. It may be (1) a particular part of the instrument, or (2) the instrument as a whole, or (3) the versions of the text in different languages, or (4) the texts of several interrelated and interdependent instruments.[3]

A modest advantage of this general approach is that it does attempt to provide a series of explicit operations through which the decision-maker may conduct a systematic search of available evidence. To be sure, the indices pointed to are scarcely complete enough to provide the kind of reminder which is intended in the procedural principle of contextuality.[4] Unfortunately it omits indispensable reference to such operations as estimating the parties' anticipated degrees of generality, explicitness, and ambiguity in all relevant words and deeds, examining additional sources of evidence of their shared expectations in the larger features of the context, and of surveying the complement of community policies required for integrating the parties' expectations with preferred public order. In short, the decision-maker's attention is not called, even in a preliminary way, to the vast range of procedures necessary for examining the many relevant features of the total context of commitment.

Judge Lauterpacht, in another example, criticized earlier decision-makers for "unduly simplifying the difficult process of interpretation" by failing to take into account "evidence of the intention of the parties more tangible than exclusive reliance on the assumed natural

3. Hudson, *The Permanent Court of International Justice, 1920–1942* 646–47 (1943).

4. For a similar discussion of a limited analysis of "contextual" factors, see Fitzmaurice, "The Law and Procedure of the International Court of Justice: Treaty Interpretation and Certain Other Treaty Points," 28 *Brit. Yb. Int'l L.* 1, 11, 18–20 (1951).

meaning of the clause in question." [5] In so doing he proposed a similar set of procedural canons in these terms: "in so far as the process of interpretation must start from *somewhere,* it is not unreasonable that it should begin with what appears to be the natural, the common, the 'plain' meaning of the terms used . . . It is therefore legitimate to insist, in the interest of good faith and of a requisite minimum of certainty in legal transactions, that the burden of proof should rest upon the party asserting that the term in question is used not in its ordinary but in an unusual connotation or that the 'clear meaning' is not what on the face of it it appears to be." [6]

A surprisingly traditional approach, as noted above, has recently been proposed by the International Law Commission.[7] While the approach recommended in its Report can scarcely be said to be a procedural one in any genuine sense, the principles of interpretation which it offers have numerous procedural consequences. At the most general level, these consequences involve both limitation upon the scope of contextual examination and a minimization of the utility of principles in aid of decision.

The immediately most significant of these limitations is of course that upon the scope of contextual analysis. What is perhaps most revealing in this respect is the explicit statement by the Commission that what it calls a *contextual* analysis is in reality only a *textual* one; witness the definition of "context" in Article 69 of the proposed Code: "The context of the treaty, for the purposes of its interpretation shall be understood as compromising, in addition to the treaty, including its preamble and annexes, any agreement or instrument related to the treaty and reached or drawn up in relation to its con-

5. Lauterpacht, *The Development of International Law by the International Court* 55 (1958).

6. Id. at 58. For a similar view, see McNair, *The Law of Treaties* 175–76 (1938):

> [t]his so-called rule of interpretation [the plain terms canon] like others is merely a *prima facie* guide and cannot be allowed to obstruct the essential quest in the application of treaties, namely, to search for the real intention of the contracting parties in using the language employed by them . . . The doctrine embodies a presumption but not an irrebuttable one, and it is reasonable to suppose that the Court will lay the burden of proof upon the party seeking to rebut the presumption.

7. Report of the International Law Commission, "Law of Treaties," U.N. Gen. Ass. Off. Rec., 19th Sess., Supp. No. 9 (A/5809) (1964).

clusion."[8] The Commission makes quite clear that most sources of extrinsic evidence, "including the preparatory work of the treaty and the circumstances of its conclusion," are excluded from this definition.[9] They are, in fact, relegated to the secondary role of "further means of interpretation," which are to be resorted to only if the "contextual," i.e. textual, analysis leaves the meaning of the provision under consideration obscure. In this important sense, then, the Commission recommends a return to the traditional limitation upon contextual analysis which in effect seeks to confine effective interpretation to the four corners of the text of an agreement.

Quite consistently with this approach, the Commission fails to recommend the deliberate and systematic employment of principles in aid of decision. In its view, the use of principles should be a matter of convenience rather than of necessity: "Recourse to many of these principles [of interpretation] is discretionary rather than obligatory and the interpretation of documents is to some extent an art, not an exact science."[10] While the Commission may be lauded for its indirect recognition of the necessity of judicial discretion in interpretation, it nowhere explains how a decision-maker who does not discipline his choice by principles can be assured of the rationality of his choice, and its assumption that the comprehensive use of principles might impair or detract from rationality in decision would appear unfortunate. It is quite unnecessary myopia to think of principles of interpretation as hard imperatives, yielding no discretion, rather than as guidelines to relevant context and economy in the examination of context.

From the vague injunctions expressed in the "expanding focus" approach we may now turn to another, parallel and equally timid, effort to enlarge the context required to be examined in interpretation, sometimes called the "principle of integration," which stipulates quite generally that an interpreter should "read the instrument as a whole"[11] and "look to the context." This principle prescribes, in one version, that "Treaties are to be interpreted as a whole, and

8. Id. at 25.

9. Ibid.

10. Id. at 26.

11. For detailed exposition and advocacy of this view, see De Visscher, *Problèmes d'Interpretation Judiciaire en Droit International Public* 59–61 (1963), and Degan, *L'Interpretation des Accords en Droit International* 95–98 (1963).

particular parts, chapters or sections also as a whole." [12] In another formulation, Schwarzenberger concludes that "The meaning of words is always relative to their context, and the words employed in a treaty may make sense only in the wider context of sentences, paragraphs, articles and the treaty as a whole." [13] It should be clear that, in its traditional formulation, the principle of integration makes reference to a broad range of operations covered, at least in part, by other principles. At one extreme, it resembles the widely cited statement of the plain meaning doctrine in the *Polish Postal Service in Danzig* case: "Words must be interpreted in the sense which they would normally have in their context." [14] At the other extreme, it resembles one version of the doctrine of effectiveness: "treaties should be interpreted as a whole, having regard to the purposes embodied therein." (Judge Azevedo in the *Second Peace Treaties* case).[15] Such a wide range of application indicates the difficulty which past decision-makers have had in separating out the specific operation which they wish to associate with the concept of "reading a provision in its context," or "reading a treaty as a whole." As we shall presently see, their efforts to do so have not to date been very successful.

The most frequently cited statement of the rule that provisions directly involved in a dispute should be considered in light of the entire agreement is contained in the *International Labor Organization (Agriculture)* case, in which the Permanent Court commented that "the Treaty must be read as a whole, and . . . its meaning is not to be determined merely upon particular phrases which, if detached from the context, may be interpreted in more than one sense." [16] It should be noted that all of the potential operations involved in widening the interpreter's focus of attention, of reading from specific phrases to entire provisions and beyond, are referred to in the Court's formula.

Other formulations make somewhat less generous reference to ex-

12. Fitzmaurice, "The Law and Procedure of the International Court of Justice, 1951–54: Treaty Interpretation and Other Treaty Points," 333 *Brit. Yb. Int'l L.* 203, 211 (1957).

13. 1 Schwarzenberger, *International Law* 505 (3d ed. 1957).

14. P.C.I.J., Ser. B, No. 11, p. 39 (1925).

15. *Interpretation of Peace Treaties with Bulgaria, Hungary and Romania* (Second Phase), [1950] I.C.J. Rep. 221, 250.

16. Supra note 1, at 23.

tratextual factors and the unique circumstances of the claims being presented. In the *Free Zones* case,[17] for example, the Court did not feel the necessity of insisting upon an examination of provisions beyond Article 435, which it described as a "complete whole" with respect to the demands of the parties to the dispute. Nevertheless, it felt required to relate portions of the article to each other: "[The Court finds it] impossible to interpret the second paragraph without regard to the first paragraph." [18] The respective paragraphs contained the mutual declaration of intention on the part of France and Switzerland to reform the Zones of Savoy and Gex in light of the fact that the previous arrangement under the treaties of 1815 was "no longer consistent with present conditions." [19] Paragraph (1) took note of the already concluded "abrogation" of the previous agreement relating to Savoy, and paragraph (2) proposed that both countries "come to an agreement . . . settling between themselves the status" of Upper Savoy and Gex. In light of Switzerland's subsequent rejection, in referendum, of the proposal for realigning the districts —together with France's declaration of intention to enforce it despite the rejection—the initial question became one of determining whether paragraph (2) had "automatically" abrogated the 1815 treaties with the repetition of the phrase found in paragraph (1) to the effect that they were "no longer consistent with present conditions." The Court concluded at an early point that a comparison of the two paragraphs necessitated a negative answer to the question, since the "abrogation" in (1) was *not* automatic, but depended upon, and referred to, the new agreement reached concerning Savoy: "there is no reason for regarding the expression 'are no longer consistent with present conditions' as *ipso facto* involving, in the second paragraph of the article the abolition of the free zones, since in the first paragraph its meaning is not such as automatically to involve the abolition of the neutralized zone." [20] In subsequent decisions, the Court maintained substantially the same position.[21]

Similarly, the Court in the case of the *Treaty of Lausanne* [22]

17. *Free Zones of Upper Savoy and District of Gex,* P.C.I.J., Ser. A/B, No. 46 (1932).
18. Id. at 140.
19. *Free Zones,* Order of Court, P.C.I.J., Ser. A, No. 22, p. 9 (1929).
20. Id. at 17.
21. Supra note 17, at 171–72.

turned to a comparison of the second and third subparagraphs of Article 3 (2) of the Treaty for the purpose of determining whether the two paragraphs together "throw any light upon the scope of Article 3." [23] It held that the reference of the phrase "decision to be reached" in subparagraph 3—upon which the "final fate" of the Iraqi-Turkish border dispute was made to depend in the absence of a special agreement by the parties—was to the decision of the Council of the League of Nations to which the dispute was referred in the previous subparagraph:

> this decision may be either an agreement between the Parties or, failing such agreement, the solution given by the Council. Now a decision on which the final fate of the territories in question depends can only be a decision laying down in a definitive manner the frontier between Turkey and Iraq binding upon the two States. This interpretation of the third subparagraph, which is indicated by the terms therein employed, is entirely in accordance with the conclusions drawn from the preceding subparagraphs and from Article 3 as a whole.[24]

The Court went on to compare Article 3 with other articles of the Treaty, and concluded that the article, taken as a whole and in its context in the agreement, conferred upon the League Council the right to make a final and binding determination of the legitimate border between Turkey and Iraq.[25]

In more general reference, the Permanent Court in the *Postal Service in Danzig* case held that its conclusion that Poland could implement its Danzig postal operations by establishing collection boxes and other essential services was "supported by . . . the various articles taken by themselves and in their relation to one another." [26] Again, in the *Memel Territory* case,[27] the Court analyzed the treaty in dispute in more abstract terms: "The Convention of Paris of 1924 and the Statute annexed to it, must be considered as a whole in order

22. *Article 3, Paragraph 2, of the Treaty of Lausanne (Frontier Between Turkey and Iraq)*, P.C.I.J., Ser. B, No. 12 (1925).
23. Id. at 21.
24. Ibid.
25. Id. at 33.
26. Supra note 14, at 39–40.
27. *Interpretation of the Statute of the Memel Territory,* P.C.I.J., Ser. A/B, No. 49 (1932).

to understand the regime which the Four Powers and Lithuania intended to establish for the Memel Territory." [28] In this case, the Four Powers (Britain, France, Italy, and Japan) had assigned to Lithuania, in Article 7 of the Memel Convention, exclusive jurisdiction over all affairs in the Memel territory not within the competence of local authorities. The event which engendered the present dispute occurred when the Governor of Memel dismissed its territorial President, thus possibly contravening Article 17 of the Convention which provided that the President "shall hold office so long as he possesses the confidence of the Chamber of Representatives." [29] In petitioning the Court, the Four Powers urged that Article 17 established an *absolute* prohibition upon the disputed act, one not subject to the requirements of the remaining sections of the Memel Convention limiting the President's protection to those courses of action which are expressly permitted within the overriding jurisdiction of Lithuania. The Court rejected this view, commenting that "Article 17 must be read as restricted to executive power in respect of matters within the competence of the Memel authorities, otherwise it would be in flagrant contradiction with the provisions of Article 7." [30] In response to the Four Powers' claim that even if *some* controls are retained by Lithuania in Article 17, the dismissal of the territorial President is not one of them, the Court again said that the "protection" provision "cannot . . . be isolated from the rest of the article in which it figures," the aim of which is to establish executive powers in Memel within the limits established by the Statute: "To place upon these words the meaning . . . [urged by the Four Powers] would result in a President being able to violate the Statute and to flout the authorities of the Lithuanian Government so long as he carried the Chamber with him. Such an interpretation would destroy the general scheme of the Convention . . . under which Memel was to enjoy autonomy within defined limits, but was placed under the sovereignty of Lithuania." [31]

Perhaps the most notable example of the Court's refusal to extend its analysis to the several provisions of an agreement occurred in the *Wimbledon* case,[32] in which it held that Part XII, Section VI, of the

28. Id. at 22.
29. Id. at 25.
30. Id. at 26.
31. Id. at 27.
32. *The S.S. "Wimbledon,"* P.C.I.J., Ser. A, No. 1 (1923).

Treaty of Versailles, relating to the regulation of the Kiel Canal, was, in its words, "self-contained," and that therefore resort to previous sections was not permissible. Such resort would, the Court contended, cause the relevant provisions of Section VI to "lose their raison d'être" in light of the clear intention of the drafters to restrict all regulations concerning the Kiel Canal to one section of the Treaty:

> in this special section rules exclusively designed for the Kiel Canal have been inserted; these rules differ on more than one point from those to which other internal navigable waterways of the [German] Empire are subjected by Articles 321 to 327. This difference appears more especially from the fact that the Kiel Canal is open to the war vessels and transit traffic of all nations at peace with Germany, whereas free access to the other German navigable waterways referred to above is limited to the Allied and Associated Powers alone . . . The provisions relating to the Kiel Canal in the Treaty of Versailles are therefore self-contained; if they had to be supplemented and interpreted by the aid of those referring to the inland navigable waterways of Germany in the previous Sections of Part XII, they would lose their 'raison d'être', such repetitions as are found in them would be superfluous and there would be every justification for surprise at the fact that, in certain cases, when the provisions of Articles 321 to 327 might be applicable to the canal, the authors of the Treaty should have taken the trouble to repeat their terms or reproduce their substance.[33]

The Court thus accepted as evidence of the parties' intention to except the Kiel Canal from the treatment accorded other waterways in Articles 321–27 the increased scope and degree of repetition which were exhibited in Section VI, Articles 380–86. This indicated, to the majority at least, that the imposition of other restrictions on travel through the canal which could be inferred from the earlier articles would not be appropriate.[34]

In the recent *Lawless* case,[35] the European Court of Human

33. Id. at 23–24.

34. Ibid. Cf. the Court's rejection of an alleged parallel between articles in the *Chorzow Factories (Indemnities)* case, P.C.I.J., Ser. A, No. 17, p. 42 (1928).

35. (Merits), *European Court of Human Rights Reports,* Ser. A, p. 27 (1961); also reported in 4 *Yearbook of the European Convention on Human Rights* 438 (1961).

Rights undertook an orderly if somewhat limited expansion of its focus of attention to relevant context. While we make more extensive reference to its procedures in this respect elsewhere,[36] its approach is worth underlining here. Simply stated, the issue in the case was whether under the European Human Rights Convention a state could without trial impose preventive detention upon a suspected revolutionary. The Court held that under most circumstances preventive detention without trial was not permissible under Article 5 of the Convention, but in the special circumstances presented in the case—where the security of the State was reasonably thought to be in jeopardy—such unusual action was permissible under the "derogation" powers of Article 17 of the Convention.

The procedural examination, particularly of issues relating to Article 5, was undertaken by the Court in a quite systematic manner. It began by examining Article 5, paragraph 1 (c), which provided that the detention of a person accused of a crime, or allegedly any detention for preventive purposes, should not be carried out except for the "purpose of bringing him before a competent legal authority."[37] The ambiguity of the textual connection between preventive detention and the requirement of trial was resolved by the Court in a series of consistently more inclusive procedures. First, another article relating specifically to arraignment and trial was examined and found to refer to the entirety of legal actions covered in Article 5, Paragraph 1 (c), and not to a subgroup of them. Then the objectives of the entire Convention—that of preserving individual liberties in the face of demands for security by the state—were examined and weighed in favor of judicial guarantees concerning preventive detention.

The final step in the process, involving a discussion of extratextual materials relating to the preparatory work on the Convention, was rejected by the Court with the traditional maxim that the text itself was clear and that as a result such reference was not permissible.

The most thorough and successful examples of interpretation which examines the larger context of agreement by appropriately economic procedures are, as previously indicated, to be found in the recent jurisprudence of certain international tribunals, particularly the International Court of Justice. These examples exhibit a sys-

36. See below, p. 304 and p. 321.

37. *European Court of Human Rights Reports,* Ser. A, p. 46 (1961).

tematic canvass of alternatives in choice among competing interpretations in a relatively comprehensive survey of relevant context. They also eschew the dogmatic establishment of hierarchies among aspects of the context under examination. While as yet tribunals have appeared somewhat reluctant to extend this method in the fullest and most effective degree, a definite trend seems to be developing which might lead in the desired direction of the comprehensive and economic examination recommended in the principle of procedural contextuality.

The most important case in which the International Court of Justice has employed a variety of principles in a relatively comprehensive and orderly canvass of relevant features of the context is that of the celebrated *Certain Expenses of the United Nations*,[38] already briefly discussed above.[39] The question of interpretation raised by the General Assembly in its request for an advisory opinion was, as previously indicated, whether certain expenditures authorized by the General Assembly

> to cover the costs of the United Nations operations in the Congo (hereinafter referred to as ONUC) and of the operations of the United Nations Emergency Force in the Middle East (hereinafter referred to as UNEF) "constitute 'expenses of the Organization' within the meaning of Article 17, paragraph 2, of the Charter of the United Nations".[40]

In justifying its conclusion that the questioned expenditures did come within the competence of the General Assembly to budget and apportion, the Court focused initially upon the relevant words of Article 17, which read:

> 1. The General Assembly shall consider and approve the budget of the Organization.
> 2. The expenses of the Organization shall be borne by the Members as apportioned by the General Assembly.[41]

Immediately invoking a presumption in favor of the most general reference of the critical words "budget" and "expenses," the Court

38. [1962] I.C.J. Rep. 151.
39. See Ch. 4. p. 165. For further explication of the facts in the *Expenses* case, see below in the discussion of the lexical operation, p. 323.
40. [1962] I.C.J. Rep. 151, 156.
41. Id. at 157.

stated that it could qualify this reference by such limiting notions as "regular" or "administrative" only "if such qualification must necessarily be implied from the provisions of the Charter considered as a whole, or from some particular provision thereof which makes it unavoidable to do so in order to give effect to the Charter." [42] A search of the other Charter provisions by the Court yielded no grounds for implying such a qualification, but on the contrary demonstrated both that the framers had known how to make express qualification when necessary and that a variety of expenses had inevitably to be "included within the 'expenses of the Organization' just as much as the salaries of staff or the maintenance of buildings." [43]

Turning next to the "general structure and scheme of the Charter," the Court invoked both the "general purposes" and the continuous practice of the organization in support of its initial presumption in favor of competence. The generous use made by the Court of inferences from the major purposes of the organization we have already outlined. The particular argument that the General Assembly had no competence to apportion because the operations in question were "actions" beyond its competence to authorize was disposed of by a finding that the operations were not, since undertaken with the express consent of the states involved, "enforcement actions" within the meaning of the Charter. The concluding segments of the opinion supporting the Court's position by inferences from the practice of the organization do not, it must be confessed, exhibit the highest artistry in craftsmanship, but the opinion as a whole can appropriately be regarded as another hopeful departure from the all too frequent dogmatic insistence upon the arbitrariness of textual exegesis.

Even the separate opinions of Judges Spender and Fitzmaurice in the *Expenses* case may afford modest hope that the doctrine of extreme textuality is approaching rigor mortis. In previous cases the position repeatedly upheld by both these judges has been that of the traditional Vattel school, which forbids recourse to extrinsic materials if the plain meaning of the text is found clear and dispositive of the issues facing the Court. In this case both judges offer some verbal, but a very limited procedural, qualification of this hoary mythology.

Thus Spender begins his general observations on interpretation with the statement that words "communicate their meaning from the

42. Id. at 159.
43. Id. at 161.

circumstances in which they are used" [44] and insists that the "stated purposes of the Charter should be the prime consideration in interpreting its text." He even writes, in glowing paraphrase of Chief Justice Marshall:

> Its provisions were of necessity expressed in broad and general terms. It attempts to provide against the unknown, the unforeseen and, indeed, the unforeseeable. Its text reveals that it was intended—subject to such amendments as might from time to time be made to it—to endure, at least it was hoped it would endure, for all time. It was intended to apply to varying conditions in a changing and evolving world community and to a multiplicity of unpredictable situations and events. Its provisions were intended to adjust themselves to the ever changing pattern of international existence. It established international machinery to accomplish its stated purposes.[45]

It does not escape him that the plain meaning "injunction is sometimes a counsel of perfection" and that the "ordinary and natural sense of words may at times be a matter of considerable difficulty to determine." [46] In the end, however, he concludes with the same old misdirection: "If the meaning of any particular provision read in its context is sufficiently clear to satisfy the Court as to the interpretation to be given to it there is neither legal justification nor logical reason to have recourse to either the *travaux préparatoires* or the practice followed within the United Nations." [47] The confusions and inadequacies in this recommendation from a procedural perspective have already been sufficiently emphasized.

Similarly, Fitzmaurice, with hardly a bow to plain and natural meaning, devotes the great bulk of his separate opinion to considering the practice of the organization and to inferences from the *travaux préparatoires.* In his formulations about the relevance of practice, however, he comes perilously close to stipulating something analogous to the *opinio juris* requirement about customary law: he insists that states which make payment under allocations imposed by the General Assembly may do so without having any subjectivities or

44. Id. at 184, 185.
45. Id. at 185.
46. Id. at 184.
47. Id. at 185–86.

creating expectations that payment is lawfully required.[48] The important point is of course what expectations are reasonably created in the general community (including states other than the payer) both by the adoption of the General Assembly resolution and by all the payments which are made under it. It may be recalled that under the aegis of customary international law behavior accompanied in the beginning by expectations of all parties that it was unlawful has on occasion come to be regarded as creating expectations about lawfulness.[49] The formulation about the permissibility of recourse to the *travaux préparatoires* offered by Fitzmaurice also, finally, continues to resemble that of Spender: recourse may be had to "the preparatory work of the San Francisco Conference" because "there is a sufficient element of ambiguity about the exact intention and effect of Article 17, paragraph 2, to make its interpretation on the basis of the rule of the 'natural and ordinary meaning' alone, unsatisfactory." [50]

Another recent case in which the International Court of Justice approximates the operations specified by the principle of procedural contextuality is that concerning the *Constitution of the Maritime Safety Committee of the Inter-Governmental Maritime Consultative Organization* (IMCO).[51] The principal issue in this case, as noted above, was whether Liberia and Panama should be seated on the Maritime Safety Committee of IMCO pursuant to Article 28 (a) of the Convention of March 6, 1948, which established IMCO. The article, which we shall quote again, reads as follows:

> The Maritime Safety Committee shall consist of fourteen Members elected by the Assembly from the Members, governments of those nations having an important interest in maritime safety, of which not less than eight shall be the largest ship-owning nations, and the remainder shall be elected so as to ensure adequate representation of Members, governments of other nations

48. Id. at 201.
49. For further exposition of this process, see McDougal, Lasswell, and Vlasic, *Law and Public Order in Space* 115–17 (1963). It is important to note, in this respect, that Fitzmaurice gives high priority to subsequent events and expectations by commenting that they may be "good presumptive (and . . . in certain cases . . . virtually conclusive) evidence of what the correct legal interpretation is." Supra note 38, at 201.
50. Id. at 209.
51. [1960] I.C.J. Rep. 150.

> with an important interest in maritime safety, such as nations interested in the supply of large numbers of crews or in the carriage of large numbers of berthed and unberthed passengers, and of major geographical areas.[52]

The Court was asked to appraise the failure of the Assembly of IMCO to elect Liberia and Panama to the Committee in spite of the fact that they were third and eighth, respectively, in registered shipping tonnage. While the criteria for the questioned election were not clarified, the nations in fact elected turned out to be nations one through ten in tonnage on Lloyd's Register of Shipping (1958), omitting only Liberia and Panama. These two countries contended that this procedure and result was contrary to the terms of Article 28 (a), which in their view should have made the election of the eight highest-tonnage nations obligatory. The opposing argument was that nowhere in the article was registered tonnage made the exclusive index of "ship-owning nations," and that other indices such as ownership by nationals or actual involvement in the shipping business should have been and were used as standards in rejecting Liberia and Panama. The Court held that the election of the first eight nations in tonnage was obligatory.

In its survey of the context, the Court employed most of the principles of interpretation, even though it did so in a somewhat confusing manner and order. The confusion arose in part out of the customary bow given by the Court to the plain meaning principle. It observed that "The words of Article 28 (a) must be read in their natural and ordinary meaning, in the sense which they would normally have in their context. It is only if, when this is done, the words of the Article are ambiguous in any way that resort need be had to other methods of construction." [53] Despite this observation and its conclusion that the words used in Article 28 (a) in their ordinary meaning clearly required the election of the eight largest shipowning nations, the Court went on to analyze the structure of the provision and of the Convention, the preparatory work, the parties' objectives and subsequent actions, and other similar conventions for their relevance to the interpretation of 28 (a). That it saw no contradiction in this approach is perhaps explainable by the lack of clarity concerning

52. Id. at 154.
53. Id. at 159–60.

what was accomplished by invoking the plain meaning principle in the first place. It did not explain, to be sure, the preferred indices for "largest ship-owning nations." What the Court seems to have done is to use the plain meaning canon in a very limited sense in order to establish the fact that eight of the Committee members should be the "largest ship-owning nations" by an index yet to be determined. The selection of an index, however, is obviously the focal point of dispute in the case, and any other determination equally obviously trivial. The announcement of the application of the plain meaning doctrine with such a fanfare under these circumstances can only be misleading; the unwary reader could easily believe that the case turned on it. This is especially true when the Court announces (1) that recourse to other methods of interpretation is prohibited if the text is clear in its ordinary meaning, (2) that the ordinary meaning is in fact clear, but (3) goes ahead anyway to invoke numerous other principles without mentioning the discovery of any relevant ambiguity which under its own rule would permit it to do so. In this particular case the invocation of the plain meaning rule thus appears as something of a red herring, a more or less gratuitous bow to an old tradition without any real significance to the outcome of the dispute.

While the Court was thus somewhat hesitating and unsure in its introduction of a total contextual survey and a wide use of interpretative principles, there can be little doubt that in this case a wide range of principles were used in a comprehensive way. Preparatory work, for example, was extensively surveyed in an effort to interpret the relevance of the various drafts of the Convention to the ultimate text.[54] Other articles of the Convention were likewise reviewed and the interpretations given them were adduced as evidence of "largest ship-owning nations" being tied to the listings in Lloyd's Register of Shipping.[55] The most significant survey in this respect, however, occurred when the Court examined international practice (including United Nations Assembly practice) and maritime usage in the employment of these terms. It pointed out that in electing two members with "a substantial interest in providing international shipping services" to IMCO's sixteen-member Council, explicit reference was made to registered tonnage as the justification for electing Italy and Japan. Similarly, it pointed out that registered tonnage continued to

54. Id. at 161–65.
55. Id. at 167–68.

be used by IMCO as a means of apportioning the expenses of the organization, an important use of this index since it should be assumed that assessments would be made on the basis of greater or lesser interests in shipping. With respect to the Maritime Safety Committee, the Court noted that the list used to determine the order of voting was one made up by the Secretary-General which coincided exactly with the Lloyd's Register.[56]

In order to determine maritime usage, the Court turned to other conventions containing specific provisions relating to ship ownership. Thus it noted that the 1930 Load Line Convention provided that "a ship is regarded as belonging to a country if it is registered by the Government of that country," a provision that appeared in similar terms in many other conventions of that time and down to the time of the present dispute.[57] From this evidence it concluded that there could be no doubt that registered tonnage—in the absence of specific evidence to the contrary—must have been the index which the parties to the IMCO Convention had in mind in providing that the eight "largest ship-owning nations" were to be elected to the Maritime Safety Committee.

The Court turned to still another principle in reaching its decision by proposing that "the interpretation the Court gives to Article 28 (a) is consistent with the general purpose of the Convention and the special functions of the Maritime Safety Committee."[58] The overall purpose of the organization, it observed, is to promulgate proposals and policies for maritime regulation. "In order effectively to carry out these recommendations and to promote maritime safety in its numerous and varied aspects," the Court concluded, "the cooperation of those States who exercise jurisdiction over a large portion of the world's existing tonnage is essential."[59]

A survey of the sort carried out by the Court in this instance would appear to be fully in accord with the dominant, contemporary trend toward more and more inclusive interpretative procedures, regularly if not systematically applied in the process of decision. None of the Court's interpretative procedures were made to depend—despite the Court's forbidding initial approach—upon features of the context

56. Id. at 168–69.
57. Id. at 169–70.
58. Id. at 170.
59. Id. at 170–71.

which might or might not preclude their use. Indeed, most of the traditional sources of evidence, including preparatory work, the provision in dispute, the entire treaty text, the apparent purposes of the parties, the subsequent actions of the parties, and customary institutional practices were as a matter of course examined and appraised by the Court.

The two cases concerning the *Temple of Preah Vihear* are other recent examples in which the Court had opportunity to employ extensive and systematic procedures in examination of context. In the 1961 case,[60] which we review in detail below, the Court refused to stop short with a literal wording by which Thailand accepted the compulsory jurisdiction of the nonexistent Permanent Court of International Justice, in light of a clear and admitted intent to submit to the authority of the new International Court of Justice. In brief review, the Court held that the plain meaning of Thailand's acceptance was clear, but went ahead nonetheless to rest its decision on extratextual factors, such as the name of the addressee of the acceptance and the fact that the only Court to which such an acceptance could have been directed was the International Court.[61] The order which the Court adopted was puzzling in the extreme: first, a largely unsystematic analysis of the relevant facts and precedents, including both textual and extratextual materials; secondly, an announcement that the text was clear and that such a survey was not necessary, citing as evidence two further extratextual references; and finally, a reminder that in case of an ambiguity in the text outside references *may* be made which support the already clear text anyway (by which point such references had *already* been made in considerable abundance). Thus, while the Court may in this instance be complimented on its willingness to examine, and rest its decision in large part on, a wide contextual analysis in line with its own expanding precedent, the doctrine it announced seems under the circumstances an entirely inappropriate and anachronistic attempt to conform to the jurisprudence of the permanent Court. Ironically, even the judges themselves appeared to be willing to affirm in word, though not in deed, their allegiance to a nonexistent court.

The more interesting of the *Preah Vihear* cases from a procedural

60. [1961] I.C.J. Rep. 17.
61. Id. at 34.

point of view, however, is the 1962 case (Merits).[62] The issue involved in the case was whether the temple and grounds at Preah Vihear, a site on the border between Thailand and Cambodia of considerable historical, religious, artistic, and, potentially, military value, was properly to be considered in Thailand or in Cambodia. A treaty of 1904 between Thailand (then Siam) and Cambodia established a line in accordance with the watershed, which apparently placed the temple in Thailand. At approximately the same time, a map drawn up by the French at Siam's request, but in no way authorized by the boundary Commission set up under the treaty, showed the temple to be located in Cambodia. The "natural" boundary, an escarpment abutting the Cambodian plain which both parties proposed generally to establish, placed the temple in Thailand. Very little administrative activity was carried on by either side in the area, but one confrontation between the two nations favored Cambodia on this point; on the other hand there was an undescribed claim of some "sovereign" acts engaged in by Thailand. The Court held in favor of Cambodia.

Two primary issues were stated by the Court: (1) whether or not the maps purporting to show the boundary between the two countries were recognized as an authoritative representation of the Commission's official delimitation, and (2) whether subsequent acts by Thailand constituted a later acceptance of Cambodia's claim and therefore precluded Thailand from now claiming the temple.

On the first issue the Court held that the circumstances surrounding the completion and distribution of the maps "called for some reaction, within a reasonable period, on the part of the Siamese authorities, if they wished to disagree with the map or had any serious question to raise in regard to it."[63] Its evidence for this obligation was primarily the elaborateness with which the maps were announced and circulated: "the maps were given wide publicity in all technically interested quarters . . . to the [four major] Siamese legations . . . and to all the members of the Mixed Commission, French and Siamese"[64] Of the 160 sets of maps, 50 copies were reserved for Thailand's use and some went to the interior and foreign

62. *Temple of Preah Vihear* (Merits), [1962] I.C.J. Rep. 6.
63. Id. at 23.
64. Ibid.

affairs ministers, provincial governors, and the like. Clearly the maps, in consequence of these and other actions, were invested with considerable authority and apparently came quite close to being officially adopted by the 1904 Commission as representing the true boundary (a scheduled meeting to adopt them was never held). The Court, with little hesitation, reviewed this evidence and decided that it was strongly in Cambodia's favor, establishing a presumption that some reaction on the part of Thailand's representatives was required and in its absence Thailand "must be held to have acquiesced." [65]

The Court's approach on the first point, therefore, was to examine somewhat piecemeal the various events surrounding the work of the Commission under the 1904 treaty, and the actions of the parties concomitant to receiving the maps several years later. It undertook still another such review of Thailand's actions since that time in deciding, with regard to the second point, that Thailand had subsequently accepted the maps as authoritative delimitations, even if initially it had not. The majority recounted the visit to the temple by Prince Damrong of Thailand, a former minister of the interior and then president of the Royal Institute, in 1930. He was met on this occasion by the French Resident of the adjoining province, under a French flag. Said the Court: "The Prince could not possibly have failed to see the implications of a reception of this character. A clearer affirmation of title on the French Indo-Chinese side can scarcely be imagined. It demanded a reaction. Thailand did nothing." [66] Other evidence was cited by the Court, including a Thai pamphlet in 1941 stating that as a result of the war Thailand had "retaken" Preah Vihear; a postwar Conciliation Commission meeting at which no claim to keep the temple was made despite Thailand's agreement to return the boundary to its pre-1941 position; and Thailand's failure to answer Cambodia's consistent claims to authority over Preah Vihear since 1949, based explicitly on the maps in question. The Court's conclusion, based upon an extremely disorganized historical and contextual examination, was that this subsequent conduct would suffice to establish Cambodia's claim even if Thailand had not originally accepted the maps as the authoritative delimitation of the border.

In its presentation of the historical data relevant to the second

65. Ibid.
66. Id. at 30.

issue the Court may therefore be criticised both for the mode of its presentation of the facts of the case and for failing to extend its survey far enough. In its introduction to the case, the majority held that it would exclude from its consideration all evidence of "the situation that existed between the parties prior to the Treaty of 1904." [67] The reason given for this exclusion was that "the present dispute has its *fons et origo* in the boundary settlements made in the period 1904–1908, between France and Siam (as Thailand was then called) and, in particular, that the sovereignty over Preah Vihear depends upon a boundary treaty dated 13 February 1904, and upon events subsequent to that date." [68] As Judge Fitzmaurice pointed out in his concurring opinion, however, there was at least one element prior to 1904 which might have been decisive, and hence should have been considered: "namely that, previous to the boundary settlements of the period 1904–1908, the Temple of Preah Vihear was situated in territory that was, at that time, under Siamese sovereignty, because of a treaty of 15 July 1867 between France (acting on behalf of Cambodia) and Siam . . . had established a frontier line running well south of the Dangrek range of mountains, across the Cambodian plain." [69] Since the 1904 treaty shifted the boundary northward into formerly Siamese territory, "there arises a presumption *in favorem ejus qui dat* that Thailand did not relinquish any territory she cannot be proved to have relinquished." [70] While Fitzmaurice did not believe that this factor directly affected the decision in the case (he concurred with the Court), he believed that it did among other things shift the burden of proof and should thus have been considered by the Court in reaching its decision and giving its opinion.

Apparently both parties, but more particularly Thailand, had relied before the Court on arguments relating to alleged historical and religious ties to the temple, and to the archeological evidence for this. The Court excluded a full consideration and discussion of these factors because it said it was "unable to regard them as legally decisive." [71] It is interesting, and should be underlined, that the Court did not examine these factors because they were *not dispositive of the*

67. Id. at 16.
68. Ibid.
69. Id. at 52.
70. Ibid.
71. Id. at 15.

issue. Surely the Court would not establish this criterion as a regular procedural "safeguard"; no feature of the context need, or should be given a conclusively dispositive effect; the various features are *examined* for their potential relevance only, and may afterward be discarded. Fitzmaurice, who despite his earlier position agreed with the Court, attempted to explain this curious exclusion:

> Such matters may have some legal relevance in a case about territorial sovereignty which turns on the weight of factual evidence that each party can adduce in support of its claim, and not on any more concrete and positive element, such as a treaty. In the present case it is accepted, and indeed contended by both Parties, that their rights derive from the treaty settlement of 1904, and on the subsequent events relative to or affecting that settlement.[72]

Neither the Court nor Fitzmaurice, it seems, were willing to consider the possibility that the evidence rejected might be relevant to determining the parties' understanding of the treaty. Therefore, this case must be interpreted as an attempt to decide—on "plain meaning" or other grounds—about the relevance of such arguments without describing or discussing them, or relating them to the treaty. When resort was in fact made to extratextual factors, it was not for the purpose of interpreting the treaty as much as it was to establish facts independent of the treaty. Apparently the Court did not consider the procedural alternative of beginning with the treaty itself, and systematically expanding its enquiry in search of an answer to its reference. What the Court did was to minimize the importance of the treaty, while engaging in an unrelated and unsystematic survey of conflicting facts in the context. The maps, in effect, were not seen as an aid in *interpreting* the treaty, but rather as a *revision* of it. This point, however, and the facts relevant to determining its validity, were never seriously considered by the Court. The closest it came was to say that "the map (whether in all respects accurate by reference to the true watershed line or not) was accepted by the Parties in 1908 and thereafter as constituting the result of the interpretation given by the two Governments to the delimitation which the Treaty itself required." [73] Thus it did not seem to matter to the Court *what* the

72. Id. at 53.
73. Id. at 34.

terms of the focal agreement were. They could be consistent, or inconsistent, with the map; the fact was the Court considered the map as "the treaty" between the parties. The conflict with another relative "plain meaning" in the treaty itself was simply ignored.

This case, then, must be considered on balance a poor example of contextual examination. The Court appears to have abandoned an "expanding focus" approach in favor of an arbitrary selection of a few important factors in the context, with the exclusion of others. It is ironic that in this radical departure from more recent tendencies the first source of evidence that it excluded was the focal agreement itself, and the extratextual materials relevant to interpreting it.

The best recent example, apart from the jurisprudence of the International Court of Justice, of the comprehensive employment of procedures promoting a full contextual review is to be found in the award of the tribunal in the *Saudi Arabia–Aramco* arbitration.[74] In this case a broad survey of alternative interpretative strategies was reviewed in a highly systematic manner. As mentioned previously, the principal issue was whether the Saudi Arabian government had, by a 1933 concession agreement with a predecessor of Aramco, conferred upon the Company an exclusive right to the transportation by sea from Saudi Arabia of the oil which it extracted under the agreement. Article 1 of the concession agreement made a comprehensive statement of the rights conferred.

> The Government hereby grants to the Company on the terms and conditions hereinafter mentioned, and with respect to the area defined below, the *exclusive right,* for a period of sixty years from the effective date hereof, to explore, prospect, drill for, extract, treat, manufacture, transport, deal with, carry away and export petroleum, asphalt, naphtha, natural gases, ozokerite and other hydrocarbons, and the derivatives of all such products.[75]

The dispute before the tribunal arose in 1954, when the government signed an agreement with A. S. Onassis giving him, in return for the establishment of a national maritime service, a "right of priority" for

74. Award of Tribunal, Aug. 23, 1958; reported in 27 *Int. Law Rep.* 117 (1963). The encomium we here offer is for the technique of the tribunal and not for the interpretation it finally achieved.
75. Id. at 68; 27 *Int. Law Rep.* 175.

the transportation by sea of some of the oil products extracted from Saudi Arabia. Aramco objected to this latter agreement on the ground that it was incompatible with the exclusive rights allegedly granted by the 1933 concession agreement. The government requested Aramco and Onassis to negotiate the alleged incompatibility, but when negotiations failed, the parties agreed to submit the issue to arbitration.

The government's principal contentions were: (1) that the concession agreement did not explicitly mention the right to transportation by sea as one of the "exclusive" rights granted and, hence, by application of the principle of restrictive interpretation no such right should be implied to limit Saudi Arabia's exercise of the powers ordinarily inherent in every sovereign state; and (2) that Aramco had indeed recognized its lack of exclusive right by its failure to build, buy, or charter any tankers for the sea transport of oil during the more than twenty years of operations under the agreement (i.e., it was left to buyers of the oil to arrange their own transport). In reply, Aramco relied primarily upon: (1) the alleged plain meaning of the words of Article 1—"transport, deal with, carry away, and export"—as including an exclusive right of transportation by sea; (2) the alleged necessity for the company to have an exclusive right to sea transportation if it were effectively to carry out the principal aims of the agreement; and (3) the reputed common practice in the international oil industry of stipulating delivery f.o.b. country of origin—thus giving buyers their choice of modes and contracts of transport.

At the beginning of its exegesis in interpretation of the concession agreement, the tribunal affirmed the need for a full contextual survey to ascertain "the common intention of the parties at the time their agreement was signed." It also commented that the task of interpretation is "not governed by rigid rules": "it is rather an art, governed by principles of logic and common sense, which purports to lead to an adaptation, as reasonable as possible, of the provisions of a contract to the facts of a dispute." [76]

In exemplification of what we have described as "identifying the focal agreement," the tribunal next found that the "starting point of any process of interpretation is the text agreed upon by the Parties." [77] Such a text "must be consulted and accepted in the first place,

76. Id. at 65; 27 id. at 172.
77. Id. at 67; 27 id. at 173.

and the words used by the Parties must be given their natural meaning." The tribunal refused, however, to be ensnared into the obscurantism demanded by followers of Vattel who, as we have seen, urge a severe telescoping of the process of interpretation after a simple analysis of these "plain and natural" meanings. The criterion suggested for abandonment of the Vattel principle was the reasonably flexible one of abandoning it whenever "each party is convinced, in good faith, that the interpretation suggested by the other is not exact," and is not merely alleging that the provision "is ambiguous simply because it is embarrassing and seeks to have it say what it does not." [78] In such a case—of which the instant case was held to be an example—"Vattel's maxim does no longer suffice for the solution of the dispute, and recourse must be had to all the means of interpretation of legal acts." [79]

Having made a preliminary identification of the main provisions of the focal agreement, the tribunal next proceeded sytematically to assess possible alternative references of these provisions by application of the whole arsenal of familiar principles. In accordance with its initial emphasis upon the agreement text, the tribunal first analyzed the critical words of Article 1 through a description of the customary process of oil extraction, refining, transportation, and marketing. The import of this description suggested that a step-by-step grant was intentionally made of exclusive rights to perform or control all phases of the oil marketing process. Thus, exploration was mentioned before drilling, extraction before manufacture, and transportation before export. A thorough semantic analysis of the conventional usage of each of the four principal terms employed in the grant was found to confirm the inference drawn from this ordering.

The tribunal therefore concluded—again provisionally—that the intention of the government, as understood by the Company, had been to grant comprehensive rights to the Company to do anything it deemed necessary to produce and sell all the oil products specified in the agreement. This included, by necessary deduction, the right to arrange the type of transportation most likely to satisfy buyers and increase market opportunities. The tribunal found that the contention of the government that the reference of the words in Article 1 could be exhausted without including external transportation by sea

78. Ibid.; 27 id. at 174.
79. Ibid.; 27 id. at 174.

was contrary to the plain meaning of the text: "The Arbitration Tribunal feels unable to adopt such an argumentation without straining the meaning of the texts in a strange manner and overlooking the respective positions of the Parties at the time the contract was signed." [80]

The latter emphasis led the tribunal, quite naturally, to a consideration of the respective positions of the parties at the time of the 1933 agreement. It was noted that at that time no one knew whether there was any oil in Saudi Arabia, and that the government was anxious to provide whatever incentives were necessary to insure maximum exploration and development:

> A Government desirous to exploit the possible resources of its subsoil as yet unexplored was in contact with an experienced corporation, prepared to run the enormous risks of an enterprise whose result could not be foretold. Both were conscious of the fact that success depended, not only upon the discovery of oil deposits, but also and chiefly upon the sale of oil and its products to foreign countries, since demand for oil in Saudi Arabia was negligible. They were aware of the necessity, to this end, of giving the concessionaire freedom to arrange transportation abroad according to methods which had already been put to the test, without Government interference.[81]

Developing this theme, the tribunal noted that no interference with the Company's operations had ever been offered in any area, whether on land or sea, by the government for over twenty years and even at the time of the agreement the government proposed no interference with the transportation of oil through pipelines to Jordan, Syria, and Lebanon.

For reinforcement of its assessment of the plain meaning of the words of grant, the tribunal offered a brief preliminary invocation of the principle of effectiveness, commenting that the agreement by admission of both parties "may contain implied rights in the concessionaire's favour, if this is necessary to give the contract all its efficacy." [82] It concluded that in fact the restriction of granted rights

80. Id. at 72; 27 id. at 178.
81. Id. at 73–74; 27 id. at 179–80.
82. Id. at 77; 27 id. at 183.

to all relevant acts except external transport by sea would in fact deprive the contract of much of its efficacy:

> In an enterprise of world-wide importance, whose success is entirely dependent on the flow of oil and oil products to foreign markets, it is impossible to imagine that the Parties would have wanted to give the concessionaire an exclusive right to transport restricted to territorial waters, while denying this right as regards transportation overseas, which is the only kind of transportation which is of real interest to the concessionaire.[83]

The tribunal also buttressed its argument from the text of Article 1 both by reference to other agreements between the parties and to another article of the same concession agreement, Article 22. This article provides, in part, as follows: "It is understood, of course, that the Company has the right to use all means and facilities it may deem necessary or advisable in order to exercise the rights granted under this contract, so as to carry out the purpose of this enterprise." [84] The tribunal commented, "These rights are couched in the widest terms, which merely confirm the interpretation arrived at by a grammatical and literal analysis of Article 1." [85] In particular, the tribunal saw a mutual reinforcement of Articles 22 and 1. Article 22 helps to clarify the meaning of Article 1 in that it specifies that Aramco may use "all means and facilities it may deem necessary or advisable" in order to operate the concession (it is in this sense a built-in principle of effectiveness formulated by the parties themselves) ; on the other hand, Article 1 was seen, somewhat circularly, by the tribunal to shed light on the scope of Article 22: inasmuch as Article 1 was interpreted as a grant of exclusive competence to the Company over transportation by sea, the scope of the "means and facilities" mentioned in Article 22 had necessarily to include "all means of effecting such maritime transportation" [86]—e.g., f.o.b. sales.

In expanding its inquiry beyond mere textual examination the tribunal made abundantly clear that it was not to be satisfied by a simple "expanding focus" approach which stops short with the four corners of an agreement. Not only did it, as we have just seen, em-

83. Ibid.; 27 id. at 183.
84. Id. at 77; 27 id. at 177.
85. Id. at 81; 27 id. at 187.
86. Id. at 82; 27 id. at 187.

ploy a number of principles of interpretation in its initial assessment of the words of the agreement, but it also made an explicit and thorough attempt to assess the bearing of various other interpretative principles urged by the parties. Extensive reference was made to the general institutional patterns in the setting in which the agreement was concluded, the necessity of historical interpretation, the principles of effectiveness and of restrictive interpretation, the principles of *contra proferentem* and *in dubio mitius,*[87] and the principles of subsequent conduct.

With respect to institutional practices, the tribunal examined the common practice in the oil industry of arranging f.o.b. sales. It commented that it could not overlook "the practices and usages of commerce, known by both Parties at the time the Agreement was signed, unless it be prepared to content itself with abstract reasoning and to lose sight of reality and of the requirements of the oil industry." [88] The conclusion which the tribunal felt obliged to reach was that both parties must have envisioned such arrangements at the time the agreement was concluded, and that as a result they must have incorporated such arrangements into their expectations at that time, namely, that the Company would follow the institutional practice of allowing buyers to arrange their own transportation.

To reinforce this inference from the general setting of the agreement, the tribunal made brief reference to the history of interactions between the parties. It was emphasized that in 1933 Saudi Arabia did not possess any tankers and thus could not have anticipated engaging in any transport of its own. Its consideration of a special arrangement with an outside shipper, furthermore, did not occur until the 1950s. In addition, the Company from the beginning did engage in considerable transportation through chartering of tankers, then later through a pipeline. No complaint was raised at any time prior to 1954 about any of these actions of Aramco. The tribunal concluded that "All this development which took place in order to facilitate connections with the rest of the world, obviously has its starting-point in circumstances which, since the very beginning, exercised a commanding influence upon the Parties and led them to grant a concessionnaire a right of maritime transport." [89]

87. Id. at 91–92; 27 id. at 196.
88. Id. at 82; 27 id. at 188.
89. Id. at 84; 27 id. at 189.

The traditional content principles of effectiveness and restrictive interpretation were, as we saw above, dealt with at some length by the tribunal in apparent deference to the considerable emphasis placed upon them by the parties. While for the purpose of appraising procedures it is needful only to call attention to this discussion as an effort on the part of the tribunal to canvass a broad range of relevant features of the context, it may be emphasized that the approach of the tribunal was an entirely open and empirical one. No attempt was made to exclude evidence from such sources as irrelevant or without significance for decision, even though it was clear that the "grammatical" analysis carried out initially by the tribunal raised a presumption which was ultimately adopted as the decision in the case. The tribunal genuinely sought to assess all evidence and basis of inference for their relevance to its stipulated goal, making but a polite bow to the traditional exclusiveness or preeminence of the plain and natural meaning principle.

The final interpretative operation of the tribunal was to engage in a minute examination of the bearing of the conduct of the parties subsequent to the agreement upon their shared expectations of commitment. The potential relevance of this conduct was precisely indicated:

> It has been admitted on several occasions by doctrine and judicial practice alike that . . . one may 'resort to the manner of performance in order to ascertain the intentions of the parties' . . . In this manner the notion of 'practical and quasi-authentic interpretation,' also known as 'contemporary practical interpretation,' has been evolved . . . Rather than a means of interpretation of agreements, the manner in which the Parties have actually conducted themselves in carrying out the contract is, in the Tribunal's opinion, a mode of proof permitting to ascertain the true intention of the Parties at the time the contract was entered into and the real meaning they have given and still give to its provisions by their actual behavior.[90]

The specific "actual behavior" to which the tribunal turned consisted both of actions—primarily on the part of Aramco—and of communications between the government and Aramco. It was

90. Id. at 93; 27 id. at 197–98; quoting from *Brazilian Federal Loans Issued in France,* P.C.I.J., Ser. A, No. 21, pp. 117–19 (1929).

pointed out, for example, that prior to 1947 Aramco organized its transportation both through chartered vessels and through f.o.b. sales. In 1940 the government requested periodic reports of the methods employed and Aramco complied. For the following fifteen years the government acknowledged such information with no objection to the methods being employed. A supplementary agreement was, moreover, concluded between Aramco and the government in 1950 which reviewed and confirmed the lawfulness of the transportation practices up to that time. The government explicitly agreed that it had received "a complete satisfaction of all outstanding claims and demands . . . with respect both to the past and to the future," and that Aramco might "continue to conduct its operations . . . in the same manner as in the past." [91] The tribunal concluded that the attitude expressed by the government in this agreement constituted "an approval of the methods used by Aramco," as well as "proof of the common intention of the contracting parties to include the right of sea transport in the exclusive right granted to Aramco by Article 1 of the 1933 Concession Agreement." [92]

Whatever one may think of the merits of the interpretation thus finally achieved by the tribunal, a better example of the systematic and disciplined employment of a comprehensive set of principles for the orderly examination of potentially relevant features of the context could scarcely be desired. The utmost security for fair and rational decision which appropriate procedures can afford was achieved by the tribunal in high degree.

THE OPERATION OF ADJUSTING EFFORT TO IMPORTANCE

Adjusting the degree of effort which will be expended to the importance of the issues presented for resolution in particular cases is, in one sense, a necessary operation of all decision-making processes. Since interpreters must program the time and energy to be made available for any given dispute or series of disputes, a valuation is required of the relative significance of the issues to be decided. The difficulty of this choice for prospective observers is to find appropriate indices of the interpreter's decision to subordinate his demands

91. Id. at 97; 27 id. at 201.
92. Ibid.; 27 id. at 202.

for a thorough contextual analysis to the shortage of time and the relatively greater importance of other matters pressed upon him. Past decision-makers have unfortunately left relatively few indications of their implicit adjustment of effort to importance. The statements which have been made, moreover, are not likely to be very convincing as evidence of a rational appraisal of the time available and the significance of the values at stake.

An example may be taken from Lord Asquith's decision in the *Abu Dhabi* arbitration.[93] The question in this case was whether a 1939 agreement between Abu Dhabi and an American petroleum company conferred oil rights in an area beyond the territorial sea of Abu Dhabi. Article 2 of the concession agreement provided that the area in which rights were granted included Abu Dhabi, "its dependencies and all the islands and the sea waters which belong to that area." [94] A dispute arose over the meaning to be attached to the term "sea waters"—whether they were to be limited to the territorial sea belt around the country, or whether they extended further out to sea as part of a hypothetical continental shelf. The decision in limiting the grant to the territorial belt turned on an analysis of the alleged plain meaning of "sea waters." This term was held to include in its plain or ordinary meaning only the territorial belt, on the grounds that the continental shelf doctrines were a later development and could not have been in the minds of the parties. The tribunal rejected a similar argument that the Sheikh of Abu Dhabi knew none of these meanings in granting the rights. In its examination of the evidence, the tribunal refused to comment upon evidence of the parties' knowledge and expectations outside the four corners of the outcome document. Lord Asquith concluded that "Chaos may obviously result" if, instead of asking what the words used mean, the enquiry extends at large to what each of the parties meant them to mean, and how and why each phrase came to be inserted." [95] If an observer could scarcely be convinced that "chaos" could result from asking "what each of the parties meant" in a dispute, especially if he is committed to ask such questions in pursuing the overriding goal of interpretation, such a statement makes more sense as an implicit ad-

93. (1951) *Reported sub nom Petroleum Development Ltd. v. Sheikh of Abu Dhabi* in 1951 *Int. Law Rep.* 144.
94. 1951 *Int. Law Rep.* 144, 147.
95. Id. at 49.

justment of the decision-maker's available effort and time. Taken in this way, the sole objection which may be raised is that the judgment was not made more explicit—that is, more directly informative of the actual choice being asserted.

The implicit use of a principle of economy can be seen in the initial case decided by the European Court of Human Rights, the *Lawless* case.[96] In this controversy the Court was called upon to assess the legality of the Irish government's preventive detention of G. R. Lawless, a member of the revolutionary I.R.A., in light of its obligations under the European Communities' Convention for the Protection of Human Rights and Fundamental Freedoms. Lawless' detention for several months in 1957 was carried out pursuant to Section 4 of the Irish Offenses Against the State Act, which provided in essence that persons suspected of activities "prejudicial to the preservation of public peace and order or to the security of the State" may be detained after notice of public emergency until the threat to peace subsides.[97] Lawless claimed, inter alia, that this Act was invalid since it conflicted with Article 5 of the European Convention on Human Rights which was designed in large measure to prohibit arrest and detention save in instances where specific criminal acts had been alleged and ordinary judicial processes and guarantees were immediately available to the defendant. Since Lawless had not been charged with commission of a criminal act but only on suspicion of engaging in or preparation for engaging in criminal or revolutionary activities and had not been brought to trial, the Irish government relied primarily upon its rights of derogation from the obligations of Article 5 guaranteed to it under Article 15 of the Convention. Article 15 provides in part that

> In time of war or other public emergency threatening the life of a nation any High Contracting Party may take measures derogating from its obligations under this Convention to the extent strictly required by the exigencies of the situation, provided that such measures are not inconsistent with its other obligations under international law.[98]

The Court held, first, that Ireland's preventive detention of Lawless was not consistent with the guarantees of Article 5, and, secondly,

96. *European Court of Human Rights Reports,* Ser. A, p. 23 (1961).
97. Id. at 34.
98. Id. at 54–55.

that his detention was consistent with, and indeed authorized by, the rights of derogation provided in Article 15. In justifying its first conclusion, the Court resorted to the time-worn notion that the text of Article 5 was "sufficiently clear in itself" according to its plain and natural meaning, and that as a result nothing more than a "grammatical" (i.e. textual) analysis was required.[99] None was in fact undertaken by the Court, even though both the evidence from prefatory work on the Convention introduced by the Irish government and its refutation by the European Commission on Human Rights (whose adverse decision Lawless was here appealing) were briefly alluded to in the Court's summaries of their positions. The Court's peremptory manner in dealing with the preparatory work in this case makes it quite clear that its invocation of the traditional rule against resort to preparatory work was, as a procedural principle, designed to abrogate its obligation to discuss the Irish government's contentions with respect to it. The opinion made quite clear that such evidence had been presented in argument and thus considered by the Court; there is even a hint that the Court implicitly accepted the Commission's rejection of the Irish contentions. Conceivably, however, in the interests of economy of time and effort on the part of the Court, careful examination and appraisal was avoided by the Court by the use of the traditional rule.

The precise significance of this aspect of the *Lawless* case is obscured by several diverse factors: first, it marked the debut of the European Court of Human Rights, and as a result was important to the Court regardless of the issues involved; second, it involved a fairly standard attempt of an established government to quell revolutionary activity, before it erupted, by rather severe police action, and thus may well prove important as precedent to the Court; finally, however, the case was raised, before the Commission and the Court, largely *ex post facto*—since Lawless had been released approximately one year before either decision by signing a modified loyalty oath to support the Irish government and refrain from engaging in any further "illegal" acts. Thus Lawless' claim before the Court was solely for compensation for detention and attorney's fees incurred in the attempt to secure his freedom. One can only guess that this factor may have weighed heavily in the Court's decision to deal with the issues presented in as summary a manner as possible. Should this be the

99. Id. at 52.

case, we would here be faced with a genuine example of the most common use of the economy principle, namely, an attempt to adjust the Court's efforts to the importance of the present controversy. It must be emphasized, however, that such an alternative is entirely speculative since the Court did not discuss its refusal to debate the effect of preparatory work in these or any other policy-directed terms.

The second major issue in the case, whether there was a sufficient "public emergency threatening the life of the nation" to justify the action taken against Lawless as "strictly required by the exigencies of the situation" under Article 15 of the Convention, was also determined by the Court by means of a "grammatical" analysis. In the ordinary meaning of "public emergency" such actions were "strictly required," according to the Court. Even though no evidence from preparatory work had been adduced in refutation of this point, the Court's summary announcement that "after an examination," it had found this "to be the case," [100] is entirely comparable to its approach to Article 5. The little summary detail given of the Court's "examination" (we would call this reference to their procedures) indicates that in the interest of some unnamed policy, possibly that of economy, the Court decided not to inquire into or discuss the matter further.[101]

In the writings of publicists, the only author to give careful attention to the problem of adjusting effort to importance has been Judge Lauterpacht. His discussion, moreover, was limited to the reasons of "economy" in the International Court's refusal to consider the preparatory work of modern multilateral conventions.[102] In the course of this discussion, Lauterpacht commented upon the relevance of adjusting effort to importance in disputes before the present Court:

> Thorough examination of the bulky record of preparatory work imposes a considerable strain upon international tribunals . . .

100. Id. at 56.

101. Other instances may be cited in which decision-makers have rejected the demands made by participants to consult additional indices of expectation and of community policy in possible recognition of the necessity of adjusting effort to importance. However, since no direct reference to procedural economy is usually made, the connection is largely speculative. Cf. the *Reparations* case, [1949] I.C.J. 174, discussed in Lauterpacht, op. cit. supra note 5, at 131–33; see also the cases collected by Schwarzenberger, op. cit. supra note 13, at 498–508.

102. Lauterpacht, op. cit. supra note 5, at 130–31.

> How can the Court be expected to engage in detailed research covering, on occasions, bulky volumes containing records of the proceedings of the Conference and of its numerous committees and subcommittees? . . . Should the business of the Court expand in a conspicuous fashion as the result of any increased willingness of States to submit disputes to adjudication, the question would arise as to the necessity of changes in the methods of the work of the Court.[103]

As one of these methods, however, Lauterpacht did not favor a restriction upon the examination of preparatory work: "The physical difficulty and inconvenience of undertaking that task cannot, consistently with the authority of international justice, be considered as providing a reason for discarding an instrument likely to assist in revealing the intention of the parties."[104] Despite his recognition of the potential problems created by limitations of time, Lauterpacht did not insist upon the relative importance of the issues presented in various cases as a determining factor in the interpreter's decision to exclude the consideration of relevant features of the larger context. His solution, which was to expand the number and facilities of international tribunals,[105] thus bypassed the issue presented to decision-makers for whom such an alternative is not available, and who must program their efforts on the basis of the nature and significance of the issues presented to them. The statements of other publicists upon this aspect of the problem of preparatory work are even less directly relevant.[106]

THE OPERATION OF IDENTIFYING THE FOCAL AGREEMENT

Past decision-makers have commonly sought to identify the participants' focal agreement as the initial step in the interpretative process.

103. Id. at 131, 132–33.
104. Id. at 132.
105. Id. at 133.
106. Cf. especially Fitzmaurice, supra note 4, at 15–17; Beckett, "Comments on the Report of Lauterpacht," 46 *Annuaire de l'Institut de Droit International* 435, 440–44 (1950).

Silving, "In the Nature of a Compact—A Note on Statutory Interpretation," 20 *Rev. del Collegio de Abrogadoz de Puerto Rico* 159, 169 (1960), writes: "Viewed

We have characterized the substantive problems involved as those of the preferred mode of expression and of the distinctive phase of agreement. Although little interest in establishing procedures to distinguish and examine "mode" and "phase" features of the process of agreement has been exhibited in past trends of decision and opinion, the observer may assume that these features have been examined without explicit discussion in order to facilitate the tentative identification of the focal agreement. As we saw above, interpreters have consistently invoked the often unclear distinction between the agreement proper and its context. Explicit consideration, however, of the various modes of expression and phases of agreement alleged to comprise the focal commitment of the participants—as recommended in the operation of identifying the focal agreement—is not commonly evident in past practice. The difficulty which the International Court of Justice had in the *Preah Vihear* case (Merits) [107] in identifying the focal agreement has already been noted. This case involved two potential "agreements" between Siam and Cambodia, one expressed in a 1904 Boundary Delimitation Treaty establishing a "watershed" criterion for locating the boundary between the two countries, and the other reflected in a course of conduct involving a set of maps made by France at Siam's request and annexed to the Treaty. By the watershed criterion, the area which later came under dispute between the parties—the temple and grounds at Preah Vihear—fell in Siam (later Thailand). By its position on the maps, the area fell in Cambodia. Thus the Court was faced with a clear choice of two conflicting focal agreements. The majority eventually decided the case in Cambodia's favor, but only over the strong protest and dissent of Judge Wellington Koo and two other judges.

In this instance the determination of the focal agreement was the crucial choice in the case. To this extent the preliminary assessment and designation of the focal agreement had to be, as the judges realized, extremely tentative. It turned out to be so tentative, however, that it is doubtful that the majority considered which instrument, in fact, it did assume to be the focal agreement. One would have thought, from the past jurisprudence of the Court, that a presumption should have favored the 1904 Treaty text, forcing Cam-

in the light of realistic jurisprudence, the "plain meaning rule", however logically dubious it may be, serves a useful purpose. It is an economy device, helping to dispose of issues which do not merit special elaboration."

107. [1962] I.C.J. Rep. 6.

bodia to prove its case that a clearly contradictory expectation had resulted from the receipt of the maps. Such was not the choice, however. The Court assumed that the receipt of the maps imposed a burden upon Thailand to protest what was claimed to be a mistake in the location of the temple. The question was never raised, apparently, as to why Cambodia was not under a similar obligation to deny that the "watershed" criterion placed the temple in Thailand, and to communicate this assertion to the then Siamese government. Thus, without systematically and consciously carrying out the operation of identifying the focal agreement, the Court appeared to place the burden of the case upon Thailand for no immediately obvious reason. This led to a considerably curtailed examination of the context —particularly the cultural and political context at the time of the signing of the agreement in 1904 and immediately after—and to a decision in favor of Cambodia which was not given adequate support. If an appropriate identification and examination of the two agreements had been made, this apparent arbitrariness might have been avoided.[108]

THE HISTORICAL OPERATION

Decision-makers have often taken into consideration the historical development of agreements as well as broader features of the historical background of the participants which ultimately affected the agreement process. Under the rubric of "historical interpretation" this operation has also gained the general approval of publicists as a significant and indeed necessary technique of interpretation.[109] We referred above, for example, to the efforts of Garner and the Harvard Research to call attention to the necessity of examining the "historical background of [a] treaty"; to the American Law Institute's insistence that "the background of, and the circumstances attending, the negotiation of the agreement" should be considered in interpret-

108. For a fuller exposition of this case, see above, p. 290, and below, p. 344.
109. As usually formulated, the principle of "historical interpretation" manifests the same confusion in reference to content and procedure principles which we found in previous analyses: Schwarzenberger, op. cit. supra note 13, at 514–17; Hudson, op. cit. supra note 3, at 655–57; Chang, *The Interpretation of Treaties by Judicial Tribunals* 95–140 (1933); Crandall, *Treaties: Their Making and Enforcement* 377–82 (1916).

ing an agreement; and to numerous other expressions of approval by publicists of the method of historical interpretation.[110] It has remained largely, however, the work of national and international tribunals to develop methods of analysis for calling attention to and weighing the relevant historical factors which may affect the parties' genuine shared expectations of agreement.

In the early *Aroa Mines (Ltd.)* case[111] the tribunal was called upon to describe the historical evolution of the 1903 protocol between Great Britain and Venezuela in the course of interpreting Article 3 of the protocol, in which Venezuela admitted liability "in cases where the claim is for injury to, or wrongful seizure of property" belonging to British nationals.[112] The issue before the tribunal was whether the Venezuelan government was responsible for injuries caused by acts of revolutionaries. It commented initially that although the unambiguous *prima facie* meaning of the provision appeared to include liability for these acts, there might exist a "latent ambiguity" which could only be discovered by considering the sequence of events leading up to the protocol itself. It was only "when viewed historically with a wise regard for all the conditions antecedent, proximate and immediate" that this ambiguity was manifest, and that as a result "construction becomes necessary."[113] The tribunal then proceeded to examine "the historical status and circumstances surrounding the parties at the time the treaty was made," including the correspondence between Britain and other nations (Germany, Italy) which asserted their common rights vis-à-vis damage caused by Venezuelan *authorities,* but made no mention of damage caused by insurgents.[114] From this material the tribunal concluded that Britain had at no time claimed, nor had Venezuela admitted, the latter's liability for damage not inflicted directly by its own representatives.

The Permanent Court weighed the relevance of chronological se-

110. Harvard Research in International Law, *Law of Treaties: Draft Convention With Comment,* 953–56 (1935); American Law Institute, *The Foreign Relations Law of the United States, A Restatement* 132–34 (Tentative Draft No. 3, 1959); De Visscher, op. cit. supra note 11, at 74.

111. Reported in Ralston and Doyle, *Venezuelan Arbitrations of 1903* 344 (1904).

112. Id. at 292.

113. Id. at 358.

114. Ibid.

quences on a number of occasions. One brief example was provided in the *Polish Nationals* case,[115] where the Court made a chronological survey of the events leading to the formation of a free city in Danzig:

> The separation of Danzig from Germany was contrary to the wishes of the German people. Almost the whole of the population of that city was German, and the Peace Conference, in order to assure Poland free and secure access to the sea, decided to make Danzig a Free City without incorporating it in Poland. In this respect, some apprehension might be entertained lest the Polish people in Danzig would be exposed to discriminatory measures . . . It is natural to suppose that it was with a view to preventing any such discriminatory measures that the authors of the Treaty of Versailles thought it desirable to prescribe as one of the objects of the treaty between Poland and Danzig . . . that a clause prohibiting such discriminatory measures should figure therein.[116]

In light of this background, the Court concluded that the claims advanced by Poland for special favors on behalf of its citizens residing in Danzig could not be based upon such concepts as the continued protection of their "free national development" and the preservation of Polish as their mother tongue, but purely upon positive discrimination by Danzig officials against people of Polish origin solely because they were Poles. To grant, within the limits specified in the agreement, equal treatment of Poles and persons of German origin was the goal, and the limit of application, of the nondiscrimination provision, as seen in light of the historical circumstances leading up to the conclusion of the agreement.

Similarly, in the case concerning the *Jurisdiction of the European Commission of the Danube*,[117] the Court indicated its willingness to examine the historical background of the Definitive Statute of the Danube as well as the Treaty of Versailles. The issue in this case was whether the Commission possessed its customary powers in a short sector of the Danube between Galatz and Braila in Romania. The Commission, in existence since 1856, had operated under numerous agreements, the latest of which was the Definitive Statute of 1921.

115. P.C.I.J., Ser. A/B, No. 44 (1932).
116. Id. at 27–28.
117. P.C.I.J., Ser. B., No. 14 (1927).

This Statute, in relevant part, held that the authority of the Commission "extends, under the same conditions as before, and without any modification of its existing limits, over the maritime Danube." [118] The operating assumption of the Commission as to what constituted the "maritime Danube" appeared to include the disputed sector; and the only agreement which was geographically specific on the Commission's jurisdiction—the Treaty of London of 1883—also included the sector (although Romania was not a party to it). First the Court attempted to determine, through an extensive historical examination of the conventions relating to the regulation of the Danube, what authority had been granted the Commission and other regulating powers, and what had been specifically denied. Beginning with the Congress of Vienna in 1815, tracing the various conventions down to the Definitive Statute, the Court found no evidence that either technical or juridical powers had specifically been withheld from the Commission in the disputed area. Thus the history of its operations in the area became crucial, since they would be the "same conditions" reestablished by the Definitive Statute, which Romania had signed. Another historical examination was thus undertaken—assisted in this instance by a previously published survey—to determine if in fact such authority had been exercised. As a result of this survey the Court concluded that prior to the Statute "the European Commission exercised the same powers between Galatz and Braila" as were exercised indisputably elsewhere, and that the Definitive Statute had indeed affirmed these powers.[119]

The International Court of Justice has attempted to carry out historical examinations, in varying degrees of thoroughness, in a number of its decisions. In the *Minquiers* case,[120] for example, the Court could hardly avoid making a thorough historical examination in light of the requests of France and Great Britain. In their 1950 protocol, they requested the Court to determine "which of the Parties

118. Id. at 24 n.

119. Id. at 55. Other historical operations of the international courts may be observed in *Customs Regime Between Germany and Austria,* P.C.I.J., Ser. A/B, No. 41, p. 42 ff. (1931); *The Corfu Channel* case (Merits), [1949] I.C.J. Rep. 4, 25 ff.; and *International Status of South-West Africa,* [1958] I.C.J. Rep. 128, 135 ff. For additional examples, see *Gold Looted by Germany from Rome in 1943* (1953), reported in 1953 *Int. Law Rep.* 441, esp. 444–63; *Petroleum Development (Qatar) Ltd. v. Ruler of Qatar* (1950), reported in 1951 id. 161.

120. *The Minquiers and Ecrehos Case,* [1953] I.C.J. Rep. 47.

has produced the more convincing proof of title" to the Minquiers and Ecrehos islands, parts of which proof extended—in the absence of a single, explicit focal agreement—as far back as the thirteenth century.[121] Although the Court contended that "What is of decisive importance, in the opinion of the Court, is not indirect presumptions deduced from events in the Middle Ages, but the evidence which relates directly to the possession of the Ecrehos and Minquiers groups"[122] in subsequent centuries, it nonetheless made an extensive survey of the participants' respective signs of possession from the earliest to present times. It concluded that the historical ties of Great Britain were greater than those of France, and that in consequence the islands belonged to Great Britain:

> The Court . . . finds that the Ecrehos group in the beginning of the thirteenth century was considered and treated as an integral part of the fief of the Channel Islands which were held by the English King . . . British authorities during the greater part of the nineteenth century and in the twentieth century have exercised State functions in respect of the group . . . [Similarly,] the Minquiers in the beginning of the seventeenth century were treated as part of the fief in Noirmont in Jersey, and . . . British authorities during a considerable part of the nineteenth century and in the twentieth century have exercised State functions in respect of this group.[123]

A more direct example of the Court's exploring the historical background of an agreement may be found in the *Anglo-Iranian Oil Co.* case,[124] in which the Court made a thorough survey of the background of Iran's denunciation of all "capitulatory" treaties prior to its declaration of acceptance of the compulsory jurisdiction of the Court with respect to subsequent disputes concerning "situations or facts relating directly or indirectly to the application of treaties or conventions accepted by [Iran] and subsequent to . . . ratification."[125] The Declaration, submitted in 1932, was preceded by five years by Iran's rejection of all previous "capitulatory" agreements. The purpose of the Court's examination of this rejection was to de-

121. Id. at 52.
122. Id. at 57.
123. Id. at 67, 70.
124. (Preliminary Objection), [1952] I.C.J. Rep. 93.
125. Id. at 103.

termine the extent and scope of Iran's later declaration which was obscured, as we saw above, by the ambiguous reference of the final phrase to "situations or facts" or to "treaties or conventions." [126] The Court concluded that the historical material considered in relation to Iran's motives in revoking all "capitulatory" agreements prior to 1927 supported Iran's contention that it had accepted the Court's jurisdiction only with respect to treaties or conventions signed subsequent to the declaration. In the Court's view, interpretation of the declaration which Great Britain proposed would have the effect of defeating Iran's goal of rejecting prior treaties as it demanded in 1927.[127]

Occasionally the Court has undertaken its principal historical operation in assessing a period subsequent to the focal agreement itself. While in content such action is traditionally conceived of as the examination of "subsequent conduct," it of course involves an historical operation which the Court may or may not wish to make clear. With few exceptions, however, a demand to make the historical operation explicit has not been evident in its decisions, or the decisions of other national and international tribunals.[128] Some, if not much, evidence of a change in this tendency was exhibited in the recent case concerning *Certain Expenses of the United Nations.*[129] Since in that case an important source of evidence relating to the legitimacy of the U.N. Suez and Congo expenditures was the practice of the United Nations in budgeting similar expenditures throughout its history, it is not surprising that the Court turned to such evidence to conclude that the expenditures were in fact legitimate.

The Court announced its intention to examine this evidence in some specifiable order by reaffirming its frequently cited doctrine in the *Second Admissions* case to the effect that it would consider "the manner in which the organs concerned 'have consistently interpreted the text' in their practice." [130] Although there is a suggestion here that a genuine historical survey of such practices might be needed, it

126. For discussion of the syntactical problems presented by this case, see Miller, infra n. 221.

127. Id. at 105.

128. One such exception may be found in the *Saudi Arabia-Aramco* arbitration, supra note 74, described above, pp. 295–302.

129. [1962] I.C.J. Rep. 151.

130. Id. at 157, quotation from *Competence of the General Assembly for the Admission of a State to the United Nations,* [1950] I.C.J. Rep. 4, 9.

was scarcely undertaken in any systematic manner. In its examination of the "practice of the Organization . . . from the outset" with respect to establishing a limitation of General Assembly budget assessments to "regular" or "administrative" (as opposed to special or "operational") budgets, the Court referred to the Assembly's first session in 1950 and made a hodgepodge of references to various Assembly meetings, special agency meetings, and programs established at different but unmentioned times.[131] The closest approach to an orderly sequence analysis was made casually in the Court's reference to the "consistent practice of the General Assembly to include in the annual budget resolutions, provision for expenses relating to the maintenance of international peace and security" of an "unforeseen and extraordinary" kind.[132] Here it pointed out that in successive years such resolutions had passed unanimously, save in 1952–54, because of conflicts over assessments for Korean war decorations.[133] Other references to the "practice of the Organization throughout its history" proved to be even more insubstantial.[134]

An interesting, though very brief attempt to carry out the historical operation was undertaken in the course of various opinions in the *South-West Africa* cases (Preliminary Objections).[135] In two of the objections to the Court's jurisdiction raised by the Union of South Africa some historical analysis was made. For example, in concluding that the Mandates were "treaties in force" as required for jurisdiction under Article 37 of its Statute, the Court briefly examined the sequence of events leading up to the transfer in 1945 of all League obligations to the United Nations. The sequence of events—which the Court found crucial—involved the establishment of the United Nations and the transfer of obligations such as the Mandates *prior to* the dissolution of the League. Thus the Mandate agreements were "treaties in force" at the time of the transfer. A similar analysis was carried out in deciding that the requirement that appellants be "Members of the League of Nations" had been fulfilled by Ethiopia and Liberia as ratifiers of the United Nations Charter.[136]

131. Id. at 159–60.
132. Id. at 160.
133. Id. at 161.
134. Id. at 165.
135. [1962] I.C.J. Rep. 319.
136. See especially id. at 335–42.

Unfortunately, the Court's analyses on both these points were somewhat offhand and unsystematic. The majority took no more than a few paragraphs to trace the history of the establishment of the Mandates system, and but a little longer to trace the dissolution of the League as it affected the Mandate agreements. Judge Jessup undertook to correct these defects in his separate but concurring opinion, and indeed his contextual review is prolific and thorough.[137] It is regrettable, however, that Jessup appears not to have attempted to carry out a genuine historical operation, since his comments do not follow any noticeable sequence and were ultimately only descriptive of a number of features of the context left unexplored by the majority. The same lack of order is notable also in other opinions, particularly in the joint dissenting opinion of Judges Spender and Fitzmaurice.[138]

Other examples of historical operations, even if somewhat attentuated, may be found in two recent cases before the International Court of Justice, namely the *Northern Cameroons*[139] and *Barcelona Traction* cases.[140] In the *Cameroons* case, particularly, in interpreting certain agreements the Court made an effort to survey and to analyze the long sequence of events leading to the termination of the British mandate and trusteeship of the Northern Cameroons. Beginning with the separation of the Cameroons territory after the First World War into French and British Mandates and extending through the period of gradually realized self-government in the 1950s, the Court attempted to achieve an understanding of the background of the dispute that had arisen between the Republic of Cameroons (formerly the French Mandate and Trust Territory) and Great Britain. The dispute, furthermore, revolved around a sequence of events which the Court rightly wished to set straight before proceeding to assess the claims presented. This sequence involved: (1) the granting of independence by France to Cameroun on January 1, 1960; (2) the gradual preparation for independence for the British holdings in the Cameroons during this period, and to that

137. See especially the historical analysis in Jessup's opinion, id. at 387–401, and later at 417–22, 431–33.

138. Brief historical references are included beginning id. at 465 and 502, respectively.

139. *The Northern Cameroons* (Preliminary Objection), [1963] I.C.J. Rep. 15.

140. *The Barcelona Traction, Light and Power Co., Ltd.* (Preliminary Objections), [1964] I.C.J. Rep. 6.

end its agreement to separate its administration of the Cameroons from its administration of Nigeria by October 1, 1960; (3) the holding of separate plebiscites in the British areas of Northern and Southern Cameroons in February 1961 to allow the people to determine whether they wished to join the Republic of Cameroons or Nigeria. When these plebiscites were held, Southern Cameroons voted to join the Republic of Cameroons, but Northern Cameroons voted to join Nigeria. Representatives of the Republic of Cameroons thereafter filed suit with the Court, claiming in essence that the failure of Great Britain, under its Trusteeship Agreement with the Cameroons, to fulfill its obligation to separate Northern Cameroons and Nigerian administration by October 1960 unfairly influenced the plebiscite and resulted in the vote to join Nigeria. Another sequence of events ultimately influenced the outcome in this case, namely, the ending of the British Trusteeship two days after the filing of the Cameroon application before the Court. The Court concluded, inter alia, that the only alleged legal wrong for which the Republic of Cameroons sought redress lapsed with this termination, and that therefore it would be inappropriate for the Court to decide on the merits of the Cameroon claim since, due to the termination, no action toward reparation or compliance would now be possible. The Court also alluded to the failure of the Cameroon claim for nullification of the Northern Cameroons plebiscite before the United Nations General Assembly, implying that the appropriate forum, in the absence of a continuing Trust Agreement, would necessarily be a political or diplomatic one.

In the *Barcelona Traction* case, in interpreting Article 37 of its Statute (relating to compulsory jurisdiction), the Court refused to delve into the background of facts relating to the merits of the dispute—quite likely because it was in process of deciding to hear the case on its merits—though it did rather extensively carry out an historical operation with respect to the development and final formulation of the article under scrutiny. This article provides that

> Whenever a treaty or convention in force provides for reference of a matter . . . to the Permanent Court of International Justice, the matter shall, as between the parties to the present Statute, be referred to the International Court of Justice.[141]

141. Id. at 27.

In this case the provision sought to be brought within Article 37 was contained in the Hispano-Belgian Treaty of 1927, where the two governments provided that in all disputes between them "either Party may . . . bring the question direct before the Permanent Court of International Justice by means of an application." [142] A principal issue was whether this provision had lapsed in 1946 with the termination of the Permanent Court, or whether on the other hand it was renewed in 1955 (when Spain joined the United Nations) by virtue of Article 37. The Court decided that it had been renewed, and that in consequence it had jurisdiction to hear the case on its merits.

One of the main grounds of this holding was presented in the Court's analysis of the historical background of Article 37, even though ultimately greater weight was given to allegedly "plain and natural" meaning. What was sought by the drafters of the article, the Court concluded, was a simple and direct way to transform the old court into the new one without creating unnecessary administrative and diplomatic changes. To this end, provisions were inserted into the Statute to transform both unilateral and bilateral or multilateral acceptances of compulsory jurisdiction of the Permanent Court *automatically* into similar acceptances for the International Court. The principal aim, therefore, of Article 37—in a most important sense the reason for its existence—was to eliminate the bothersome necessity of having all countries with "referral" clauses in their treaties renegotiate these clauses to change the name of the court. The drafters were quite aware, in the Court's view, of precisely the type of problem that arose in the instant case and sought explicitly to deal with it. By simple extrapolation, it would seem unnecessarily defeating of this aim to hold that one type of situation—where one of the parties did not join the United Nations immediately prior to the termination of the Permanent Court in 1946—would be the only exception to this rule. This would especially hold true, the Court observed, when there is no mention in the article of original or charter membership, and when the only direct demand is that the two members have a "treaty or convention in force" for referral and decision by the Court.

142. Ibid.

THE LEXICAL OPERATION

The investigation of semantic problems of various types has naturally constituted a major portion of the work of past decision-makers. One result observed above with respect to content principles has been the unfortunate deference paid the plain and natural meaning doctrine in rejection of other indices of expectation.[143] Among the possible lexical operations open to the interpreter, however, relatively few have been examined in much detail. Thus the effects upon linguistic usage of similarities or differences in culture, class, interest, personality, and previous exposure to crisis have been infrequently discussed and presumably little understood.

The most frequent application of the lexical operation has been in analyses of the cultural features of the largest shared audiences of particular communications made in the agreement process. In recent years a more general form of this concern has emerged in which the explicit specification of lexical operations in relation to the largest shared audiences has become paramount. Several examples of this concern may be briefly mentioned.

In the *Preah Vihear* case (Preliminary Objections),[144] the Court emphasized in a brief but effective way its determination to carry out the lexical operation in more than a perfunctory manner. This case, several times referred to above, was concerned with whether Thailand had accepted the compulsory jurisdiction of the International Court by virtue of its 1950 declaration in which it renewed its 1940 submission to the compulsory jurisdiction of the Permanent Court. Since Thailand did not join the United Nations until approximately six months after its inception, it relied on the Court's decision in *Israel v. Bulgaria*—which held that Article 36, paragraph 5, of the Court Statute only operated to transform acceptances of compulsory jurisdiction if those acceptances had been made prior to the date on which the Permanent Court ceased to exist and the International Court began—in contending that its 1950 declaration was an ineffective attempt to renew an untransformed and thus lapsed 1940 sub-

143. For recent affirmations of the procedural limitations of this view, see Bernhardt, *Die Auslegung völkerrechticher Verträge* 30–39, 58–66 (1963). See also De Visscher, op. cit. supra note 11, at 52, for a somewhat more moderate view.

144. [1961] I.C.J. Rep. 17.

mission. Essentially, Thailand was arguing that despite its admitted intention to accept the International Court's jurisdiction, it did not succeed since by virtue of *Israel v. Bulgaria* it only succeeded in "renewing" a lapsed commitment to a court no longer in existence.

The Court rejected Thailand's argument. In its view Thailand's 1940 acceptance had indeed lapsed, not only because of the holding in *Israel v. Bulgaria* but also because Thailand did not send in its renewal until two weeks after the ten-year period stipulated in the 1940 declaration. Thus, by May 20, 1950—the time of Thailand's resubmission—there was, literally speaking, no acceptance to "renew." Sheerly on its face, then, the Court agreed with Thailand that it had mistakenly "renewed" a lapsed submission to a nonexistent court. The Court was not, however, willing to let the matter rest at this point; clearly it regarded Thailand's contention absurd when seen in context.

From a procedural point of view, the Court simply looked at the most relevant feature of the context—namely the demise of the Permanent Court in 1946 and the subsequent establishment of the International Court of Justice—and came to the conclusion that the only sensible effect of a 1950 declaration would be to submit to the compulsory jurisdiction of the only court which in 1950 could have received a submission "in accordance with Article 36" of the United Nations Charter, i.e. the International Court of Justice. As the Court said: "If the 1950 Declaration is considered in this way, it can have no other sense or meaning than as an acceptance of the compulsory jurisdiction of the present Court, for there was no other Court to which it can have related." [145]

The issue of the *prima facie* or literal meaning of Thailand's declaration was faced directly by the Court. Referring to its earlier opinion in the *Anglo-Iranian Oil Co.* case, the Court held that "the principle of the ordinary meaning does not entail that words and phrases are always to be interpreted in a purely literal way." [146] Also, the Court recalled that earlier it had held that the principle of ordinary meaning "did not apply where it would lead to 'something unreasonable or absurd.' " [147] It held that this was such a case, for two reasons: (1) the obviously bizarre fact of a submission to a defunct

145. Id. at 32.
146. Ibid.
147. Id. at 33, quoting from *Polish Postal Service in Danzig,* P.C.I.J., Ser. B, No. 11, p. 39.

court, and (2) the equally clear contradiction of that submission by a reference to its action as being carried out, as we mentioned above, "in accordance with Article 36, paragraph 4, of the Statute of the International Court of Justice." The Court thus held that by clear intention Thailand—in its 1950 declaration—intended to accept the compulsory jurisdiction of the International Court.

What the Court did not draw attention to was that in fact, as a matter of procedure, recourse had to be made to a larger portion of the context than the four corners of the document in order to reject the alleged "literal" meaning. Even though in its operations the plain and natural meaning doctrine was affirmed, its affirmation also led to a clear precedent in procedure that the broader context may be resorted to in order to overcome what might appear a literally clear text. In that way the Court did more than it modestly announced, namely, applying its "normal canons of interpretation"; it emphasized in a more than usual way the necessity of recourse to the larger context as a procedural step in interpretation. The fact that it chose to justify this step by the fiction that "words are to be interpreted according to their natural and ordinary meaning *in the context in which they occur*"[148] is in this light of little consequence.

The European Court of Human Rights in the *Lawless* case[149] provided some evidence on two points of a more liberal if not more explicit and systematic attempt to carry out the lexical operation. The case, which we have summarized above, involved the legality of the Irish government's preventive detention of G. R. Lawless, an I.R.A. revolutionary, in alleged conflict with its obligations under the Convention for the Protection of Human Rights and Fundamental Freedoms.[150] The Court, as we have seen, held (1) that the de-

148. Id. at 32 (emphasis added).

149. *European Court of Human Rights Reports,* Ser. A, p. 27 (1961).

150. Id. at 46; primarily its obligations under Article 5, paragraphs 1 (c) and 3:

> 1. Everyone has the right to liberty and security of person. No one shall be deprived of his liberty save in the following cases and in accordance with a procedure prescribed by law:
>
> . . .
>
> (c) the lawful arrest and detention of a person effected for the purpose of bringing him before the competent legal authority on reasonable suspicion of having committed an offence or when it is reasonably considered necessary to prevent his committing an offence or fleeing after having done so;
>
> . . .

tention of Lawless without affording him a judicial hearing was contrary to paragraphs 1 (c) and 3 of Article 5 of the Convention, and (2) that Ireland's deviation from these provisions was permissible under Article 15 of the Convention, which permits parties to derogate from their obligations under circumstances where public peace and security are threatened.[151]

The lexical operation was carried out first by a "grammatical" analysis of the paragraphs of the Convention most directly concerned (1c and 3 of Article 5; 1 of Article 15), then of their interrelationships, and their relationships to their articles read as a whole. A further part of this grammatical analysis consisted ultimately of a comparison of the effects of Articles 5 and 15 taken as a whole, and of their relationship to each other. As a final step in this analysis, the Court took into consideration the objects of each article, and the general aims of the Convention as a whole. While the presentation of this analysis proceeded along the lines of the contentions advanced by the parties in an article-by-article manner, the opinion of the Court was eventually thorough and quite explicit on these points.

The second part of the lexical operation, where the Court attempted to deal with extratextual materials, was done much less thoroughly and with the additional disadvantage of the Court's acceptance of the traditional maxim that in the absence of confusion in the natural and ordinary meaning of the text such extratextual reference was not permissible. Despite an acceptance of both the principle and the fact of clarity in the ordinary meaning of the text in the present case, the Court still managed, first, to review the Irish government's evidence with respect to some preparatory work for the Convention, and, secondly, to review the European Commission's rejection of the Irish conclusions from this evidence in its report filed

---

3. Everyone arrested or detained in accordance with the provisions of paragraph 1 (c) of this Article shall be brought promptly before a judge or other officer authorized by law to exercise judicial power and shall be entitled to trial within a reasonable time or to a release pending trial. Release may be conditioned by guarantees to appear for trial.

151. Article 15 (1) reads: "In time of war or other public emergency threatening the life of the nation any High Contracting Party may take measures derogating from its obligations under this Convention to the extent strictly required by the exigencies of the situation, provided that such measures are not inconsistent with its other obligations under international law."

before the Court. It continued, however, to refuse to comment on either the evidence, the Irish contentions with respect to it, or the Commission's report, on the ground that this was not permissible under the traditional rule. What this amounts to, in our view, is a brief, implicit, and highly unsystematic attempt to carry out the lexical operation in a manner which would nonetheless satisfy the old maxim. The Court thus succeeded in giving the impression that it could work without the rule, even though it still felt the need to offer a bow in its direction. It also succeeded in this way in obscuring the lexical operations which it actually performed with respect to Articles 5 and 15.

An interesting example of the thoroughness with which the lexical operation can be carried out and the clarity with which it can be described may be found in the case concerning *Certain Expenses of the United Nations,*[152] reviewed in detail above. In its holding that the expenses incurred in the Congo and Suez operations were "expenses of the Organization" under Article 17 (2) and were not "actions" under Article 11 (2) of the Charter, the Court referred initially to the "plain" and *prima facie* meaning of the text to arrive at its decision. In referring to the text of Article 17 (2), it commented that "on its face, the term expenses of the Organization means all the expenses and not just certain types of expenses which might be referred to as 'regular' expenses." [153] Despite this, the Court refused simply to stop on such a presumption, observing that it had "not been asked to give an abstract definition of the words "expenses of the Organization." [154] The majority went on to review other paragraphs of the same article, other articles, and the entire Charter as well as early work carried on under it, its general purposes, and the more stable practices established under it. To be sure, the Court concluded that all other features of the context were consistent with the plain meaning of Article 17 (2), but fortunately it omitted the traditional disclaimer that further evidence could not lawfully be examined if the ordinary meaning was found clear.

Most importantly for our present purposes, the Court made clear its procedures for establishing and confirming the meaning of Article 17 (2). While admitting that it "would be possible to begin with a

152. [1962] I.C.J. Rep. 151.
153. Id. at 161.
154. Id. at 158.

general proposition to the effect that the 'expenses' of any organization are amounts paid out to defray the costs of carrying out its purposes," the Court commented: "The next step would be to examine, as the Court will, whether the resolutions authorizing the operations here in question were intended to carry out the purposes of the United Nations." [155] The Court did in fact proceed step by step to examine the various sources of evidence itemized above to see if the expenditures were made in carrying out the purposes of the United Nations. Its conclusion that the expenses were subject to apportionment by the General Assembly was thus based upon a systematic review of the other features of the context, and in an entirely reasonable order from the more specific to the more general, and from the more distant in time to the more recent.

A less systematic and considerably different approach was taken by the Court in its decision that the operations in question were not exclusively Security Council "actions" under Article 11 (2). On this issue the Court's sole bow to the plain meaning rule was by way of evasion, in commenting that there was no evidence that the operations were Article 12 "actions" reserved to the Security Council but might as well be Article 14 "measures" permitted to the General Assembly. The largely unstated assumption of the Court appeared to be that the operations in question could, by the reasonable application of the plain meaning rule, be given either label. In pointing out conflicting interpretations in this and other areas, the Court was able to turn to other evidence which led to its conclusion that the Suez and Congo operations were not exclusively covered by Article 12. The end result was a determination of the meaning of Article 12 by reference to numerous features of the context. The Court concluded that it covered only "enforcement" or "coercive" action and not that taken with the consent and at the request of the state in which the action is taken.

One specific cultural feature which has received considerable reference in past practice has been that of differences in languages and the multiple problems of translation and linguistic priority which these differences have created in interpreting agreements.[156]

155. Ibid.

156. For a general discussion of this problem, usually referred to in the traditional literature as that of "versions in different languages," see Hardy, "The Interpretation of Plurilingual Treaties by International Courts and Tribunals,"

Decision-makers have developed a surprisingly large number of doctrines and precedents designed to relate differences in linguistic usage to particular claims presented. These doctrines, unfortunately, do not usually direct the decision-maker's attention specifically to the relevance of differences in cultural patterns upon language. In a general way, however, they focus attention upon one manifestation of these differences.

Early attempts to establish rules for the resolution of variations in linguistic usage was more general in form, usually embracing cultural differences which may arise even within the same language group. Hall, for example, argued that "When terms used in a treaty have a different legal sense within the two contracting states, they are to be understood in the sense which is proper to them within the state to which the provision containing them applies." [157] Although it is not clear why he wished to distinguish disputed claims by favoring the party to which a given provision "applies," Hall apparently intended to favor the usage of the party that would be forced to assume active burdens under an agreement.[158] The same position was taken previously by Fiore, who held that "Words which have a different legal meaning in each of the contracting states must be considered as used in the sense ascribed to them in the state which, by the treaty, undertakes an obligation." [159]

---

37 *Brit. Yb. Int'l L.* 72 (1961); 5 Hackworth, *Digest of International Law* 265–67 (1943). Harvard Research, op. cit. supra note 110, at 971–73; Hudson, op. cit. supra note 3, at 648–49; 2 Hyde, *International Law Chiefly as Interpreted and Applied by the United States* 1493–94 (1945); Chang, op. cit. supra note 109, at 141–58; Crandall, op. cit. supra note 109, at 389–94.

157. Hall, *A Treatise on International Law* 346 (7th ed. 1917).

158. The following example is offered: "by the treaty of 1886 it was stipulated between Austria and Italy, that inhabitants of the provinces ceded by the former power should enjoy the right of withdrawing with their property into Austrian territory during a year from the date of the exchange of ratifications. In Austria the word inhabitant signifies such persons only as are domiciled according to Austrian law; in Italy it is applied to everyone living in a commune and registered as a resident. The language of the treaty therefore had not an identical meaning in the two countries. As the provision referred to territory which was Austrian at the moment of the signature of the treaty, the term inhabitant was construed in conformity with Austrian law." Id. at 347.

159. Fiore, *International Law Codified* 342–43 (Borchard transl. 1918). The danger in both Hall and Fiore's view, aside from the obvious difficulty of determining which participant the agreement "applies" to (or which participant "un-

The focal point of modern disputes over the most economic methods of settling claims concerning texts in different languages was established by Oppenheim in his contention that "each party is only bound by the text in its own language" unless "the contrary is expressly provided." [160] This position has been generally rejected by recent writers.[161] The Harvard Research Draft has summarized the trend of opinion in these terms:

> When the text of a treaty is embodied in versions in different languages, and when it is not stipulated that the version in one of the languages shall prevail, the treaty is to be interpreted with a view to giving corresponding provisions in the different versions a common meaning which will effect the general purpose which the treaty is intended to serve.[162]

Although it is difficult to discern a consistent pattern of practices in past trends of authoritative decision,[163] one feature in past practice which exceeds the contribution of any commentator to date should be separated out for special emphasis. Decision-makers have pointed to at least two conditions which may be relevant to determining the preferred version of an agreement text. These are, respectively, the language in which the agreement was originally

---

dertakes an obligation") is that it may easily be used to defeat the expectations of the participants that the usage current in the petitioning, or benefiting, state was adopted in their commitment. The same considerations, as we shall presently see, apply to the rules developed in past practice relating more specifically to the comparison of texts drafted in different languages.

160. 2 Oppenheim, *International Law* 862 (Lauterpacht, 7th ed. 1948).

161. See especially Hardy, supra note 156, at 116–17, who concluded that "the decisions of international tribunals . . . do not confirm the existence of this alleged rule." See also Hudson, op. cit. supra note 3, at 649 n., who called the position "clearly erroneous" as a representation of past trends of decision in national and international tribunals.

162. Harvard Research, op. cit. supra note 110, at 971. The view which Hudson ultimately adopted was even less committal: "The versions in all languages must be considered together, and a meaning is to be given to the composite of them. Ordinarily, neither version should be subordinated to the other, and neither should be regarded as a translation of the other." He argued that even when the parties expressly stipulated that one version should prevail in case of conflict, "the version in the other language should still be taken into account in interpretation." Op. cit. supra note 3, at 648–49.

163. See summaries in Harvard Research, op. cit. supra note 110, at 971–73; Hudson, op. cit. supra note 3, at 649; and Hardy, supra note 156.

negotiated and composed, and the relative degree of explicitness and clarity among the various versions of the text in relation to the dispute which has arisen.[164] On appropriate occasions, past decision-makers have been willing to look to these factors, among others, in determining the participants' expectations as to which version of the text should prevail.

In an early case, the United States Supreme Court commented that since no advance priority could be attached to the Spanish and English versions of the United States–Spanish Treaty of 1819, "one version neither controls nor is to be preferred to the other . . . [b]oth being originals and of equal authority, we must resort to some other mode than the inspection of the treaty to give it a proper construction." [165] The Court then proceeded to take note of the fact that the document was negotiated and composed in Spanish, under the responsibility of the Spanish government: "The King of Spain was the grantor, the treaty was his deed, the exception was made by him, and its nature and effect depended on his intention." On this basis, the Court concluded that the Spanish version of the text should prevail.[166] Similarly, the Permanent Court, in the *Exchange of Greek and Turkish Populations* case,[167] referred to the fact that the Lausanne Convention of 1923 had been drawn up in French in resolving the dispute which had arisen over the term "établissement" in Article 1 of the Convention. It concluded that when "the Convention was drawn up in [one language] . . . regard must be had to the meaning of the disputed term in that language," and proceeded to examine the etymology of the term in French in creating a presumption that the term was used in its ordinary meaning in that language.[168]

Past decision-makers have relied upon one version of an agreement in order to resolve apparent ambiguities in other versions in different languages on numerous occasions. In an early exchange between the United States and the Netherlands, Secretary of State Hughes declined to affirm the English version of the two governments' treaty of

164. For a thorough discussion of past trends in these areas, see Hardy, supra note 156, esp. at 82–98, 112–19.
165. *United States v. Arredondo and others,* 6 Pet. 691, 737–38 (1832).
166. Id. at 741.
167. P.C.I.J., Ser. B, No. 10 (1925).
168. Id. at 18, 18–20.

1913 in light of a narrower provision in the Dutch version: "When a treaty is executed in more than one language, each document is to be regarded as an original, and the sense of the agreement should be drawn from the two texts collectively. Thus, if one is ambiguous, either party may turn to the other text for guidance if it reveals the common design." [169] The English document committed the parties to investigate jointly "all disputes," while the Dutch text referred only to future disputes. Although "all disputes" does not appear to be ambiguous on its face, Hughes argued that only the Dutch text was "explicit," and should be seen as limiting the apparent grant in English.[170] A similar dilemma was resolved by the German Constitutional Court in the case of *Reparation Commission v. the German Government* [171] by reference to a formula relating the two major issues faced in the American dispute: "If there are two texts equally clear but not agreeing with one another, it would be arguable that the text involving the smaller obligation for the party obliged ought to be preferred. But if one text is clear and the other is not, the necessary solution is to interpret the less clear text in the light of the other text." [172]

Although in later decisions courts have not insisted that preference for an unambiguous text is "necessary," special deference has been given to such texts on several occasions. In the case of *In Re Esau,* for example, the tribunal looked to the Russian text to resolve the ambiguities in Article 6 (b) of the Nuremburg Charter in their English and French versions.[173] And similarly, in the *Pyrene Company* case, the Queen's Bench Division indicated its willingness to examine the French version of the provision involved in order to "help solve an ambiguity" in the English text.[174]

169. Reported in Hackworth, op. cit. supra note 156, at 265.
170. Ibid.
171. (1924), reported in 1923–24 *Annual Digest of Public International Law Cases* 334.
172. Id. at 336.
173. (1949), reported in 1949 *Int. Law Rep.* 482.
174. *Pyrene Co. Ltd. v. Scindia Navigation Co. Ltd.,* [1954] 2 Q.B. 403; reported in 1954 *Int. Law Rep.* 297, 299. Cf. also *Claim of the Standard Oil Company to Certain Tankers,* reported in 22 *Am. J. Int'l L.* 404 (1928) and 2 U.N. Rep. Int'l Arb. Awards 777, sub nom. *The Deutsche Amerikanische Petroleum Gesellschaftoil Tankers;* and other cases collected by Hackworth, op. cit. supra note 156, at 265–67, and Chang, op. cit. supra note 109, at 141–58.

The most widely discussed application of the rule that the more restrictive of two provisions in different languages should be adopted as the "common" intention of the parties is to be found in the *Mavrommatis* case.[175] In this case the Permanent Court laid down the rule in these terms: "[w]here two versions possessing equal authority exist one of which appears to have a wider bearing than the other, it is bound to adopt the more limited interpretation which can be made to harmonize with both versions." [176] The terms in dispute in the two texts were the English "public control" and its French counterpart *"contrôle public"* of Article 11 of the Palestine Mandate.[177] According to the Court's reading of the "ordinary" meaning of these terms, the English phrase was limited to public *ownership,* while the French phrase extended as well to public *regulation* of concessions such as those held by Mavrommatis. It concluded, in contrast to the rule which it laid down, that the wider of the two significations should be adopted according to the intentions of the parties.[178]

The *Mavrommatis* case illustrates a common deficiency in past attempts to formulate a general prescription for regulating priorities among texts in different languages or with different meanings in varying cultures sharing the same language. Precisely the same problem is encountered in attempting to favor the "burdened" or "obliged" parties, or the most limited of several versions, or the drafter, or the least ambiguous text.[179] To be sure, each of these factors may be important in certain circumstances, and it will be useful to call the decision-maker's attention to them. Their significance to the shared expectations of the parties to any particular agreement must, however, be regarded as a function of the various features of the context to which attention was called by the jurists and publicists reviewed above. It should be quite clear that these particular indices cannot be usefully generalized into rules whose application may be precisely specified in advance. A less misleading approach would see

175. *The Mavrommatis Palestine Concessions,* P.C.I.J., Ser. A, No. 2 (1924).
176. Id. at 19.
177. Id. at 20–23.
178. Ibid.
179. The latter position has frequently been adopted in past decision, as we have seen, but has not, to our knowledge, been emphasized in the writings of publicists to date.

these indices as items to which the decision-maker's attention should be drawn in their *probable* relevance to the genuine shared expectations of the participants.

References to the effects of class, personality, interest,[180] and crisis differences upon linguistic usage have not been found in a degree meriting separate comments. Some discussion of these features in their relation to contextual analysis was offered in the previous chapter.

THE LOGICAL OPERATION

Apart from general authorization of the employment of logical techniques and the manufacture of a number of pseudo-logical principles, scholars and decision-makers appear to have done little to promote the employment of logical operations in the interpretation of agreements. Many of the principles which have been formulated are not merely inadequate reflections of modern logical operations, but can scarcely be said, in any technical sense of the term, to be logical operations at all.

The principle which has been most frequently discussed and applied in past practice is that of *expressio unius est exclusio alterius.* This principle—which as usually stated prescribes that whenever a given reference has been expressly included in an agreement, all other related references must be regarded as having been excluded—has recently been supported by a prominent international jurist as being one of the "processes of logic . . . [which is] apparently unassailable," [181] and has been characterized in international decision as "a rule of both law and logic." [182] It may be easily seen, by restating the rule in logical terms, that it has no foundation in any current or past principles of logic, and that therefore the justification for the rule, if indeed there is one, must be discovered elsewhere.

The rule of *expressio unius* may be stated in implicative form as

180. But see the *Abu Dhabi* arbitration, supra note 93, where an issue concerning interest was indirectly raised by an inquiry into whether the lawyers of both sides, but particularly those of Abu Dhabi, were aware of the "continental shelf" and "territorial sea" doctrines at the time of initial agreement.

181. Lauterpacht, op. cit. supra note 5, at 59. See also Degan, op. cit. supra note 11, at 112–14.

182. *Decision in Life-Insurance Claims,* reported in 19 *Am. J. Int'l L.* 593, 602–03 (1925).

follows: If any given individual or class expression (x) occurs in an agreement, then it must be inferred that any other similar individual or class expression (y), (z), etc., was intentionally excluded from the operation of the agreement by the parties. What is involved in this formulation of the rule may perhaps be most easily observed in certain particular invocations of it. Thus in the dispute concerning *German Demands on Denmark,*[183] a peace settlement which regulated the payment of war damages among the respective countries contained the provision that "all goods seized on German territory" prior to a certain date would be subject to restitution. Counsel in the case argued that the *expressio unius* rule should be applied to exclude all other seizures, especially those on the high seas:

> Inasmuch as the Preliminaries specify the restitution of goods seized on land before a certain period, they, by necessary implication, exempt goods seized on the high seas from the operations of their provisions. In other words, . . . the well-known doctrine *"expressio unius est exclusio alterius"* is applicable to this as to other contracts.[184]

Similarly in the *David J. Adams* case[185] the tribunal was called upon to interpret a provision that prohibited the entry of American fishermen into certain territorial waters of Canada, except "for the purpose of shelter . . . repairing damages . . . purchasing wood . . . and obtaining water."[186] Despite the fact that other acts, such as the purchase of bait for which the *Adams* was seized, had been permitted for some time, the tribunal, applying the *expressio* doctrine, held that in light of the express prohibition of any "other purpose" than those mentioned, the seizure was authorized.[187]

In order to demonstrate the fallacy in the claim that the *expressio*

183. Reported in McNair, op. cit. supra note 6, at 203–04.
184. Id. at 204. For the outcome of the dispute reported, see id. at 203–04.
185. (1921), reported in Briggs, *The Law of Nations: Cases, Documents and Notes* 892 (2d ed. 1952).
186. Id. at 893.
187. Id. at 894–96. As these examples demonstrate, the special function of the doctrine has traditionally been to limit the extension by analogy of rights and duties which agreements have explicitly granted. The rational performance of this function, as we now proceed to show in more detail, has been unduly impeded by the conception which past decision-makers have had of the origin of the doctrine, and of its justification in policy.

unius rule can be justified by purely logical considerations, it should suffice to restate the rule in terms of the logical relationships which it establishes. It says, in effect, that under any circumstances in which the relation of implication (If . . . then) is discovered, it may be legitimately transformed into a coimplication (If and only if . . . then). To use the previous examples, the relation of 'If land seizure . . . then restitution' is to be transformed into 'If and only if land seizure . . . then restitution,' and the relation of 'If entry for shelter, repairs, wood or water, then no violation,' may be transformed into 'If and only if entry for shelter, repairs, wood or water, then no violation.' Without quarreling with any particular applications of the rule, it can be noted that its justification in logic—stated as a general preference for coimplication over implication—must obviously be rejected. The failure of international jurists and publicists to recognize that the rule is not one of logic has, however, resulted in a needlessly foreshortened examination of more adequate lexical and contextual justifications for its application.[188] In the absence of any general basis for applying the rule to all cases, its usefulness can only be determined after a careful consideration of all relevant features of the context designed to discover whether the participants themselves intended their specifications to be exclusive, and thus coimplicative, or whether they were intended to be only illustrative, leaving open the possibility that other related but unexpressed alternatives were included.

The necessity of recourse to the context was implicitly recognized by the tribunal in the case concerning the *Guillemot-Jacquemin Claim.*[189] In this case the tribunal was called upon to interpret the following provisions from Part A, Annex XVI, of the 1947 Peace Treaty:

> (1) Any contract which required for its execution intercourse between any of the parties thereto having become enemies . . . shall . . . be deemed to have been dissolved as from the time when any of the parties thereto became enemies.
>
> . . .
>
> (3) Nothing in Part A of this annex shall be deemed to in-

188. For an introduction to the literature which most directly emphasizes the respective roles of lexical and broader contextual features of language, see above, Ch. 2, notes 2 and 19, and more recent analytical approaches as exemplified in Hart, *The Concept of Law* (1961), and other writings by the same author.

189. (1949), reported in 1951 *Int. Law Rep.* 403.

> validate transactions lawfully carried out in accordance with a contract between enemies if they have been carried out with the authorization of the . . . Allied . . . Powers.[190]

The principal issue in the case was whether the plaintiff, a French national, having leased property in Rome to Italian nationals during the war, could claim the invalidation of the lease under paragraphs (1) and (3) in order to regain possession of the property prior to the stated date of termination. The tribunal upheld the lease, interpreting paragraph (1) to apply only to contracts concluded before the war.[191] The provision would appear to have been designed to invalidate such prewar contracts, but the tribunal's conclusion that it does not apply to contracts concluded *during* the war is clearly an application of the *expressio unius* rule. It involves an inference from 'If before, then not valid' to 'If not before, then valid,' which changes the provision from its *prima facie* implicative form into a coimplication.

Although the tribunal did not discuss this application of the *expressio* rule, it did discuss and refuse to apply an equivalent allegedly "logical" expression, namely, the *deductio a contrario*.[192] The *a contrario* rule was invoked by the plaintiff, who contended that the statement "contract between enemies" in paragraph (3) included any contract signed during the war; since it validated a type of claim that was *not* the plaintiff's, it followed that the plaintiff's claim was thereby invalidated. Although the tribunal rejected this argument, it can easily be shown that this principle is formally synonymous with that applied to paragraph (1): 'If not plaintiff's, then valid' to 'If plaintiff's, then not valid,' which is exactly the same shift as that involved in the *expressio unius* rule. Here the Court accepted it without comment, but refused to apply its equivalent under other conditions, commenting that its application would violate the "wish" of the drafters.[193]

Contrary to what at first may appear to be an inconsistency in the application of the principle, the tribunal gave implicit credence to the necessity of recourse to the context for the determinative, and naturally variable, factors in applying it. The *a contrario* rule was rejected because the immediate context in Part A indicated that the

190. Id. at 403 n.
191. Id. at 404–05.
192. Id. at 404.
193. Ibid.

necessary prerequisite for its application (that "contract between enemies" possesses a different meaning in paragraphs 3 and 1, respectively) had not been met. The *expressio* rule was applied to paragraph (1), on the other hand, because the assumption of 'If not before, then valid' seemed to the tribunal a more reasonable one in light of the wording of (1), which appeared to suggest that the parties intended to invalidate only those contracts which were concluded prior to the change of conditions in the formal creation of "enemies," i.e., at the declaration of war.

Past decision-makers have declined to apply the *expressio unius* rule in one context which deserves mention. Simply stated, it is that whenever the generic class of several specifications is explicitly included in an agreement, preference should be accorded it and the *expressio* rule should not be applied to the specifications. In this form, the rule resembles another principle with a long tradition and a much stronger foundation in logic, namely, the *a fortiori* principle.[194] An example of this form may be found in the *Duc du Guise Claim,*[195] in which the Franco-Italian Conciliation Commission construed the following provision of Article 78 of the Peace Treaty: "The Italian Government shall nullify all measures, including seizures, sequestration or control, taken by it against United Nations property." [196] The Commission, in accepting the plaintiff's claim despite the fact that it did not qualify under one of the specifications, commented that "The Treaty does not require the Italian Government to nullify [only] measures of seizure, sequestration or control, but all measures including seizure, sequestration and control. The latter are not enumerated to indicate the kind of measures which must be annulled, but purely so as to establish quite clearly that they are included in the requirement of the paragraph." [197] In cases of this type, the general class of events ("all measures taken") is described as "including" the various members specified, which are added for emphasis or clarity and are obviously not intended to be exclusive.

194. This type of argument may be characterized, as the example suggests, in terms of the relationship of inclusive classes. If Class A contains Class B, then it follows logically that 'If B, then A.' For further discussion of this point see Copi, *Symbolic Logic* 66–75, 319–31 (1954).

195. (1951), reported in 1951 *Int. Law Rep.* 423.

196. Id. at 424 n.

197. Id. at 425.

To apply the *expressio unius* principle to the specific members would be in direct disregard of what has been expressly included in the more general expression.[198]

In recent times, one version of the *expressio unius* doctrine was employed in a quite different context in the *First Admissions* case,[199] in which the International Court of Justice made an advisory interpretation of Article 4, paragraph 1, of the United Nations Charter:

> Membership in the United Nations is open to all . . . peace-loving States which accept the obligations contained in the present Charter and, in the judgment of the Organization, are able and willing to carry out these obligations.[200]

The principal question presented to the Court was whether certain conditions (the reciprocal admission of another state) could be added by a member of the Security Council to those already contained in paragraph 1. The Court answered in the negative, commenting that "The terms 'Membership in the United Nations is open to all . . . peace-loving states which' . . . indicate that States which fulfill the conditions stated have the qualifications requisite for admission." [201] Thus the Court construed the provision as saying: If and only if a state is peace-loving and willing and able to accept all Charter obligations, then it is qualified for membership. In other words, the stated conditions and *only* the stated conditions may be invoked. This conclusion was supported by reference to the supplementary provision of the Security Council rules of procedure calling on it to "decide whether in its judgment the applicant is a peace-loving State and is able and willing to carry out the obligations contained in the Charter, and accordingly whether to recommend the

198. Examples of this argument may be found explicitly stated in the *Chorzow Factory* case, supra note 2, at 23, 33; *Legal Status of Eastern Greenland,* P.C.I.J., Ser. A/B, No. 53, p. 73 (1933), (these cases are collected with comment in Schwarzenberger, op. cit. supra note 13, at 513–14). See also *Frontier (Local Authorities) Award* (1953), reported in 1953 *Int. Law Rep.* 63. Judge Alvarez used the argument in another context in the *Second Admissions* case, supra note 130, at 18.

199. *Conditions of Admission of a State to Membership in the United Nations,* [1948] I.C.J. Rep. 57.

200. Id. at 62.

201. Ibid.

applicant State for membership."[202] Although the Court placed considerable emphasis on this provision, it is clear that the necessity of applying the *expressio* doctrine to justify the conclusion reached is equally as great as it was in relation to Article 4(1). The term "accordingly" could be interpreted either as equivalent to "then" or to "then and only then" in referring an applicant for membership. The important point is that the alternatives may be specified in terms of the logical relations of implication and coimplication, but the ultimate choice—unaided in this case by precise textual indications—must be made after a thorough contextual survey of relevant indices of the participants' expectations as well as relevant community policies. The criticism which may be leveled at the Court in this instance was that it remained satisfied with wholly textual considerations, thus failing to make an adequate contextual examination to resolve the logical ambiguities in the Charter provisions.[203]

Traditional concepts of legal syntax concerning the relationships of conjunction and disjunction have also been developed in past trends of decision. Relative to semantic and other inquiries the frequency with which decision-makers have been faced with ambiguities resulting from such relationships has not been as great. A number of significant examples, however, may be noted. In the *Chorzow Factory* case, for example, such an ambiguity allegedly occurred when the Permanent Court was called upon to interpret Article 23 of the Geneva Convention of 1922.[204] This article related to the requirements concerning arbitration of disputes arising under the Convention: "Should differences of opinion resulting from the interpretation and application of Articles 6 to 22 arise . . . they should be submitted to the decision of the Permanent Court of International Justice."[205] The Court, in referring to other arbitral clauses con-

202. Id. at 63.
203. Another principle which is often proposed as a related, even complementary, "logical" principle to that of *expressio unius* is that of *ejusdem generis.* This latter principle is, at least potentially, a direct complement to the *expressio* rule in that it permits the inclusion of similar types of events which would be, in theory at least, excluded by the *expressio* doctrine. In fact, however, the *ejusdem* principle is seldom employed in this manner, and is more often used to assist in examining and weighing the parties' emphases upon different levels of generality in the various provisions of an agreement. For this reason, the principle has been included for discussion above under the principle of generality, Ch. 4, p. 201.
204. P.C.I.J., Ser. A, No. 9 (1927).
205. Id. at 12 n.

taining similar grants, concluded that "the contracting Parties agreed to submit to arbitration any differences as to the interpretation *or* application of the particular treaties" (emphasis added), thus construing the "and" of Article 23 as an inclusive disjunctive "or." [206] A similar conclusion was reached concerning Article 23 in the case concerning *Certain German Interests in Polish Upper Silesia*,[207] where the Court commented on "the word *et* which, in both ordinary and legal language, may, according to circumstances, equally have an alternative or a cumulative meaning." [208] In both of these cases, the choice of the "alternative" meaning of *and*, which we have outlined above in logical terms as inclusive disjunction, was adopted despite claims on the part of one of the participants that a "cumulative" meaning be preferred (creating a conjunctive relationship) to prohibit or restrict the application of the arbitration requirement. In selecting the alternative meaning, the Court—with no suggestion that the choice was dictated by "logic"—made explicit its belief that the parties had no intention of limiting the relevance of Article 23 to cases in which both interpretation and application were involved. It stated that, as a matter of policy which by now has become well settled, "There seems to be no reason why States should not be able to ask the Court to give an abstract interpretation of a treaty; rather would it appear that this is one of the most important functions which it can fulfill." [209]

Further problems involving conjunctive and disjunctive, as well as other, relations have arisen which have required for their solution the application of the more specific policies discussed above. Thus in the case of *Scala v. Nappi*,[210] the Italian Court of Cassation invoked the general aims of the 1947 Treaty of Peace in resolving the syntactical ambiguities of Annex XVI, Part B (1):

> All periods of prescription or limitation of right[s] of action . . . involving United Nations nationals and Italian Nationals . . . shall be regarded as having been suspended, for the duration of the War, in Italian territory on the one hand, and on the other hand in the territory of those United Nations which grant,

206. Id. at 21.
207. P.C.I.J., Ser. A, No. 6 (1925).
208. Id. at 14.
209. *Certain German Interests in Polish Upper Silesia* (The Merits), P.C.I.J., Ser. A, No. 7, pp. 18–19 (1926).
210. (1950), reported in 1949 *Int. Law Rep.* 316.

on a reciprocal basis, the benefit of the provisions of this paragraph.[211]

The Court in its decision was concerned with the status of (1) Italian nationals residing in the United States, and (2) Italian *and* United States nationals residing in the United States with respect to their ability to bring suit against an Italian national in Italy. It held that the provision applied only to foreign nationals as prescribed, regardless of residence. Of the many possible logical circuits involved in B (1), the following three may be taken as the ones most relevant to the Court's decision: [212]

(a)	All limitations are suspended in wartime for	Persons who are foreign and Italian nationals	Bringing suit in Italy
(b)	All limitations are suspended in wartime for	Foreign nationals	Bringing suit in Italy
(c)	All limitations are suspended in wartime for	Italian nationals	Bringing suit in Italy

The Court eliminated alternative (c) because "the protection of the interests of their own nationals is the sole concern of their home State" and therefore (c) "could not form the subject-matter of an international agreement [since it involves only] Italian municipal law." [213] The justification for eliminating alternative (a) is not made clear by the Court, but it appears to hold that it is logically required to do so by the rejection of (c).[214] The final selection of alternative (b) is said to coincide with the intentions of the signatory powers: "[t]his provision is intended to ensure reciprocity . . . between the States signatories of the Treaty. In accordance with

211. Ibid.

212. For further elucidation of the use of the circuit analogy for detecting syntactic ambiguities, see Layman E. Allen, "Interpretation of the California Pimping Statute," 1960 *M.U.L.L.* 3. See also Allen, "Toward a Procedure for Detecting and Controlling Syntactic Ambiguity in Legal Discourse," in 3 *Advances in Documentation and Library Science,* Part 2 (1961).

213. Id. at 317.

214. "Nor is it correct to contend that the persons concerned have acquired United States citizenship, for the Court below has found that they have not lost

the usual character of international conventions, Italy had bound herself by the above-mentioned clause to accord the treatment laid down therein to the nationals of the other contracting States." [215] Why such treatment should exclude persons who are "nationals of other contracting states" *and* nationals of Italy is not, in the material reported, satisfactorily explained.[216]

A similar instance of syntactical ambiguity, resulting from the alternative references of a modifier to a series of disjunctive phrases, is contained in the case of *In Re Esau*.[217] This case involved the planning, by Esau, of a large theft of gold and scientific instruments taken from Holland to Germany during the Second World War. His defense was that the theft was justified by military necessity as outlined in Article 6 (b) of the Nuremberg Charter: "violations shall include . . . plunder of public or private property, wanton destruction of cities, towns or villages, or devastation not justified by military necessity." [218] The tribunal's analysis of the alternatives presented by this provision may be illustrated in the following diagrams:

(1)	Plunder of property Wanton destruction of towns Devastation }	Not justified by military necessity }	Violation
(2)	Plunder of property Wanton destruction of towns Devastation ——→	Not justified by military necessity }	Violation

Italian nationality. They cannot, therefore, receive the treatment laid down by the Treaty of Peace in favour of nationals of states other than Italy." Id. at 317.

215. Id. at 316–17.

216. Ibid. An excellent recent example of a similar kind of syntactical ambiguity may be found in *Kolovrat v. Oregon,* 366 U.S. 187 (1961), analyzed in detail in Allen, "Some Uses of Symbolic Logic in Law Practice," 1962 *M.U.L.L.* 119.

217. (1949), reported in 1949 *Int. Law Rep.* 482.

218. Id. at 482–83.

It may plausibly be contended that under the first, but not the second alternative, explicit proof of the absence of military necessity would be required for any act of "plunder," "wanton destruction," or "devastation." The tribunal held that the final phrase relating to military necessity "could not . . . logically refer to plunder, etc." since those acts were already outlawed under the laws of war.[219] To be sure, its choice of terms in insisting that the reference as diagrammed in (2) cannot be made *logically* is unfortunate, since it should be obvious from the diagram itself that both alternatives are logically feasible. On the other hand, its contention that *any* plunder of property or wanton destruction of communities is outlawed by the laws of war is well documented in past practice, within the limits of what is considered reasonable in light of wartime conditions; these limits are established, however, by reference to requirement of military necessity.[220] Such a conclusion would transform alternative (2) into an equivalent version of (1). Under these circumstances, it may be suggested that the questions of policy raised by the Court in its suggested shift in the burden of proof between the two alternatives, and the wide discretion left in the application of the central terms in either instance, might have been given a more explicit survey in lieu of the claim that the outcome was dictated "logically." [221]

A more recent example of a relatively direct description of logical procedures used in decision-making was provided in the *Lawless* case.[222] In this case, as we have seen, the legality of the Irish government's preventive detention of revolutionaries in time of crisis was disputed before the European Court of Justice by Lawless, who was a member of the I.R.A. and who admitted to previous and fairly consistent revolutionary activity. He claimed that the government's action conflicted with the Convention for the Protection of Human

219. Id. at 483.

220. For a more extensive discussion of this point, see McDougal and Feliciano, *Law and Minimum World Public Order,* Ch. 6, esp. at 671 ff. (1961).

221. For further recent examples of syntactical ambiguities in international agreements, see *Geneva Protocol* case (1948) in 1948 *Int. Law Rep.* 4; *Holder v. Ministère Public* (1944), reported in 1946 id. 90; *UNESCO (Constitution)* case (1949), in 1949 id. 331; *Abu Dhabi* arbitration, supra note 93. See also Miller, "Two Examples of Syntactic Ambiguities in International Agreements," 1962 *M.U.L.L.* 72, for an analysis of the widely discussed syntactic ambiguity in the *Anglo-Iranian Oil Co.* case, [1952] I.C.J. Rep. 93.

222. *European Court of Human Rights Reports,* Ser. A, p. 27 (1961).

Rights and Fundamental Freedoms, to which Ireland was a party. The Court held that the detention of Lawless without an opportunity for judicial determination of his case was indeed contrary to paragraphs 1 (c) and 3 of Article 5 of the Convention which require all alleged offenses and preventive-measure cases to qualify for immediate judicial hearing. It also held that Ireland's derogation from these provisions was permissible under Article 15 of the Convention, which permits nation-state parties to abrogate their obligations under Article 5 under circumstances where the peace and security of the nation are at stake.

The logical issue was raised in the first of the Court's determinations, namely, in its decision that Ireland had violated the express provisions of Article 5. In this respect the crucial provision was subparagraph 1 (c) :

> Article 5 (1) Everyone has the right to liberty and security of person. No one shall be deprived of his liberty save in the following cases and in accordance with procedure prescribed by law:
>
> (c) the lawful arrest or detention of a person effected for the purpose of bringing him before the competent legal authority on reasonable suspicion of having committed an offence or when it is reasonably considered necessary to prevent his committing an offence or fleeing after having done so.[223]

The question before the Court, in its own words, were "whether in Article 5, paragraph 1 (c), the expression 'effected for the purpose of bringing him before the competent judicial authority' qualifies only the words 'on reasonable suspicion of having committed an offence' or also the words 'when it is reasonably considered necessary to prevent his committing an offence.' " Its first approach was simply to state with emphasis its own conclusion in such a way as to make the decision appear quite straightforward: "The wording in Article 5, paragraph 1 (c), is sufficiently clear to give an answer to this question." [224] This answer was that the expression in question "qualifies every category of cases of arrest or detention referred to in that subparagraph." [225]

223. Id. at 46.
224. Id. at 51.
225. Ibid.

This familiar approach, which the Court later referred to as a "grammatical" one, was made to appear quite perfunctory for apparently persuasive purposes. But the fact that the Court did not consider the matter so simple can be seen from the way it further, systematically, enlarged its enquiry. First it brought to bear another paragraph (paragraph 3 of Article 5), which provided that everyone arrested pursuant to 1 (c) "shall be brought promptly before a judge or other officer authorized by law to exercise judicial power and shall be entitled to trial within a reasonable time or to release pending trial."[226] This paragraph clearly referred to the entirety of paragraph 1 (c) (the precise reference was to "everyone arrested or detained in accordance with the provision of paragraph 1 (c)"), and not simply to part of it.[227] Thus the Court undertook its second procedural step, that of enlarging the scope of its inquiry to the entirety of paragraph 1.

The final step in the Court's analysis, before it drew up short of considering extratextual materials, was to consider the scope and purpose of the entire Convention: "The meaning thus arrived at by grammatical analysis is fully in harmony with the purpose of the Convention which is to protect the freedom and security of the individual against arbitrary detention or arrest."[228] The Court concluded that if the course recommended by the Irish government were to be followed, this purpose would be thwarted by exempting persons jailed on preventive grounds from judicial guarantees.

Unfortunately, as we have seen, the relative clarity in the execution of the logical operation by the Court in the *Lawless* case is by and large an exception among past decisions. Even if a rather arbitrary limit was placed upon the examination of extrinsic evidence, the Court's procedures were quite straightforward and presented in a relatively orderly fashion. The logical operation, indeed, was seen in an increasingly widening context of other features of the agreement process. While by no means exemplary, this case stands in contrast to most past uses of the logical operation. From our survey we have seen that the techniques developed by modern logicians, even in the least detailed prescriptions of propositional calculus presented briefly in the previous chapter, have yet to be applied in past trends of deci-

226. Id. at 46.
227. Ibid.
228. Id. at 52.

sion. The resulting confusion and lack of clarity as to what constitutes a logical inference is sadly characteristic of the efforts of most past decision-makers.

Although the comparison of international and national tribunals yields few surprises in that neither have as yet systematically adopted and applied modern logical techniques, the comparison of national and international publicists and commentators yields a quite different picture. An extensive literature on the applications of modern logical methods to municipal legal problems has recently developed.[229] In at least two countries legal problems have received the attention of professional logicians.[230] Some municipal law logicians, in providing "applications" of modern logical techniques, have discussed syntactical ambiguities in international agreements.[231] International law publicists, however, have on the whole remained free of their influence, a condition for which no satisfactory explanation easily appears. The simplicity of the more common logical problems, however, can scarcely justify the inadequate tools of analysis developed in past practice. Such tools have not been adequate, as we saw above, to solve the problems already encountered; to confront future contingencies it is imperative that the full range of modern methods known to logicians be made available and applied in decision.

THE OPERATION OF ASSESSING GESTURE AND DEED

The assessment of gesture and deed has received little express treatment in past practice, especially in relation to the understandings prevailing at the distinctive phase of agreement as a result of culture, class, interest, personality, and exposure to crisis factors. Occasional comments by scholars to the effect that gestures and deeds are customarily clear and unequivocal have tended to discourage the consideration of operations designed to investigate actual conditions.[232]

229. For a detailed bibliography of modern legal syntax literature, see 1959 *M.U.L.L.* 17.

230. Cf. M. R. Cohen, "The Place of Logic in the Law," 29 *Harv. L. Rev.* 622 (1916); Fitch, "Book Review," 17 *J. of Symb. Logic* 73 (1952); Kraszewski, reviewing of works by Gregorowicz, Wolter, and Ziembinski, 23 id. 73 (1958); Allen, supra notes 212 and 216, and "Logical Theory: Deontic Logic," 60 *M.U.L.L.* 13 (1960); Dickerson, *Legislative Drafting* (1954).

231. Cf. Allen, supra note 216.

232. Cf. Fitzmaurice, supra note 4, at 20–21.

The fact that gestures and deeds, as we pointed out above, partake of the same degrees of explicitness, complementarity, equivocality, and completeness as words, and thus require assessment in the same manner, has had little recognition. Exceptionally, the difficulties involved in making inferences from gestures and deeds have been given implicit recognition by decision-makers applying the content principle of subsequent conduct.[233] As we have already seen, however, the operation of assessing this type of inference has frequently been mismanaged by a general devaluation of evidence from behavior precisely because of the difficulties in fact of its rational assessment as an index of the parties' shared subjectivities. It need not be reemphasized that such a devaluation is hardly compatible with a genuine attempt to ascertain the shared expectations of the parties.

Various examples of the examination of important events subsequent to a focal agreement could be offered to illustrate the operation of assessing gesture and deed. The clearest and most relevant instances are, however, to be found in cases where the focal agreement appears to be ambiguous or inconsistent, and a long history of interactions between the parties is available for making inferences. From the vantage point of the scholarly observer, moreover, if the utility of this particular recommended operation is to be appropriately appraised, this history of interaction must be openly and thoroughly discussed by the court in its opinion. Such a case was the 1961 decision of the International Court on the *Case Concerning the Temple of Preah Vihear*.[234] This case involved, as related above, a 1904 treaty between Thailand (then Siam) and Cambodia (then part of French Indochina) which had established a "watershed" criterion for delineating the frontier and constituted a Commission to implement it. Shortly after 1940 Thailand asked France to survey portions of the frontier and draw up maps of them. This was done but was never sanctioned by the Commission, whose work was terminated just as the maps were delivered. In brief, the "watershed" criterion left the temple at Preah Vihear in Thailand, but the maps showed it to be in Cambodia. After a number of diplomatic and other strategic moves on both sides, Cambodia brought the case before the Court.

Faced with one text that was clearly authoritative (the treaty) and one which was not (the maps), the Court's first question was

233. Discussed above, p. 132.

234. [1962] I.C.J. Rep. 6.

whether the deeds of Thailand after receiving the maps indicated that it had accepted them as the authoritative delimitation of the frontier. The Court's most extensive assessment of the gestures and deeds of the parties, however, occurred with respect to a second issue —namely, whether Thailand's conduct concerning the maps during a period of over fifty years now precluded it from claiming jurisdiction even if originally the maps had not been accepted as authoritative. The Court answered in the affirmative on both issues and decided in favor of Cambodia.

With regard to the first of the questions raised, the Court held that the *omission* of an expected act—an official response by Thailand to the receipt of the maps—was of importance since it constituted an implicit acceptance of the line there delineated. Several ceremonial acts accompanying the receipt of the maps were also held to be important: a prompt and generous note of thanks, wide publicity of the maps in all interested circles, notices sent to the four major Siamese legations and to all members of the Commission on both the French and Siamese side. These acts added, in the majority's view, to the "official" nature conferred on the maps by the Siamese. This "officialness" in turn placed upon the Siamese a burden of reacting to the maps even though they were not Commission documents and France had requested no formal acknowledgement of their receipt or their contents.

As some of the dissenting judges point out, the majority opinion overlooks several important points. First, with regard to the supposed "acceptance by silence," it was never clearly established that an obligation existed on the part of the Siamese to read the maps. With respect to the view that any interested party would have been aware of the maps' "error," Judge Wellington Koo points out:

> No question about the Temple had been raised by either France or Siam during the negotiations for the Treaty of 1904 or subsequently in the meetings of the Mixed Commission of Delimitation. It had never been in issue between the two Parties at any time before 1908 [when the maps were received by Siam].[235]

In elaboration of this theme the Judge continued:

> Moreover, the Annex I map was drawn on the scale of 1:200,000, which means that the distance of 500 metres on the ground

235. Id. at 84.

> lying between the alleged frontier line and the temple area is represented on the map by a width of only 2.5 millimetres. And because the Temple is perched on the summit of the promontory of Preah Vihear, the mark indicating the Temple is buried in a tangle of contour lines in a small part of the map. Even if one looks specially for the mark, it is by no means easy to find it.[236]

The point here is that even if an obligation existed to look generally at the maps, since there were eleven total maps and Preah Vihear was but a dot on one of them seen with difficulty, only a person specially alert to the placement of the temple would have noticed it. And the temple had at no time during the negotiations been an issue between the parties, so it would have been quite reasonable for a reader of the maps to miss the "error" entirely.

The ceremonial acts surrounding the maps' receipt in Siam were, similarly, thought by the majority to be unambiguous but challenged by the dissenters. One noted that the Interior Minister's note of thanks was "certainly not unusual," especially in light of the fact that he had been sent an extra copy for his own use "as an act of special courtesy." And as far as the wide distribution of the maps within Siam was concerned, this act was held not unusual "when it is recalled that at the time Siam did not yet have a good modern map showing the whole frontier region between Siam and French Indochina, and that the Siamese Government had previously requested the President of the French Commission to have one made by the French topographical officers." [237]

Perhaps the most interesting conflict in interpreting the deeds of the Siamese during this period occurred over Prince Damrong's visit to the temple in 1930, to which reference has already been made. Although the Prince was by then no longer Foreign Minister but rather President of the Royal Institute, and although he announced upon arrival at the temple that his tour had to do only with his archeological interest in the temple and had "nothing to do with politics," the Court took the position that his trip "clearly had a quasi-official character." [238] The Prince was met at the site by the French Resident for the adjoining Cambodian province, wearing his full military regalia.

236. Ibid.
237. Ibid.
238. Id. at 90, 30.

The French flag was flying over the temple. One of the persons accompanying the Resident, a French archeologist, toasted the Prince's arrival by referring to his archeological skills and his interest in "another of the monuments of our Cambodia." The Court believed that these signs of assertion of sovereignty over the temple were sufficient to put the Prince on notice; and his quasi-official role should have led him to warn the Siamese government of the Cambodian actions. Instead, all he appeared to do was to thank the Resident and send him some photographs of the occasion.

The dissents, particularly that of Judge Wellington Koo, dispute the quasi-official role of Prince Damrong's visit and his obligation to urge the filing of a formal protest. There would appear to have been reasonable grounds for doubt on this score, however politic a thing it might have been to notify the Siamese officials involved more directly in such matters. There is no evidence, however, that the Prince did *not* do so, except that the Siamese government did not take steps to challenge the French-Cambodian assertion. Still, the more important issue in this area relates not to the nature of the Prince's visit, nor to his notifying the Siamese government, but rather to the available modes of action open to the Siamese in the face of such a display of French power. Judge Wellington Koo points out the dilemma of the Siamese in this respect by quoting from a comment made by Prince Damrong's daughter, who accompanied him on the trip: "It was generally known at the time that we only give the French an excuse to seize more territory by protesting. Things had been like that since they came into the river Chao Phya with their gunboats and their seizure of Chanthaburi." [239] The same judge also observed that this "was a situation not peculiar to Siam. It was, generally speaking, the common experience of most Asiatic States in their intercourse with the Occidental Powers during this period of colonial expansion." [240] Thus in his view, and very plausibly, the most likely reason that the Siamese did not protest this display of French-Cambodian sovereignty over Preah Vihear was that they realized it would accomplish nothing and perhaps only result in their losing further territory. Thus their silence on the matter scarcely exhibited unequivocal consent to the assertion; it signified only that they wished to keep whatever land they had in the face of a threat from an aggressor with

239. Id. at 91.
240. Ibid.

whom they realized they could not compete. Upon such a view, therefore, the majority's interpretation of the Siamese "silence" omits consideration of this important cultural factor. A further verification of this "cultural imbalance" view of French-Siamese relations during this time can be found in the fact that when Siam became a power more nearly equal vis-à-vis Cambodia after the downfall of France to the Germans in 1904, it immediately posted a military guard over the temple, and retained the guard for the more than twenty years until the present suit. The majority, again overlooking the cultural factor of French influence, regarded this move only as a "local action," and in a way a denial at the governmental-diplomatic level of Cambodian jurisdiction (despite its great reliance on the actions of the French Resident in 1930). In fact it is not clear what sort of action at the governmental level in 1940 would have been appropriate, since Cambodia was not at that time an independent nation (it did not become so until 1953), and France had no interest, and for some time no recognized government to take an interest in Cambodia. Thailand did only what it could, namely, to send first a guard and then a detachment of troops (in 1954) to the temple area. These measures could be considered, as Judge Wellington Koo indicated, to have been under the circumstances the most "positive acts [which] clearly evidence the absence of any intention on the part of Siam or Thailand to acquiesce in or accept the . . . [original 1908] map line." [241]

Another instance of clear-cut need for an operation assessing the effects of gesture and deed was presented in the *Brazilian Loans* case.[242] In this case the Permanent Court was called upon to weigh the effect of a long-standing practice of payment in paper francs of interest on Brazilian bonds despite an initial treaty provision for payment in "gold francs." The Court, following a practice employed in several other cases, held that such evidence from the behavior or deeds of the parties could not be considered when the text was clear in its plain and natural meaning.[243] Thus the operation of assessing deed was obviated—though doubtlessly in the service of an unexplained policy—by the search for a "plain" meaning.[244]

241. Id. at 86–87.

242. *Brazilian Federal Loans Issued in France,* P.C.I.J., Ser. A, No. 21 (1929).

243. Id. at 118 ff.

244. But see the Court's references to the pattern of practices with respect to regulation of business hours in the *Competence of the International Labour Or-*

Even failure to act must of course be included among the "acts" requiring assessment under this principle. Thus in the *Saudi Arabia–Aramco* arbitration,[245] discussed in detail above, the tribunal discounted the past failure of Aramco to employ even a single vessel to transport the oil extracted under its concession agreement with Saudi Arabia in assessing the extent of its right to exclusive control over sea transportation to foreign markets. A crucial difference, however, between the tribunal's approach in this case and that of the Court in the *Brazilian Loans* case was that the assessment of gesture and deed was not precluded by a narrow textual limitation. It can be inferred from the brief discussion offered that the tribunal in fact made careful examination of this "act" in relation to other features of the total context.

In another recent case, the *Barcelona Traction* case (Preliminary Objections),[246] the International Court of Justice had opportunity to assess a complicated combination of words, gestures, and deeds, all affected by overtones of authority. A suit filed in 1958 by Belgium against Spain for an alleged miscarriage of justice against Belgian nationals with interests in the Barcelona Traction, Light and Power Company was withdrawn in 1961. The Belgian notice of withdrawal stated only that "at the request of Belgian nationals the protection of whom was the reason for the filing of the Application in the case [and] availing itself of the right conferred upon it by Article 69 of the Rules of Court [it was] not going on with the proceedings instituted by that Application." [247] It was understood and admitted by both parties, however, that the reason for the withdrawal at this time was that the private Belgian and Spanish interests concerned had decided to negotiate for a settlement. These negotiations were, as events transpired, unsuccessful, and in consequence the proceedings were reopened in June of 1962.

Spain claimed that the previous discontinuance per se precluded any further action by Belgium, and that in addition its finality was

---

ganization to Regulate, Incidentally, The Personal Work of the Employer, P.C.I.J., Ser. B, No. 13, p. 19 (1926), where the operation is not subject to similar restrictions in terms of "plain" meaning.

245. Supra note 74. See also the discussion of such "silent gestures" by the tribunals in the early *Chamizal Arbitration Between the United States and Mexico* (1911), reported in 5 *Am. J. Int'l L.* 782 (1911), and in the *Corfu Channel* case, supra note 119.

246. [1964] I.C.J. Rep. 6.

247. Id. at 17.

understood by both parties as a prerequisite for the negotiations. Belgium denied any such understanding, and contended that its discontinuance rested solely upon hopes for the success of the negotiations. When they failed the only recourse was to reopen the suit. The Court held that the discontinuance did not foreclose further action by Belgium.

The Court saw no reason to hold that a discontinuance was per se final and irrevocable: errors in procedure, failure to give appropriate notice, failure to exhaust local remedies, discovery of new evidence, any of these possibilities might appropriately lead to a discontinuance and a subsequent reapplication. The Court thus concluded that "The existence of these possibilities suffices in itself to show that the question of the nature of a discontinuance cannot be determined on any *a priori* basis, but must be considered in close relationship with the circumstances of the particular case." [248] The Court was quite clear on the implications of this view for interpretation: "The real question is not what the discontinuance does—which is obvious—but what it implies, results from or is based on. This must be independently established, except in those cases where, because the notice itself gives reasons, or refers to acts or undertakings of the parties, or to other circumstances, its import is clear and apparent." [249] Such evidence was not forthcoming, the Court concluded, from either side in the present dispute. Not only were the exchanges of the private Spanish and Belgian interests inconclusive, they also failed to show that such exchanges could or did in any way bind their respective governments. Thus the act of discontinuance was neither on its face, nor in the detailed expectations of the parties, ultimate and irrevocable.

THE OPERATION OF ASSESSING SCIENTIFIC CREDIBILITY

Few controversies have arisen concerning alternative methods for determining the usages current in the different communities or audiences which might affect the expectations of the parties to an international agreement. Hence decision-makers have not found it necessary to assess the scientific credibility of the various possible

248. Id. at 19.
249. Id. at 21.

sources of information. Frequently disputes in which the plain and natural meaning principle is invoked involve potential appeals to different standards of community-wide meanings, but the outcomes of these disputes have not yet been made to turn on the credibility of various sources of evidence. Modern techniques of content analysis, and other techniques of determining relevant community usages appear not to have been exploited by decision-makers or publicists.[250]

THE OPERATION OF ESTIMATING AGREEMENT PROBABILITY

The pragmatic dimension of communication analysis, to which agreement probability relates, has been examined in part by decision-makers as one aspect of the overall contextual approach. The contextual survey of the participants' shared demands and expectations, tracing these factors from early through current conditions, has nonetheless failed to make use of available operations in examining the "causes" of a communicated message. Past techniques developed for examining the "consequences" or "effects" of communication have failed to produce any more adequate results. The main references to the effects of communication have resulted, as we saw above, in analyses of its effects on the decision-making process and upon the participants as manifested in their subsequent courses of conduct. But the predominant emphasis of the pragmatic dimension of analysis has most frequently been limited to considerations of the "reasonableness" of reliance upon the communicated message.[251] The operations designed to assess this feature of the agreement process, however, are scarcely representative of the operation of estimating agreement probability to which we refer.

Several attempts were made in the *South-West Africa* cases (Preliminary Objections) [252] to estimate the probability of agreement as

250. The best summary of quantitative content analytic techniques is Berelson, "Content Analysis," in 1 *Handbook of Social Psychology* 488 (Lindzey ed. 1954). See discussion and further references in Ch. 2, above.

251. Cf. especially *Eastern Greenland* case, supra note 198, at 69–71, where the issue of reasonable reliance upon a communicated message was raised explicitly. For cases arising in the context of subsequent behavior in actual reliance upon a message, see above, p. 132.

252. [1962] I.C.J. Rep. 319.

between South Africa and other interested nations under the League of Nations Mandate system. South Africa, for example, had advanced the contention in its first objection to the jurisdiction of the Court that the Mandates were not "treaties," in order to escape Article 37 of the Court's Statute. The Court took cognizance of the conduct of the parties with respect to similar agreements and declarations in reaching the conclusion that indeed the Mandates were treaties: the fact that certified copies of most treaties were filed with the appropriate authorities, as copies of the Mandate agreements were filed with the Secretary-General of the League of Nations; the fact that many treaties speak in their preambles of obligations "undertaken" according to explicit "provisions," as was done in the preamble to the Mandate; and the fact that several formalities, such as signatories and the actions of states pursuant to the obligations undertaken by these signatories, usually attend treaties as was the case with the Mandates. In the fourth objection raised by South Africa in the same case, the Court again resorted to traditional practice to determine whether the instant dispute was one which "cannot be settled by negotiation." [253]

South Africa had argued that no negotiations on this specific point had occurred between itself and the plaintiff states, and that therefore the dispute could easily be negotiable. The Court, however, called attention to the fact that many agreements were today either formally or informally negotiated and arbitrated in the daily diplomatic work of the organs of the United Nations, and that in the General Assembly several years of discussions of this issue had lead to no result. In 1954, in fact, a representative of the Union government had explained to the Special Committee on South-West Africa convened to study the Union's administration of the Territory, that it was "doubtful whether there is any hope that new negotiations . . . will lead to any positive results." [254] Whence followed several more years of fruitless efforts at further informal negotiation. By taking notice of the fact that negotiations on treaty issues naturally proceed according to current customs within the United Nations institutional structure, the Court resolved the apparent paradox that a non-negotiable issue had been raised between several parties which had

253. Id. at 344–46.
254. Id. at 345.

never entered into direct negotiations on the issues involved in the dispute.

THE OPERATION OF ESTIMATING THE EFFECTS OF DECISION

An observer may assume that most past decision-makers have considered the interpretative process as a means of clarifying and stabilizing the expectations of both the participants to an agreement and future community decision-makers. The indices of this consideration, however, are at present unsatisfactory, as we observed above in outlining the principles of decision.[255] We may project that, as a result of realistic assessments of competence, decision-makers have sought to limit the scope of judgment to affect the minimum range of values necessary to resolve conflicting claims of participants and to avoid similar conflicts in the future. On the other hand, in deference to the rational development of maximum world public order, they have on occasion generalized to include the projection of wider community policies when in their estimation the situation made such formulation desirable. The techniques which may have been developed for these estimations have nonetheless rarely been explicitly discussed, and the observer must only speculate as to which operations may have actually been involved. It is reasonable to assume, however, that studies of current predispositions and probable responses to alternative decisions have not been made to any notable extent.

The issue of the possible effects of decision did arise, even if in a decidedly negative way, in the *Northern Cameroons* case (Preliminary Objections).[256] In this instance the International Court was called upon to ignore any such effects and to render a decision in spite of them. The conditions which led to this request were, as we have seen, as follows: The applicant Republic of Cameroons filed suit against Great Britain for alleged violations of its Trust obligations with respect to the territory of Northern Cameroons. These "violations" related to the alleged failure of Great Britain to separate its administration of Northern Cameroons and Nigeria in compliance with a General Assembly resolution requesting that it do so by

255. See above, p. 61.
256. [1963] I.C.J. Rep. 15.

October 1960. The Republic of Cameroons claimed that this failure influenced the people of Northern Cameroons to vote—in a plebiscite held in February 1961—to join Nigeria rather than the Republic. The request made by the Republic that the Court ignore the effects of its decision arose from the fact that two days after filing its claim before the Court in April 1961, Great Britain's Trusteeship in the Cameroons was terminated by the United Nations General Assembly, and Northern Cameroons was recognized—pursuant to its vote—as a part of Nigeria. Since the agreement which was the basis of the Republic's claim was thus terminated, it was difficult for the Court to see what kind of reparations or specific performance could be enforced against the former holder of the Trust. The Republic of Cameroons, in fact, asked for neither reparations nor a voiding of the allegedly "influenced" election; it requested merely a holding that the violation had occurred.

After commenting that it could "in an appropriate case, make a declaratory judgment," the Court noted that if it was satisfied "that to adjudicate on the merits of an Application would be inconsistent with its judicial function, it should refuse to do so." [257] The Court pointed out that even in the case of a declaratory judgment it is required to take into account the effects of its decision. Quoting from a previous case, it observed that the intention of a declaratory judgment is "to ensure recognition of a situation at law, once and for all and with binding force as between the Parties; so that the legal position thus established cannot again be called in question and in so far as the legal effects ensuing therefrom are concerned." [258] Effecting a declaration of law "once and for all" between the parties in the instant case, however, was impossible, since the dispute concerned an already terminated treaty for which "there can be no opportunity for a future act of interpretation or application of that treaty in accordance with any judgment the Court might render." [259] Presumably both the effort of the Republic of Cameroons to "minimize the importance of the forward reach of a judgment of the Court," and the Court's above-mentioned fear of rendering a decision "inconsistent with its judicial function" relate to the probable use the Re-

257. Id. at 37.

258. Ibid. Quotation from *Interpretation of Judgments Nos. 7 and 8 (The Chorzow Factory)*, P.C.I.J., Ser. A, No. 13, p. 20.

259. Ibid.

public intended to make of such a decision if rendered in its favor.[260] Having lost a vote in the General Assembly to nullify the Northern Cameroons plebiscite, the Republic of Cameroons might have sought to use a favorable Court decision as a new lever in the Assembly to reverse the initial vote. In response, the Court made clear that it did not believe that one of its functions was to facilitate this sort of effect: "it is not the function of a court merely to provide a basis for political action if no question of actual legal rights is involved." [261] It implied that while such "political" effects need not be ignored, the minimal conditions for a judicial controversy must first be met, namely, that "one or the other party, or both parties, as a factual matter, are in a position to take some retroactive or prospective action or avoidance of action, which would constitute a compliance with the Court's judgment or a defiance thereof. This is not the situation here." [262]

A more nearly paradigm awareness of the effects of a decision was shown by the Court in the *Barcelona Traction* case (Preliminary Objections).[263] Here the issue was one of jurisdiction revolving around Article 37 of the Statute of the Court, which provides that "Whenever a treaty or convention in force provides for reference of a matter . . . to the Permanent Court of International Justice, the matter shall, as between the parties to the present Statute, be referred to the International Court of Justice." [264] A treaty in force between Spain and Belgium did so provide, and the decision the Court had to make hinged in part on whether Spain's late acceptance of Article 37 (it did not join the United Nations until 1955) allowed the relevant portion of the treaty to lapse. The Court held that it did not lapse, and that in fact Article 37 was designed to avoid such lapses and such forced renegotiations of referral or arbitration clauses—without any stipulation as to when the parties might join the United Nations.

In so doing, the Court recalled its decision in *Israel v. Bulgaria,* where it held that a *unilateral* acceptance by Bulgaria of the compulsory jurisdiction of the Permanent Court in 1921, followed by its acceptance of a similar "transfer" article (Article 36) through join-

260. Ibid.
261. Ibid.
262. Id. at 37–38.
263. [1964] I.C.J. Rep. 6.
264. Id. at 17.

ing the United Nations in 1955 was not sufficient to establish jurisdiction by the International Court. It distinguished *Israel v. Bulgaria* from the case before it in a number of ways, but one of the more important distinctions related to the relative effects of alternative decisions in the two cases. As it said:

> The case of *Israel v. Bulgaria* was in a certain sense *sui generis* . . . [whereas] any decision of the Court, relative to Article 37, must affect a considerable number of surviving treaties and conventions providing for recourse to the Permanent Court . . . It is thus clear that the decision of the Court in the present case, whatever it might be, would be liable to have far-reaching effects.[265]

While the Court was anxious to avoid allowing its consideration of the different effects of the two decisions "to influence the legal character" of the later decision, nevertheless it believed that such a consideration "does constitute a reason why the decision should not be regarded as already predetermined by that which was given in the different circumstances of the *Israel v. Bulgaria* case." [266]

THE OPERATION OF EXAMINING THE SELF FOR BIAS

In past discussion, as already noted, very little recognition has been given to methods of discounting the possible effects of the various kinds of potential bias. On the whole, writers and decision-makers have contented themselves with comment upon possible sources of bias and with attempts to set up administrative guarantees to minimize it at the institutional—rather than the individual—level.

Judges have occasionally commented in a rather general way upon the sources of their own bias, but have suggested virtually no realistic steps to discount it. In the *Anglo-Iranian Oil Co.* case,[267] for example, dissenting Judge Levi Carneiro made passing reference to the effect of his own cultural experience: "It is inevitable that everyone of us in this Court should retain some trace of his legal education and his former legal activities in his country of origin." [268] Judge

265. Id. at 29.
266. Id. at 30.
267. [1952] I.C.J. Rep. 93.
268. Id. at 161.

Carneiro's bias in this case favored Great Britain, because, as he explained, his own country (Brazil) provided "strict guarantees for the payment to the expropriated property owner of just . . . compensation." [269] This experience was apparently not described, however, for corrective purposes, for Judge Carneiro went on to refer to its effect as "inevitable, and even justified, because in its composition the Court is to be representative of 'the main forms of civilization and of the principal legal systems of the world.' " [270] The few extrajudicial comments of other decision-makers and publicists appear to share this view of the inevitability of culturally conditioned values.[271] It is not surprising, therefore, that in the wake of such a position procedures for bringing such values into consciousness and discounting their "inevitable" consequences have been overlooked.[272]

Other measures designed to deal with bias have been directed not so much to its elimination as to its acceptance after the manner of Judge Carneiro. The principal effort has been to work out some institutional arrangement to reduce or balance the various relevant biases, or to eliminate the biased offender, and so on. In both international courts, for example, attempts were made to control the modes of election, tenure, and payment to reduce possible sources of political and economic pressure on its judges.[273] In addition, conflict-of-interest and recusation provisions are a common feature of these as well as other courts, in which (1) the nonjudicial activities and interests of the judges are limited for purposes of avoiding unnecessary conflicts of interest, and (2) the conditions of prior involvement as an adviser or advocate in an issue before the Court are spelled out and procedures established for the purpose of keeping a

269. Ibid.

270. Ibid., quoting from the Court Statute, Art. 9.

271. See the Permanent Court Report on national representation by Loder, Moore, and Anzilotti, P.C.I.J., Ser. E, No. 4, p. 75 (1927–28). See also Jessup, "The Customs Union Advisory Opinion," 26 *Am. J. Int'l L.* 105 (1932), and Borchard, "The Customs Union Advisory Opinion," 25 id. 711 (1931). See, generally, D. M. Flemming, *The United States and the World Court* (1945).

272. For a survey of recent trends in accounting for national bias, see generally R. P. Anand, *Compulsory Jurisdiction of the International Court of Justice* 44 ff. (1961); also Anand, "International Courts and Contemporary Conflicts" 309–79 (unpubl. thesis, Yale Law School, 1964).

273. See the historical material on this point collected in Anand (1964), id. at 314–27.

judge with such involvement from sitting on the case. Under the latter rules, a number of judges on both the Permanent and International Courts have asked or been requested not to sit on cases where prior advocacy has been involved.[274]

The most controversial measure adopted by both the international courts for dealing with national interest—one might say national bias—has been the provision for ad hoc national judges to be appointed in cases involving major interests of unrepresented localities. The issues involved in this procedure have stimulated an intense and lengthy discussion among the various commentators on the work of the Permanent and International Courts. Lauterpacht, writing in 1933 of the Permanent Court, objected that the presence of ad hoc judges changed the nature of the Court deliberations into a dispute among advocates: "They tend to degenerate into a contention between the conflicting claims of the parties. The fine scales of justice are loaded with the crude and incongruous element of partisan interest." [275] As Lauterpacht suggests, ad hoc judges have been accused of failing to possess the impartiality necessary to qualify them as judges. Indeed, the facts show that ad hoc judges have voted for their country about 85 per cent of the time in cases before the Permanent and International Courts.[276] Defenders of the plan say that not only is such a vote as should be expected, but also that the ad hoc judges serve the valuable function in Court deliberations of making certain that their country's position is well represented. As such, their position should not be thought to be impartial, but rather to be the representative of their country's interest in the decision-making processes of the Court.[277] For our purposes, here, however, this dispute

274. Id. at 327.

275. Lauterpacht, *The Function of Law in the International Community* 233 (1933).

276. Cf. 2 Liacouras, *The International Court of Justice* 527b (Preliminary ed. 1962).

277. For an extensive discussion of the issues concerning the election of ad hoc judges, see Anand (1964), supra note 272, at 341–78. For a general discussion of cultural bias, see id. at 309 ff.

On one occasion for separate judicial discussion of this provision, in the *Austro-German Customs Regime* case, P.C.I.J., Ser. A/B, No. 41 (1931), the Court was asked to determine whether Austria had the right to appoint a judge ad hoc in light of its position as the major party in the case. The Court held, under the provision limiting each group of parties-in-interest to one judicial rep-

need not receive further elaboration since in any case the selection of ad hoc judges, while in a vague sense in recognition of the problem of cultural or national bias, is in no way a constructive step toward the examination of bias in the individual decision-maker. It involves, if anything, an avoidance of the task in the implicit recognition of the "inevitability" of the priority of national interests in international decision-making. It in no way alleviates the resulting confusion that the false dichotomy between "national" and "international" interests is seldom clarified by an appropriate conception of common interests. The absence of procedural devices explicitly recognized and sought for the purpose of reducing or totally nullifying individual bias reflects the neglect of many procedural principles by international tribunals, and especially the omission of critical and sustained intellectual inquiry into the procedures actually employed, and the possibility of adapting them to the fundamental objectives of the task of interpretation.

---

resentative, that since Germany had filed much the same type of claim as Austria, and since Germany was already represented on the Court, Austria was not entitled to a separate judge. In determining the similarity of interests, the Court relied upon the fact that "the arguments advanced by the German and Austrian governments lead to the same conclusion" (p. 90). The dissenting judges reasoned that since the legitimacy of the Customs Regime had only been questioned because of the special obligations "not to alienate its independence" placed upon Austria by the Treaty of St. Germain, the similarity in the conclusions of both Austria and Germany should be subordinated to the difference in obligation between them (p. 91).

6. PAST INADEQUACIES AND FUTURE PROMISE

The review of past practice in the interpretation of international agreements that we have offered in the preceding chapters discloses a remarkable, and, in many respects, lamentable state of affairs. If one were to limit the summary to what decision-makers say that they do, or what scholarly commentators allege them to do, the situation would be a picture of confusion, modified by abundant contradiction and disturbing irrelevance. Fortunately, our recommended mode of approach to the assessment of a flow of decision does not allow us to rest on these conclusions and to terminate the inquiry on this nihilistic note. Human beings often *do* better than they *say*, even though we are perhaps more accustomed in everyday life to encounter continuing demonstrations of the opposite failing. Decision-makers in the international community, faced by the urgencies of applying authoritative and controlling prescriptions to concrete circumstances, and perceiving that some interpretation of an alleged agreement is essential, have repeatedly met the challenge in ways that cannot fail to win the confidence of those who explore the record with care and competence. Many of the procedures actually employed increase the probability of a result that corresponds to a close approximation to the actual shared expectations of the parties to whatever agreements are involved.

It cannot, however, be asserted in the light of the trend of decision that the favorable, if largely unacknowledged, features of the process have produced a consistent level of performance on whose absence of eccentricity one is entitled to rely. The melancholy truth is quite otherwise; it is only possible to conclude that the past and present stream of interpretation is inadequate. Patent discrepancies exist between what is too often done in fact, and defensible conceptions of what is, or ought to be, accepted practice.[1]

1. The opinion of the Court and several of the separate opinions, both concurring and dissenting, in the recently decided *South-West Africa* cases (*Ethi-*

PAST INADEQUACIES

Under the heading of articulate confusion must come the not infrequent evidences of doubt or disbelief in the necessity for the exercise of an interpretative role. In seeming justification of abstinence from the assumption of the interpreter's responsibility is the reiteration of Vattel's maxim that "It is not permissible to interpret what has no need of interpretation." [2] Of all the empty verbalisms on which it is possible to rely for intellectual padding, and seeming confirmation, this is among the most vacuous. No standard is affirmed for identifying "what has no need of interpretation" (or, of course, what has such a need).

Into every vacuum, even a verbal one, some substance is likely to seep; and if the seepage is unintended and unperceived, noxious consequences may follow. Among the reiteraters of Vattel's maxim, we can observe the unmistakable spore of unacknowledged failure, a failure which would appear inevitably to accompany bringing an analytic sequence to a premature end. If an opportunity for interpretation is seized or evaded, this is perceived and asserted to suffice; hence the maxim is used to justify whatever the interpreter does. But is this judgment grounded on an inspection of the pertinent setting? Does it register a disciplined inference; or is it an excuse to avert the

---

opia v. South Africa; Liberia v. South Africa) (Second Phase) offer dramatic documentation of the continuing need both of a more sophisticated understanding of the task of interpretation and of a more comprehensive and viable set of principles of interpretation. Decision of the International Court of Justice, July 18, 1966. [1966] I.C.J. Rep. 4.

The attribution, by Anthony Lewis in the *New York Times,* of this decision to a legal philosophy comparable to that of Mr. Justice Frankfurter in constitutional cases within the United States does little justice to the memory of a great judge. *New York Times,* July 19, 1966, p. 16, cols. 4, 5.

In a recent arbitration between Italy and the United States the tribunal was apparently confronted by arguments largely in terms of "textuality" but managed to work its way through a doctrinal quagmire to a consideration of the expectations which the parties reasonably created in each other. *Advisory Opinion of the Arbitral Tribunal Constituted in Virtue of the Compromises Signed at Rome on 30 June 1964 by the Governments of the United States of America and of the Italian Republic,* July 17, 1965.

2. Supra, pp. 78–82.

decision-maker's eye from the problem at hand? The maxim provides no guidance to the mind; it is a gloss on arbitrariness.

Curiously linked with the assumption that interpretation is so easy that it often need not even be made is the diametrically opposed view that the idea of attempting to give coherence and stability to the task of such subtlety as that of interpretation is utterly misconceived. Sometimes the pessimism about the possibility of interpretative principles is grounded in the garb of "science," and depends, among other allegations, on the indisputable commonplace that the subjective processes of one person are not open to direct observation by anybody else. Since science is alleged to depend on direct observation, and shared expectations cannot be observed directly, interpretation is therefore declared to be a scientific impossibility.

Such a position, it is perhaps redundant to point out, depends on the false premise that science is free of concepts, and operates entirely with objective measures. The theoretical conceptions of physical scientific investigation are guides to the selection of what is to provide a basis of inference about such categories as mass and energy. In the human sciences concepts such as "intention" or "expectation" are guides to the choice of signs and of other behavioral bases for inferring the presence or absence of subjective events. It is common observation that persons who are brought up in the same culture, or who are exposed to similar circumstances in life, operate with concepts regarding the subjectivities of their culture mates, concepts that enable them to infer many of the intervening subjective events that are likely to give rise to predictable future behavior. To attempt to move from "muscle movements" to "muscle movements" and to dispense with the guidance of hypothetical images of intervening subjectivities is to adopt a procedure that is poorly adapted to the requirements of negotiation, bargaining, persuasion, litigation, or enlightenment. To throw away the evaluations acquired as part of experience is to gouge out an eye when an eye exercise would improve some limitation of vision.

Of all the self-defeating complications that have appeared in the flow of decision the most fertile root of confusion is the spurious simplicity of the "textualist" approach to the interpreter's problem. The "textualist" position is phrased in many equivalent or interlocking ways. "It is the treaty which is the subject of interpretation and not the intention of the parties"; "The text must be presumed to be the intention of the parties"; "le texte signé est, sauf de rares exceptions, la seule et la plus récente expression de la volonté commune des parties." [3] But the textualist position does too much violence to common sense to stand without prompt qualification. Any experienced decision-maker or scholarly commentator thinks immediately of a vast array of factors, knowledge of whose influence in historic situations is indispensable to understanding the manifest vocabulary of an agreement that is alleged to be made articulate in a text. Hence the bold affirmation of the text-bound principle is counterbalanced by declarations in support of a *contextualist* position that affirm the importance of taking account of the setting in which a presumptive agreement was made and the process by which it was achieved, all of which may be included in the reference of the customary term of art, the *travaux préparatoires.*

However, the permissive slide along the gradient from text to context does not typically proceed according to a plan that includes a provisional map of the territory that furnishes an adequate basis either for the choice of route or the selection of a stopping place. In the absence of a preliminary reconnaissance of the context in which the controversy has arisen, provisionally assessed according to factors that may in the particular sequence of events affect the expectations of the parties, the decision-makers are self-condemned to steer a capricious interpretative course. The capriciousness is exaggerated whenever a decision-maker seeks to adhere with tenacity to a literal version of the textualist approach, and does his best to keep his attention glued to the controverted language.[4]

The obvious fact is that the phrase-focused interpreter cannot entirely blind himself to the larger features of the dispute, although his cadaver-like obedience to the textualist command may result, when his glance strays toward *travaux préparatoires,* in sensations akin to those said to be enjoyed by a peeping Tom.[5] At the margin of full waking attention the decision-maker may allow himself to learn

3. Supra, p. 209.

4. The theme of textuality receives a recurrent emphasis in the separate opinion of Judge Van Wyk in the 1966 *South-West Africa* cases [1966] I.C.J. Rep. 65.

5. In his dissenting opinion in the 1966 *South-West Africa* cases Judge Mbanefo relies upon a highly restrictive conception of the relevance of *travaux préparatoires.* [1966] I.C.J. Rep. 500. The more generous conception of Judge Jessup ([1966] I.C.J. Rep. 352) would appear more accurately reflective of contemporary practice, and certainly Judge Mbanefo could have found many better sticks with which to beat the Court's decision than an outmoded expression of the *travaux* principle, more honored in utterance than in observance.

enough about the relative strength of the contending parties at the time of negotiation, and other realistic detail, to accept—or to question—his first reading of the provisions of the treaty. Whether the interpreter fully admits the necessity to himself or not, the judgment of the supposed "plainness" or "simplicity" of meaning of the words depends on these illicit glimpses of the context. When relevance is a grudging concession to that which cannot be avoided, realism of interpretation is not done away with entirely; rather, it is either mutilated or shriveled to a caricature of its potentiality.

The erratic invocation of traditionally formulated principles of interpretation confirms the strange reluctance with which decision-makers have allowed themselves a degree of access to pertinent reality. There is premature de-emphasis on the handling of evidence outside the clauses of the treaty before the tribunal. Witness the declaration in the *Lotus* case: "If the plain and natural meaning of a provision is clear, it is not permissible to have recourse to *travaux préparatoires.*" [6] This putative denial of "recourse," with all its ambiguities of reference, is a self-stultifying conception. Even a preliminary examination of the pre-outcome phases of a treaty may raise a presumption that the purposes of the parties were quite different from those that find lucid and conventional expression in the final document. A parallel prematurity of de-emphasis on the relevant, as we saw, also often emerges in reference to the examination of acts subsequent to the supposed conclusion of an agreement, the post-outcome phase.[7]

Given the dogmatic frame of reference characteristic of textualism, the grudging allusions to sources of interpretative inference outside the language of the treaty imply a hierarchy of worth among the several sources; and such a claim to establish a universal hierarchy is a clumsy and arbitrary deformation of the varied patterns of interrela-

6. Supra, p. 96.

7. In the 1966 *South-West Africa* cases the International Court of Justice limits the subsequent conduct which it regards as relevant by stating its goal as that of identifying only past, rather than contemporary, expectations. "The Court must," it insists, "place itself in the point of time when the mandates system was being instituted and when the instruments of mandate were being framed." [1966] I.C.J. Rep. 23. The demand by Judge Jessup in his dissenting opinion for interpretation in accord with contemporary expectation and conditions would appear more in accord with contemporary community expectations about the requirements of rational and authoritative decision. Cf. Judge Padilla Nervo, id. at 463; Judge Tanaka, id. at 294.

tionship that are inseparable from the social and political process, and which it is the responsibility of decision-makers to disclose and act upon. In some contexts, competent examination shows, the most reliable clue to the shared expectations of the parties comes from the *travaux;* in other contexts it may come from subsequent conduct. And what is most reliable is best to be ascertained by a mode of interpretation that brings these several features of the context into the picture at an early stage in the inquiry before any rigid biases in favor of the universal primacy for the interpreter of the seeming clarity of the text slam the doors of the mind of decision-makers against perceiving the order of relevance that correctly applies to the situation before them. No arbitrary hierarchy of source categories is genuinely valid or arbitrarily useful for interpretative purposes; what is pertinent is a comprehensive list of the sources to be scrutinized in every case in order to ascertain their perhaps unique significance in the immediate controversy.

Even the terms that have been customarily segregated to the role of designating a category of source for the use of an interpreter are employed in ways that often defeat the goals of interpretation. Some versions of the *travaux* principle fail to direct the interpreter's attention to relevant factors outside the official record of negotiation: the parties' historical perspectives, and especially the long-range goals of the participants; the level of crisis at the time of negotiation; the institutional patterns of which the negotiations formed a part, and so on.

If principles of interpretation related to sources of interpretation have implied an impossible hierarchical order, other principles—explicitly concerned with the interpreter's attribution of importance to purposes—have erred in a different direction. In traditional principles relating to source the bases of inference referred to can at least be identified, which is an obvious precondition of dealing with them at all. The traditional principles of effectiveness and restrictive interpretation excell in the bland ambiguity with which they have been invoked. Both principles purport to deal with the parties' major aims and purposes in a largely complementary fashion. They are, as was demonstrated, often formulated together: "The parties' major purposes in concluding an agreement must be effected whenever they are consistent with their express or implied reservations." [8]

8. Supra, p. 156 ff.

There appear, however, to be no guiding lines proffered for distinguishing the transition from "major" to "minor" objectives. The use of the restrictive principle has also given rise to a relatively distinctive set of problems. It is in this connection that prominence is often given to the asserted identity of a party to the controversy as a nation-state, accompanied by the insistence that any doubt should be resolved in favor of the sovereign state. Passing over any objection that one may entertain concerning the vagueness of the concept of sovereignty, this version of the principle of restrictive interpretation is objectionable since it forecloses, or at least discourages, the consideration of indices of the party's intention to withdraw its claims or its control over some value in order to acquire others. Seen in this light, there appears to be little basis in policy for establishing any presumption whatever in favor of the "burdened" state (i.e., the potentially burdened, defending, state) in a conflict, since any agreement involves both benefits and burdens which are bargained for equally. If they are not exchanged on equal grounds, we may assume that the parties would not have failed to say so. In either case, however, it should be the communicated intentions of the parties which prevail, and the crucial flaw in the traditional restrictiveness principle is precisely that it makes no reference whatever to these intentions. It is instead an entirely unsupportable dogmatic policy for overturning, or policing, the parties' genuine shared expectations of commitment. We have recommended, in its place, a principle of restrictive interpretation designed to assist the decision-maker in his attempt to ascertain these expectations. Seen in this perspective it becomes an indispensible complement to the principle of effectiveness in implementing the interpreter's initial, and in this context, primary goal.

The reformulation which we have offered of both the principle of effectiveness and that of restrictive interpretation raises directly the issue most often misunderstood in past decision and opinion, namely, that two complementary principles may be proposed which call attention to similar, possibly identical features of the context and suggest similar operations to examine those features, and yet may at the same time be effectively employed in decision to weigh the various indices examined.[9] In past decision the phrasing of interpretative

9. In the 1966 *South-West Africa* cases the opinion of the Court emphasizes the principle of restrictive interpretation in a degree which almost wholly disregards its complement, the principle of major purposes. [1966] I.C.J. Rep. 25. An in-

principles as logical opposites has led many commentators to reject both versions as unnecessary barriers to decision. This conception, which implicitly demands exceptionless and monolithic rules regulating the application of complementary principles, has sometimes resulted in the hasty rejection of principles altogether and, on other occasions led to fruitless attempts to establish hierarchies of principles in order to avoid what is otherwise conceived of as interpretative chaos. In these demands, therefore, we have seen both sides of the same counterfeit coin in traditional conceptions of interpretative principles: the demand for the construction of systematic preferences between principles of content (or among contextual features), and the rejection of the employment of complementary principles in decision.

In the course of our review of the characteristic problems faced with considerable frequency in past decision, we noted the treatment given to "syntactic" (rather than "semantic") problems in international agreements. While we concluded that decision-makers have persistently failed to make use of available techniques of logical analysis, we did come across a significant and allegedly "logical" principle in the well-known doctrine of *expressio unius exclusio alterius.* Our initial criticism of this doctrine, however, related precisely to its status as a rule of logic. We argued that it simply makes no sense, to translate the rule into logical terms, to "prefer coimplication to implication." This is, we have asserted, the only "logical" version of the *expressio* possible. But even if logical status were not claimed for it (this is the case, for example, in the comparable rule of *ejusdem generis:* specific statements are to be preferred to general ones), the rule would still be objectionable upon *any* standard of justification, since the inclusion or exclusion of other alternatives in the minds of the parties realistically depends, and in a way unspecifiable in advance, upon *all* of the factors in the total context. If one retains the basic premise that the genuine shared expectations of the participants should be given highest deference within the context of world community policies, the most obvious result of a rule automatically excluding implied alternatives, or automatically preferring specific statements to general ones, would be a conflict with the par-

---

sightful contrast is offered by Judge Tanaka in his dissenting opinion in eloquent statement of the importance of "teleological" interpretation. Id. at 276.

ties' legitimate expectations to the contrary, and thus a conflict with the overriding goal of interpretation.

Yet, however beset with confusion and contradiction the interpreters of international agreements have been in discharge of their responsibility to invoke lucid principles to state and justify what they are doing, decision-makers have as a rule followed procedures that could be better described, and that have been of key importance in keeping alive such confidence and acceptance as they have received.[10] Built into the practices of litigation and negotiation are ways of organizing the focus of attention of decision-makers that increase the likelihood that the significant contextual features of the controversy will be brought to their focus of attention in an orderly sequence. The judges or other officials involved may be but dimly aware of the relevancy of these routines to the requirements of realistic interpretation. It may seem obvious that the contending parties will be represented by counsel, and that the counselors will prepare their presentation after inquiries that may hit upon items in the *travaux* or subsequent conduct, for example, that tend to overturn any hasty acceptance of inferences in regard to the expectations of the parties that depend entirely on a close reading of the final text.

Any failure on the part of the legal community to recognize the importance of such preparatory work for the task of contextual interpretation is likely to lead to unfortunate results in various circumstances. If decision-makers perceive the practice of representation by counsel as a formality without meaning for interpretation, they may neglect to look past the formalities to question the competence of counsel or to take sufficient initiative in conducting an independent check of the context to provide reassurance regarding competence, or to supplement the inadequacies of counsel. Similarly, in cases that involve relatively summary procedure and put the total burden on the decision-maker, significant features of the context relevant to the problem may be overlooked.

The inadequate attempts that have been made to formulate procedural principles have tended to nullify the contextual advantages of employment of counsel and of access to reasoned decision. The formulations have begun at the wrong end of the relevant sequence.

10. The potentialities that inhere in the systematic application of the contextual and historical principles are excellently indicated in Judge Jessup's dissenting opinion in the 1966 *South-West Africa* cases. [1966] I.C.J. Rep. 323.

Instead of emphasizing the relevances of the contextual whole to the part, the usual point has been to stress the possible adequacy of the part as a short-cut means of comprehending the whole. Scholarly statements of a theory of interpretation have fallen into this pit by outlining alleged rules of interpretation that begin with some version of "primacy of the text" to be read according to "plain and natural meaning." Successive rules may give vague procedural directions to widen the relevant context in an orderly sequence. They assume, however, that it is possible for the interpreter, without investigating the entire setting, to obtain—by occult means, it appears —insight that requires no further verification. Hence a curious belief pervades the process that an interpreter can know enough at each step to reach a valid decision and need not go further in inspecting the enlarging map.[11]

FACTORS CONDITIONING PAST INADEQUACIES

It may seem surprising to some that persons and institutions of such conventional eminence as those charged with responsibility for the application of international agreements should, on close analysis, display a record marked by chronic confusion and contradiction. If the situation is to be changed in any fundamental respect the factors that have conditioned the interpretations formulated in the past flow of decision must be identified and evaluated.

One possible explanation would connect the vagaries of the interpretative process with a characteristic feature of the world arena so deeply embedded in the structure of international affairs that no

11. In the 1966 *South-West Africa* cases the International Court of Justice declined "to engage in a process of 'filling in the gaps'" upon the apparent assumption that the decision it made did not have the consequence of filling in gaps. [1966] I.C.J. Rep. 48. At the same time the Court took a very limited view of the relevance of basic community policies to the primary, supplementing, and integrative goals of interpretation and application. Application with explicit, rather than unconscious, reference to the larger features of the context it appeared to confuse with "legislation."

A much more realistic, and more frequently honored, perspective is announced by Judges Padilla Nervo and Tanaka in their dissenting opinions, in which they insist upon the relevance of basic constitutive policies (as reflected in the United Nations Charter and other sources) for both supplementing and policing the shared expectations found by primary interpretation. [1966] I.C.J. Rep. 441, 248.

change is to be expected until the structure is itself profoundly reconstructed. The hypothesis is that in a divided world the discordant state of matters related to interpretation is to be accounted for as a strategem deliberately adopted by decision-makers as a means of preserving a wide range of freedom of judgment behind a smokescreen of doctrinal ambiguity.

We cannot at present assess this hypothesis on the basis of systematically gathered data obtained by interviewing a representative sample of officials who have acted as decision-makers in the world community at various times in the last few generations. Nor is it possible to turn to a body of memoir and diary material that contains clear indications of the perspectives actually entertained by representative officials. Historical researches supply, as yet, only occasional hints of the subjective events that helped to shape the final outcome of recorded controversies. Under these circumstances we cannot hope to arrive at a satisfactory evaluation of the suggestion that jurists have deliberately cultivated ambiguity in the field of interpretation, as in every field of law, hoping thereby to achieve a result that harmonizes most closely with their genuine goals as professional servants of the law. The squid function, according to this view, is a legitimate camouflage of the judicial, or other interpretative, mind in a world in which inclusive interests must often establish themselves indirectly before they are strong enough to withstand the counterattack of particular or special interests.

Despite our long-range commitment to a conception of human dignity that enjoins candor on decision-makers we do not find it hard to believe that jurists may, in good faith, consider the possible wisdom of adopting evasive tactics in the hope of relieving themselves from the pressure of elements that they believe to be misguided. There are, however, grounds for doubting the accuracy of the image of a galaxy of canny jurists engaged in outsmarting the rest of the world in the interest of judicial integrity.

One ground for doubting this image of the super-sophisticated jurist is that when we examine the history of individual decision-makers before their ascendancy to an international tribunal, for instance, we have so far uncovered little evidence of precocious emancipation from traditionally distorting dogmatisms in regard to legal doctrine. The books and law journal publications by these distinguished gentlemen have not been designed to shake the conventional approach of colleagues and students toward the language of legal doctrine. Whatever the criticisms, further, that may have later been made of these rising jurists, such criticisms have rarely if ever included the complaint that they cherished heretical notions that they found it expedient to conceal. Moreover, we find it somewhat improbable that interpreters of international agreements, active over many decades, could have engaged in an all-inclusive conspiracy of benevolent deception without at least an occasional case of open self-congratulation or inadvertent disclosure.

An additional ground for skepticism is the abundant evidence that confirms the remarkable success of the legal profession in indoctrinating its practitioners with a set of perspectives and operating techniques that generate and sustain chronic confusion on problems of interpretation. We have called attention to the fact that confusions of this kind antedate the rise of modern studies of communication, and continue wherever knowledge of modern communication analysis has not spread. Our scrutiny of decision and commentary alike give less credibility to the hypothesis of conspiracy than to the perhaps less dramatic suggestion of genuine intellectual confusion.

The hypothesis of honest confusion gains weight when we consider the astonishing conflict of view that obtains among some of the most distinguished authorities who have dealt at length with the theory of interpretation. At the beginning of the present work we quoted at length from the extremes in modern commentary in order to depict the prevailing state of contradiction. We infer that genuine intellectual difficulties must be involved when eminent figures commit themselves to such diverse positions as that, on the one hand, interpretation is as automatic as the working of a well-designed and operated slot machine, and, on the other, that all interpretation is a genteel hoax.

The important task is to identify the character of the intellectual difficulty whose consequences are so strikingly manifest. Judgment is lagging behind available knowledge, less in the sense that specific items are overlooked or obscured, than that new bodies or methods of thought are insufficiently taken into account. In the theory and practice of interpretation the principal intellectual obstacle would appear to be the failure by decision-makers and publicists to conceive of the agreement-making process—to say nothing of the processes of claim and decision—as a process of *communication,* and to view this process in its widest extent through the powerful lenses of modern communication studies.

To acknowledge that the interpreter is inextricably involved in interrelated processes of communication is not only to commit him to the goal of full contextuality (i.e., to examining without advance bias all features of the context relevant to decision), but also to the acquisition of an appropriate framework for conceiving the context he is requested to analyze. The *conception* of agreement as a process of communication, then, involves viewing all signs and acts of collaboration between the parties as an effort on their part to mediate all relevant subjectivities of commitment. This means in turn that such signs and acts of collaboration are not to be interpreted in isolation or as ends in themselves, but as instrumentalities for achieving the goal of communicating demands to appropriate audiences, and eventually for mediating expectations concerning the content of the agreement. Seen in this way, communication involves the transmission of signs through channels to targets or audiences with the goal of mutual understanding on the part both of the sender and receiver of the messages. It is the possible inadequacies in transmission —usually through the inherent shortcomings in the capability of words and other signs to communicate shared subjectivities—that place the communications analyst on guard that only a total contextual survey, systematically examining "who said what to whom through what channels and with what effects," will suffice in performing his difficult task of determining the genuine shared expectations of the parties.

It would be quite impossible, we believe, for a competent analyst who is acquainted with the study of language and gesture to commit himself seriously to the one-sided assertions that clutter the literature of interpretation. The "plain language" case would be seen in context as a rare set of circumstances more often approximated, or imagined, than achieved. Similarly, the idea that meanings are utterly chaotic and consequently that communication is a delicate plant which seldom flowers in actual life is an hypothesis more appropriate to the exegesis of modern poetry than to interpreting the prose of important international agreements.

Delay among the jurists is to be explained, in part, by the rapidity with which contemporary studies of communication have taken shape, and by the many tributaries that contribute to the general stream. The strategy of communication management—variously called advertising, propaganda, public relations, psychological warfare, or peacefare—is highly developed in the world arena; and one result has been the fostering of systematic investigations of the phenomena of public opinion and mass persuasion. The social and behavioral sciences have developed at an increasing tempo; and communication is a process of cardinal concern for all. Mathematicians and logicians have treated forms of analysis that have revolutionized the traditional boundaries of these disciplines.[12] It is obvious from the review of past decision that these intellectual advances have been ignored or neglected by decision-makers and commentators who, we predict, will in the long run benefit most from their existence.

If decision-makers and commentators had exposed themselves more promptly and fully to the growing field of communication knowledge, they would long since have perceived the far-reaching consequences of distinguishing between *content* and *procedure* in facing a problem of application and interpretation. Communication studies have found it indispensable to distinguish between classifying the "manifest" meaning of words and using procedures that enable the classifier-interpreter to become aware, in the first place, of the manifest content.

The venerable principle of effectiveness would undoubtedly have been reconsidered in the light of the contrast between content and procedure. Our review showed that it has been conceived almost entirely as a maxim that presupposes the decision-maker's knowledge of all relevant indices of the parties' expectations. Such a principle must be amplified, if it is to provide useful guidance to decision in these crucial areas by indicating how the interpreter's focus of attention is

12. The *International Encyclopaedia of the Social Sciences,* soon to be published, will reflect the transformation in theory construction, procedures of observation, and findings that have taken place since the publication of the first *Encyclopaedia of the Social Sciences* in the early 1930s (1930–34). The historical growth and contemporary state of the human sciences are characterized in Hoselitz (ed.), *A Reader's Guide to the Social Sciences* (1959); Lerner (ed.), *The Human Meaning of the Social Sciences* (1959); Lerner and Lasswell (eds.), *The Policy Sciences* (1951).

A compact introduction and evaluation of newer developments can be found in Allen and Caldwell (eds.), *Communication Sciences and Law: Reflections from the Jurimetrics Conference* (1965); Baade (ed.), *Jurimetrics* (1963).

to be directed, and toward what, in the making of dependable inferences about controverted expectations. Certainly it is not enough to admonish the interpreter to give effect to shared expectations. Procedural suggestions are needed to aid in scrutinizing the context to establish the contents in fact shared by the parties. Plainly, two interdependent sets of principles are called for, one characterizing what is relevant to the task that confronts the interpreter; the other proposing a set of operations whereby the relevant content can be processed and weighed for the purpose of ascertaining the parties' genuine shared expectations.

More mastery of communication knowledge might, further, have changed the whole approach to the discovery of supposed "truth." The task of formulating principles for the discovery of "truth" has traditionally been conceived in terms of content. It is commonplace, for example, to declare that contradictory statements should be noted or that differences in levels of abstraction should be taken into account in a judgment of truth about expectation. It is, however, insufficiently stressed that an inclusive context is to be explored—by procedures that are described—if the decision-maker is to increase the likelihood that his estimates of "truth" are to be the best attainable within the limits of time (and other facilities) at his disposal. When we consider the sequence of subjective events that is involved in judgment, it is clear that most of the time-honored maxims relate to the content of the *terminal* subjectivities in the sequence. For instance, "do not assert that contradictory statements are true" is an acceptable—not to say truistic—maxim. But if the likelihood that the terminal subjectivity—the final assertion about the expectations of participants who have expressed themselves in contradictory fashion—will be "true" is to be increased, it is important to discipline the subjectivities that precede and lead up to it. The challenge of stating a procedural principle is to provide a guide for the focus of attention of the decision-maker as he strives to bring his final judgment in a concrete case in harmony with the genuine shared expectations of the parties. To rely upon principles of content alone is to avoid the most difficult part of the decision-maker's responsibility.

A corollary of the conclusion that past decision-makers, unchallenged by contemporary knowledge of communication, have relied too confidently on principles of content—inadequately conceived—is that they failed to provide precise indication of the contextual features referred to by each principle. They have failed to outline, in other words, the minimal operations involved in focusing attention upon the various features of a context. The operations to which reference is occasionally made do not distinguish the contextual features relevant to one principle, or group of principles, from those relevant to another.

Closely connected with the deep-laid bias in favor of articulating principles of judgment in terms of content is the bias in favor of "hierarchical" modes of arranging whatever principles are employed as guides or justifications. In the simplest terms our criticism is that no fixed hierarchy of propositions can be advantageously established in advance of decision. The weighting of each principle will vary with each case, independent of any super-principle other than the goal of ascertaining actual shared expectations. The appropriate weighting emerges in the course of adhering to procedural arrangements for allowing a clear map of relevance to emerge at the focus of attention of the decision-maker.

Unawareness of the advancing front of knowledge must also help explain other persistent misconceptions that affect and afflict interpretation. Acquaintance with modern logical operations, for example, could easily avoid such ludicrous pseudo-logical rules as that of *expressio unius exclusio alterius.* Knowledge of the multitudinous functions of language, carefully delineated by modern semiotics or semantics, would discourage such capricious restrictions on the examination of the context as the plain and natural meaning rule. A study of the subjective variables involved as causes and consequences in a process of communication would have fixed attention on the need for consistently applying a much broader version of the *travaux* principle than has actually been relied on. Such a study would have established the need for the principles of effectiveness and of restrictive interpretation, not for the purpose of *imposing* a supposed communication upon the parties, but as a means of inferring the subjectivities which were in fact shared. It would have emphasized the need to formulate principles that would help to relate the characteristics of the various participants in the agreement-making process (objectives, base values, and so forth) to the outcome.

That the high task of interpreting international agreements could be carried on in an atmosphere clouded by unnecessary confusion and contradiction is a grave reflection against the education of the established decision-makers. The search for explanatory factors does unmistakably carry us back to dubious indoctrination and poorly selected exposures during the relatively impressionable years of advanced preparation. But why have these inhibiting forces been strong enough to override initiatives toward enlarging the realism of professional training? Evidently the success of those who move into the active decision process is sufficiently great to sustain expectations that no change is necessary, and might even prove disadvantageous.

This would appear to bring us back to a somewhat altered version of the explanation which we evaluated at the start. Must we not conclude that the interpreters of international agreements are unconsciously adapted to the political arena in which they operate, obtaining survival advantages for themselves by employing a set of intellectual tools that provides a symbolic screen of confusion, contradiction, and concurrence?

It is a possible conclusion, therefore, that what a shrewd conspiratorial approach has failed to accomplish has been achieved in a degree by largely unconscious reliance on procedural practices that have functioned to some effect side by side with doctrinal principles that have made remarkably little sense.

It may be that in no other aspects of decision is the simultaneously rational–nonrational character of legal process more obvious. The decision-makers who are authorized by general expectation to settle controversies over international agreements are presumed to act in a comprehensive frame of doctrine that provides a network of prescriptive norms to be applied in specified factual contingencies. This is the conspicuous indication of the intellectual component of the situation. The prescriptive norms fall in two broad categories that by tradition are called "substantive" and "procedural"; and we shall presently see that these time-honored distinctions are intimately related to, though not identical with, the separation between "content" and "procedure" referred to in the present analysis.

Observe that the doctrines or principles of interpretation that have been employed in such erratic fashion in the trend of decision are primarily called "substantive" principles in the traditional terms of art. They refer to the classification of statements; hence they relate to the manifest content of communications. We called attention to the scarcity of interpretative doctrines or principles that dealt, not primarily with the classifying of content, but with the agenda of the decision-maker in exposing himself to statements or to other objects of reference in the process of arriving at a final result. It was taken for granted that controversies over agreements would be conducted by appropriate decision-makers according to established expectations about agenda (including rules of evidence). Hence the procedural principles that have in fact often been employed are largely obscured, since they are fused with general practices of the tribunal, and are not labeled as in any way distinctively oriented toward an interpretative task.

Another example of the overcondensation that leads in many cases to inadvertent error is the continuing failure to distinguish between two steps that are invariably taken when a general term—such as a doctrinal prescription—is applied to a particular controversy. Every term of general reference, since it is abstract, is open to several versions of how it should be used in referring to specific contingencies. Hence the applier-interpreter must take the first step, which is to select subordinate terms of more restricted reference. These are the "operational indices" that are now eligible for employment in the discourse of the decision-maker. The second step is to choose from among the potential indices the term or terms that are held to be appropriate to the controversy under consideration. It is not to be taken for granted that all the indices apply to all the contingency patterns that come within the zone of reference of the basic concepts that figure in prescriptions. To identify "one index with one concept" is to treat the two as complete equivalents. This is rarely helpful to the decision-maker who is acutely aware of the point that general words are important guides to thought and action precisely because they are not *wholly* bound to single circumscribed references.[13] The decision-maker must use his judgment in assessing the adequacy of particular indices to his subjective model. Since the details of the social process are contextual, they are liable to change their relationship to one another as the situation changes. Hence, although there may be much stability in a series of concrete circumstances, the decision-maker—the concept user—must persist in evaluating the degree of congruence (or deviation) that occurs. The se-

13. Cf. De Visscher, *Problèmes d'Interpretation Judiciare in Droit International Public* (1963) at p. 28: "The confrontation of a concrete fact with an abstract norm is at the base of all juridical interpretation. From the abstraction of the precept interpretation derives the individual application."

quence of steps—invention of indices, selection of index pertinent to a particular case—is an operation of fundamental importance in identifying and characterizing the manifest content of thought as latent or partial communication.

Whatever their limitations, the rational component of the decision process is mainly exemplified and implemented by the procedures, since they provide an agenda whose cumulative impact is to bring the context of agreement to the focus of attention of the decision-makers. This comes about, as previously suggested, both by the provision of skilled counsel and by the maintenance of orderly and reasoned decision, hence increasing the likelihood that significant features of the pre-outcome and post-outcome phases of agreement are brought to the decision-maker's notice.

At the same time, it is evident that the principles of procedure have been insufficiently specialized to meet the requirements of a comprehensive conception of relevance to the needs of interpretation. Hence the inbuilt rationality of "due process" has failed to provide for the scrutiny of the total situation that would conform to the postulated goal of discovering shared expectations.

The non-rational component of the decision process is indicated by the acceptance by the parties of results that are achieved by procedures that fall far short of the requirements of reality testing, and which are justified by assertions that are often confused and contradictory. Since many acceptances are not the result of intimidation, the factors that lead to compliance can be assumed to include many motivations that are not fully considered and evaluated. These motives are among the most potent supports of any legal system, since they include automatic demands within individual personalities to conform to the decisions of authoritative and controlling figures.

POSSIBLE FUTURE DEVELOPMENTS

The preceding review of the trend of decision has kept our eyes turned toward the past in much the same way that interpreters of controverted agreements must focus on past events in attempting to reach a satisfactory hypothesis concerning the expectations of the parties. With us, as with the decision-makers responsible at the application phase, the inspection of the past is a springboard toward the future. Our self-appointed task is to commit ourselves to a set of recommendations about interpretation, and to do so in the light of assumptions about probable future consequences for the value goals which we join with others in postulating for the world community. The deciders of a specific controversy also face the future in the double sense that the actual conduct of proceedings is intended to culminate in the near future in a decision, and that the decision is presumably taken with future preferences and contingencies in view. No matter how minute the preoccupation of a decision-maker or commentator may become with the present or past, these references to elapsed events are prelude to intended or unintended future effects. Whether planned or not, the decision-maker has one direction in which to affect the course of history; the direction can only be forward. Strictly speaking, every act of thought is in the ever receding present; and all present images prepare future act completions whether the manifest content to which they refer is past, present, or future.

Before we focus again on recommended goals, objectives, and strategies of interpretation it will be illuminating to step back a moment and consider the probable future course of decision-makers who must interpret international agreements. The proper approach, for reasons other than modesty, is to assume for the time being that our own recommendations will have nothing to do with the coming sequence of interpretation. The appropriate point for assessing possible effects of this category will be when alternative recommendations are under review.

There is not much to be said if we assume that the world community will exterminate itself, or even that it will engage in violent acts that inflict profound damage on life and the accumulated capital of civilization. Let us therefore assume a future in which the public order system of today retains its essential features with one important change, namely, a slow movement by consent toward at least a minimum order of world security.

The question is whether any factors in the social context are likely to affect the responsible interpreters of international agreements. Our analysis of the factors that help to account for the degree of confusion and contradiction found in past decisions laid heavy emphasis on unfamiliarity with the point of view, the methods and the findings, of modern research in the social and behavioral sciences, and more particularly in the study of communication. A remarkable acceleration has occurred in recent years in the scientific investigation of nature, man, and society; and we regard it as highly probable that this accelerated development will continue, even though the rate of acceleration may presently fall.

We have earlier called attention to sources that summarize the progress of the most relevant sciences. Such data cannot but add credibility to the prediction that the decision-makers of the world community are likely to be more and more influenced by the sciences of communication, and will show the effect by adopting more sophisticated principles in the task of interpretation. Since interpreters are, to a significant extent, recruited from professionally trained people, and since professional and pre-professional curricula are commonly responsive to the general intellectual environment, the training of future interpreters may include a more competent grasp of communication theory and data. Hence the whole process of agreement formation, of claims rising from alleged agreement, and of decisions involving agreement probably will be permeated by the new learning.

A conspicuous feature of accumulating knowledge is the systematic survey of past vocabulary for the purpose of discovering the frequency of various usages, prevailing at specified times and places, analyzed according to culture, class, interest, personality, and level of crisis. The execution of such a program calls for the examination of samples of books, periodicals, newspapers, letters, diaries, documents, legislative debates, administrative hearings and proceedings, court records, and so on. Not long ago such a suggestion would have seemed utopian. There have, however, been exceptionally rapid innovations that bring these operations well within reach. Machines are being perfected to scan printed records and to record them according to codes that permit distributions and trends to be followed in detail.[14]

The advisers of agreement-makers will have more and more exhaustive information at their disposal for testing the size and composition of audiences who are familiar with possible words to be incorporated into the text of agreement. They will be able to anticipate

14. The contemporary techniques involved are outlined and applied in Stone, et al., *The General Inquirer: A Computer Approach to Context Analysis—Studies in Psychology, Sociology, Anthropology, and Political Science* (1966).

the predispositions with which future decision-makers will respond to a claim that is put forward in case a dispute arises between parties over interpretation. It will be feasible to anticipate in some detail the response of decision-makers since data storage and retrieval systems will cover the doctrinal justifications and the procedures used in all controversies of record.

One consequence of the expansion of a data-rich civilization is that contextuality becomes an accepted routine of thought and manipulation. Machine auxiliaries cannot be effectively employed unless they are given instructions that can only achieve explicitness when defined as part of a whole configuration. The demand for economy in data gathering and manipulation attaches a premium to comprehensive systems, and to systems that can readjust through time by continuing "translation forward."

It must not be supposed that data in regard to gesture will be neglected as investigation widens and deepens. It is possible to employ moving picture cameras to record the spontaneous gestures (and body postures) of every society, and of every component group. The film can be coded by automatic scanners.[15]

Such intimations may be enough to indicate the grounds of our inference regarding the possible impact of knowledge upon interpretation. We are suggesting that these developments cannot but influence the arena in which decision-makers perform their tasks. We affirmed that the degree of past acquiescence to the response of official decision-makers was linked in part with the existence of professional perspectives that created and tolerated much confusion and contradiction, and with built-in procedures of settlement that actually overcame many limitations on rationality at the doctrinal level.

What happens to the political structure of the arena if the spread of knowledge undermines the willingness of community members and advisers to acquiesce in responses by decision-makers that strike them as unnecessarily erratic? Will not their disrespect for the competence of a tribunal that lags behind available knowledge influence

15. Techniques for the study of posture, gesture, and locomotion have been contributed to by a wide variety of people, notably by students of the ballet, athletic performance, and cross-cultural contact. See especially Birdwhistell, *Introduction to Kinesics: An Annotation System for Analysis of Body Motion and Gesture* (1952).

the perspectives of clients, and spread further discontent with institutions that pretend to speak in the name of such world public order as exists?

The political consequences will be of great relevance in the next few decades in which hitherto dependent, colonial or underdeveloped, nations are striving to consolidate their position in the world system. No doubt they will be sufficiently astute to employ skilled counselors from the more industrial powers until they have an adequate supply of specialists among their own nationals. These foreign counselors must protect their competitive position with the client by making use of the best available methods and by criticizing adversely any decision-maker who makes himself vulnerable by failing to adapt to the perspectives of new knowledge.

Despite the tendency in some communities to confuse seniority with adequacy, it is not unreasonable to predict that the approach of international tribunals will be modified by new personnel (and re-education) to take advantage of the implications of communications research for interpretation.

RECAPITULATION OF RECOMMENDED ALTERNATIVES

The projection outlined in the preceding section at least warrants the hypothesis that important conditioning factors are at work and in all probability will continue to influence the course of future decision-making along lines that are congenial to the approach outlined in our opening chapters. By this time the implications of the original sketch are presumably more obvious than they were at the start. As a means of reviewing the recommended principles of application and interpretation, let us consider a hypothetical controversy over the interpretation of an international agreement and outline, in highly skeletonized form, the procedures we recommend for the application of public order prescriptions to a concrete set of circumstances.

We shall not linger over the goals of interpretation, deferring any further discussion of these overriding aims until our concluding pages. Recall only that we distinguish (1) primary interpretation, (2) supplementing interpretation, and (3) policing and integrating interpretation, a. negative, b. affirmative.

Of fundamental relevance is the point that the principles of content and procedure are simultaneously employed by the decision-maker with varying degrees of emphasis throughout the entire course of his efforts to cope with the problem before him. The principles of content, it will be recalled, serve as reminders of the subject matter to be brought to the focus of attention at one time or another before a final commitment is made. The procedural principles provide an agenda for the sequence in which the subject matter is made accessible to the decision-maker's center of attention, and the subprocedures by which competing subject matters are evaluated. Clearly, these recommendations are directed mainly to the audience chiefly responsible for official decision, or for the critical evaluation of decision. The degree to which they serve the manipulative strategies of a counselor or advocate depends on his estimate of their significance for the decision-maker whose judgment is his target.

At the very beginning of a decision process a responsible decision-maker will apply to the immediately manifest (and the available latent) content of his subjectivity the principle of *impartiality*. This means that a decision-maker will make himself conscious of, and counterbalance as far as possible, any disposition to deny equality of consideration to the parties before him. Among the interfering predispositions may be exposure to biased perspectives connected with conditioning by culture, class, interest, and personality factors, and also by the crisis levels connected with each factor.

If this content principle is to be given effect it must be implemented by the operation of *examining the self* for predispositions incompatible with the goal of human dignity. As specifics we cite the possible use of the technique of free association (or free fantasy) for the purpose of allowing available latent content to come to the surface where it is open to critical scrutiny. The critical scrutiny includes candid and competent attempts to weigh the validity of hypotheses in regard to formative influences in the direction of adherence to equality of basic respect for all people. It may be that the problem is to obtain insight into the fact of bias, as a first step toward deliberately modifying one's outlook. For human beings in an anti-black or anti-white, anti-Muslim or anti-Jewish environment, for instance, this is no trivial undertaking. Candid people admit to themselves the long-drawn-out nature of this problem of self-modification. The purpose of the present principle is to keep the challenge fresh—

no matter how exalted or how exempt from merely "human" weaknesses a decision-maker may seem to be.

The suggestion outlined here does not exclude nor is it identical with, the practice of lifelong meditation, as exemplified by an outstanding international official like the late Dag Hammerskjöld. Hammerskjöld followed the well-established convention of appraising himself according to various rectitude criteria. He did not, however, bring to his aid, it appears, the prolonged free association methods devised by modern psychologists or psychiatrists; nor did he look at himself in the realistic frame of reference now partially available as a result of the systematic analysis of culture. Whatever aid he received from these meditations came from the philosophic, theological, and literary components of civilization, which provided the procedural device—meditation—on which he relied. It is not necessary to pass final judgment on the merits of meditation versus free association or of meditation *plus* free association *plus* systematic appraisal in terms of culture.

Many controversies that reach a tribunal cast their shadow far ahead. Decision-makers are well aware of the identity of the contending parties, of their relative strength, and of the importance that seems to be attached to the resolution of the dispute. It may be obvious from the beginning that a result adverse to one party will have grave repercussions for world security and for the continuation of the tribunal itself. We have underlined the point that decisions are always steps into the future; hence part of the relevant context must necessarily lie in the future (or, better, comprise the future). Among our recommended principles of content is the principle of *enforceable decision,* or the expectation that authoritative outcomes will be put into effect. In estimating post-outcome response to the applier-interpreter's decision the calculation must include the prospects of compliance and noncompliance, and of the generalization of noncompliance to the point of destroying current institutions of public order. We recommend an early start on the operation of *estimating the effect of decision.*

It may seem odd to call attention to this dimension of the decision-maker's problem even before the details of the controversy have been investigated. On reflection, however, it will be apparent that decision-makers live in the everyday world of news and comment, and cannot cut off from their attention communications that are understood by any informed person to possess implications for world security. The present suggestion is based on the policy of encouraging insight rather than suppression or repression; the latter cannot work while the former may. If applier-interpreters alert themselves to the probable power consequences of the alternatives open to them, they may be skillful enough to find a mode of conflict resolution—capable of being implemented by various interpretations—that involves minimum concession to survival expediency as a value, among other values, at stake.

The first step toward examining the details of the controversy is procedural: *identify the focal agreement.* As we have had occasion to reiterate, it is not to be assumed that the interpreter can read a controverted text and divine the answer to the issues in dispute. There is, however, the problem of adopting a working hypothesis about the manifest content of the agreement arrived at by the parties at the outcome phase. In order to proceed in a coherent manner, the decision-maker needs to formulate a definite set of statements, fully recognizing that this initial hypothesis is subject to drastic revision and may be altered almost beyond recognition when the whole context is explored.

It is often possible to accept as the focal agreement the clauses of a treaty. Some controversies relate, however, to allegedly informal understandings in which the expectations of the parties have grown up over time and have never been phrased in an official document. From the claims presented by the parties it may be feasible to formulate a preliminary statement of the supposed communication.

The operation of establishing the focal agreement brings sharply into view the rival interpretations that are pressed by the parties on the decision-maker. It may be that the "issue" seems clearly drawn, depending, for instance, on disagreement about the usual meaning of a word at the time the agreement was made. But the decision-maker's choice of issue is a crucial step in organizing the flow of communication (and other exposures) during the proceedings. Before crystallizing on the phrasing of an "issue," it is prudent to scan the context with the full checklist of recommended principles in view. All sorts of unarticulated inferences arise in the mind of a decision-maker as he becomes acquainted with the controversy before the tribunal. The role of a checklist of principles is to bring these inferences into the center of attention and to provide selective guidance in the task of identifying a factor that seems to deserve further consideration. This contributes to the operation of *adjusting effort to importance,* which continues throughout the proceedings.

The principles of content provide an essential map for the systematic inventory of factors affecting the expectation of the parties. These principles are organized, as illustrated in detail above, to bring into consideration the actual process of agreement: *participants, objectives, situations, base values, strategies, outcomes, effects.*

In regard to participants, for instance, the principle of *involvement* asks for information enabling the interpreter to determine the intensity of participation of various parties in the agreement process, and therefore to defer to the parties most involved. The *relevance of characteristics* is a reminder of the point that the expectations of parties can be established to some extent by taking note of the standard perspectives and operations of the groups to whose culture they have been exposed. These inferences apply to groups or individuals.

In assessing the probable objectives sought by the parties to an agreement we emphasize the *relevance of value range.* The relative significance of wealth or power considerations, for example, can be critically evaluated by noting their presence or absence at the time of economic or military threats or opportunities, and the articulation of concern with various objectives by influential participants in the decision process of the parties. The principle of *projecting expectations* underlines the importance of interpreting according to the major objectives expected by the parties to be given effect by the agreement. Some detailed suggestions have already been made about the criteria of "major" and "minor" objectives. The principle of *anticipated solution* recommends giving priority to solutions that were anticipated, and not rejected, during the agreement process, yet were not incorporated in a final text.

In regard to the situation in which the process of agreement-making and performance go forward, the general principle is that of *assessing the particular interactions among the parties in the light of the generally prevailing pattern of the setting.* We have spelled this out to some extent in regard to *spatial features, time features, institutionalization,* and *crisis level.*

Base values are pertinent to the task of interpretation since the relative equality or inequality of power, wealth, and other values is highly suggestive in evaluating the credibility of assertions about the expectations with which the parties concluded an agreement. Hence the proposed principle of *assessing the value position of the parties.*

Several inferences depend on knowledge of the strategies employed by the parties during the pre-outcome phase of the process of agreement. In this connection we stress the principle of *including all strategic acts,* which implies among other points that deeds as well as signs are considered. Sometimes the parties to an agreement rely heavily on language in arriving at an outcome; at other times the reliance may be on overt acts. When analysis of different categories of communication results in contradiction or confusion, we recommend relying on the *preferred mode of expression* in the process of agreement. Controversies sometimes give prominence to supposed logical contradictions, ambiguities, or gaps. We recommend the *examination of logical relationships,* with the proviso that the purpose is to ascertain the logical expectations current at the time. We also call attention to the principle of *adapting the level of generality or particularity to the other features of the context.* For instance, importance should be given to emphasis on goal, and to repetition, prominence, and elaboration.

In interpreting the outcome phase itself, we propose the principle of giving priority to the *distinctive phase of agreement.* The point is that when sources of equal credibility yield contradictory results concerning the expectations that prevailed at the pre-outcome and outcome phases of the process of agreement, assign primacy to the latter. When a clearly delimited outcome phase occurs, it is especially likely that the parties will give their fullest attention to what is communicated under such circumstances. The advantages of favoring the outcome phase weaken as expectations are created by "customary" interaction over a long period.

The relevance of effects (post-outcome events) can be ascertained by *following subsequent conduct* and also by *assessing impacts on the value position of the parties.* We reiterate that it is not to be assumed that parties, who in general are seeking to improve their net value position, will make overwhelmingly disadvantageous agreements.

Any examination of the process of agreement is always engaged in assessing the interplay of many factors that condition one another. We suggest two principles to serve as reminders in scanning pre-outcome, outcome, and post-outcome phases: the principle of the *largest shared audience;* the principle of the *probability of agreement.* The first assumes, in the absence of persuasive evidence to the contrary, that the words used in communication are to be interpreted as they are generally understood by the largest audience contemporary to the agreement to which all parties belong. The latter takes account of the fact that particular agreements are almost always one of a stream, and that standard expectations are likely to grow up about the obligations assumed by those who make them. The principle is even more helpful when the parties have themselves entered into a number of arrangements of much the same kind.

The foregoing discussion has successively brought into view the various phases of the agreement process. In connection with several points that have been raised by the principles of context, we recommend the use of procedures designed to bring to the notice of interpreters the best evidence on the basis of which inferences can be made about rival interpretations. One procedural suggestion is already strongly implied in the enumeration of agreement phases. It can be formulated as the *historical operation,* namely, the act of considering the focal agreement in the light of the content by moving the attention backward in time to the beginning of the agreement sequence, and forward to the present from the outcome. In practice this usually implies leaping all the way back to the start and moving toward the outcome, which is ordinarily more convenient and illuminating than sampling the past at random.

We refer also to the *lexical operation,* which includes all the techniques by which the semantic meaning of words is established. Many modes of content analysis have been devised to aid in the solution of similar questions. There is also the *logical operation,* which includes the analysis of any family of statements according to their internal relations (e.g. contradiction, level of abstraction). It will be recalled that we emphasized that the relevant task is to establish the "semantic" dimension of the "logical" usage current when the agreement was being made. Modern logical tools may disclose implications that were undreamed of when the parties were hammering out their understanding. We do not neglect to note the operation of *assessing gestures and deeds,* since several techniques are already at hand for accomplishing this purpose, making it possible to choose among inferences that depend on judgment of the methods used. There is a frequent need for the operation of *assessing the scientific credibility* of contradictory results.

With the exception of some principles mentioned at the beginning of this enumeration the principles mentioned, whether of content or procedure, have referred to the process of agreement and have dealt almost exclusively with the decision-maker's objective of *primary interpretation*. Our comprehensive list includes additional points about the decision process itself. For instance, the *objectives* of decision-makers add to primary interpretation the principle of *supplementing expectations in harmony with public order goals,* the principle of *constitutive priority,* and the principle of *promoting stable future expectations.*

In very broad terms we assume that the total act of application-interpretation will conform to a procedure that moves in succession through the consideration of these objectives. It is meaningless to proceed to later questions until the expectations of the parties have been established to the best of the ability of the decision-maker.

There is, however, a tremendous gap in our present recommendations in reference to supplementation, constitutive priority, and future stability of expectation. We do not here outline procedures by which all the prescriptions comprising the relevant system of public order are to be assessed for relevance to a controversy in hand.

Decision-makers and commentators are of one voice in affirming the view that as responsible authorities they cannot dream of giving effect to whatever expectations a particular congregation of parties happens to share. A typical assertion is that a treaty ought to be interpreted "In the light of the rules of international law in force at the time of its conclusion." [16] No guidance is offered about the most efficient means of linking a current dispute with the entire structure of international law. The matter is left with this remarkably inclusive principle of content standing unsupported by proposals for coping with the selective obligations implied. The scholarly observer might at least undertake, as we hope to undertake at some future time, to present a comprehensive and orderly treatment of the system of worldwide (and regional) prescription that is addressed to the selective tasks involved.[17]

16. Supra, pp. 100–11.

17. A framework of inquiry, with some illustrative detail, is offered in McDougal, Lasswell, and Reisman, *The World Constitutive Process of Authorita-*

Appropriate principles for the guidance of supplementation and integration are still another matter. It is evident that the objective of primary interpretation, if executed in a specific controversy, will make it possible to establish the presence or absence of particular gaps or ambiguities in the expectations entertained by the parties. Hence an essential precondition will be met for supplementing these expectations in ways that meet two requirements: they harmonize with primary expectations and also with the international system of public order. The act of supplementation presupposes that the international system has been appropriately scanned.

The objective of promoting stable future expectations in regard to various categories of agreement calls for more than perfunctory consideration by decision-makers. It is correct to assert that in the course of the process of decision attention may be directed to questions which, if officially clarified, would probably contribute to the stabilization of expectations among parties to future agreements. What procedures are best adapted to evaluating assertions and counter-assertions of the kind? Questions of this order we must for the present leave to one side, pending a more exhaustive analysis of what is involved in estimating the future.

Principles pertaining to the process of decision relate to *base values* and *strategies* as well as to objectives and official participants. In this summary we have not yet mentioned the principle of *explicit rationality,* affirming the importance of making explicit the principles of interpretation and application that influence the decision reached by the applier-interpreter. The procedures involved in reviewing past dispositions to accept or reject various formulations of principle are procedures congenial to the conventionally trained judge or scholar who is learned in the law.

Above all we must reiterate that the particular recommendations briefly recapitulated above are to be understood as implementing our overriding concern for context as against text; or, rather, for the location of a text, if any, in a valid configuration of past, present, and future events. The *contextual principle* is two-pronged in implication, since it *provides a set of principles relating to both content and procedure.*[18]

---

tive Decision (a chapter in Black and Falk, *The Future of International Law,* forthcoming, 1967). Separate publication in 19 *J. of Leg. Ed.,* issues 3 and 4 (1967).

18. It is sometimes debated whether principles of interpretation are, or should

THE FUTURE PROMISE OF INTERPRETATION

It is conceivable that the interpreter's contribution to world public order will be of greater rather than lesser significance in the years immediately ahead. These years of incessant and accelerating change will undoubtedly either be a time of transition toward disaster or, in happier contrast, will mark a steady movement toward forming a more perfect union of mankind. There is an obvious link between stable expectations and the evolution of an inclusive system of security.

Our projection of future events provided substantial support for the forecast that as the world revolution of science and technology diffuses toward universality the sciences of communication will spread. Hence it is not oversanguine to conclude that a potent set of conditioning factors will work in favor of a more disciplined process of interpretation.

One would be inexcusably credulous, however, to assume that these consequences will be automatically registered in the decision process of the world community. Acts of choice are essential. Therefore a major purpose of the present enterprise is to invite reflection on the strategies best adapted to the great responsibilities of applier-interpreters in the international arena.

If confidence is to be built in the integrity of the decision process, it will be a gradual achievement. To no inconsiderable extent confi-

---

be made, "binding" prescriptions. International Law Commission, Report, U.N. Gen. Ass. Off. Rec. 19th Sess., Supp. No. 9, at 25; American Law Institute, *Foreign Relations Law of the United States* (1965) at 452. Ordinarily we would regard any question about whether principles which at best can only serve as presumptive guides to potentially relevant features of the context can be made "obligatory" or "binding" as of somewhat transempirical character. It is, however, apparently contemplated that the highly textualist, hierarchical articles of the International Law Commission's draft convention are to be submitted to the states of the world in treaty form.

If the employment of any principle is to be made "obligatory" upon decision-makers, it would appear much the better alternative to prescribe the contextuality principle and its whole family of ancillary principles. Such a posture of authoritative expectation would at least make it more difficult for decision-makers to *justify* arbitrary interpretations: it might even make it more difficult for them to make such interpretations. Certainly any proposal which would have the effect of canonizing principles which arbitrarily preclude examination of the full relevant context of an agreement should be rejected.

dence will be a result, generalized by the parties to particular agreements, of the experience of discovering that the challenge to interpret is met with skill and devoted loyalty to the overriding goals of public order. If we are to judge from the past consolidation of public order systems, the permeation of confidence throughout the body politic is fostered when those who lose a particular controversy remain impressed by the competence and integrity of the process itself. Losers must come to admit to themselves, at least, that by acting in accord with discernible norms they can expect to be on the winning side in future disputes. It will not do for them to try to welch on an agreement, since community decision-makers will be too intent on ascertaining the prior state of shared expectation, and too cognizant of relevant procedures of inference, to allow it. Similarly, it will not be smart to connive to frustrate the goals of the entire system of public order by entering into agreements to bring about results incompatible with these goals. Decision-makers will be too identified with the aims of the whole to acquiese, unless the immediate decision-making situation has become a crisis in which the survival of the framework of unity is at stake, and other considerations must regretfully be relegated to a subordinate place or sacrificed completely.

We have insufficiently emphasized the volume of international agreements that have been made, especially in recent decades; and the increased volume that can be anticipated in coming years. Similarly, insufficient stress has been laid on the large number of controversies that arise concerning the interpretation of agreements and that are not carried to litigation before the most prominent international tribunals. Thousands of disagreements are resolved by negotiation; and the advisers make use, not only of bargaining (or threatening) points extraneous to the scope of the original agreement, but of such authoritative expectations as have spread among competent legal advisers. Whatever influences the expectations of this professional elite will undoubtedly continue to affect the positions urged upon clients at every stage of any process of agreement (or of claim rising from contradictory versions of the original perspectives of the parties). That decision-makers affect one another cumulatively as a by-product of the communication process to which they contribute is a proposition that requires no corroborative data.

It may also be noted that the importance of international agreements is not dependent on a "feudal," "capitalistic," or "socialistic" form of society in the component communities of mankind. In a diversifying world of science and technology, new groups that possess relatively distinctive demands, expectations, and identities are always making their appearance whatever the formalities used to allocate base values. Decisions made at the "top" must always depend for effect on the stream of decision taken by innumerable mid-elite persons and structures, to say nothing of rank-and-file attitudes of cooperation or resistance. In international relationships the "top" may nominally make the decision; it is, however, part of the expectations of the participants most directly concerned that the genuine understanding is the one reached by spokesmen of component territorial or pluralistic groups. Any failure to act within this frame of reference fractures the web of international cooperation and leads to value deprivations, immediate and retaliatory, all along the line. All communities, whatever their form, have a vital stake in enlarging and improving the value shaping and sharing processes of the larger earth-space arena which comprehends them.

We call attention, thus, to the special opportunities available to any decision-maker who is burdened with an applier-interpreter role in an international controversy. These decision-makers may fortify the tendencies on behalf of worldwide peaceful cooperation or they may confirm and exacerbate division and antagonism. The principles of content and procedure that are appropriate to the problem at hand, if clearly asserted during the entire decision process, reaffirm the goals of public order and spell out in detail their meaning, not only for the benefit of immediate parties to the controversy, but the guidance of the advisers of future agreement-makers. Counselors are, after all, specialized and often unofficial mediators between public order and particular clients.

The contextual approach to the interpretative task indicates why it is pertinent for all parties to participate in an effort to retrace the steps that led to the original agreement. Allowing that each party conducts his recapitulation as selectively as possible with an eye to choosing the statements most likely to influence the decision-maker favorably toward his claim, the reliving of the past performs a function that is somewhat equivalent to the patient's rehearsal of a traumatic experience under the supervision of a physician. In the act of exploring the background in detail, a reconstruction of the self occurs; reality is tested and many ego-generated fantasies are given up.

The concurrent effect of a three-party review of competing versions of reality (two parties plus a decision-maker), if conducted according to the principles of content and procedure outlined here, is to modify all concerned and to improve the chances that the modification will be toward sharing a common high regard for the decision process. Consider what happens when an individual or the members of a group engage in an isolated account of their side of a controversy. We are not surprised if positions grow more rigid and self-righteous. If no uninvolved third party is present and dissenting parties engage in a face-to-face rehearsal of their separate versions of the past, the result may be similar. When a decision-maker is present who is authorized and trained to speak for the common interest, and who has no direct involvement with the dispute, a review of the past dialogue between contending parties may end quite differently. The parties often discover weak spots in their own assumptions; and they may perceive more fully than before factors that perhaps clarify the position of the other. A party also gains in self-respect if his recapitulation wins the support at vital points of competent and uncommitted decision-makers. In any case few participants are so blind to the problematic character of life that they cannot concede to themselves, even when they lose, that competent and responsible decision-makers may also serve their interests in future contingencies.

All the specific strategies recommended here are subject to continuing reappraisal in the light of experience in the world community. The significant and enduring goal is to realize as fully and expeditiously as possible an inclusive public order that gives effect to the dignity of man. Hence in controversies over international agreements the most general aim is to apply these agreements in terms of all community policies, including the policy of according the highest possible deference, compatible with other constitutional policies, to the genuine shared expectations of the particular parties. In the public order we recommend, applier-interpreters must, therefore, be committed to *primary interpretation,* or the giving of deference to the genuine shared expectations of the particular parties to an agreement; to *supplementary* interpretation, or the completion of ambiguous or vague expectations according to the goals of public order; and to *policing and integrative interpretation,* which includes, *negatively,* giving no effect to the expectations of the parties when they conflict with the goals of the system of public order, and *affirma-*

tively, encouraging conformity of future agreement-making with the goals of public order.

We are under no illusion, of course, that establishment of appropriate goals for interpretation and the formulation of a more adequate body of interpretative principles—in terms of content *and* procedure—will necessarily bring about the realization of a world public order of human dignity. So comprehensive and revolutionary an achievement will require many changes in the predispositions current at any given present in the future of the world arena. Given the appropriate predispositions, the improved flow of communication to, from, and among authoritative and controlling decision-makers could further the overriding goal.

It would, however, be a crude mistake to assume that because a single factor in the total process of decision—and of decision within the whole social context—cannot be guaranteed to be of Messianic significance that it is of trivial consequence for the future of law and man. On the contrary: without more adequate conceptions of interpretation the flow of decision is likely to adapt itself at unnecessary human cost to the challenges that arise in the controversies that express and in turn affect the reconstruction of world public order in an era of explosive scientific and technological growth.

It is possible even in an era of accelerating change to maintain some stability of expectation among those who enter into agreement with one another. It is not only possible: it is an indispensable conditioning factor among the equilibrium of factors that must interact to achieve and sustain world public order of any kind, minimum or optimal. Unless shared expectations about future policies are sustained during these years of transition from traditional relationships, the mutual confidence necessary to protect the current degree of approximation toward a more secure world, and to arouse more validated perspectives of confidence in what can occur, is incapable of realization.

The role of interpretation is precisely the nurturing of confidence by seeking to ascertain and to effectuate in greatest measure the expectations of agreement-makers. For the peaceful supersession of the present anarchic and bellicose state of world political confrontation it is important to substitute a decision process inclusive in scope, in potent control of coercion, and persuasively achieved. If such a constitutive process is brought into existence it must be able to rely upon interpreters who give the utmost effectiveness to prescriptive agreements on behalf of at least minimum public order. The institutions of intelligence and recommendation must likewise rely upon interpreters who seek to sustain basic stability of life in the world arena, and apply the techniques available to expedite rather than to nullify steps in this direction. In the concrete controversies and initiatives that relate to the invocation of prescriptive norms, it must be possible to assume interpreters who seek to comprehend all expectations compatible with inclusive public order, and who, if confronted with concrete questions of application, proceed in the same disciplined framework. Both appraisal and termination—two other phases of the total process of decision—are expedited by interpreters who perceive the relevant context and act in accord with basic goals.

For purposes of optimal order the role of interpreters is, if possible, of even more moment. Optimal public order takes freedom of choice with great seriousness, and contravenes the aims and anticipations of particular agreement-makers with reluctance. The conception of human dignity places the utmost responsibility upon community decision-makers since they are expected to practice self-restraint upon any proclivities they may have to augment the scope of centralized power.

The stress that is properly put upon procedural principles in adequate interpretation clarifies the task of decision-makers who seek in complete good faith to live up to the content principles involved. More than that: awareness of the procedural choices at stake enable counsel for claimants to strengthen the courage and sense of obligation of decision-makers who waver in devotion. When such community spokesmen are confronted with features of the context that would otherwise drop out of sight, they are being invited to live up to the true role of adequate defenders of world public order.

Proper principles of interpretation, therefore, are indispensable instrumentalities of change in the direction of a more perfect public order. Whether the role of the participant in the total process of decision is that of claimant, counsel, decision-maker, or commentator, it is within the capacity of all to discipline good intentions—or even to nullify weak or bad intentions—by insisting upon sound principles of content and procedure in giving appropriate deference to the legitimate expectations both of the parties to international agreements and of the larger community in which they are included.

TABLE OF CASES

Acquisition of Polish Nationality, 161–62, 228, 256 n.
Aleksich v. Industrial Accident Fund, 205 n.
Ambatielos case, 181 n., 206
Ambatielos case (Preliminary Objection), 240–41
Ambatielos Claim, 213
Anglo-Iranian Oil Company case (Preliminary Objection), 149, 156 n., 181 n., 195–96, 200 n., 210, 212 n., 244, 257, 313–14, 320, 340 n., 356–57
Aroa Mines (Ltd.) case, 310
Article 3, Paragraph 2, of the Treaty of Lausanne (Frontier Between Turkey and Iraq), 143, 151 n., 178–79, 235 n., 278–79
Asakura v. Seattle, 162 n.
Asylum case (Colombia v. Peru), 129
Autonomy of Eastern Carelia, 212 n.
Awards of Compensation Made by the United Nations Administrative Tribunal, Effect of, 162 n., 164 n.

Barcelona Traction, Light & Power Company, Ltd. (Preliminary Objection), 155, 316, 317–18, 349–50, 355–56
Bluff v. Father Gray, 9 n.
Brazilian Federal Loans Contracted in France, Payment in Gold of, 137–38, 143, 301 n., 348, 349
Brigitte Bardot M.P.?, 9 n.

Certain Expenses of the United Nations, 165–66, 283–86, 314, 323–24
Certain Questions Relating to Settlers of German Origin in the Territory ceded by Germany to Poland, 161
Chamizal Arbitration Between the United States and Mexico, 139–40, 349 n.
Choctaw Nation v. U.S., 162 n.
Chorzow Factories (Indemnities) case, 281 n.
Claim of the Standard Oil Company to Certain Tankers, 328 n.
Colombian Bond cases, 176 n.
Competence of the General Assembly for the Admission of a State to the United Nations, 7, 126 n., 127 n., 214, 222 n., 238–39, 250, 314–15, 335 n.
Competence of the International Labor Organization (Agriculture), 143, 146–47, 235 n., 273 n., 277
Competence of the International Labor Organization to Regulate, Incidentally, the Personal Work of the Employer, 138–39, 162 n., 167 n., 348–49 n.
Compromises Signed at Rome on 30 June 1964 by the Governments of the United States of America and of the Italian Republic, Advisory Opinion of the Arbitral Tribunal Constituted in Virtue of the, 361 n.
Conditions of Admission of a State to Membership in the United Nations, 129, 205, 236–37, 250, 335–36
Constitution of the Maritime Safety Committee of the Inter-Governmental Maritime Consultative Organization, 126 n., 162 n., 192, 212 n., 222 n., 242–44, 286–89
Corfu Channel case (Merits), 140, 162 n., 312 n., 349 n.
Corfu Channel case (Preliminary Obection), 241–42
Customs Regime Between Germany and Austria, 153–54, 192, 312 n., 358–59 n.

Daniel v. Commission for Claims on France, 85 n.
David J. Adams, In the Matter of the, 259, 331
Decision in Life-Insurance Claims, 330 n.
Delimitation of the Czechoslovak-Polish Frontier (Question of Jaworzina), 133 n., 137, 162 n., 256 n.
Diversion of Water from the Meuse, 256 n.
Duc du Guise Claim, 334

Eastern Greenland, Legal Status of, 198, 245 n., 335 n., 351 n.
Eck v. United Arab Airlines, Inc., 143 n.
Employment of Women During the Night, 126 n., 159–60, 218 n., 226 n., 229–31, 235, 245 n., 252
Exchange of Greek and Turkish Populations, 228–29, 245 n., 255 n., 327

Faber v. United States, 151 n.
Factory at Chorzow (Jurisdiction), Case Concerning the, 84–85, 162 n., 167–68, 256 n., 273, 335 n., 336–37
Factor v. Laubenheimer, 162 n., 200 n., 204
Flegenheimer Claim, 266 n.
Ford v. United States, 151 n.
Franciska, The, 253 n.
Free Zones of Upper Savoy and District of Gex, 152–53, 154 n., 160, 193 n., 226 n., 278
Free Zones case, Order of Court, 278 n.
Frontier Between Turkey and Iraq (Article 3, Paragraph 2, of the Treaty of Lausanne), 143, 151 n., 178–79, 235 n., 278–79
Frontier (Local Authority) Award, 335 n.

Geneva Protocol case, 340 n.
Genocide case (Reservations to the Convention on the Prevention and Punishment of the Crime of Genocide), 156 n., 187–88, 257
Geofroy v. Riggs, 162 n.
Georges Pinson case, 105 n., 180
German Demands in Denmark, 331 n.
German Interests in Polish Upper Silesia (Jurisdiction), 245 n., 255 n., 337
German Interests in Polish Upper Silesia (Merits), 154, 190, 205 n., 237
G. L. Elton (U.S.) v. United Mexican States, 254
Gold Looted by Germany from Rome in 1943, 162 n., 312 n.
Goldsmith v. United States, 204, 205 n.
Greco-Bulgarian "Communities" case, 161, 255 n.
Guillemot-Jacquemin Claim, 200 n., 332–33

Hartford I. M. Company v. Cambria M. Company, 79 n.
Hauenstein v. Lynham, 162 n.
Heirs of Jean Maninat, 153
Hilder and Others v. Dexter, 153 n.
Holder v. Ministère Public, 340 n.

In Re Esau, 200 n., 328, 339–40
In Re Ross, 162 n.
Interpretation of Judgments Nos. 7 and 8 (The Chorzow Factory), 354 n.
Interpretation of Peace Treaties with Bulgaria, Hungary and Romania (Second Phase), 101, 168, 169, 181, 190 n., 210, 212, 226 n., 244, 277
Interpretation of the Greco-Turkish Agreement of December 1st, 1926, 245 n.
Interpretation of the Statute of the Memel Territory (Preliminary Objection), 126 n., 235 n., 279–80
Island of Timor case, 84, 189–90
Israel v. Bulgaria, 155, 156, 319–20, 355, 356

Jaworzina Boundary (Delimitation of the Czechoslovak-Polish Frontier), 133 n., 137, 162 n., 256 n.
Jordan v. Tashiro, 162 n.
Jurisdiction of the Courts of Danzig, 190–91
Jurisdiction of the European Commission of the Danube, 126 n., 137, 147, 212 n., 254–55, 311–12

Kolovrat v. Oregon, 339 n.
Kozuh v. Uff. Stato Civile de Milano, 162 n.
Kronprinz Gustaf Adolf case, 105 n., 176

Lawless case (Merits), 281–82, 304–06, 321–22, 340–42

Lighthouse Case Between France and Greece, 195, 234, 245 n.
Lotus, The S.S., 96, 116, 125, 126, 128, 129, 130, 179 n., 226, 231–33, 235, 240, 250, 364
Lusitania cases, 79 n.

Maltass v. Maltass, 123, 124
Marryat v. Wilson, 85 n.
Mavrommatis Jerusalem Concessions, 182, 190 n.
Mavrommatis Palestine Concessions, 190 n., 329
Maximov v. United States, 86–7
Med Guds Hielpe, The, 203 n.
Minority Schools in Upper Silesia, 256 n.
Minquiers and Ecrehos case, 190 n., 312–13

Naomi Russell (U.S.) v. United Mexican States, 85 n., 254 n.
Nationality Decrees Issued in Tunis and Morocco (French Zone) case, 147, 182, 259
Nielson v. Johnson, 162 n.
North Atlantic Coast Fisheries, 175–76, 208, 212 n.
Northern Cameroons (Preliminary Objection), 316–17, 353–55
Norwegian Loans, Case of Certain, 181 n.

Oscar Chinn case, 105 n.

Palumbo Claim, 200 n.
Petroleum Development (Qatar) Ltd. v. Ruler of Qatar, 312 n.
Petroleum Development (Trucial Coast) Ltd. v. Sheikh of Abu Dhabi, 8 n., 303, 330 n., 340 n.
Pertulosa Claim, 80 n., 85 n.
Phosphates in Morocco (Preliminary Objection), 179–80 n.
Polish Nationals in Danzig, 233–34, 311
Polish Postal Service in Danzig, 126 n., 135–36, 149 n., 160, 180 n., 222 n., 225–26, 277, 279, 320
Polish War Vessels, Access to, or Anchorage in, the Port of Danzig, 179, 193 n., 208, 212 n.
Pyrene Company Ltd. v. Scindia Navigation Company Ltd., 328

Radio Corporation of America v. The National Government of the Republic of China, 176–77
Reparation Commission v. the German Government, 328
Reparations for Injuries Suffered in the Service of the United Nations, 105 n., 156 n., 162–64, 194, 306 n.
Re Rizzo and others, 85 n.
Reservations to the Convention on the Prevention and Punishment of the Crime of Genocide, 156 n., 187–88, 257
Reserved Fisheries Arbitration, 254
Rights of Nationals of the United States of America in Morocco, 156 n., 210, 211, 213, 256–57

Santovincenzo v. Egan, 162 n.
Saudi Arabia v. Arabian American Oil Company, 150, 170–71, 180, 266 n., 295–302, 314 n., 349
Scala v. Nappi, 337–39
Scott v. The Thames Conservancy, 9 n.
Serbian Loans Issued in France, Payment of Various, 126 n., 202–03, 235 n.
Shanks v. DuPont, 162 n.
Ships Taken at Genoa, 205 n.
Shoshone Indians v. U.S., 162 n.
Sinclair v. Atkinson, 33 n.
South-West Africa, International Status of, 140–41, 195, 312 n.
South-West Africa cases, 108 n., 360–61 n., 363 n., 364 n., 366 n., 368 n., 369 n.
South-West Africa cases (Preliminary Objection), 85–86, 125 n., 150–51, 245–49, 315–16, 351–52
State v. Western Union Telegraph Company, 205 n.
Statute of the Saar Territory, 162 n.

Tacna-Arica Question, 153 n.
Temple of Preah Vihear (Merits), 290–95, 308–09, 344–48
Temple of Preah Vihear (Preliminary Objection), 290, 319–21
Terrace v. Thompson, 162 n.
Territorial Jurisdiction of the International Commission of the River Oder, Case Relating to, 131 n., 180 n., 189 n., 255

Towne v. Eisner, 219 n.
Treatment of Polish Nationals and Other Persons of Polish Origin or Speech in the Danzig Territory, 190 n., 193 n., 273 n.
Treaty of Neuilly, Article 179 (Interpretation), 256 n.
Tucker v. Alexandroff, 162 n.

UNESCO (Constitution), 340 n.
United States v. Arredondo and others, 327 n.
United States v. Classic, 99 n.
United States v. Texas, 153 n.
Universal Adjustment Corp. v. Midland Bank, Ltd., of London, 151

Valentine v. U.S. ex rel. Neidecker, 162 n.
Venezuelan Bond cases, 79 n.
Vryheid, The, 253

Warren v. U.S., 162 n.
Wimbledon, The S.S., 126 n., 178, 227–28, 245 n., 280–81

NAME INDEX

Abelson, Robert P., 75 n.
Adams, James Truslow, 99 n.
Albert, Ethel M., 52 n.
Albert, Lee A., 33 n.
Alfaro, Ricardo, 88 n.
Alford, Neill H., 267 n.
Allen, Layman E., 57 n., 73 n., 328 n., 339 n., 343 n., 373 n.
Altamira, Judge P. G., 152–53
Alvarez, Alejandro, 127 n., 214–15, 239, 263, 335 n.
American Law Institute, 104–05, 106, 109 n., 119, 120, 123–24, 222 n., 309–10, 391 n.
Anand, Ram P., 260 n., 357 n., 358 n.
Andreae, F., 252 n.
Anzilotti, Judge D., 159, 160, 195, 218 n., 229, 230–31, 245 n., 252, 357 n.
Ashby, H. Ross, 38 n.
Asquith, Lord, 8 n., 303
Ayer, Alfred J., 54 n.
Azevedo, Judge A. P., 127 n., 214–15, 239, 263, 277

Baade, Hans, 373 n.
Barton, Allen H., 75 n.
Barton, R. F., 54 n.
Basdevant, Jules P., 181 n.
Bateson, Gregory, 37 n.
Bavelas, Alex, 75 n.
Beck, James M., 99 n.
Beckett, Sir Eric, 9 n., 91, 92–3, 115–16, 117, 127 n., 130, 131–32, 186–87 n., 187, 212 n., 222 n., 224–25, 250, 307 n.
Bentivoglio, Ludovico M., 6 n.
Berelson, Bernard, 75 n., 351 n.
Bernhardt, Rudolf, 6 n., 91 n., 93 n., 127 n., 134 n., 199 n., 224 n., 319 n.
Beth, Loren P., 32 n.
Bickel, Alexander P., 33 n.
Birdwhistell, Ray L., 74 n., 381 n.
Bishin, William R., 33 n.
Black, Charles L., 33 n.
Bloomfield, Leonard, 69 n.
Borchard, Edwin P., 79 n., 158 n., 325 n., 357 n.
Brehm, Jack W., 75 n.
Brierly, James L., 83 n.
Briggs, Herbert W., 27–28 n., 258 n., 259 n., 331 n.
Bross, William, 66 n.
Brown, Judson S., 51 n.
Brown, Roger, 37 n.
Bruner, Jerome S.. 38 n.

Caldwell, Mary E., 373 n.
Carlston, Kenneth, 5 n.
Carneiro, Judge Leo, 356–57
Cartwright, Dorwin, 37 n.
Casey, Ralph D., 37 n.
Chang, I., 82 n., 83, 114, 116, 120, 123, 128 n., 158 n., 219 n., 220, 225 n., 226 n., 231 n., 233 n., 250 n., 309 n., 325 n., 328 n.
Cherry, Colin R., 54 n.
Cheshire, G. C., 218, 220 n.
Churchill, Winston S., xi
Clark, Charles, 33 n., 87
Clark, Grenville, 3 n.
Cohen, Felix S., 33 n., 63 n.
Cohen, Morris R., 33 n., 343 n.
Copi, Irving M., 73 n., 334 n.
Corbin, Arthur L., 33 n.
Crandall, Samuel B., 79 n., 83 n., 105 n., 109 n., 158 n., 309 n., 325 n.
Cross, Rupert, 33 n.

Davison, W. Phillips, 14 n.
Degan, V. O., 6 n., 32 n., 38 n., 49 n., 91 n., 159, 224, 253, 276 n., 330 n.
Deutsch, Karl, 37 n., 54 n.
De Visscher, Charles, 3 n., 6 n., 105 n., 124 n., 135 n., 159, 195, 199 n., 225 n., 276 n., 310, 319 n., 377 n.
DeVries, E., 40 n., 68 n.
Dickerson, F. Reed, 343 n.
Dogan, Mattei, 51 n.
Doob, Leonard W., 37 n.
Doyle, W. T. S., 310 n.

Edwards, Allen F., 74 n.
Edwards, Ward, 51 n.
Efron, David, 74 n.
Ehrlich, Ludwig, 6 n., 82 n., 112–13, 128 n.
Eldersveld, Samuel, 37 n.
Engel, Salo, 40 n., 98 n., 187 n.
Erickson, Erik H., 51 n.
Eulau, Heinz, 51 n.

Fairman, Charles L., 7 n., 9–10, 116, 233 n., 252 n.
Falk, Richard A., 390 n.
Feliciano, Florentino P., 3 n., 11 n., 14 n., 107 n., 340 n.
Fenwick, George C., 78 n., 158 n.
Fifoot, C. H. S., 218 n., 220 n.
Fiore, Pasquale, 79 n., 82 n., 83 n., 108 n., 109 n., 118 n., 158 n., 174 n., 209 n., 217, 218, 222 n., 253, 325
Fiske, Marjorie, 77 n.
Fitch, Frederic B., 73 n., 343 n.
Fitzmaurice, Sir Gerald M., 8, 80 n., 83, 83–84 n., 96 n., 98 n., 115–16, 117, 124 n., 127, 130, 132, 132 n., 133 n., 141, 156 n., 157, 172–73, 174 n., 181 n., 182, 201 n., 202, 207, 209–10, 213 n., 214 n., 222 n., 224, 226 n., 231n ., 248–49, 250 n., 253, 274 n., 277 n., 284, 285–86, 293, 294, 307 n., 316, 343 n.
Flemming, D. M., 357 n.
Frankfurter, Felix, 361 n.
Freud, Sigmund, 50 n.
Freund, Paul M., 33 n.
Friedmann, Wolfgang, 156 n.
Fromm-Reichmann, Frieda, 51 n.

Gardner, Richard N., 170 n., 218 n.
Garner, J. W., 109, 156, 309
Gerard, Ralph W., 38 n.
Gidel, M. Gilbert, 88 n.
Goldberg, Arthur, 86 n., 165 n.
Goodhart, Arthur L., 33 n.
Gordon, Edward, 7 n.
Gould, Wesley L., 14 n.
Gregorowicz, Jan, 343 n.
Griswold, Dean Erwin P., 32 n.
Gross, Leo, 166 n.
Grossen, Jacques Michel, 6 n.
Grotius, Hugo, 144, 158, 174 n., 175, 182, 216, 217, 220
Grzybowski, Kazimierz, 259 n.
Gudschinsky, Sarah C., 69 n.
Gutmann, Bruno, 54 n.
Guttsman, W. L., 51 n.

Haber, David, 245 n.
Hackworth, Green H., 133 n., 201 n., 219 n., 325 n., 328 n.
Hall, John F., 51 n.
Hall, Robert A., 69 n., 73
Hall, William E., 79 n., 105 n., 109 n., 157 n., 217, 218, 325
Hallowell, Irving, 70 n.
Halsburg, Lord, 153 n.
Hambro, Edvard, 124 n., 128 n., 133 n., 169, 174 n., 221 n.
Hamilton, Walton H., 32 n., 99 n.
Hammerskjöld, Dag, 384
Haraszti, Z., 6 n.
Harding, J. D., 200 n.
Hardy, Jean, 324 n., 326 n., 327 n.
Hart, H. L. A., 74 n., 101, 332 n.
Hartley, Eugene L., 37 n.
Hartley, Ruth E., 37 n.
Harvard Research in International Law, 5 n., 7, 27 n., 81 n., 83 n., 98 n., 104 n., 109 n., 120–21, 123, 124, 126–27, 134, 135, 156, 157, 158, 188, 218 n., 221 n., 231 n., 258 n., 309, 325 n., 326
Hay, George, 253 n.
Hayakawa, Samuel I., 67 n.
Hebb, David O., 38 n.
Henle, Paul, 70 n.
Herbert, A. P., 9 n.
Hexner, Ervin P., 39–40 n., 98 n., 187 n.
Hoebel, E. Adamson, 54 n.

Hogg, James F., 45 n., 125 n., 128 n., 130 n., 174 n., 181 n., 195 n., 197 n., 201 n., 223, 226 n., 231 n., 236 n., 250 n.
Hoijer, Harry, 70 n.
Holmes, Oliver Wendell, 41 n., 218, 219 n.
Holsti, Ole R., 75 n.
Hoselitz, Berthold F., 373 n.
Hovland, Carl I., 75 n.
Hsu Mo, Judge, 206
Huber, Max, 90
Hudson, Manley O., 83 n., 84, 105 n., 124 n., 128 n., 133 n., 135, 141, 174 n., 186, 187, 209 n., 219 n., 222 n., 225 n., 226 n., 231 n., 236 n., 250 n., 253, 262, 274, 309 n., 325 n., 326 n.
Hughes, Charles E., 327–28
Hurst, Sir Cecil, 152–53
Hyde, Charles Cheney, 83 n., 93–94, 105 n., 113, 114, 116, 117, 119–20, 122, 125, 128 n., 129, 130, 133, 142, 143, 156 n., 158 n., 173, 174 n., 182, 212–13, 218 n., 219 n., 225 n., 226 n., 231 n., 249, 325 n.
Hyman, Herbert H., 75 n., 77 n.

Iklé, Fred L., 14 n.
Institute of International Law, 88 n., 96 n., 127 n., 130 n., 221–22, 231 n.
International Law Commission, 5–6 n., 88–90, 91 n., 223–24, 275–76, 391–92 n.

Jakaboski, Theodore M., 152 n.
Janis, Irving L., 75 n.
Janowitz, Morris, 55 n.
Jenks, C. Wilfred, 5 n.
Jensen, Otto C., 57 n.
Jessup, Philip C., 5 n., 86, 125 n., 316, 357 n., 363 n., 364 n., 368 n.
Johnson, Wendell, 67 n.
Johnstone, Quinton, 33 n.
Jones, Ernest M., 27 n.

Kaplan, Abraham H., 4 n.
Katona, George, 75 n.
Katz, Daniel, 37 n.
Katzenbach, Nicholas deB., 4 n.
Kelley, Harold H., 75 n.
Kelsen, Hans, 98, 187 n., 215 n.
Kelsey, Francis W., 158 n.
Kendall, Patricia L., 77 n.
Kerley, Ernest L., 267 n.
Klaestad, Helge, 181 n., 244
Klapper, Joseph T., 75 n.
Kluckhohn, Clyde, 52 n.
Klüver, Heinrich, 38 n.
Knapp, Jerome W., 85 n.
Koffka, Kurt, 50 n.
Köhler, Wolfgang, 50 n.
Kozhevnikov, F. I., 6 n.
Krastin, Karl R., 64 n.
Kraszewski, Zdzislaw, 343 n.

Landis, James M., 33 n.
Lasswell, Harold D., 3 n., 4 n., 13 n., 21 n., 33 n., 37 n., 46 n., 51 n., 65 n., 75 n" 77 n, 268 n., 286 n., 373 n., 389 n.
Lauterpacht, Sir Hersch, 9, 80, 81 n., 82 n., 83, 88, 92 n., 93 n., 96 n., 98 n., 101, 101 n., 102–04, 105 n., 109 n., 113, 116, 123 n., 126, 128 n., 129, 130, 149, 156, 156–57 n., 158, 159, 169 n., 172 n., 173–74, 175, 181–82, 195 n., 207, 208, 209, 213, 219–20, 224, 231, 231 n., 233 n., 250 n., 251 n., 252 n., 253 n., 263–64, 265, 274–75, 306–07, 326 n., 330 n., 358
Lawrence, Thomas J., 7 n.
Lazarsfeld, Paul, 75 n.
Lee, Alfred McL., 37 n.
Lee, Irvin J., 67 n.
Lefley, Ray, 74 n.
Leites, Nathan, 75 n.
Lenhoff, Arthur, 33 n.
Lerner, Daniel, 68 n., 75 n., 373 n.
Levi, Edward, 33 n., 57 n.
Lewin, Kurt, 50 n.
Lewis, Anthony, 361 n.
Liacouras, Peter J., 91 n., 259 n., 260 n., 358 n.
Lifton, Robert, 70 n.
Likert, Rensis L., 75 n.
Lindzey, Gardner, 75 n., 351 n.
Lissitzyn, Oliver J., 7 n., 94–95 n.
Llewellyn, Karl, 32 n., 33 n., 54 n.
Loder, B. C. J., 357 n.

MacKay, D. M., 38 n.
Malinowski, Bronislaw, 54 n.
Marriott, James, 253 n.
Marshall, John, 285
Marvick, Dwaine, 51 n.
Mayo, Louis H., 27 n.
Mbanefo, Louis, 363 n.

McCulloch, Warren S., 38 n.
McDougal, Myres S., 3 n., 4 n., 11 n., 13 n., 14 n., 21 n., 27 n., 65 n., 77 n., 107 n., 170 n., 171 n., 218 n., 268 n., 286 n., 340 n., 389 n.
McGuire, William J., 75 n.
McMahon, J. F., 85 n.
McNair, Lord, 83, 85 n., 96 n., 108 n., 109, 127 n., 133 n., 134, 145, 146, 154, 156, 172, 174 n., 181 n., 200 n., 201, 202, 203, 204 n., 205 n., 222 n., 253, 258 n., 259 n., 275 n., 331 n.
Meerloo, A., 70 n.
Merrill, Maurice H., 32 n.
Merton, Robert, 77 n.
Mildew, Lord, 9 n.
Miller, Arthur S., 32–33 n.
Miller, George A., 37 n.
Miller, James C., 340 n.
Moore, John Bassett, 79 n., 85 n., 176 n., 254 n., 357 n.
Morris, Charles W., 37 n.
Moses, Fritz, 68 n.

Nathanson, Nathaniel, 165 n.
Neri, S., 6 n.
Newman, James, 70 n.
New York Times, 165 n.
Niemeyer, G., 4 n.
North, Robert C., 75 n.
Nussbaum, Arthur, 5 n.

O'Connell, D. P., 40 n.
Oldfathers, Charles H., 158 n.
Oppenheim, Lassa F. L., 9, 80 n., 105 n., 108, 113, 209 n., 253 n., 326
Osgood, Charles E., 75 n.
Owle, Justice, 8 n.

Padilla Nervo, L., 108 n., 364 n., 369 n.
Pal, Radhabinod, 106 n.
Parker, Judge Edwin B., 79 n.
Patterson, Edwin, 33 n.
Pei, Mario, 18 n.
Pereterskii, Ivan S., 6 n.
Philbrick, Frederick, 67 n.
Phillimore, Sir Robert J., 79 n., 109 n., 112, 118 n., 158 n., 174 n., 185, 217
Piaget, Jean, 50 n.
Pickford, Glenna R., 69 n.
Pitts, Walter, 38 n.
Pollux, 169 n.
Pool, Ithiel deS., 68 n., 75 n.
Pospisil, Leopold, 54 n.
Pound, Roscoe, 32 n., 219 n.
Pribram, Karl, 38 n.
Probert, Walter, 67 n.
Pufendorf, Samuel, 158, 217
Pye, Lucian W., 51 n.

Radin, Max, 33 n.
Ralston, Jackson H., 153 n., 310 n.
Raman, K. V., 5 n.
Rapaport, Anatol, 66 n.
Read, J. E., 129, 181 n.
Reisman, Michael W., 27 n., 389 n.
Roosevelt, Franklin D., xi
Rosenberg, Milton J., 75 n.
Rosenne, Shabtai, 3 n.
Rostow, Eugene V., 33 n.
Ruesch, Jurgen, 37 n.

Samore, William, 260 n.
Sapir, Edward, 37 n., 70 n.
Schachter, Oscar, 39 n., 63 n.
Schatzman, Leonard, 68 n.
Schechter, Alan S., 10 n., 117
Schein, Edgar H., 70 n.
Schücking, W., 105 n.
Schwarzenberger, Georg, 7 n., 82 n., 83 n., 104, 113, 118, 124 n., 127 n., 128 n., 131, 132, 133–34, 142, 174 n., 195, 218 n., 220 n., 231 n., 233 n., 253 n., 277, 306 n., 309 n., 335 n.
Schwelb, Egon, 40 n.
Scott, James B., 84 n., 175 n.
Shannon, Claude, 54 n.
Shils, Edward A., 51 n., 75 n.
Shurshalov, V. M., 6 n., 151–52, 193–94
Silving, Helen, 6 n., 33 n., 307–08 n.
Sinclair, I. M., 85 n.
Smith, Bruce L., 37 n.
Sohn, Louis, 3 n.
Spender, Sir Percy, 248–49, 284–85, 286, 316
Spier, Hans, 70 n.
Spinks, Thomas, 253 n.
Sprout, Harold, 55 n.
Sprout, Margaret, 55 n.
Stein, Morris, 51 n.

Stevens, Robert, 33 n.
Stone, Harlan F., 99 n.
Stone, Julius, 7 n., 101, 103–04, 105, 114–15, 116, 117, 128 n., 169, 170, 218 n., 221 n., 223, 225 n., 231 n., 252 n., 264
Stone, Philip, 75 n., 380 n.
Strauss, Anseim L., 68 n.
Suárez, Francisco, 217
Suci, George J., 75 n.
Sullivan, Harry Stack, 37 n.
Sutherland, Arthur E., 32 n.

Tammelo, Ivar O., 7 n.
Tanaka, Totaro, 108 n., 364 n., 367 n., 369 n.
Tannenbaum, Percy, 75 n.
Ten Broek, Jacobus, 32 n.
Tobin, H. J., 144, 146, 154
Tolman, Edward C., 50 n.
Toscano, Mario, 4 n.
Toulmin, Stephen, 74 n.
Trubek, David, 33 n.

Ullmann, Steven, 69 n.

Van Wyk, J. T., 363 n.
Vattel, Emmeric de, 7, 8 n., 32, 78, 78 n., 79, 80, 80 n., 81, 81 n., 82, 83, 84, 90, 109 n., 112, 122, 158, 172, 174 n., 175, 182, 209 n., 216–17, 249, 284, 297
Verba, Sidney, 55n .
Verdross, Alfred, 106 n., 108 n.
Verzijl, J. H. W., 9, 180, 252 n.
Vidich, A., 51 n.
Vlasic, Ivan A., 4 n., 13 n., 21 n., 65 n., 268 n., 286 n.
Von Neumann, John, 38 n.

Waldock, Sir Humphrey, 89
Weaver, Warren, 54 n.
Wechsler, Herbert, 33 n.
Wellington, Harry H., 33 n.
Wellington Koo, T. K., 308, 345–46, 347, 348
Wertheimer, A., 50 n.
Westlake, John, 7 n., 83 n.
White, Ralph, 51 n.
Whorf, Benjamin L., 70 n.
Wigmore, J. H., 79, 80 n., 93–94, 117, 118, 218
Williams, John, 66 n.
Williams, Gwladys L., 217 n.
Winiarski, B., 166 n.
Wolff, Martin, 5 n.
Wolter, W., 343 n.
Wright, Quincy, 118 n., 145, 146, 148, 154, 189 n.

Yü, T. C., 7 n., 79, 79 n., 81, 82 n., 83 n., 84, 93 n., 113–14, 116, 122, 124 n., 128 n., 218 n., 218–19, 226 n., 231 n., 252 n.

Zaninovitch, M. George, 75 n.
Ziembiński, Z., 343 n.
Zinnes, Dina A., 75 n.
Zipf, George K., 43

SUBJECT INDEX

Adjusting effort to importance: operation described, 65–66; trend of decision, 303–07; Lord Asquith avoids "chaos" by rigid textuality, 303–04; Lawless case approach, 304–06; direct admission by Lauterpacht, 306–07

Anticipated solution: principle described, 53; trend of decision, 186–88

Application: process of, ix–x, xvii–xix; of international agreements, 5, 6

Assessing scientific credibility: procedure principle of, 74–75, 350–51

Base values: in process of agreement discussed generally, xii, 11, 52–53, 193–94; outlined, 18; principles relating to described, 55–56; trend of decision, 194;
in process of decision, 263–65

Beckett, Sir Eric: 9 n., 91, 92–93, 115–16, 117, 127 n., 130, 131–32, 186–87 n., 187, 212 n., 222 n., 224–25, 250, 307 n.

Bias: principle described, 77; trend of decision, 356–59; cultural factors, 356–57; conflict of interest, 357; judges ad hoc, 358–59

Claim process: claimants, 22; objectives, 22–23; specific types of controversy, 23–25; strategies and outcomes, 26

Communication: mediated subjectivities, ix, 37; signs and symbols, x, xi, 37–38; process of, x–xiv, 34, 36–37, 45, 371–72

Constitutive priority: principle of, 261–62

Constitutive process, 4, 27 ff., 36, 41

Content principles: defined, 12, 46, 47–48; summarized, 50–64; trend of decision, relating to the context, 119–44, 373–74, 383–84; trend of decision, relating to the agreement process: participants, 144–54, objectives, 154–88, situations, 188–93, base values, 193–94, strategies, 194–206, outcomes, 206–15, post-outcomes, 215–16; trend of decision, relating to the decision process: officials, 258–60, objectives, 260–63, base values, 263–65, strategies, 265–67, outcomes, 267–69

Context: of agreement, 11, 21, 34, 119, 188; general features outlined, 21; principles relating to, 59–60; similar provisions or agreements, role of comparing, 253–58

Contextuality principle: of content, described, xiv, 50, 65, 98–9, 119–23, 132–35, 372; trend of decision, 119–44; total context, 119–21; preliminary events recognized, 122–25; relation to plain meaning doctrine, 125–26; limitations criticized by Lauterpacht, 127–30; limitations explained by Beckett, 131–32; subsequent events recognized, 135; authentic interpretation, 137–42;
of procedure, described, 65, 273–75; trend of decision, 173–302; expanding focus approach, 274, 276–77; jurisprudence of the International Court, 283–95; improved procedures in Saudi Arabia-Aramco arbitration, 295–302

Crisis level: past experience, 15, 17; content principle, described, 55; trend of decision, 192–93

Decision process: decision makers, 27–28, 45 ff.; objectives, 29–30; arenas, 31; base values, 31; strategies, 31–32; outcomes, 32–34; effects, 34; trend of decision, 258–69

Distinctive phase of agreements: described, 12, 13–21, 58; trend of decision, 206–15; relationship to merger principle, 207–08; relation to outcome text, 209–15; Fitzmaurice's views, 209–10

Effectiveness of decisions, 63–64, 263
Effectiveness principle: described, 32, 98, 156–59; trend of decision, 98, 159–86; value range, 154–56; outlined by Lauterpacht, 156–57; major purposes, 157–71; relation to "plain" meanings, 159–67; other restrictions, 161–62; *Peace Treaties* case restriction, 168–69; doubt of Stone, 169–70; "teleological" interpretation, 170–71, 214–15
Effects: in process of agreement, general features, 20, 42, 76–77; particular relevance, 20; subsequent practices, 132–44; in process of decision, trend of decision, 353–56
Ejusdem generis, doctrine of: trend of decision, 201; one version, 201–03; its complement, 203–05; as semantic operation, 367–68
Expectations: genuine shared, discussed generally, 6, 8, 11–12, 33, 81; assessment of as goal, 36, 40–42, 81; stability of, 63, 262–63; need to supplement and police, 101–11
Explicitness in decision, 265–66
Expressio unius est exclusio alterius: principle described, 330; as "unassailable" logical principle, 330; trend of decision, 331–36; limitations, 332–36; syntactic operation, 367–68

Fairman, Charles: contends "formal maxims do not decide concrete cases," 9
Fitzmaurice, Sir Gerald: 8, 80 n., 83–84, 96 n., 98 n., 115–16, 117, 124 n., 127, 130, 132–33, 141, 156–57, 172–73, 174 n., 181–82, 201–02, 207, 209–10, 213 n., 214 n., 222 n., 224, 226 n., 231 n., 248–49, 250 n., 253, 274 n., 277 n., 284–86, 293–94, 307 n., 316, 343 n.
Focal agreement: operation described, 36, 56, 66–67, 385; trend of decision, 307–09

Generality: level of, 18–19, 52, 57–58; trend of decision, 200–06; doctrine of *ejusdem generis,* 201–06
General patterns in the setting: principle described, 53–54; trend of decision, 188–93
Gesture and deed: mediation of subjectivities through, ix, xi, 18–19, 36–37; mode of expression, 56–57, 197–99; operation of assessing, 73–74, 343–50
Goals of interpretation: discussed, xiv, 6, 10, 35, 39–41, 41 n., 42–44; summarized, 44–45; trend of decision and opinion, 82–111; goal of ascertaining expectations affirmed by commentators, 82–84; by courts, 84–87; exceptions, 88–94; position of Lauterpacht and Stone on supplementing interpretation, 101–04; policing, 105–11

Harvard Research in International Law, 5 n., 7, 27 n., 81 n., 83 n., 98 n., 104 n., 109 n., 120–21, 123–24, 126–27, 134–35, 156–58, 188, 218 n., 221 n., 231 n., 258 n., 309, 325 n., 326
Historical operation: described, 67; trend of decision, 309–18; consistent if limited and unsystematic procedures in Permanent Court, 311–12; broader view in present Court, 312–18
Human dignity, 6, 30, 40, 45, 52, 66, 77, 106, 370
Hyde, Charles Cheney, 83 n., 93–94, 105 n., 113–14, 116–17, 119–20, 122, 125, 128 n., 129–30, 133, 142, 143, 156 n., 158 n., 173, 174 n., 182, 212–13, 218 n., 219 n., 225 n., 226 n., 231 n., 249, 325 n.

Impartiality: principle described, 61, 382; trend of decision, 258–60
Information theory, 54
Institute of International Law, 88 n., 96 n., 127 n., 130 n., 221–22, 231 n.
Institutionalization, 17, 54, 190–92
Intentions of parties: goal of interpretation, 82
International Law Commission: on goals of interpretation, 88–90; report supports plain meaning approach, 223–24; limited view of context, 275–76
Involvement: principle of, described, 50, 144; trend of decision, 144–48

Jus aequum, rule of: proposed by Schwarzenberger, 118 n.

Largest shared audience: principle described, 59–60; trend of decision, 216–52

Lauterpacht, Sir Hersch: contends principles of interpretation "cloak results arrived at by other means," 9; position on goals of interpretation, 102–03; criticizes plain meaning doctrine, 127–30; outlines principle of effectiveness, 156–57

Lexical principles: semantic analysis, xii–xiii; principle of procedure, 319; relation to largest shared audiences, 319–22; use in decision, 320–30; thorough lexical operation in *Expenses* case, 323–24; relation to texts in different languages, 325–26; Oppenheim's early view, 326; Oppenheim rejected, 326–27; position of the Permanent Court, 327; recent views, 328–30

Logical principles: syntactic analysis, xii–xiii; principle of content described, 57; trend of decision, 199–200; principle of procedure, 330–43; *expressio unius* rule, 330–36; conjunction and disjunction, 336–37; circuit analogies, 338–40; need for explicit policy choices, 340; recent approaches, 340–43

McNair, Lord, 83, 85 n., 96 n., 108 n., 109, 127 n., 133 n., 134, 145–46, 154, 156, 172, 174 n., 181 n., 200 n., 201–03, 204 n., 205 n., 222 n., 253, 258 n., 259 n., 275 n., 331 n.

Minimum order, 1–3, 11–14, 107, 340, 379

Mobilization of authority functions, principle of, 64, 267–69

Mode of expression: principle described, 56–57; trend of decision, 197–99

Necessity of interpretation: Vattel principle, 7, 32, 78–79, 79 n., 80–82, 90, 122, 216–17, 249, 297, criticized, 79–80; some interpretation is always necessary, 78, 79–82

Objectives: in process of agreement, xi, 11, 16–17, 51–52, 154, 156–57, 171–76; trend of decision, 154–88; value range, 154–56; major purposes, 157–71, 365–66; relation to "plain" meanings, 159–67; other restrictions, 161–62; *Peace Treaties* case restriction, 168–69; doubt of Stone, 169–70; "teleological" interpretation, 170–71, 214–15; restrictive interpretation as complementary interpretive principle, 171–74; as policy, 175–79; recommended rise as complementing principles, 183–86; anticipated solutions, 186–88

in process of decision, 29–30, 260–63; primary and supplemental interpretation, 260–61; constitutive priority, 261–62; stability of expectations, 262–63; adjusting effort to importance, 302–07

Open texture of concepts: defined by Hart, 100

Outcomes: of communication, xiii;

of agreement, described, 11, 13, 19; of relevance, 19–20; of principles relating to, 58–59; trend of decision, 206–16; distinctive phase principle, 206–14; identifying the focal agreement, 307–09;

of decision, described, 64; trend of decision, 267–69

Participants: in process of agreement, characteristics described: group, 11, 15, 51; individual, 15, 42, 51; trend of decision, 144–54; degree of involvement, 144–48; group characteristics, 148–51; individual characteristics, 151–54;

in process of decision, 27–28; officials, 258–59

Persuasion: by agreement, 1; and coercion, 1, 6, 13–14; as goal, 6

Plain and natural meaning principle: described, 7, 8, 32, 41, 95–96, 111, 116–18, 369; affirmed by International Law Commission report on the law of treaties, 88–89; rejected by large majority of commentators, 96–97, 218; as standard meaning for largest shared community audience, 43; trend of decision and opinion, 216–52; employed to restrict contextual analysis, 216; early views, 216–17; current American views, 218–20; supported by the Institute of International Law, 221–22; by the International Law Com-

mission, 223–24; relation to preliminary work, 226–29; relation to major objectives, 229–31; rejections, 231–36; conflicting views expressed by the International Court, 236–44; increasing contextuality, 244–49; projected trend, 249–52
Policing, xvii, 41–42, 100, 105–11, 261–62, 382, 394
Preliminary work. See *Travaux préparatoires*
Prescribing function, discussed, 4
Primary interpretation, xvii, 29–30, 44, 61–62, 260, 382, 394
Principles of interpretation: no fixed hierarchies of, xiv–xv, 36, 49, 95–6, 115, 365; function of, 6–9, 12, 45–77, 111–18; summary of proposed, 50 ff.; view that "settled and fixed" rules decide cases, 112; view that rules are useless, 112–15, 362
Principles of interpretation, proposed principles of content relating to process of agreement: involvement, 50, 144–48; relevance of characteristics, 51, 148–54; relevance of value range, 51–52, 154–56; projecting expectations, 52–53, 156–86; anticipated solution, 53, 186–88; situations, 53–54, 188–93; value positions of the parties, 55–56, 193–94; strategic acts, 56, 194–96; preferred mode of expression, 56–57, 197–99; logical relationship, 57, 199–200; level of generality, 57–58, 200–06; distinctive phase of agreements, 58, 206–15; subsequent conduct, 58–59; largest shared audience, 59–60, 216–52; impact on value positions of parties, 59; probability of agreement, 60, 252–58
Principles of interpretation, proposed principles of content relating to process of decision: impartiality, 61, 258–60; primary interpretation, 61–62, 260; supplementing expectations, 62, 260–61; constitutive priority, 62–63, 261–62; stable future expectations, 63, 262–63; making decisions effective, 63–64, 263–65; explicit rationality, 64, 265–66; mobilization of authority functions, 64, 267–69
Principles of interpretation, proposed principles of procedure: contextuality, 65, 273–302; adjusting effort to importance, 65–66, 307–09; identifying focal agreement, 66–67, 307–09; historical, 67, 309–18; lexical, 67–71, 319–30; logical, 71–73, 330–43; assessing gesture and deed, 73–74, 343–50; assessing scientific credibility, 74–75, 350–51; estimating agreement probability, 75–76, 351–53; estimating effects of decision, 76–77, 353–56; examining self for bias, 77, 356–59
Principles of interpretation, traditional: plain and natural meaning, 7, 8, 9, 12, 32, 41, 95–96, 111, 116–18, trend of decision, 216–52; "it is not permissible to interpret what has no need of interpretation," 7, 32, 78–79, 79 n., 80–82, 90, 122, 216–17, 249, 297; effectiveness, 9 n., 32, 98, 156–59, trend of decision, 154–88; restrictive interpretation, 9 n., 32, 157, 171–75, 183–86, trend of decision, 175–82; *travaux préparatoires,* 32, 98–99, 119–23, 145, trend of decision, 123–32, 282–302; subsequent conduct, 32, 98–100, 132–35, trend of decision, 135–44; *ejusdem generis,* 201–05; *expressio unius est exclusio alterius,* 330–36
Probability of agreement: content principle described, 60, trend of decision, 252–58; procedure principle described, 75–76, trend of decision, 353–56
Procedure, principles of: defined, 12, 46, 48–49; outlined, 65–77; trend of decision, 270–359; contextuality, 273–302; effort, 303–07; identifying focal agreement, 307–09; historical, lexical, logical operations, 309–43; gesture and deed assessment, 343–50; scientific credibility, 350–51; agreement probability, 351–53; estimating effects of decision, 353–56; examining self for bias, 356–59; inadequately employed, 376–78; recommended use, 383–90
Projecting expectations: principle described, 52–53; trend of decision, 156–86; summary and recommendation, 386
Public order: of preferred values of human dignity, ix, xv, 6, 30, 40, 45, 52, 66, 75–77, 106; supplementation of expectations through reference to, xviii, 29, 44, 61–2, 104–5, 394–96; world, 4–5, 6, 34, 40, 44, 47, 62, 66, 184, 186, 261–62, 391

Relevance of characteristics, 51, 148–54
Restrictive interpretation: discussion, 32, 157, 171–75, 183–86; trend of decision, 175–82; protection of state sovereignty, 175–79; limitations, 179–82; minor objectives, 365–67

Similar provisions: comparing in interpretation, 253–58
Situations: as fora, xi; general features, 17; particular features, 17–18; arenas, 31; principles relating to, 53–55; trend of decision, 188–93; spatial position, 189; time factors, 189–90; institutionalization, 190–92; crisis level, 192–93
Social process, ix, 3, 4 ff., 14, 21, 26, 34, 45, 65, 184–85, 214–15, 365; shaping and sharing of values in, 1; postulate of maximation of values discussed, 10–11; values in, 42, 51–52; clarification of community values, 13, 47–49; public policy role described, 42, 46, 63, 76
Spatial and temporal factors in interpretation, 17, 54, 189–90
Stability of expectations, 42, 63, 262–63
Stone, Julius, 7 n., 101, 103–04, 105, 114–15, 116, 117, 128 n., 169, 170, 218 n., 221 n., 223, 225 n., 231 n., 252 n., 264
Strategic acts: principle described, 56; trend of decision, 194–96
Strategies: of communication, xii, 18–19; of interpretation, summarized, 47–49; trend of decision, 194–206; principles as, 56–57; two diametrically opposed views, 6–11; strategic acts, 56, 194–97; mode of expression, 56–57; 197–99; shortcomings of signs and deeds, 18–19; of decision, 64–65, 265–66
Subjectivities, x, xi, xiii, xv, 10–11, 38–39, 100; not available to direct observation, xv–xvii
Subsequent conduct: discussion of, 32, 98–100, 132–35; employed in decision, 135–44; accepted uniformly, 135; authentic interpretation, 135–37; practical interpretation, 137–42; reservations of Hyde, 142–43
Supplementing interpretation, 29, 44, 61–62, 99–105, 260–61, 382, 394

Textuality, xv–xvii; principle of, 209–15, 362–63
Travaux préparatoires: discussion of, 32, 98–99, 119–23, 145; employed in decision, 123–32; *Lotus* doctrine, 125–26; *Lotus* criticized, 126–30; contextual operations, 282–302, 363–65, 368–69

Value position of the parties to an agreement, 55–56, 59, 193–94
Value range: relevance to decision, 51–52, 154–56, 386
Vattel principle that "it is not permissible to interpret what has no need of interpretation": 7, 32, 78–79, 79 n., 80–82, 90, 122, 216–17, 249, 297, 361
Verzijl, J. H. W.: contends principles of interpretation are often "worthless," 9